EXPOSING
── THE ──
FALLACIES
── OF THE ──
PRE-TRIBULATION
RAPTURE

A BIBLICAL EXAMINATION
OF CHRIST'S SECOND COMING

BILLY BROADWATER

WESTBOW
PRESS°
A DIVISION OF THOMAS NELSON
& ZONDERVAN

WestBow Press books may be ordered through booksellers or by contacting:

WestBow Press
A Division of Thomas Nelson & Zondervan
1663 Liberty Drive
Bloomington, IN 47403
www.westbowpress.com
1 (866) 928-1240

Scripture taken from the King James Version of the Bible.

ISBN: 978-1-4908-3523-5 (sc)
ISBN: 978-1-4908-3525-9 (hc)
ISBN: 978-1-4908-3524-2 (e)

Library of Congress Control Number: 2014907756

Print information available on the last page.

WestBow Press rev. date: 03/10/2017

"Nothing in the world is more dangerous than sincere ignorance..."

Martin Luther King

I tell you that he will avenge them speedily. Nevertheless when the Son of man cometh, **shall he find faith on the earth**?

Luke 18:8

CONTENTS

ACKNOWLEDGMENTS

I would like to make my opening remarks by saying how grateful I am for the many people who have labored diligently in the Word of God and for their unfailing devotion to the truth. By nature, religion and its subsequent doctrinal pursuits are difficult and controversial. If you have ever taken part in a conversation involving such pursuits, you have become reasonably acquainted with the debates that follow.

My appreciation goes to Marvin Rosenthal and the late Robert Van Kampen, because of their extensive research pertaining to the subject of the rapture which brought clarity to my understanding of the Scriptures that surrounds this topic.

I have been fortunate for the last twenty-five years to be able to teach a Bible study at the Travis County Corrections Facility. Many thanks go out to the men who challenged me in my studies not to provide generic answers to their Bible questions, but real in-depth answers. Thank you goes to Dusty, Zabion, Jerry, Albert, and many others who were an encouragement to me. Mike Vest was faithful in serving Christ with me for over ten years in the prison Bible study. Special thanks go to Clark Gorbet as a co-laborer in Christ in the prison Bible study for many years, along with the numerous conversations about Bible truths, which includes his input in this book.

Appreciation goes to Natashia Jackman for her help in editing. My son Kyle, who gave me several pointers and guidance by his writing skills. My daughter Melissa deserves credit for her help in editing as well. Heidi Walker, the author of "Before God's Wrath," gave me invaluable input throughout my book. Her understanding of the rapture topic greatly aided me in writing and layout, along with her constructive analysis that was extremely beneficial.

Lastly, but most of all, thanks go to my wife Beatrice, a loving wife who is the strong hold of my life. Her patience and grace to me have been extended beyond measure. As a construction superintendent, I usually have to work many hours each week; and she was extremely gracious to me as I worked on this book. I love you sweetheart with all my heart.

INTRODUCTION

The testimony of my faith is similar to many Christians I have heard and read. I came to know Christ in 1984, and immediately became enthralled with teachings concerning the end-times. As a new Christian, I realized that my life had been eternally changed. The future -not only in the eternal sense- but in this life, became important in a way that it had never been before. This fact brought about my concerns as to the questions surrounding His second coming. After all, the emphasis of biblical salvation is that our earthly relationship with God has been bridged back through Jesus Christ.

Like many new believers, I had the propensity to follow the predominant theory of the pretribulation rapture. It seemed appropriate as a child of God, considering that Jesus wouldn't allow his children to suffer the horrific events foretold in the book of Revelation. After all, as believers we are saved from the wrath and judgment of God.

However, as a student of the Bible, my opinions and thoughts began to develop. I was inquisitive, and I found ways to satisfy my searches by listening to biblical teachings on tape, and reading books from old-time preachers in the Independent Baptist community. I would like to thank my two former pastors. Chester Sassman of Calvary Baptist Church who was very influential in my early Christian growth when I was a Southern Baptist. Later, the late Hank Thompson of Capitol City Baptist Church encouraged me to take reading and studying the Bible seriously. John R. Rice, Dr. Lee Robertson, Lester Roloff, Al Lacey, and many others were positive influences. Others, like J. Vernon McGee was the popular radio speaker at the time with his **Thru the Bible** program. John MacArthur's radio program **Grace to You** taught a pretrib rapture. Later, David Jeremiah, who is very well-known with **Turning Point** radio, espoused with conviction persuading his listeners with the pretribulation rapture. I wish to add that I believe these are very godly men, of which I have been blessed by their teachings.

Combining all these influences, it was through their teaching on the pretrib rapture which helped shape my views. Furthermore, at the time, the Mark 1V productions of the **"Thief in the Night"** were popular movies in Christian circles. **"The Years of the Beast"** was one of the first movies of the rapture that I was introduced to. And I cannot forget mentioning Hal Lindsey's **"The Late Great Planet Earth"** as it swept across the US affecting many people's opinions on the pretribulation rapture.

Despite these many influences, still, I was unable to reconcile many biblical passages that brought more confusion than clarity. As Christians, we are commanded to follow the Scriptures. In Acts 17:11 where it states: *search the scriptures daily, whether those things were so*; I chose to allow the Scripture to manifest itself instead of habitually following the interpretations of those around me. I began to discern a pattern in God's word that refuted much of the pretribulation teaching.

My studies on the rapture continued diligently over the next ten years, with seemingly more questions than answers. My confusion on the subject took a different turn in 1995. While visiting the local Christian book store, as I frequently did, I came across a book called **"The Pre-Wrath Rapture of the Church"** as I was browsing the current-events section. The title of the book caught my attention as something different pertaining to the rapture topic. I liked the word *pre-wrath* instead of pretrib, because that's was my biggest hang-up on the rapture subject, since I was confused with the Scripture passages between God's wrath and Satan's.

This book exceeded my expectations and would begin to clear up the many discrepancies from the pretribulation teaching such as: Why is the church supposedly exempt in the Olivet Discourse in Matthew 24; How could John actually be the raptured church in Revelation 4; How could separating the rapture from the second coming be two totally separate events? The purchase of this book would prove to be the beginning of my ride down the road that ultimately led to my understanding of the Scriptures and its teachings of the end-times.

I began subscribing to **"Zion's Fire"** magazine, led by **Zion's Hope** ministries. Through **"Zion's Fire"** articles and tapes by Marvin Rosenthal on the Olivet Discourse and the book of Revelation, my belief in the rapture was forever set. Other books, authored by Robert Van Kampen, called **"The Sign"** and **"The Rapture Questions Answered,"** helped reinforce my views on the Lord's plan for his return from a prewrath perspective, not pretrib.

After all these years and my perseverance for the truth, I have written this book about the rapture. Even though I do not hold a degree in theology, I believe my years of study concerning the topic of the rapture and zeal for scriptural truth, qualifies me to write this book. I am convinced of the argument for the prewrath rapture as being the clearest, most scripturally developed teaching on the subject. It is my earnest desire that these truths expressed in this thesis will be a blessing and add clarity to your understanding of the end-times.

I will point out the many contradictory and confusing statements by the leading pre-tribulation teachers over some of the basic verses pertaining to the rapture of the church. I could have had documented many more of their contradictions in my book; however, these are sufficient enough to reflect what is central to their theory. This book focuses mainly on the fallacies of the pretribulation rapture and the scriptural rebuttal. I only ask that you keep an open mind when you consider why there is so much discrepancy between those who advocate pretribulation teachings. I must add that it was never my intention to rebuke the pretribulation rapture teaching. I was sincerely pretrib in my beliefs for a long time, so I wrote this book with no biased intentions.

I liken this debate on the timing of the rapture to that of a trial in the courtroom. I believe the pretrib teaching is trying to prove their case based solely on circumstantial evidence. Can circumstantial evidence alone prove a case? Yes! It will be proven however, there is no scriptural evidence to substantiate their view- it's all conjecture. I will also prove that pretrib teachers have tampered with the courtroom evidence (the scriptures) to build their case. Pretrib teachers have attempted to persuade others by changing to literal meaning of major eschatological passages. The smoking gun is that there are verses plainly stating the rapture will occur "after" the tribulation, yet, "before" God's wrath. The scriptures themselves gives us the cold-hard facts for a prewrath rapture.

Moving forward, I also want my book to emphasize the true meaning of Christ's return. We can debate when Christ comes, and we will; however, we cannot afford to miss the purpose of why Christ is coming back. This is paramount in the context of the passages highlighting Christ's return, which ties to the timing of the rapture.

I believe the Word of God to be the final authority in all matters. I believe, as we arrive closer to our Lord's return that Christians with an *escapism mentality* will be questioned, especially in areas of the world that become less tolerant of biblical Christianity. With the ever-changing world in which we live, many Christians are beginning to see the hostility of the anti-Christ society in light of the prophesied Scriptures. The emphasis in the prophetic Scriptures is to bring hope when believers begin to discern the "signs of the times." True believers will know and trust God in the midst of trials and troubles.

In my years of study of biblical truths, I have found that in conversations concerning the rapture that many are not really sure what they believe. Many defend the teachings of their church rather than Scripture, which is something I frequently did. Some tend to "reason" more in their belief than really substantiating a hermeneutical approach to the Bible. I fear that many other biblical doctrines receive similar treatment. No one, including this author, wants to be told we are wrong and need correcting, that's part of our sinful human nature. Furthermore, we live in a society that preaches tolerance – which typically is saying don't judge me according to my lifestyle – and any negative connotations towards a belief system (social or religious) is usually viewed as hateful and mean-spirited. I understand the title of this book has negative ring-tones that reverberate across mind and spirit of Christians that believe in a pretribulation rapture, which implies that they are wrong in their belief. That was the point in my naming of this book, which is to stir the reader to make him or her defend what they believe.

I am afraid that many Christians are of the persuasion that Jesus will not allow them to suffer physically, which is a critical factor involving the rapture debate. I call this type of Christianity, "Americanized Christianity," and it is rampant in our churches. With all the emphasis on God's blessings, we have forgotten God's warnings. Sadly, the biblical warnings against sin have been removed from many preaching sermons, and along with the true meaning of God's love which is oftentimes defined by humanistic philosophy. Many churches have become self-help centers for physical and emotional needs, instead of a called-out-assembly to proclaim God's truth; the emphasis being on extrinsic rewards rather than intrinsic guidance. Questioning the legitimacy of the pretribulation rapture view is rejected by many based on their unproven belief that they have God's blessings and will not suffer hardship.

The Apostle Peter addresses these concerns in his first epistle.

> That the trial of your faith, being much more precious than of gold that perisheth, though it be tried with fire, might be found unto praise and honour and glory at the appearing of Jesus Christ. (1 Pet. 1:7)

Peter understood that hardships would be concomitant with Christianity. Timothy wrote in 2 Timothy 2:3: *to endure hardness as a good soldier of Jesus Christ.* These men were not pessimists, but realists, understanding that biblical Christianity would run divergent to the world's philosophy. I am reminded in the book of Jeremiah chapter 23 the Lord's rebuke of the leadership in Israel. They told the people what they wanted to hear: *Hearken not unto the words of the prophets that prophesy unto you: they make you vain: they speak a vision of their own heart, and not out of the mouth of the LORD...They say still unto them that despise me, The LORD hath said, Ye shall have peace; and they say unto every one that walketh after the imagination of his own heart, No evil shall come upon you* (vv.16-17). Jeremiah's day in Israel is really no different than our day we live in now. We want to be told good things about ourselves, and that good things are going to happen to us, which is typically materialistic in its premise.

Jesus understands that the heart of man in his natural state desires what is pleasing to the flesh and not that which is spiritual. He told of this in John 6 after he healed many and fed the multitude. Afterwards, he went across the Sea of Galilee to Capernaum, and the multitudes came the next day seeking him. Jesus exposed them immediately for the reason why they came seeking him. It was because they were fed physically, and did not desire a spiritual hunger. They failed to see their lost spiritual condition and did not desire the righteousness of Christ.

> Labour not for the meat which perisheth, but for that meat which endureth unto everlasting life, which the Son of man shall give unto you: for him hath God the Father sealed. (John. 6:27)

He exposed their true desire, which was not for God and his eternal holiness. Instead, their desire was for fleshly fulfillment, which is ephemeral. The encounter culminated in John 6:66, when those who were present became offended (v.61) with Jesus's words and *went away, and walked with him no more* (v.66). This will be a key point that I will address showing the seriousness of turning from Jesus when someone is offended.

Unfortunately, preachers lead many to think of the possibility that Jesus could come back at any moment, therefore you better get saved to escape the tribulation. My friend, salvation is not based on missing the tribulation, but being made righteous so we can live in the presence of God for eternity. A person needs to be saved because they are spiritually dead, and they could die at any moment (Luke 12:19-20). Reasoning with an individual based solely on their deliverance from a physical tribulation is not a biblical salvation. What Scriptures teach consistently is that trials and tribulation bring a reality to an individual's own mortality when compared to eternity (Ps. 119:71).

A point of emphasis: concerning the first-time Jesus came to this earth, is that the Jews of the time believed he had come to deliver them from the hands of their oppressors- the Romans. In fact, Jesus came the first time to provide spiritual deliverance from their sin, which still applies to us today. Only at the second coming of Christ will there be a physical deliverance for those spiritually saved (1 Cor. 15:52-54). The end-result will be the bringing in of the millennial kingdom, but only after Christ purges this world of evil. The teaching of the New Testament provides overwhelming support that physical deliverance is not the primary key for the Christian.

> These things I have spoken unto you, that in me ye might have peace. In the world ye shall have tribulation: but be of good cheer; I have overcome the world. (John 16:33)

> Confirming the souls of the disciples, and exhorting them to continue in the faith, and that we must through much tribulation enter into the kingdom of God. (Acts 16:22)

The prewrath position puts the church in the tribulation, going against the common thought pervasive in Christianity. The world is progressively more anti-Christian, and this pattern will continue up to the end-of-the-age. The end of-the-age being the final seven-years, leading up to the establishment of Christ's kingdom on earth, as prophesied by Daniel.

Most students of prophecy agree that we are living in the end-times. Yet, with our limited knowledge, we really don't know how much longer before Christ returns. Mainline Christianity has been saying for the past hundred-years Christ's coming is near. In all honesty, it could be several hundred more years before the end of the age. However, it does seem close with the conflicts over the previous 100 years such as: WWI, WWII, Vietnam, Korean War, various wars in the Middle East and ethnic cleansing in various countries have claimed the lives of untold millions are indicative of this fact. It is reported that Russia alone is responsible for over forty million deaths post WWII. Reports in China, over thirty million have been killed with the establishment of their communist government in 1921.

Christians are still persecuted today, or at least relegated to second-class citizens in many Muslim countries. As the Scriptures teach, believers are strangers and pilgrims in this present world, which is ultimately not our true home. This is one of the dangers of not seeing the real purpose of the rapture related to the final seven-years of Daniel's prophecy. While many believe that we will not see the events in the tribulation, the setup for a great fall is in place. Multitudes will not be heeding the warnings of the events surrounding them. Nazi Germany, under the leadership of one of the greatest tyrants of all time caused untold havoc upon the world. The people of Germany thought they were electing a savior, but instead got the devil.

Here is an example of the culpability of a society through deception by this crazed tyrant.

> My feelings **as a Christian points me to my Lord and Savior** as a fighter. It points me to the man who once in loneliness, surrounded by a few followers, recognized these Jews for what they were and summoned men to fight against them and who, God's truth! Was greatest not as a sufferer but as a fighter. **In boundless love as a Christian** and as a man I read through the passage which tells us how the Lord at last rose in His might and seized the scourge to drive out of the Temple the brood of vipers and adders. How terrific was His fight for the world against the Jewish poison. Today, after two thousand years, with deepest emotion I recognize more profoundly than ever before the fact that it was for this that **He had to shed His blood upon the Cross. As a Christian** I have no duty to allow myself to be cheated, but I have the duty to be **a fighter for truth and justice**... And if there is anything which could demonstrate that we are acting rightly it is the distress that daily grows. **For as a Christian I have also a duty to my own people.**
> -Adolf Hitler, in his speech in Munich on 12 April 1922

Adolf Hitler persuaded millions that he was a Christian, only to drag multitudes to their deaths. Multitudes were blinded to the evidence that was before them, because they were deceived into believing —and many chose- a lie. The audacity to call one's self a Christian and claim they have the right to slander and oppress the Jews and others in the name of nationalism is startling.

This frightening type of sentiment is still alarmingly present today. The reward for Israel becoming a nation in 1948 is the endless attacks from her enemies and the day-to-day struggle (both politically and socially) for a right to exist peacefully. Islam, an antichrist religion, will continue to extend its tentacles of death upon every nation.

Germany was not necessarily pagan in its beliefs as a society, and was a fairly religious nation when Hitler came on the scene. However, he changed the belief system of their society to where even the churches represented Hitler's ungodly philosophies. Jesus said in Matthew:

> For nation shall rise against nation, and kingdom against kingdom: (Matt. 24:7a)

Kingdom against kingdom references not only the physical battles in war between countries; but also, the conflict between the physical (governments) and spiritual (church). Christians will continue to be isolated from society, due to the direction the world is going. This world is no friend of the believer, which usually mocks and ridicules true Christians who "stand up" for truth and righteousness, and stand against sin. We also need to be aware that the term "anti" does not always mean" against," but can take on the meaning to be "in place of." 1 John 4:3 *"And every spirit that confesseth not Jesus Christ is come in the flesh is not of God: and this is the spirit of antichrist"* And when Christ becomes "substituted" for His role as Lord, then undoubtedly biblical truth becomes blurred at best. Nationalism and its ungodly laws become the lord of that society, and sadly religions get swept away by the tide. The homosexual movement is a good example, headed by the political establishment of the liberal elite, has made major inroads in the culture and even many religious denominations are even changing their beliefs to satisfy this societal decree.

The god of this world, Satan, will continue to unleash his demonic forces upon this world, especially as he sees his time on the earth drawing to a close. The Antichrist will not only be mighty in power economically, but spiritually powerful as well. Jesus warned repeatedly in His Olivet Discourse that *"if it were possible even the elect would be deceived"* (Mt. 24:24). Antichrist will certainly talk-the-talk religiously, sadly, numerous religious folks will be duped by this slick politician. The question becomes, how many mass defections will there be when this man-of-sin is revealed during a time the Bible calls, the "great tribulation?"

> For then shall be great tribulation, such as was not since the beginning
> of the world to this time, no, nor ever shall be. (Matt. 24:21)

As I close out my introduction I want to emphasize that this book was not written as a "doom and gloom" read. Many have accused those who do not believe in a pretribulation rapture of this sentiment. It is about the truth of God's word above church tradition and man-made creeds. This book is about hope, the blessed hope for God's people that Christ is coming again. My prayer is that it will encourage Christians to stand true in the midst of hardships and deceptions that are becoming all too common. Also, I would like to add, that even though I just wrote how society is changing for the worse, I believe there are good Bible-believing, soul-winning churches doing a great work for the Lord.

Borrowing a quote from a noted Christian speaker and author on why this topic or any topic from the Word of God is important, he says, "Because Truth Matters." This is certainly the case concerning the rapture. I encourage you, while you read this book, that you will sincerely search the Scriptures and compare them in context with the other teachings on the rapture.

Bible prophecy typically is a two-edged sword within the Christian church, with a dull edge on one side and an extremely sharp edge on the other. On the dull side, prophecy is disregarded as something in the far-future, being irrelevant with no immediate effect on us. On the sharp side, some take every current-event news story as though "everything" related to the prophetic mysteries of the Bible is unfolding before our very eyes. The next big event is supposedly on the horizon. As with all theology, in Bible prophecy there needs to be a balance of sharpness, which only comes from proper spiritual discernment that will equal out the two sides.

I will be presenting the view the prewrath rapture of the church, which basically teaches in a nutshell that the church will go through the first three-and –half-years and into part of the second-half of the final seven-years. This teaching is not a midtribulation rapture or a posttribulation rapture, but is sandwiched somewhere in between the two views. I will define the terms that relate to this study in the next chapter.

I would like to emphasize one last point in our study. Since the doctrine of the second coming is woven throughout the Scriptures, it may seem that I am repetitive in some of the arguments against a pretribulation rapture. To build my case, it is important for you to understand that it is necessary to do so in order to tie-in the overall theme of the second coming. Also, I purposely printed out many of the Scriptures verses that I reference to aid you in your study on the rapture. I will be quoting from the Authorized King James Version of the Bible throughout this book. This is the most recognized version and has stood the test of time. This will also help curtail any debate which version is best translated from the Greek and Hebrew to prove the timing of the rapture. Unfortunately, too many teachers and bible scholars end up flip-flopping between numerous version in order to gain an advantage proving their rapture position. I believe this will help curtail any biased slant that the reader might perceive of me if I were to switch back and forth between Bible versions. In other words, I am allowing the Bible to be the final authority; not what I think the verse should say to aid my point of view. If I have an issue with trying to prove my point, it will certainly not be because of a Bible translation. God Bless!

CHAPTER ONE

DEFINING THE TERMS

In this chapter, we will look at some of the definitions pertaining to Bible prophecy. These definitions will be the focus of this book in framing the debate on the rapture. I wrote this book with the intent that the reader should have a basic understanding of the teaching on the rapture subject.

First let me give the proper definition about biblical hermeneutics. Here is a quote from Robert VanKampen's book "The Rapture Questions Answered" explaining the proper method of Bible interpretation.

> One's hermeneutic basically refers to how one understands something that is written or spoken. The normal method we use every day is what I refer to as the `face-value hermeneutic": we understand what we read or hear by taking what is said to us at face value-or, by taking it literally, if you prefer that word-in its most natural, normal, customary sense...
>
> I have come to realize that the only hermeneutic that makes the Bible alive and meaningful is the hermeneutic that takes Scripture exactly for what it says. That doesn't mean that we are to ignore the many obvious figures of speech and expressions that are found in Scripture, but that does eliminate spiritualization (substituting the literal sense for a deeper, spiritual meaning), allegorization (abandoning the literal sense for what the reader considers to be a more meaningful understanding), culturalization (limiting unnecessarily the literal sense to the culture of the day in which it was written), and any other scheme that distorts what the text says when understood in its most normal, natural, customary sense.[1]

Here's a simple adage that can be applied to proper hermeneutics, "When the literal sense makes common sense then seek no other sense."

1. Eschatology:

This is the study of last-things in relation to God closing out humanity's reign on earth and ushering in His ultimate authority in His kingdom.

A. Preterits View:

This view places the events of Matthew 24 (the Olivet Discourse), and the events of Revelation taking place in AD 70. They see the abomination of desolations and the destruction of the temple to have been fulfilled by the hands of the Romans. They do not believe there is a literal rapture of the church.

B. Historicists View:

This view teaches prophecy is unfolding throughout church history. Before the nineteenth century, the historicists saw the Papacy and the Catholic Church as being the Antichrist along with his religious system. There is no literal rapture of the church.

C. Futurist View:

Futurist, view prophesies given by Jesus and the events in the book of Revelation are to be fulfilled in the future; contiguous with his coming at the "end of the age." There will be a literal rapture of the church.

2. Rapture:

The rapture is a reference to the "catching up" of Christians (still living), and they are gathered together in the air to meet Christ and be presented before God in heaven. The rapture event should not be confused with the resurrection, which describes the dead being raise back to life.

> For the Lord himself shall descend from heaven with a shout,
> with the voice of the archangel, and with the trump of God: and

the dead in Christ shall rise first: Then we which are alive and remain shall be **caught up** together with them in the clouds, to meet the Lord in the air: and so shall we ever be with the Lord. (1 Thessalonians 4:16-17)

Behold, I show you a mystery; We shall not all sleep, but we shall all be changed, In a moment, in the twinkling of an eye, at the last trump: for the trumpet shall sound, and the dead shall be raised incorruptible, and we shall be changed. (1 Cor. 15:51-52)

3. Second Coming:

This is the promise given by Christ to believers, where He will return again and establish in his kingdom here on earth.

And if I go and prepare a place for you, I will come again, and receive you unto myself; that where I am, there ye may be also. (John 14:3)

And while they looked stedfastly toward heaven as he went up, behold, two men stood by them in white apparel; Which also said, Ye men of Galilee, why stand ye gazing up into heaven? this same Jesus, which is taken up from you into heaven, shall so come in like manner as ye have seen him go into heaven. (Acts 1:10-11)

The definition of the second coming is one of the fundamental differences discussed in Bible prophecy as it relates to the rapture. There are differing views (which we will see) among pretribulational teaching when explaining the second coming. Some pretribulationist teach that the second coming of Christ is not the rapture event at the beginning of the 70th week, but is the final return of Christ at the end of the 70th week. Other pretribulationist say that the second coming is one event broken up in two returns; first, the rapture of the saints at the beginning of the 70th week, and second, the return of Christ at the end of the 70th week. Prewrath teaching places the second coming of Christ after the mid-point of the 70th week, which includes his return at the end of the final seven-years. The second coming is one event broken up in several stages (rapture, trumpet and bowl judgments, return at the battle of Armageddon).

4. Daniel's Seventy Weeks:

Here is the scripture reference in the book of Daniel pertaining to the seventy-week prophecy.

> **Seventy weeks are determined** upon thy people and upon thy holy city, to finish the transgression, and to make an end of sins, and to make reconciliation for iniquity, and to bring in everlasting righteousness, and to seal up the vision and prophecy, Know therefore and understand, that from the going forth of the commandment to restore and to build Jerusalem unto the Messiah the Prince shall be seven weeks, and threescore and two weeks: the street shall be built again, and the wall, even in troublous times. And after threescore and two weeks shall Messiah be cut off, but not for himself: and the people of the prince that shall come shall destroy the city and the sanctuary; and the end thereof shall be with a flood, and unto the end of the war desolations are determined. And he shall confirm the covenant with many for **one week**: and in the midst of **the week** he shall cause the sacrifice and the oblation to cease, and for the overspreading of abominations he shall make it desolate, even until the consummation, and that determined shall be poured upon the desolate. (Dan.9:24-27)

This is the specific and final period in relation to God's people as He fulfills His plan of redemption. Biblical scholars agree the term "weeks" means "weeks of years," where one week equals seven years. The following is an example in the Bible where we see the correlation where one week equals seven years.

Genesis chapter 29 describes Jacob's love for Rachel, the daughter of Laban whom he had to serve seven years to Mary her. Because of Laban's deception about their marriage custom, Jacob ended up marrying Leah, Rachel's older sister. In a further agreement, Jacob agreed to serve Laban another seven years in order to marry Rachel.

> Fulfill her **week,** and we will give thee this also for the service which thou shalt serve with me yet **seven other years**. And

> Jacob did so, and fulfilled her **week**: and he gave him Rachel his
> daughter to wife also. (Gen. 29:27-28)

We see from this example how the seventy-weeks in Daniel's prophetic passage equals a time period of four hundred and ninety years: 7 x 70 = 490.

We will see in chapter six where four hundred and eighty-three years of Daniel's prophecy have been completed, which coincided perfectly with the final week of Christ's ministry just days before his crucifixion. Since there is only one week left on God's timetable, this would be the 70th week. There are not any disputes between the different rapture views (except preterism) about there being a final seven-year time period.

5. Tribulation:

This is the common name given by pretribulationist for the final seven-year period that will complete the 70th week spoken in Daniel 9:24-27. However, the specific name "tribulation" is **never** mentioned regarding Daniel's vision of weeks. This is extremely important to understand in the rapture debate. Pretribulation teachers, basically, only cite two verses in their frail attempt to classify the final seven-years as the "tribulation." The first is found in Daniel 9:27. The second is found in Jeremiah 30:7: *Alas! for that day is great, so that none is like it: it is even the time of Jacob's trouble; but he shall be saved out of it.* While this is a reference to Israel in the last days, still, there is no reference to the entire seven-year period. We will see later that this specific prophecy is addressed by Christ himself in the New Testament. And, most important, neither of these two verses gives credence to the name **tribulation**.

6. Great Tribulation:

The main reference given for this event is found in Mathew 24:21, which occurs at the mid-point of the 70th week of Daniel. Jesus describes this time as the ultimate persecution in all of history upon the world.

> For then shall be great tribulation, such as was not since the beginning
> of the world to this time, no, nor ever shall be. (Matt. 24:21)

The great tribulation plays a major part of the rapture debate. Pretribulational teaching says this is the "wrath of God" (as well as the term tribulation); therefore, since the church is not to be the participant of God's wrath we will be taken out (raptured) before this happens (1 Thess.5:9; Romans 2:8-9). Prewrath teaching is that this is the wrath of the Antichrist, not God; thus, the church is subject to persecution during this time. Furthermore, the common belief from the pretribulation view is that the great tribulation will last for three-and-half years, or forty-two months. Some pretribulation teachers, incorrectly, say that the entire seven-years are the great tribulation. Prewrath teaching says the great tribulation will be "cut short" due to God's supernatural intervention, therefore limiting the duration of the great tribulation of Satan's wrath, but not limiting the seven-years themselves.

7.   Abomination of Desolation:

This is an event directly associated with the great tribulation; in fact, it is the abomination of desolation that ignites the great tribulation. The Scripture reference for this event is found in Daniel 9:27, and referenced again by Jesus in Matthew 24:15, and as well as by Paul in 2 Thessalonians 2:4.

> And he shall confirm the covenant with many for one week: and in the midst of the week he shall cause the sacrifice and the oblation to cease, and for the overspreading of abominations he shall make it desolate, even until the consummation, and that determined shall be poured upon the desolate. (Dan. 9:27)

> When ye therefore shall see the abomination of desolation, spoken of by Daniel the prophet, stand in the holy place, (whoso readeth, let him understand:) (Matt. 24:15)

> Who opposeth and exalted himself above all that is called God, or that is worshipped: so that he as God sitteth in the temple of God, showing himself that he is God. (2 Thess. 2:4)

Both pretribulation and prewrath teachings agree that the Antichrist will enter the future rebuilt temple in Jerusalem and cause the sacrifices to cease at the mid-point of Daniels seventy-weeks. However, I will be presenting an optional view to this popular teaching

8. Armageddon:

This is the final battle of the Antichrist and his world armies against Jesus Christ as He descends from heaven at the end of the 70th week of Daniel, which immediately precedes the millennium.

9. Millennium:

This is a thousand-year time period that will be considered paradise on earth where Jesus Christ himself will rule and reign in His kingdom. The millennium will follow the final seven-years. Towards the completion of the thousand years, Satan will be loosed one last time and will bring a short rebellion where he is defeated and cast into the lake of fire. Immediately following, the great white throne judgment will take place, separating all the lost and the saved for eternity. The lost will find their final abode in the lake of fire where Satan resides; and for the saved, we will be in the presence of God forever.

> And I saw thrones, and they sat upon them, and judgment was given unto them: and I saw the souls of them that were beheaded for the witness of Jesus, and for the word of God, and which had not worshipped the beast, neither his image, neither had received his mark upon their foreheads, or in their hands; and they lived and reigned with Christ a **thousand years.** But the rest of the dead lived not again until the **thousand years** were finished. This is the first resurrection. (Revelation 20:4-5)

A. Pre-Millennialism: This term teaches that Jesus Christ will return and set up his kingdom on earth after the 70th week of Daniel is completed, and before the thousand-year reign of Christ.
B. Post-Millennialism: The time period that follows a golden-age on the earth of a thousand years. According to this view there will not be a final seven-year period, but Christianity will usher in this future kingdom of God on earth, supposedly, because Christianity will permeate every aspect of worldly affairs. Christ will not return until after this golden-age is completed.
C. Amillennialism: The belief that there will be "no" millennium. They define the thousand-year reign of Christ in Revelation 20 is symbolic.

We are supposedly currently living in the church-age which is the millennium itself. At some point in the future, Christ will return and the final judgment of mankind will take place then we enter eternity. There will be no kingdom for Israel to receive and enjoy the blessings that God promised them. This is the doctrinal position of the Churches of Christ, The Roman Catholic Church, Methodist and Lutheran Church.

10. Church-Age:

This is commonly taught as the time period from the day of Pentecost (Acts 2) to the return of Christ at the rapture. The church-age will vary in its duration according to the different views on the rapture, but it is agreed the church-age will be concluded when the rapture does takes place. For the pretribulationist, it will conclude before the 70th week; however, there are varying beliefs on when exactly the rapture takes place before the 70th week. Pretribulationist never nail down this time, it could be days, months, or even years. This causes major theological problems for their view that I will expose later. But one fallacy I will expose now is that pretribulationist insist that the seventy-week prophecy is strictly for the nation of Israel. If this is the case, then related to the timing of the pretrib rapture, it must occur **exactly** when the 70th week begins. If not, then the seventy-week prophecy of Daniel is incorrect. Pretribulationist cannot get around this fact. For the prewrath view, we believe the church-age will conclude sometime within the final half of the 70th week, more specifically, at the opening of the sixth seal in Revelation chapter 6.

We will now look at the various beliefs pertaining to the timing of the rapture in relation to the final seven-years.

Pre-Tribulation Rapture:

The standard pretribulation position is that the rapture (secret and invisible) will occur before the beginning of the final week, while the second coming of Christ (visible) will occur at the end of the final seven-years. As a reminder, I am purposely not calling the final week- the tribulation, but the 70th week or just seven-years. Pretribulationism describes at the rapture, Jesus coming "for" the church, and the second coming Jesus returning "with" his church. There is considerable debate to whom to attribute the pretribulation rapture to. It is believed that this doctrine was introduced by Edward Erving of Scotland around 1825. Some notable pretribulation teachers and preachers include J. Dwight Pentecost, John Walvoord, Tim LaHaye, J. Vernon McGee, Chuck Smith, Chuck Missler, Jack Van Impe, Grant Jeffrey, Thomas Ice, David Regan, David Jeremiah and Adrian Rodgers.

Mid-Tribulation Rapture:

The midtribulation position declares that the rapture will occur in the middle of Daniel's 70th week. Since the great tribulation occurs at the mid-point of the seven-years; conversely, midtrib teaches the rapture is pretribulational as well. They teach the church will suffer some persecution up to the middle of the week then be raptured.

Partial Rapture:

The partial rapture view holds to multiple raptures of believers starting at the beginning and occurring at different intervals throughout the seven-year period. The term "partial" refers to the idea that only select Christians will be raptured at a given time during the final week depending on the spiritual condition of the individual believer.

Post-Tribulation Rapture:

The posttribulation position places the rapture at the end of the 70th week just before the battle of Armageddon. Posttribulationist believe when God's wrath takes place, believers will be supernaturally protected just like Israel was when the ten plagues of destruction came upon Egypt. They take what Paul said in 1 Corinthians 15:52 that the rapture occurs at the "last trump," which they say matches the seventh trumpet in the book of Revelation. Therefore, they teach that the church will be here on earth during the entire 70th week.

Pre-Wrath Rapture:

Prewrath rapture adherents believe the Bible teaches only one second coming of Christ, and the rapture is an event associated with Christ's second coming. The prewrath teaching places the rapture occurring at some point during the second half of the final seven-years of Daniels 70th week before the first trumpet is sounded in Revelation chapter eight. At the latest, the rapture would occur no closer than about five months before the end of the 70th week, because the 5th trumpet judgment last five months by itself. At the mid-point of the 70th week the Antichrist is revealed, when this occurs it will kick-off the great tribulation where the Antichrist will begin to persecute both Israel and the church. At some point during the second half of the 70th week the great tribulation will be "cut short" and God will supernaturally intervene on earth and will begin to pour out His wrath upon the lost. This specific time period of God's wrath is called the Day of the Lord. However, before God pours out His wrath, Christ will rapture the Christians who are still alive, resurrect the believers who are dead, and seal the 144,000 (Israel) for protection. Unlike pretrib teaching, prewrath teaching states that the rapture event will be visible for the entire world to see.

Thus far, we have covered the definition of the rapture, tribulation, Daniel's seventy-weeks, and the five major views on the rapture. Now we need to look at some more Bible terms.

11. Dispensational Theology:

This is a very critical term in the debate concerning Christ's coming. Dispensationalist believe that the Bible is broken up into multiple time periods, where at different "dispensations" God did a specific work under different covenants for those living at that time. Dispensationalism espouses "progressive revelation" where God allows man to have more of an understanding of His permissive will and work on the earth. This teaching is considered to be fathered by John Nelson Darby (1800-1882), and expounded further by C.I. Scofield, who wrote the Scofield Study Bible in 1909. As a side note, it was John Darby who was responsible for spreading the pretribulation rapture doctrine in America during the mid-1800s.

Pretribulationism is based on the foundational teaching of dispensationalism. As I mentioned already, dispensationalism teaches that Daniel's seventy-year prophecy (490 years total) is strictly for Israel, leaving the final week for Israel's chastisement from God for their rebellion, which will finally bring them to repentance and acceptance of Jesus.

The key to the dispensational argument is that the church and Israel are completely distinct from each other. We agree that Israel was birthed with Abraham and temporarily set aside at Pentecost in Acts 2 when the church had begun. According to dispensationalism, it will be at the rapture of the church, God will turn His attention again towards Israel to fulfill His promises to the nation, but not before they endure seven-years of tribulation while the church is in heaven enjoying the presence of Christ. Strangely, dispensationalism teaches once the church-age ends before the 70th week, and the final seven-years are completed, only then does a new dispensation begin-the kingdom. They mysteriously bypass the 70th week as being a dispensation. Therefore, I have coined the phrase "pretrib-dispensationalism" to describe dispensationalism defined by pretribulationist.

12. Covenant:

A binding agreement between two or more parties pertaining to an oath given by one or more of the parties involved. This is based on God's promises in the Old Testament to certain individuals or groups (e. g. Abraham and Israel). Some of these covenants were strictly for Israel (e.g. the Holy Land, circumcision), and some can be applied to the New Testament Christians (e.g. Baptism, Lord's Supper). The Noahic covenant, as an example, was God's promise to the world in general not to destroy the earth again by flood. The book of Hebrews was written based mainly on the premise of the New Covenant that both Israel and the church benefit from. (cf. Heb. 8:6-13, 9:1, 15; 10:14-19) I am purposely bypassing the teaching called "covenant theology" since I am only dealing with the rapture topic as it relates to the church.

13. Imminent:

Impending, Looming. This is a term used by pretribulationist who teach the rapture of the church could happen at any-moment. They teach that all prophecy has been fulfilled pertaining to the rapture of the church, and therefore Christ's coming could be today. Pretribulationist often say, "the next event on God's calendar is the rapture of the church."

14. The Day of the Lord:

The Bible describes a future supernatural judgment event when God intervenes in the affairs of mankind on earth. When this day occurs, God will pour out His wrath and judgment upon the unbelievers. There are historic times throughout the Old Testament when God intervened, usually in judgment, however, the Bible does not describe those events as "the day of the Lord." This is very critical in understanding the rapture debate. Pretribulation teachers say the day of the Lord applies to the full seven-years, and prewrath teaching says it occurs sometime in the second half of the seven-years.

These are the main terminologies that I will be using in this study on the rapture. I brought these terms to your attention; however, I will limit our study between the two rapture views.

As I close this chapter I believe it's imperative that we "get it right" as we interpret the Scriptures in relation to the rapture. Here is one last quote from Robert Van Kampen explaining proper biblical hermeneutics.

> Remember-and this is critical-we have not found truth until we find the single common denominator that makes all of the passages fit together. Psalm 119:160 teaches us that "the sum of Thy word is truth." In other words, you don't have truth until you have processed all of the passages dealing with a particular subject and found the single solution that accommodates them all without contradiction![2]

CHAPTER TWO

PSYCHOLOGY 101

Psychology 101 is certainly a peculiar term used in a book about the Rapture. I use this term concerning the mind-games played when trying to argue one's doctrinal position. I acknowledge there are very capable pretribulationist that can articulate their position in a well-defined manner. Some statements I quote by pretrib teachers do not necessarily reflect everyone in the pretrib belief system. However, these statements cannot be swept under the rug as though they do not exist, because they do, and many within the pretrib espouses these sayings.

When engaging with others over the doctrine of our Lords coming, it was not long before I noticed how my pretribulation brethren crafted some of their arguments through human reasoning, as I mentioned in the introduction. Some would make statements like: "I just don't see how God would allow the church to suffer;" or, "I can't reason in my mind God doing that to his people." And my favorite, "Christ is not going to beat up His bride before the wedding." They even make cute remarks like, "I'm not looking for the under-taker but the upper-taker," as though such acknowledgment makes them immune to death. However, it's the intimidation factor that is silently used to make the pretribulation rapture theory seem more spiritual.

Anyone who believes contrary to the pretribulation rapture is usually viewed as someone who is not concerned with spreading the gospel or even Christ's return. Many times, we are marked as divisive to the church's teaching. Many pretribulation proponents would not dare to have others question their belief. Sadly, rather than having a biblically sound discussion regarding the concerns presented by the pretribulation rapture, it typically solicits an unwelcome response. "How could anyone believe that Jesus may not come back today" is the cry from pretribulationist. With that said, here is the first quote from perhaps the best-known prophecy teacher within pretribulationism.

In Tim LaHaye's book "Rapture Under Attack," he echoes this mentality against those who oppose a pretribulation Rapture.

> Yet for some reason, this concept, (pre-tribulation rapture) which has brought so much hope and comfort to millions of Christians throughout church history, has been under **savage attack** during the last sixty years by those who **refuse** to take prophecy as **literally** as they do other scriptures. Some of these **attacks** have taken the form of **vicious personal attacks** on those who held the position; others have even used **gross distortions in their vendetta** against it. Unfortunately, they have been amazingly successful in **causing many innocent victims to abandon their expectation of rapture** in their lifetime and in the process not only **stolen their hope** but, in some cases have **stolen their zeal** for service.[3] (parenthesis and bold letters mine)

LaHaye's statement is echoed loudly through pretribulation literature and sermons. The wording of his statements implies that anyone who questions the pretribulation position is not true in the Christian faith. We have become tormentors to the Christian's only hope for this life, which is apparently the pretribulation rapture. We are labeled, savage attackers, simply because we hold a different perspective on the Lord's return. LaHaye also claims that anyone who opposes the pretrib view is doing it in the name of vendetta (vengeance)- so much for biblical discernment!

LaHaye attempts to add validity to his statement by mentioning church history as though there was a belief in the pretrib rapture throughout church history. This is a distortion of truth, which will be presented in a later chapter (5).

Could it be that those who abandoned their former position (like me) concluded that the pretrib doctrine has fatal flaws in it? I will make a case that it is the pretrib teaching that has abandoned the literal interpretation of the Scriptures, and the gross distortions have come from the pretrib teachers themselves, as I propose in this book.

Here is another example by LaHaye playing the psychological game:

Prisoners have looked expectantly through dungeon windows. Slaves have looked up in the fields. Children have wondered at a slant of sunlight through a sudden break in the clouds. Jesus is coming soon! Maybe today. Maybe tonight. Maybe before I draw my next breath.

And yet that **comforting** belief is under greater **attack** today more than at any time in recent history. Christian mothers now **worry** that their precious sons and daughters will be **forced** to undergo the horrors of the great tribulation. Christian fathers **fret** about the **impossible task** keeping their families alive through the most gruesome period the world has ever known.[4] (bold letters mine)

Let me first comment about his statement regarding the prisoner's dilemma with incarceration. Is a prisoner with no hope of a physical release to believe they have NO HOPE other than Jesus coming back to free him? How about those confined in concentration camps during World War II, surely, they longed for their release, but when help did not come, as in most cases, what would become of them then? Many just gave up on life, yet people like Corrie Ten Boom found a renewed hope in the eternal God who promised her something far better. Are we to believe the Christians being held in those prisons, that their only hope was the rapture?

John the Baptist was not rescued from prison by Jesus; rather, he was left to face his death through beheading. Christ allowed him to experience his ordeal alone. Jesus did not come running to rescue him from, undoubtedly, the darkest day of his life. It was God who commissioned John to go and preach to Israel in the wilderness. And it was God who left him alone in that prison cell. But we do know the scriptures tell us is that Christ later stated *John was the greatest who were born of women* (Mt. 11:11). John's only questioning during his imprisonment was he wanted to make sure that Jesus was the true Christ (Matt. 11:3). John never viewed Jesus as someone who was to come and rescue him from his predicament as he suffered physically and this will be the fundamental danger in the tribulation. Many will reason amongst themselves that accepting the Antichrist's terms and conditions as God's will, being physically delivered, but in reality, will be their eternal doom. (Luke 17:33).

Second, are we to believe that a mother's only comforting hope for her child's impending death is the rapture? The uses of terms by LaHaye such as "comforting belief," is manipulating his readers to think there is "no comfort" without a pretribulation rapture. He makes void the true purpose of the rapture; which is to translate believers who are alive at Christ's second coming to be delivered from the wrath to come, not escape some trial a believer may be experiencing. It is a shame that millions of persecuted believers throughout history did not have any hope – all had to face death or severe punishment without being raptured.

What are believers to think of the impossible task of keeping their families alive through the most gruesome time ever to face in this world? The pretribulation theory teaches that after the rapture occurs, multitudes will be saved during the tribulation? How about those who become believers during the wrath of Antichrist-how do they face this impossible task? Do those who are supposedly left behind have any kind of "hope" during this awful time? Does the book of Revelation reference any hope for Christians as they face trials in the tribulation? Yes!

Here are four examples of psychological statements used by pretribulational teaching that I believe sum up their typical rhetoric:

1.   "I am not looking for the Antichrist, but Jesus Christ!"

This is a classic catchphrase of the pretribulationist argument for a pretrib rapture. It is strange that most of the rapture date-setters have been pretribulationist, and yet they claim to believe in imminence. Edgar Whisenant's book "Eighty Eight Reasons why Christ will Return in Eighty Eight" was a big bust for the pretribulational believers. It was Hal Lindsey's book "The Late Great Planet Earth" that helped mold the idea that Christ would return in 1988:

> What generation [would experience the end times predicted in Matthew 24:34]? Obviously, in context, **the generation that would see the signs** - chief among them the rebirth of Israel. A generation in the Bible is something like forty years. If this is a correct deduction, then **within forty years or so of 1948, all these things could take place.**[5] (bold letters mine)

This bold prediction was swept under the rug by many who were embarrassed by Lindsey and Whisenant's predictions. Lindsey's statement made regarding the budding of the fig tree is found in Matthew 24.

Pretribulationist consistently state that the fig tree- referenced in the Olivet Discourse- represents Israel in the tribulation. However, I will show that the fig tree pertains to the events, both, before and during the final seven-years, and that the fig tree does not solely refer to Israel.

In 1994, Harold Camping, a pretribulationist, declared that the rapture would occur on September 6th later that same year. Camping, again, predicted the rapture in 2011. He called it "Judgment Day," and affirmed it would take place on May 21, 2011. Like his first failed prediction, his second has come and gone to no avail.

In an interview, Camping apologizes for his botched prediction, yet, he twisted his blunder by redefining it as a "spiritual judgment day" rather than a physical one.

> OAKLAND, Calif. –Harold Camping, who predicted that 200 million Christians would be taken to heaven Saturday before catastrophe struck the planet, apologized Monday evening for not having the dates "worked out as accurately as I could have."…it dawned on him that instead of the biblical Rapture in which the faithful would be swept up to the heavens, May 21 had instead been a **"spiritual" Judgment Day,** which places the entire world under Christ's judgment, he said...[6] (bold letters mine)

The final analysis, Camping covered his initial false prediction by adjusting the date of Christ's return. Charles Taze Russell, founder of the Jehovah Witnesses, attempted to predict the date of Christ's visible return in 1914. When his prophecy failed, Russell also claimed that the kingdom had come via a spiritual dimension by the invisible return of Christ. Just like that, magically, the Jehovah's Witnesses supposedly became God's agent of authority to the inhabitants of the earth because they claim to be spiritual empowered. This was just another example of Christ's warning to believers to watch out for false prophets. We can positively see that one main component to false teaching is the emphasis upon special knowledge of Christ's return. Believers should take warning as Christ noted in the Olivet Discourse.

In another example, Chuck Smith, who was the father of the Calvary Chapel movement and the radio Bible teacher of **The Word for Today,** had made the same failed rapture prediction as Hal Lindsey.

> We're the generation that saw the fig tree bud forth, as Israel became a nation again in 1948. As a rule, a generation in the Bible lasts 40 years. The children of Israel journeyed in the wilderness for 40 years until that generation died.
>
> From my understanding of biblical prophecies, **I'm convinced that the Lord is coming for His Church before the end of 1981.**[7] (bold letters mine)

Chuck Smith believed, convincingly, that Christ's return would take place in 1981; however, even quoting Scripture, he was incorrect because he did not take Scripture at face value.

On one hand, I can only chuckle at the thought of the prophetic soothsayers as they continue to forecast the soon return of Christ by making obscene predictions as world-events unfold. On the other hand, I cringe at the prospect of those who will only laugh at those who drum-up excitement of Christ's coming. One of the fundamental reasons that many non-believers will scoff at Christ's second coming is due to the false predictions pretribulationist continue to make.

> Knowing this first, that there shall come in the last days scoffers, walking after their own lusts, And saying, Where is the promise of his coming? for since the fathers fell asleep, all things continue as they were from the beginning of the creation. For this they willingly are ignorant of, that by the word of God the heavens were of old, and the earth standing out of the water and in the water: (2 Peter 3:3-5)

In addition, consider the failed predictions of the Y2K in which we were bombarded with the possible "end of the world" scenarios. One of the main predictions was due to society's dependence on the computer; supposedly, the date change from 1999 to 2000 would lead to computer failures worldwide. This hysteria in the Christian community was led by the pretribulation teacher Chuck Missler. Many people stored food and the sale of personal electric generators sky rocketed, because their belief was that we were going to plummet back to the dark-ages. I know the sincerity of many, but I truly believe that much of the prophecy teaching today is only a marketing ploy so they can sell materials and literature!

"I'm not looking for the Antichrist, but Jesus Christ," is not a true statement practiced by many pretribulationist. Numerous sermons and books presented by pretribulation teachers regard current technology as the development of the mark of the beast. Most end time teaching is done by pretribulationist emphasizing the rise of the Antichrist and the mark of the beast. If these teachers are looking for Jesus Christ; why spend so much time teaching about things that point to the coming Antichrist? They deny looking for the Antichrist, but they preach and teach otherwise. Here is a small, but growing, list of some notable pretrib teachers writing books about the Antichrist.

From Daniel to Doomsday (The Countdown has Begun) written in 1999 by John Hagee.

Jerusalem Countdown (World War Three has Begun) written in 2006 by John Hagee.

Earths Final Moments (Powerful insights and understandings of the prophetic signs that surround us) written in 2011 by John Hagee.

The Coming Economic Armageddon, written in 2010 by David Jeremiah

End Time and the Secrets of the Mahdi, by Michael Yousef

Global Warning, written in 2008 by Ed Hindson and Tim LaHaye

Is the Antichrist Alive Today, written in 2002 by Mark Hitchcock

The Prince of Darkness (Antichrist and the New World Order), written in 1994 by Grant Jeffrey

Unleashing the Beast (The coming Fanatical Dictator and His Ten-Nation Coalition) written in 2011 by Perry Stone.

You can see by these pretribulation teachers, and many others, they spend a considerable amount of time writing on the Antichrist and his end-time system. If pretrib folks are looking for Jesus Christ, then back up what you believe and stop all this peripheral discussion about the Antichrist.

I would like to make one last point regarding end-time books written by pretribulationist. Unfortunately, and I can safely say, most have been written books with the intention to market their prophecy ministry to Christians. One case in point is a book written by Tim LaHaye in 1972 called **The Beginning of the End**. In this particular book LaHaye said:

> "Carefully putting all this together, we now recognize this strategic generation. **It is the generation that 'sees' the four-part sign of verse 7 [in <u>Matt. 24</u>], or the people who saw the** *First World* **War**. We must be careful here not to become dogmatic, but it would seem that these people are witnesses to the events, not necessarily participants in them. That would suggest they were at least old enough to understand the **events of 1914– 1918**, not necessarily old enough to go to war."[8] (bold letters mine)

This quote alone proves the major fallacy of LaHaye's imminence regarding signs. However, what I would like to zero in on is the revision to the same book that was resold in 1991. LaHaye uses dishonest practices and rewords the phrase we just read to make his book seem that he is keeping current with prophetic events. Here's what he said in 1991.

> "Carefully putting all this together, we now recognize this strategic generation. *It is the generation that 'sees' the events of 1948.* We must be careful here not to become dogmatic, but it would seem that these people are witnesses to the events, not necessarily participants in them. That would suggest they were at least old enough to understand the **events of 1948**."[9] (Bold letter mine)

He changes the same "sign-event" from WWI to the rebirth of Israel, thirty years later. LaHaye deception is not any different than Jehovah's Witnesses that continually "update" their prophetic calendar to mislead their followers. Any serious author (especially Christian) would not write such a deliberate fallacious statement. As a leader in the Christian community, LaHaye should uphold a higher standard than to mislead his readers with such an obvious change.

Lastly, let me make a comment dealing specifically with the appearance of the Antichrist before the rapture. This is something that I will develop in more detail later, but as prewrath we are not looking for the Antichrist instead of Christ like pretrib folks accuse us of. Let me explain by using an illustration in the Bible about this story of Peter walking on the water during the storm. If you recall, it was when Peter took his eyes (focus) off Jesus did he begin to sink and start to panic. As prewrath believers, we certainly believe in Antichrist before the rapture, but unlike pretrib, we emphasize the correct biblical meaning of watchfulness. And it's certainly not focusing on the appearance of Antichrist, but the coming of Christ, despite the coming storm caused by Satan.

2. "You can go through the Tribulation if you want to."

This scurrilous phrase is repeated by the pretribulation crowd more than any other in order to side-step the real rapture issues. This would be no different than a lost person stating: "You can believe in hell if you want to, but I don't, and I'm not planning on going there." Since someone chooses not to believe in hell, do they automatically become exempt from going there? No! The ploy of pretribulation teacher's use of crafted psychology is not any different from those who deny a literal hell.

Persecute Me Please:

> You would think the **desire to go through the tribulation** would be as popular as the desire to jump into a pit filled with vipers and broken glass. As illogical as it may seem, there appears to be a large number of Christians that fully expect to get roughed up before Christ returns.

> Many Christians **argue strongly for the right to suffer persecution** at the hands of the Antichrist and the one world government. **These Tribulation saints wannabees** constantly harp, "Because Jesus and his disciples suffered persecution we should expect no better.[10] (bold letters mine)

> Todd Standberg

In my research studying the topic on the rapture, I have yet to meet any non- pretrib person who desires to go through the tribulation. Prewrath believers certainly do not desire tribulation, but are willing to accept the evidence presented in the Scriptures at face value.

In John Hagee's book "From Daniel to Doomsday" he echoes the same pretrib sentiment about those who question the pretrib position.

> My friend, dominion theologians [the belief the church will usher
> in the kingdom of Christ] and liberal preachers are running down
> Main Street screaming, "We're going through the tribulation,"
> and those are more loyal to the message of a man than the word
> of God are joining the stampede.[11] (brackets mine)

I'm reminded of the account recorded in Matthew 16 where Jesus, for the first time, explained to the disciples that he would be killed at the hands of the religious leaders. It was at this time Peter rebuked Jesus.

> 21. From that time forth began Jesus to shew unto his disciples,
>   how that he must go unto Jerusalem, and suffer many things
>   of the elders and chief priests and scribes, and be killed, and
>   be raised again the third day.
> 22. Then Peter took him, and began to rebuke him, saying, Be it
>   far from thee, Lord: this shall not be unto thee.

This is the natural response of Peter's thinking that Jesus was special and He was above such exposure of suffering. Peter's remarks are evident to many believer's beliefs pertaining to suffering. Read on your own, Jesus's response to him, it wasn't pretty.

3. Christ is not going to beat up His Bride!

> "Arguing that the Lord would put the Bride of Christ through the
> Tribulation is like getting engaged and then beating your bride
> senseless in order to prepare her for the wedding."

> Indeed! What kind of loving Bridegroom would subject His Bride
> to the worst beating imaginable (as Jesus Himself described it).[12]

This pretrib quote pretty-much sums up their thought process about what happens to the church if we go through the tribulation. They attempt to paint a wedding day picture in your mind with the horrible conclusion of the groom beating up his bride. We will see this is not the case, but we will see Christ avenging His bride after the church is assaulted by the enemy. In Christ's loving nature, He desires that those who want the hurt His bride will "repent" and turn to Him before they are judged.

A perfect illustration of this is when Christ pleads with Saul (later named Paul) who was persecuting God's people. Acts 9:5 *And he said, Who art thou, Lord? And the Lord said, I am Jesus whom thou persecutest: it is hard for thee to kick against the pricks.* Jesus confirms to Saul, he is not persecuting just anyone, but Christ himself. When the tribulation occurs, it can't possibly be Christ persecuting His own, this would be a violation of God's nature. If the Church belongs to God, then God won't be persecuting himself, just like we witnessed in the book of Acts. This is why we will see in our study the differences between tribulation and wrath.

4. "We are not going thru God's Wrath"

This phrase comes on the heels of the last phrase "Christ is not going to beat up His Bride." I will be dealing with this statement throughout this study. This often-repeated phrase by pretrib is usually one of their first rebuttals to others who disapprove of the pretrib teaching. This is at the heart of the rapture debate, simply because the pretrib thinking is that the 70th week is strictly God's punishment on the world, so therefore we are out of here at the beginning of the tribulation. Pretribulationism does not allow any time for the final seven-years to develop with the rise of Antichrist and his short-term reign, along with the world's worshipping him before God intervenes and punish the earth. They interchangeably use God's wrath and tribulation in their terminology, leaving no distinction between the two. There is however a distinction, and I will lay out the two differences, leaving no doubt to the reader their proper use.

Fear & Intimidation:

In Jesus's earthly ministry, the religious leadership in Israel was his greatest opposition. The Pharisees were rooted and grounded in traditions, who became powerful leaders throughout Israel. In Jesus's "Sermon on the

Mount," he often repeated the statement *ye have heard it had been said*. The traditions of the Pharisees became the final authority above God's word. The Pharisees demanded obedience to their way of thinking. The classic example of this is found in John 9 when Jesus healed the blind man, and the Pharisees "demanded" an answer from the blind man how he received his sight.

> They say unto the blind man again, What sayest thou of him, that he hath opened thine eyes? He said, He is a prophet. But the Jews did not believe concerning him, that he had been blind, and received his sight, until they called the parents of him that had received his sight. And they asked them, saying, Is this your son, who ye say was born blind? how then doth he now see? His parents answered them and said, We know that this is our son, and that he was born blind: But by what means he now seeth, we know not; or who hath opened his eyes, we know not: he is of age; ask him: he shall speak for himself. These words spake his parents, because they **feared the Jews**: for the Jews had agreed already, that if any man did confess that he was Christ, he should be **put out of the synagogue**. (John 9:17-22, bold letters mine)

Do you think the Pharisees would be thankful for the healed man? No! They were the "authority" and had to maintain control, after all, they were the keepers of the law and determined the righteousness among the people (John 9:34). It was the Pharisees who sent their followers to question John the baptist: who was he and by what authority was he preaching and baptizing (John 1:21-22) - as though John was accountable to them. The spiritual foothold the Pharisees had on the people incited fear, leaving the people unable to question the actions and teachings forced upon them. Remember, it was the Pharisees who instigated the arrest and put Christ on trial, resulting in His death by crucifixion.

We are to be subject to God's truth, the scriptures, above denominational belief. As Christians, aren't we excited when someone from a false religion becomes born again and joins our fellowship? We hail them heroes as they stand for "truth" even against the backlash they receive from their church or denomination. Intimidation is a major, and equally serious, deterrent to the truth. The Pharisees were not interested in truth, only self-exaltation- they loved to be praised. In the end, as Christians, we are called to be students of truth. Jesus discussed the importance of knowing the truth in John 8.

> Then said Jesus to those Jews which believed on him, If ye
> continue in my word, then are ye my disciples indeed; And ye shall
> know the truth, and the truth shall make you free. (John 8:31-32)

Pride can be worse than any cancer that slowly and internally devastates the physical body. It is pride that keeps people from hearing and obeying the truth, which, if not treated, will slowly eat away a person's spiritual and emotional well-being. Pontius Pilot's pride made him question the very Son of God by asking Jesus; *what is truth?* (John 18:38). Pride is an invasive virus that blinds and binds the heart from receiving what is true and honest.

Believers should be allowed openly to question what a teacher teaches by the Word of God. Jehovah Witnesses are brainwashed into accepting the teachings of the Watchtower. It is well-known that Jehovah Witnesses are not allowed to read or study any teaching materials outside Watchtower literature. If they are caught, most likely they will be excommunicated and shunned from their religion, which is nothing more than mind-control of a system that subjugates their followers to a Christless eternity.

Here is an example in our rapture study of extreme intimidation in a quote by LaHaye, which has the hidden element of the mind-control philosophy.

> It is my **overwhelming conviction** that some people have left
> the pre-trib position because they have **overexposed** their minds
> to arguments for post- or mid-Trib positions and **underexposed**
> their minds to the biblical reasons holding the pre-Trib view.[13]
> (bold letters mine)

On his criticism of Marvin Rosenthal's book "The Pre-Wrath Rapture of the Church," LaHaye comments:

> Because the author **failed to have his manuscript evaluated**
> by other biblical literalist with a **better grasp** of Greek, Hebrew,
> and prophecy before **he rushed into print**, it may well serve as
> an instrument of confusion,[14] (bold letters mine)

LaHaye is more concerned with attacking the character of Rosenthal, along with Robert VanKampen, than the content of his message (ad hominem). This is merely an unfounded and immature attack against a different view, which pretrib adherents like LaHaye do not like to be questioned. We will see whether the prewrath doctrine of the rapture of the church is based on biblical accuracy and contextual harmony.

Here are a few more examples of LaHaye's blind assault:

> **Satan,** the master deceiver, does not want us to get excited about the **fact** that there are **more signs of Christ's return today than any other time in church history.** Consequently, we can expect him to send all kinds of **deceivers** into the church to **rob** us of the keen consciences of living every day in the light of Christ's possible return.[15] (bold letters mine)

> When the pre-Trib position is **attacked, undermining** the faith of a young Christian, or when a minister embraces a different **theory** and divides his church by teaching it, **Satan** notches another victory.[16] (bold letters mine)

According to LaHaye, all kinds of deceivers have entered the church like thieves and robbed true believers of their hope, all because they question the legitimacy of the pretrib rapture. I ask the question: Is it better to act in unity by believing a lie, or divided because of what is true? The rapture topic should not ultimately be a divisive issue in the church; however, Satan wins if theology takes a back seat in church teaching. Also, I'm glad he acknowledges the fact that signs are needed to occur "before" the rapture happens.

In his book *"Rapture Under Attack"* LaHaye says:

> Since writing the above words and the publication of this book in 1992, I invited a number of the leading prophecy scholars, writers and teachers of the pre-Trib view of end tine events to meet me for three days in Dallas, Texas, for in-depth discussions on prophecy. Dr. John Walvoord, the dean of all living prophecy scholars and authors was there, as were Drs. Charles Ryrie, Dwight Pentecost, Stan Tousaint, Gerald Stranton, Hal Lindsey, Dr. Thomas Ice, and many others. We all agreed that a permanent group was needed, so we formed the Pre-Trib Research Center (PTRC). Since then, almost two hundred prophecy scholars have joined from many Christian colleges, seminaries, Bible schools, churches and related ministries.

For six years this group has meet faithfully for three days annually to consider all the attacks on our position, to study its scriptural basis, and to provide biblical answers to the questions against it. It has been thrilling to see the plethora of good books, videos, and cassettes on the end times that came out of the pens of our members. Some have gone out to start whole ministries, and it is my prayer that the "Left Behind" series will end up as a major movie production that will have the same soul-winning impact on viewers that the books have had on readers.[17] (bold letters mine)

I am glad he named these leading scholars within pretribulationism, because I will quote them later to show you the confusion they cause over their own interpretations amongst themselves.

Here is one example of a video used to help explain the disappearance of millions of people due to the pretrib rapture. In "Unidentified," they depict space aliens invisibly arriving to cover up a secret rapture (pretrib doctrine). This supposedly will help the world explain to those left behind the disappearance of millions of Christians. This is nothing more than UNBIBLICAL NONSENSE of the highest degree that the pretrib teachers devise to justify their doctrine. I have even heard this talked about on radio programs while they taught on the rapture. Nowhere in Scripture is there a hint that the world is in confusion about the disappearance of Christians and children as well.

LaHaye also discards Robert Van Kampen's book "The Sign," which he strictly bases "guilt by association" for working with Marvin Rosenthal.

Writer and teacher B. W. Newton was a member of the Plymouth Brethren Church, and a close associate of John Darby who ultimately controlled the teachings of the church. Newton eventually rejected Darby's teaching on dispensationalism and pretribulationism, and was unceremoniously excommunicated by Darby. Thomas Ice, a leading pretrib advocate, comments on "why" Newton wrote and preached against Darby's doctrine:

It doesn't take much **imagination** to foresee Newton's **resentment** of Darby. According to one researcher, "He spent the second half of his life on a crusade to disprove the pre-Trib rapture and thus had repeated clashes with J. N. Darby. He wrote scores of books advocating his views."[18] (bold letters mine)

This is a weak and circumventing argument to state "it just takes imagination" to dismiss someone's belief system. In Ice's psychological analysis of Newton, he believes "resentment" is the only real reason for attacking Darby's doctrine. Again, this demonstrates that intimidation can keep the truth buried. As Christians, we are commissioned to be ready to give an answer to those who ask (1 Peter 3:15) - B.W. Newton certainly did.

As Christians, we have been mischaracterized by the liberal media, which has the power to persuade the audience to their opinions and philosophies. Typically, one side of the story is usually presented, which is slanted to their liberal, biased opinion. The rapture topic taught in many churches is treated the same way. The pretrib foothold in many churches has been a one-sided presentation with no chance of a counter-argument. Many churches have in their doctrinal statement that their members must believe the pretrib rapture to hold a position of leadership. Consequently, there are serious implications in teaching the rapture doctrine without proper study. The pretrib teaching is chameleon, ever-changing in its interpretation of scripture, which I will identify throughout this teaching. Pretrib teachers should not be offended when questioned about their belief in the rapture. I would be remiss if I did not bring up the psychological aspect of the rapture debate. With psychology aside, I trust and pray that the reader will be open to the evidence as to make a valid judgment.

CHAPTER THREE

OLD TESTAMENT OVERVIEW

As the drum beat of Bible prophecy continues to get louder and louder, I believe we are witnessing the culmination of prophetic events foretold thousands of years ago. Before we delve heavy into our rapture study, it is imperative to review the roots of Bible prophecy in order to better understand the fruits of its fulfillment. To achieve this, I believe a brief review of the Old Testament is necessary. I would like to discuss the plan and purpose for man by God throughout the Old Testament to help establish a foundation as we develop Christ's coming in the New Testament. This will certainly aid us in our study on the purpose and the timing of the rapture. In the book of Acts, Paul on several occasions, when challenged by the Jewish leadership about his new-found faith, he would rehearse Israel's journey in the Old Testament to form a background from a historical perspective to add a legitimacy to prove his point.

The Beginning

In the Genesis account of creation, we first witness God's literal, twenty-four hour, six-day creation, where afterwards, God rested (was satisfied) on the seventh day. We see Adam was created on the sixth day, along with his wife, Eve, who was to be his "help meet."

Shortly after their creation, God commanded them not to eat from the tree of knowledge of good and evil. Subtly, Satan, came to Eve in the form of a serpent and deceived her by persuading her she could make choices without any negative consequences. After that fateful choice to partake of the forbidden fruit, she gave to Adam and he did the same. The results of that decision were disastrous, and we are still faced with the consequences today. Their decision brought about a separation from God that passed unto the entire human race. Plainly, that decision brought about sin (transgression of God's law or His holiness).

> Wherefore, as by one man sin entered into the world, and death
> by sin; and so death passed upon all men, for that all have sinned:
> (Rom. 5:12)

We see God pronounced certain judgments upon Adam and Eve for their disobedience that was passed unto us. However, the one judgment I would like to focus on which impacts our study, is the one that was pronounced on Satan himself.

> And the LORD God said unto the serpent, Because thou hast
> done this, thou art cursed above all cattle, and above every beast
> of the field; upon thy belly shalt thou go, and dust shalt thou eat
> all the days of thy life:
>
> And I will put enmity between thee and the woman, **and between
> thy seed and her seed (Jesus); it shall bruise thy head**, and
> thou shalt bruise his heel. (Gen. 3:14-15)

This verse is paramount concerning God's plan of redemption for mankind. Satan would eventually bruise Christ's heel at the cross, but in return, it would also be his death-blow. It was from this announcement that Satan would attempt, throughout the Old Testament, to try and stop the prophecy in Genesis 3:15 from being fulfilled; he certainly understood the consequences. Satan won a victory in the garden by deceiving Eve, now he would be determined to stop God at all cost.

It's not too long before we see this conflict take place with the murder of Abel by Cain. Cain moved with envy against his brother, because Abel was "accepted" with God through the right offering, whereas Cain's offering was rejected by God (cf. Gen. 4:4-5; 1 John 3:12).

After the death of Abel, God blessed Adam and Eve with a new son, Seth (Gen. 4:25). It would be through the linage of Seth that the promised seed of Genesis 3:15 would come.

Noah and the Flood

From the events of Cain and Abel we now move to Noah and the story about the flood, where the Bible paints a sad picture how wicked man had become.

> And God saw that the **wickedness of man was great in the earth, and that every imagination of the thoughts of his heart was only evil continually.** And it repented the LORD that he had made man on the earth, and it grieved him at his heart. And the LORD said, **I will destroy man** whom I have created from the face of the earth; both man, and beast, and the creeping thing, and the fowls of the air; for it repenteth me that I have made them. (Gen. 6:5-7)

> And God looked upon the earth, and, behold, it was corrupt; for **all flesh had corrupted his way** upon the earth. And God said unto Noah, The **end of all flesh** is come before me; for the earth is filled with violence through **them;** and, behold, **I will destroy them** with the earth. (Gen. 6:12-13)

The inhabitants of the earth allowed their hearts to be steered away from God, which ultimately led to corruption and violence. Satan won a major step in thwarting God's plan for the promise seed of Eve by the murder of Able; now he's managed to corrupt the whole earth. However, God saw a man, Noah, whose lineage was not given over to the wickedness of the world. Even though Noah was a sinner, the Bible says he found "grace" in the eyes of God.

> But **Noah found grace** in the eyes of the LORD. These are the generations of Noah: Noah was a just man and **perfect in his generations,** and Noah walked with God. (Gen. 6:8-9)

What does it mean that Noah was perfect in his generations? The answer can be found in the New Testament.

> For if God spared not the angels that sinned, but cast them down to hell, and delivered them into chains of darkness, to be reserved unto judgment; And spared not the old world, but saved Noah

the **eighth person, a preacher of righteousness,** bringing in the
flood upon the world of the ungodly; (2 Pet. 2:4-5)

Noah the eighth person is speaking of his lineage from the time of
Enos. It was with Enos when men began to call upon God. We can see this
in Genesis's chapter 4.

And Adam knew his wife again; and she bare a son, and called his
name Seth: For God, said she, hath appointed me another seed
instead of Abel, whom Cain slew. And to Seth, to him also there
was born a son; and he called his name Enos: **then began men
to call upon the name of the LORD.** (Gen. 4:25-26)

I believe they were crying out about their desire to have a personal
relationship with the creator of the universe, God himself. This was how they
were declared righteous, as stated about Noah in 2 Peter. If we follow the
genealogy, we can see how Noah was the eighth person starting with Enos,
who was the son of Seth.

1.) Enos- 5:6
2.) Cainan- 5:9
3.) Mahalaleel- 5:12
4.) Jared- 5:15
5.) Enoch- 5:18
6.) Methuselah- 5:21
7.) Lamech- 5:26
8.) Noah- 5:28-29

Noah's righteous lineage spared mankind's fate from destruction.
Furthermore, it was through Noah's lineage that God kept his witness in the
earth. The same will take place in the final days during Daniel's 70th week
after the rapture of the saints, when God transitions from the church back
to Israel (more on this later).

The rest of the story of Noah and his family is history. The inhabitants
of the earth perished in the flood, and Noah and his family were spared the
wrath of God.

I do want to direct your attention to a verse recorded in the Bible after
the flood.

> And God spake unto Noah, and to his sons with him, saying,
> And I, behold, I establish my **covenant** with you, and with **your seed** after you; (Gen. 9:8-9)

God gave his word to Noah spoken through a covenant that He made to mankind where He would not destroy the earth again with a flood. God sealed this covenant by placing a rainbow in the sky (Gen 9:13-14).

The result of this attempt by Satan to get God to destroy mankind failed, but Satan would not give up.

The Tower of Babel

The next major attack by Satan upon man was the building of the Tower of Babel.

> And the **whole earth was of one language, and of one speech.** And it came to pass, as they journeyed from the east, that they found a plain in the land of Shinar; and they dwelt there. And **they said** one to another, Go to, **let us make** brick, and burn them thoroughly. And they had brick for stone, and slime had they for mortar. And **they said**, Go to, **let us build** us a city and a tower, whose top may reach unto heaven; and **let us make** us a name, lest we be scattered abroad upon the face of the whole earth. And the LORD came down to see the city and the tower, which the children of men builded. And the LORD said, Behold, **the people is one, and they have all one language; and this they begin to do: and now nothing will be restrained from them, which they have imagined to do.** Go to, let us go down, and there confound their language, that they may not understand one another's speech. So the **LORD scattered them abroad from thence upon the face of all the earth:** and they left off to build the city. Therefore is the name of it called Babel; because the LORD did there **confound the language of all the earth: and from thence did the LORD scatter them abroad upon the face of all the earth.** (Gen. 11:1-9)

As we stand back and analyze what their society had become, we again can see that man's heart was bent on rebelling against God once again. Just like before the flood, man's "imagination" was at the forefront of his self-destructive behavior. Satan had persuaded mankind to gather together and build a tower that was to bring spiritual harmony to the people of the earth. Perhaps this literal tower was designed to harmonize mankind into a "religious family," which was completely opposite of what Satan attempted to do before the flood. Before the flood, he instigated havoc on mankind with violence and corruption, but now his plan was to have man exalt himself. If Satan could not get man to completely kill one another, he would enslave them through unity of a false religion by getting man to worship God on his religious terms. Was not this the condition that Satan proposed to Eve in the garden? I believe we are witnessing the resurgence of this age-old lie where the ecumenical movement is engulfing many churches, led by contemporary worship. Concluding, we see God's intervention by confounding the languages of mankind and dispersing them physically across the face of the earth, thus stopping Satan again.

Abraham

We now come to another main character of the Bible, Abraham. Abraham, specifically, his faith, plays a major role throughout the Bible, where he becomes the torch bearer, not only for Israel, but the church as well.

We see through the genealogy account in Genesis that Abraham was born the son of Terah (Gen. 11:26). If find it interesting that Abraham was born in the year 1948 from the creation of Adam. Originally, Abraham's name was Abram, where his name-change would take place years later when God makes a specific covenant (promise) with him. Abraham's name means a "friend of God," giving him a new identity with his relationship to God. We further see in Genesis chapter 12 that God told him to separate himself from his family and kinsman, and move to another land. This was perhaps due to the influence of paganism within his family.

> Now the LORD had said unto Abram, **Get thee out of thy country, and from thy kindred, and from thy father's house**, unto a land that I will show thee: And I will make of thee a great nation, and I will bless thee, and make thy name great; and thou shalt be a blessing: (Gen. 12:1-2)

Through his decision to follow God, the Bible records that Abraham was justified by Faith because his actions proved he believed the promises of God. In chapter 15, we see that God sealed this promise by a covenant.

> And he brought him forth abroad, and said, Look now toward heaven, and tell the stars, if thou be able to number them: and he said unto him, **So shall thy seed be. And he believed in the LORD; and he counted it to him for righteousness…**In the **same day** the LORD made a **covenant** with Abram, saying, Unto thy **seed** have I given **this land,** from the river of Egypt unto the great river, the river Euphrates: (Gen. 15:5, 18)

The first covenant; God made with Adam (the father of the human race) was in the Garden of Eden (Gen. 3:15). Next, it was with Noah, by preserving humanity from total destruction in the flood. Later, though there was not a specific covenant mentioned, God intervened at the Tower of Babel, dispersing the inhabitants across the earth. In this covenant with Abraham, God promised that he would give him a son (Isaac), and through his seed Abraham would have a family that would be multiplied as the stars of heaven. The foundation was laid, God was now establishing His elect people-Israel, and by giving them the promise land they could be kept from the influence of an ungodly world.

> Neither shall thy name any more be called Abram, but thy name shall be Abraham; for a **father of many nations** have I made thee. And I will **make thee exceeding fruitful,** and **I will make nations of thee,** and kings shall come out of thee. And I will establish **my covenant** between me and **thee and thy seed after thee** in their generations for an **everlasting covenant,** to be a God unto thee, and to **thy seed after thee.** And I will give unto thee, and to **thy seed after thee, the land wherein thou art a stranger, all the land of Canaan, for an everlasting possession**; and I will be their God. (Gen. 17:5-8)

After Abraham left his kinsfolk in Haran twenty years earlier, God appears to him again which was to solidify the covenant of the promised seed. This is the time where God changes his name from Abram to Abraham; symbolizing Abraham's identity as the father of many nations. God refers to his future people as *many nations,* not just Israel; which would eventually incorporate the church saints from all over the earth as well (Matt. 21:43). The physical land of Israel is promised to the physical seed of Abraham, the

Jews; whereas, we know today through the New Testament that believers in Christ are of the spiritual seed of Abraham (e.g. Romans 4).

Sodom and Gomorrah

At this point I will bypass the events of Sodom and Gomorrah to keep on track the flow of the narrative in our study. However, please do not overlook the importance of what transpired in these wicked cities as it does parallel to end-time events in its application. See appendix on the prophetic significance of the destruction of Sodom and Gomorrah compared to the birth of Isaac.

From the Birth of Isaac to the Promise Land

After the destruction of Sodom and Gomorrah in Genesis chapter 19, we see the birth of Isaac in chapter 21. Isaac's birth occurred twenty-five years after Abraham journeyed from his homeland. Isaac is the father of Jacob who becomes the patriarch of Israel. To Jacob were born twelve sons (and one daughter) that eventually become the twelve tribes of Israel.

The recognition of Israel as a sovereign nation would not come until she endured hardship under the heavy-hand of the Egyptians. This prophecy of bondage of affliction was foretold to Abraham back in Genesis.

> And he said unto Abram, Know of a surety that thy seed shall be a **stranger in a land that is not theirs, and shall serve them;** and **they shall afflict them four hundred years;** And also that nation, whom they shall serve, will I judge: and afterward shall they come out with great substance. (Gen. 15:13-14)

For four-hundred years the children of Israel would live in bondage to the Egyptians, and eventually, a Pharaoh (king) would come to the throne and put tremendous hardship on them. It was during this adversity, God eventually would deliver Israel from the Egyptian bondage. Just as God rose Joseph up to a position of prominence, God also raised up Moses to lead them out of bondage into the Promised Land. Not only would Israel be led out of Egypt, but Egypt's place as a world power would never be the same- she would suffer divine destruction by the direct hand of God. We read in Exodus 1:15-16 how Pharaoh was used as a tool of Satan by trying to prevent the promised deliverer (Moses) from being born. This scenario will eventually be played-out again in the New Testament with the birth of Christ.

Because Israel's lack of faith after God's deliverance from Egypt, Israel would not enter the Promised Land until they had been disciplined by God for forty-years. However, despite Israel's rebellious condition, God would still honor His promise to Abraham and his seed to fulfill His covenant.

Israel would eventually enter the Promise Land after forty-years in the wilderness that started with the leadership of Moses, followed by Joshua. Once Israel entered, they would drive out many of the inhabitants from the land; because it was God's will that Israel be the permanent occupants of the land. This is a foundational doctrine that God establishes with Israel as she receives her identity with the Promise Land. Along with Israel's establishment in the land, God was choosing a place that he alone would be rightfully worshiped.

> And ye shall overthrow their altars, and break their pillars, and burn their groves with fire; and ye shall hew down the graven images of their gods, and destroy the NAMEs of them out of that place...But unto the place which the LORD your God shall choose out of all your tribes to put his NAME there, even unto his habitation shall ye seek, and thither thou shalt come... Because I will publish the NAME of the LORD: ascribe ye greatness unto our God. (Duet. 12:3, 5; 32:3)

Just as with Enos, when men began to call on the name of the Lord, it is God's desire that the world would see God's blessing on Israel, which in turn they (world) would call upon God. As an example, the Bible records the queen of Sheba saw the wisdom of Solomon, and how the blessings of God were upon him (I Kings 10:1-10). Sheba gave God glory by declaring: *Blessed be the Lord thy God, which delighted in thee, to set the on the throne of Israel: because the Lord loved Israel for ever...* (v.9)

Rahab is another prime example of this.

> And she said unto the men, I know that the LORD hath given you the land, and that your terror is fallen upon us, and that all the inhabitants of the land faint because of you. For we have heard how the LORD dried up the water of the Red sea for you, when ye came out of Egypt; and what ye did unto the two kings of

the Amorites, that were on the other side Jordan, Sihon and Og, whom ye utterly destroyed. And as soon as we had heard these things, our hearts did melt, neither did there remain any more courage in any man, because of you: for the LORD your God, he is God in heaven above, and in earth beneath. Now therefore, I pray you, swear unto me by the LORD, **since I have showed you kindness, that ye will also show kindness** unto my father's house, and give me a true token: And that ye will save alive my father, and my mother, and my brethren, and my sisters, and all that they have, and deliver our lives from death. (Joshua 2:9-13)

Rahab's kindness toward the spies shows that God's hand of mercy is extended toward those who are not specifically chosen (Israel). The story of Jonah preaching to the Ninevehites, which led to their repentance, is another good example.

Israel as a Nation

Israel was led politically and socially by kings, but her religious affairs were placed under the authority of the tribe of Levi, headed up by the high priest. God also established another authority with the nation of Israel, and those were the prophets. God used the prophetic office to speak straight to the people about their spiritual well-being. The prophets included such men as Samuel, Jehu, Elijah, Elisha, Isaiah, Jeremiah, Daniel, Amos, Jonah, Ezekiel, and many others.

King David will have a special role in God's plan in the future. God promised that David will set on the royal throne in Israel during the millennium.

And I will set up one shepherd over them, and he shall feed them, **even my servant David**; he shall feed them, and he shall be their shepherd. And I the LORD will be their God, and my servant David a prince among them; I the LORD have spoken it. (Ezek. 34:23-24)

God promised David that an everlasting kingdom would be established through his seed.

> And when thy days be fulfilled, and thou shalt sleep with thy fathers, **I will set up thy seed after thee**, which shall proceed out of thy bowels, and I will establish his kingdom. He shall build an house for my name, and I will **stablish the throne of his kingdom forever.** I will be his father, and he shall be my son. If he commit iniquity, I will chasten him with the rod of men, and with the stripes of the children of men: (2 Samuel 7:12-14)

Solomon, David's son, would reign and build the first temple of Israel for the Lord. After Solomon, the kingdom was divided around 931 BC under the revolt of Jeroboam which led to the ten tribes to the North (Israel); and Rehoboam and two tribes that dwelt in Jerusalem (Judah and Benjamin). The Northern kingdom went into Assyrian captivity in 722 BC and the Southern kingdom followed in 586 BC to Babylon.

Israel in Babylon Captivity

From the writings of Jeremiah, Daniel understood the seventy-years of captivity which was foretold by God was about to end.

> Thus saith the LORD of hosts, the God of Israel, unto all that are carried away captives, whom I have caused to be carried away from Jerusalem unto Babylon;... And seek the peace of the city whither I have caused you to be carried away captives, and pray unto the LORD for it: for in the peace thereof shall ye have peace...For thus saith the LORD, That **after seventy years be accomplished at Babylon** I will visit you, and perform my good word toward you, in causing you to return to this place. (Jer. 29:4, 7, 10)

> In the first year of his reign I Daniel understood by books the number of the years, whereof the word of the LORD came to Jeremiah the prophet, that he would accomplish **seventy years** in the desolations of Jerusalem. (Dan. 9:2)

As the seventy years of captivity were drawing to a close, Daniel proceeded to confess the sins of the nation before God.

> We have sinned, and have committed iniquity, and have done
> wickedly, and have rebelled, even by departing from thy precepts
> and from thy judgments: (Dan. 9:5)

From this setting, God would send the angel Gabriel to Daniel to reveal some of the most highly prolific prophetic verses concerning God's plan for Israel. I will deal later with the specifics of this prophecy, primarily the seventy-week prophecy in Daniel chapter 9.

The Completed Work of God

As foretold in Isaiah 7:14, God would send the promised deliverer through the birth of the male child, Jesus. In the genealogy account in Matthew chapter 1, we are given the "royal lineage" of the birth of Christ from Abraham to Joseph. In Luke's genealogy, we have the birth of Christ traced back through the account of Adam. This lineage is based on the "human lineage" of Christ, where he is called the son of man. This typifies that not only was He Israel's messiah, but also to everyone else who would put their faith and trust in Him as Lord of their life.

We see early in the New Testament where Satan attempted to stop the promise seed (Jesus) by having Herod kill all the male children two years old and under. (Herod is a type of the Antichrist, who, in sometime in the future, will attempt to stop God from fulfilling his final plan to bring in the kingdom.)

Jesus ultimately fulfilled the promise in Genesis 3:15 at Calvary by being the righteous (perfect) sacrifice for God. He was raised from the dead three days later proving that He was in fact the sinless Son of God. This was the ultimate death-blow to Satan, and he knows it. In the meantime, he will turn his attention to stopping the final plan of God which is to bring about His earthly kingdom at the second coming of Christ. In truth, Satan had this death sentence pronounced upon him before the foundation of the world. God said in Isaiah 14 and Ezekiel 28, when Satan rebelled against God, that he would come to a final judgment where he will be punished for eternity. Therefore, Satan will at all cost try to thwart God's final judgment on him.

In Isaiah 9:6-7, it references Christ and the prophecy surrounding His first coming; however, there is an incomplete portion of this prophecy that was not fulfilled. This pertains to Christ's rule and reign on Earth. The first-time Christ came was for the redemption of mankind from sin bringing spiritual victory. His next return will be the establishment of his kingdom on earth that promises to bring full spiritual and physical deliverance.

> For unto us a child is born, unto us a son is given: and the government shall be upon his shoulder: and his name shall be called Wonderful, Counsellor, The mighty God, The everlasting Father, The Prince of Peace. Of the **increase of his government and peace there shall be no end, upon the throne of David, and upon his kingdom, to order it, and to establish it with judgment and with justice from henceforth even forever.** The zeal of the LORD of hosts will perform this. (Isa. 9:6-7)

As I have already emphasized, Christ's establishment as the future king does not only pertain to Israel, but the Gentiles as well.

> And in that day there shall be a root of Jesse, which shall stand for an ensign of the people; to it shall the **Gentiles** seek: and his rest shall be glorious.... I the LORD have called thee in righteousness, and will hold thine hand, and will keep thee, and give thee for a covenant of the people, for a light of the **Gentiles**;... Thus saith the Lord GOD, Behold, I will lift up mine hand to the **Gentiles**, and set up my standard to the people: and they shall bring thy sons in their arms, and thy daughters shall be carried upon their shoulders. (Isa. 11:10; 42:6; 49:22)

As foretold by Christ in Matthew 24, Luke 21, and Mark 13, and detailed in the book of Revelation, God will bring to pass his completed work on Earth. Christ will rule and reign on Earth someday, it's a forgone conclusion, until then, we will continue to witness in these last days the culmination of the conflict of the ages.

CHAPTER FOUR

EARLY ROOTS OF BIBLE PROPHECY

As Christians, today, especially with the propensity to understand Bible prophecy, I would like to look briefly how religious movements in early America influenced our thinking through the rise of teachers who claimed to understand Bible prophecy and end-time events. Even though we are in the 21st century, we are not that far removed from our spiritual heritage and the influence of this time period. As examples, Charles Finney (1792-1875), in his evangelistic meetings started what many Baptists churches still practice today, which is the altar call (i.e. have people come forward to the altar for various reasons, mainly for prayer and salvation). The doctrine of tithing is another example which many churches practice today. This teaching did not enter the protestant and evangelical churches until the late 1800s.

The 1700s and 1800s proved to be crucial periods in America's religions concerning eschatology. The Shakers predicted the return of Christ in 1792. Jonathan Edwards, who preached the famous sermon "Sinners in the Hands of an Angry God," is even recognized by secular writers as having a considerable impact in America. He is well-known for bringing about revival in America known as the Great Awakening. Edwards was convinced that the first Great Awakening in the 1730s and 1740s was the beginning of converting the world to Christianity that would usher in a golden age of the millennium.

The second Great Awakening which took place during the early 1800s was started by Finney; it again promised a golden millennial-age that would lead to the return of Christ. It was reported that millions of new members were enrolled into existing evangelical denominations, and new religions were formed out of this movement. Several of these religions claimed to restore some "lost" truth that the church had supposedly abandoned. Even though some of these religions I reference do not have a direct impact on our rapture study, it shows man's hunger for understanding prophetic events and the return of Christ. Jesus warned in Matthew 24 that many false prophets would arise in the last days and draw men after them (Matt. 24:4-5, 11). As I stated in my opening remarks, false teachers and false predictions seem to go hand-in-hand.

The Mormons

The Mormons were a group that came into existence in 1830 under the leadership of its founder, Joseph Smith. Smith's belief that he was to establish "Latter-Day Saints" as the true Christian faith, because Christianity had strayed from the truth, which resulted in drawing many people to follow him.

Supposedly, Smith translated the book of Mormon from the "golden plates" he discovered in the wilderness with the help of the angel Moroni. Joseph Smith claimed that he was commissioned by God to establish the "new Jerusalem" called Zion, and even built their first temple in 1835 in Kirkland, Ohio. The Mormons re-established the priesthood that was designated solely to the nation of Israel (minus animal sacrifices). They teach that a new dispensation for the true church had begun with Joseph Smith and his new religion. The Mormons later moved to Utah under the leadership of Brigham Young, after Smith's untimely death, and built their main temple where they currently worship and practice such things as baptism for the dead- proxy.

Here are a few prophecies by Joseph Smith who predicted Christ's return:

> I was once praying very earnestly to know the time of the coming of the Son of Man, when I heard a voice repeat the following: **Joseph my son, if thou livest until thou art eighty-five years old,** thou shalt see the face of the Son of Man; therefore let this suffice, and trouble me no more on this matter.[19] (bold letters mine)

> I prophesy in the name of the Lord God, and let it be written- **the Son of Man will not come in the clouds of heaven till I am eighty-five years old.**[20] (bold letters mine)

In 1835, Smith, at the age of 30, declared during a church meeting that the "command of God is that Jesus will return in fifty-six years,"[21] and Smith would still be alive when Christ would return. Joseph Smith died in 1844 at the age of 39, only nine years after giving his prophecy, proving him as a false prophet, along with many of his other failed predictions.

The Millerites

William Miller was a Baptist preacher who in the 1830s and 1840s preached heavily on the advent of Jesus Christ. He gained many followers who became known as the Millerites. Their primary emphases became the imminent return of Jesus Christ. In 1842, the magazine "**The Signs of the Times**" began to publish Miller's theory that Christ would come back sometime in 1843. This movement spread nationwide, and caused many people to become enthralled with the prospect of the promised return of Christ. When this prophecy did not happen, it became known as the "Great Disappointment." Miller, like many who do not learn from their mistakes, recalculated his timetable and figured he was off by one year. This came and went as well, becoming known as the "Second Great Disappointment." Many abandoned the Millerites, and from this debacle some of these followers started their own assembly, which became known as the Seventh-day Adventist Church.

Seventh-day Adventist

The Seventh-day Adventists took the date of the second "Great Disappointment" and reinterpreted Miller's prediction and said it did occur. They claimed this event was not to rapture the saints from the earth; but that God had spiritually cleansed His heavenly temple and established His true church on the earth.

Ellen G. White became the central figure of the Seventh-day Adventist Church, claiming to be their true prophet of God. She stated of William Miller's 1843 prophecy concerning Christ's coming:

> I have seen that the 1843 chart [William Miller's] was directed by the hand of the Lord and that it should not be altered, that the figures were as he wanted them.[22]

Since then, they claimed that the true people of God would be identified by keeping the Ten Commandments, along with keeping the Jewish Sabbath on Saturday. Tithing became the bases for their members to give to their church, which prospered the church immensely. Adventists believe that they are the chosen remnant identified in Revelation 12:17, which are the ones to proclaim the three angel's messages of Revelation 14. The result of their interpretation of this passage is that Christianity has already taken the mark of the beast by worshipping on Sunday instead of the Saturday Sabbath.

In 1833, Ellen G. White, when the Leonid meteor shower occurred that year (as it does every year), declared that: "This is the last of the signs of Christ coming!"[23] As a side note: Joseph Smith also claimed the same meteor shower was a sign that proved he was the true prophet of God.

In 1844 Ellen G. White wrote:

> I saw the state of the different churches since the second angel proclaimed their fall. They have been growing more and more corrupt. Satan has taken full possession of the churches as a body. Their professions, their prayers and their exhortations are an abomination in the sight of GOD.[24]

Here are a few quotes by White making predictions, only proving her to be a false teacher.

In 1856 Ellen G. White prophesized:

> I was shown the company present at the Conference. Said the angel: Some food for worms, some subject to the last plagues, some will be alive and remain upon the earth to be translated at the coming of Jesus.[25]

1862 Prophecy concerning the United States:

> This nation will yet be humbled into the dust. When England does declare war, all nations will have an interest of their own to serve, and there will be general war.[26]

Jehovah Witnesses

The roots of the Jehovah Witness go back to a man named Nelson Barbour, (1824-1905). Barbour attended Temple Hill Academy from 1839-1842. Barbour became a Seventh-day Adventist after the Great Disappointment of 1843.

Barbour, not learning from mistakes made during the Great Disappointment, fell into the same trap, and in 1871 published a small book titled "**The Midnight Cry,**" which said that Christ would come in 1873. When 1873 arrived- and Christ did not- he readjusted his timetable to 1874, which failed as well. Just like the Adventists, Barbour claimed Christ came "invisibly" in order to justify his false prediction. His magazine "**The Midnight Cry**" was an offshoot of his book, and later it was re-labeled "**Herald of the Morning.**" It was through this magazine how Charles Taze Russell (founder of the Jehovah's Witnesses) met Nelson Barbour in 1875.

After several years of working together, Russell and Barbour had to part ways, due to a disagreement over certain Bible doctrines. Russell resigned from the ministry and started his own magazine in 1879, titled, "**The Watchtower.**" Russell agreed with the teachings of Barbour on biblical prophecy, and it was not long before Russell started adopting his own views on the literal return of Christ.

It would be Russell's infamous prediction that Christ would come in 1914, fulfilling the end of the "time of the Gentiles," that would leave his mark on failed Bible predictions-The Watchtower Assembly (Jehovah Witnesses) would follow suit by many more failed predictions as well. Here is a quote in the very first Watchtower publication about Christ's return.

> Again, we may rest assured that when Jesus said, "All the tribes of the earth shall mourn and wail because of Him" when they see Him coming, He did not refer to the conversion of sinners-Do the tribes mourn and wail because of the conversion of a sinner?-And if it refers, as almost all admit, to **Christ's personal presence on the earth**, it teaches that all on earth will not love His appearing, as they certainly would do if all were converted. But, "If I go away, I will come again," *cannot* **refer to a spiritual coming again**, because, spiritually, He never went away, as He said, "Lo, I am with you alway, even to the end *of* the world," [age.] Therefore, Jesus taught His second **PERSONAL** coming.[27] (bold letters mine)

Here is another statement by Russell in the "**Watch Tower Magazine**" predicting the same event.

> As most of our reaers are aware, we believe the word of God furnishes us with indubitable proof that we are *now* living in this

"Day of the Lord"; **that began in 1873, and is a day of forty years duration** as was *"the day of temptation* in the wilderness, "when Israel proved God and saw His works *forty years.* Heb. iii. 9[28] (bold letters mine)

The significance of the year 1873 in his statement showed that he still believed in Barbour's failed prediction. This, along with other teachings, such as the dimensions of the "great pyramid" in Egypt, were used by Russell to predict the date of Christ's second coming. When the visible return of Christ failed to happen in 1914, the Jehovah Witnesses reinterpreted Russell's prophecy to be an "invisible" return- sound familiar?

1879: Jehovah Witnesses taught:

Christ came in the character of a Bridegroom in 1874…at the beginning of Gospel Harvest.[29]

1902: Jehovah Witnesses taught:

In view of this strong Bible evidence concerning the Times of the Gentiles, we consider it an established truth that the final end of the kingdoms of this world, and the full establishment of the kingdom of God, will be accomplished by the end of A.D. 1914[30]

John Darby- Father of Dispensationalism

John Darby was born November 18, 1800 in Westminster, London. He was educated in Westminster School and Trinity College, in Dublin, Ireland, where he became an ordained minister in the Anglican Church in 1826. By 1828, John Darby had already dissociated himself from his church, and later joined the Plymouth Brethren in circa 1830. He began attending the Powerscourt Conferences, which centered on Bible prophecy.

It was another preacher, Edward Irving, from London, England who should be credited with the doctrine of the pretribulation rapture. In his journal, "**The Morning Watch**" (1830), Irving began to publish his teachings on the pretribulation rapture. In fact, in 1825 Irving predicted that Christ would return by 1864. In 1826 he started the "School of the Prophets," obviously with a heavy emphasis on Bible prophecy.

It would be another notable event that struck a chord among the Irving's followers that supposedly validated his pretribulation teaching. A Scottish teenager, Margot McDonald, was having visions, and thru these visions the pretribulation rapture teaching was apparently verified as true. Irving took this as a sign of God's approval upon his teaching.

Darby was influenced by Irving's teaching on the rapture at his Bible studies as he taught at the Powerscourt Conferences. Darby took hold of this pretribulation rapture and combined it with his new teaching-dispensationalist theology; and began to preach this dogmatically.

The result, Darby developed a "seven-age dispensation" that categorized the Bible into these particular groups. Bible teachers acknowledge Darby's theory of the seven-age dispensation; however, in all reality, Darby espoused an "eight-age" dispensation, with one special dispensation that separates the 70th week by itself. The 70th week is cardinal to the pretrib theory.

1.) Innocence- in the Garden of Eden
2.) Conscience and Moral Responsibility- After the fall
3.) Human Government- After the flood
4.) The Promise- Abraham
5.) The Law- Beginning with Moses up through to the Church Age
6.) The Church- Began in Acts chapter two
7.) Israel in the 70th Week
8.) The Kingdom- Revelation chapter twenty

Dispensationalism categorizes different Old Testament historical periods, which I believe was developed solely, or at least in part, to support Darby's pretribulation rapture theory. To excuse the church from the tribulation, i.e. 70th week, a distinction between Israel and the church was developed. According to Darby's dispensational doctrine, as he makes a distinction between Israel and the church, he also taught two salvations, one designed for Israel and one for the church. This led to internal divisions within the Brethren Church. Theologian Bernard Ramm wrote:

> The sharp division of the Church and Israel, each going its own course through history into eternity is a remarkable piece of theological heresy.[31]

Napoleon Noel wrote in his book "**The History of the Brethren**" that Darby had complete control of the doctrinal position of the church. A classic example of Darby's control is when he excommunicated George Muller- the famous preacher and a father to many orphans - from the Plymouth Brethren Church. Muller disagreement with Darby on his teachings on pretribulationism and dispensationalism led him to leave the Brethren Church. Here is Muller in his own words:

> My brother, I am a constant reader of my Bible, and I soon found that what I was taught to believe (by Darby's Doctrine) did not always agree with what my Bible said. I came to see that I must either part company with John Darby, or my precious Bible, and I chose to cling to my Bible and part from Mr. Darby.[32] (parenthesis mine)

It was through his course of travels throughout America in the 1860s and 70s when John Darby began to spread his dispensational doctrine. More notable, it was during the Niagara Bible Conference at Niagara-on–the Lake, Ontario, that Darby's teaching took a foothold here in America. This conference was led for two decades by the pastor of Walnut Avenue Presbyterian Church in St. Louis, Missouri, James Brooks. As an ardent supporter of John Darby's dispensationalism, Brooks adopted Darby's view of the pretribulational rapture in his articles "**The Truth**" and the "**Watchword**." These conferences had a heavy influence over many people, but two men in particular that would have a profound impact on Protestantism- Dwight L. Moody and C. I. Scofield.

In 1878, Brooks produced his fourteen-point statement of faith which dominated the Niagara Conferences, and this became known as the Niagara Creed. Many within the conference used this as a stepping-stone to hammer-out their views on dispensationalism. As dispensationalism became the predominate view, the conference in 1897 almost split, primarily, over the difference between a pretribulational or posttribulational rapture.

It was at the Niagara Conference of 1901 that Scofield became persuaded to write his "Reference Bible." The Darby infused doctrines of dispensationalism and pretribulation rapture were the emphasis of *Scofield's Reference Bible*. The *Scofield Reference Bible* was published in 1909, and would indoctrinate many evangelical churches in America, especially among the Baptist Churches.

Louis Sperry Chafer, who founded Dallas Theological Seminary in 1924, was heavily influenced by the *Scofield Reference Bible*; and brought the Darby doctrine of dispensationalism to his seminary. This seminary has had both positive and negative influences in Christian circles. The seminary became the breeding-ground for dispensationalism and the pretribulation rapture that would spread throughout many Christian denominations.

Because of dispensationalism, it is believed that Darby's theory of a secret rapture was introduced around 1839. The connotation of the pretribulation teaching implies an invisible, secret rapture, even though Scriptures do not explicitly teach this. This fallacy is forced upon the Bible through the interpretations of Darby's doctrine of a secret rapture; because, if Scriptures are interpreted literally then pretribulationism suffers doctrinally.

After World War I many evangelicals began using the pretribulational rapture as their platform to teach their salvation message- that Jesus may appear at "any moment." This has been the dominant teaching of many evangelical sermons ever since, warning folks they better get saved before the coming tribulation.

Plainly, the pretribulation rapture, along with the dispensation teaching, is a new doctrine that came into being from the teaching of a few men. The recorded historical account of the church throughout its history gives no credence to a pretribulational rapture as many pretribulationist assert.

As a former pretribulationist, I was not taught any historical background for this belief system. It's my firm belief -although not speaking for everyone - that many who hold to the pretrib rapture are not familiar to the factual background and how it impacts the rapture debate. S.P. Tregelles (1813-1875), who was associated with Darby and the Plymouth Brethren for years, eventually he rejected the pretribulation rapture and became a posttribulationist. He wrote a book in 1864 *"The Hope of Christ's Second Coming,"* which is a rebuttal to the new teaching of the pretribulation rapture and the doctrine of dispensationalism. His writings are great sources for the historical arguments against the fallacies of the pretrib rapture.

One area of history that I purposely left out in our study is the belief of the early church fathers in the 1st and 2nd centuries on eschatology. I have read arguments from both, post and pretrib teachers, and while I believe many of the church fathers held the belief that the church will endure the tribulation before Christ returns; I will leave it to the reader to do his or her research. There is one significant writing that most scholars agree was written in the first century as a Christian treatise- **The Didache**. It is also known as the "**The Teaching of the Twelve Apostles**." There is reference made pertaining to end-time teaching that states the Antichrist will come before Christ's return.

> Watch for your life's sake. Let not your lamps be quenched, nor your loins unloosed; but be ye ready, for ye know not the hour in which our Lord cometh. But often shall ye come together, seeking the things which are befitting to your souls: for the whole time of your faith will not profit you, if ye be not made perfect in the last time. For in the last days false prophets and corrupters shall be multiplied, and the sheep shall be turned into wolves, and love shall be turned into hate; for when lawlessness increaseth, they shall hate and persecute and betray one another, **and then shall appear the world-deceiver as Son of God,** and shall do signs and wonders, and the earth shall be delivered into his hands, and he shall do iniquitous things which have never yet come to pass since the beginning. Then shall the creation of men come into the fire of trial, and many shall be made to stumble and shall perish; **but they that endure in their faith shall be saved from under the curse itself**. And then shall appear the signs of the truth; first, the sign of an out-spreading in heaven; then the sign of the sound of the trumpet; and the third, the resurrection of the dead; yet not of all, but as it is said: The Lord shall come and all His saints with Him. Then shall the world see the Lord coming upon the clouds of heaven.[33]

It is my sincere intent to allow the weight of the Scriptures to be the final authority on any biblical topic, which is where we find and weigh the evidence.

CHAPTER FIVE

DISPENSATIONALISM– THE TROJAN HORSE

We will now examine the underlying contributor to the pretribulation rapture - dispensationalism. Dispensationalism is the Trojan horse that came through the back door into the church by its founder John Darby in the 1800s. We will see that pretrib-dispensationalism (my term) is built upon conjecture without biblical facts in determining the different so-called dispensations throughout the Bible. The common element that many folks fail to see is the significance how the doctrine of dispensationalism affects the rapture debate.

As mentioned in the previous chapter, I believe the dispensational doctrine was created solely for the purpose to make the Bible seem as though it authenticates a pretribulation rapture. Here is Tommy Ice explaining the true purpose of why dispensationalism was created.

> Dispensational Futurism
> Increasingly scholars began to take literally the Old Testament
> Promises to restore the Jews to their land so that end-time
> prophecy could be fulfilled. Scholars also begin to realize that
> if they took these prophecies to apply literally to Israel, then this
> meant that the church had a different and distinct program than
> Israel within God's plan...[34]

What the prophecy scholars (Darby and other pretrib teachers) realized is that for there to be a pretrib rapture there would have to be a mandatory separation between the church and Israel, so a "program" was created via dispensationalism. I say again, this theory (pretrib-dispensationalism) was developed solely to rationalize the pretribulation rapture theory. Also, the key end-time prophecy that needed to be fulfilled was Israel's return to the promise land. We will see in the chapter on imminence, that, this, along with other prophecies, nullifies the pretrib rapture. Prewrath believers do not dispute God has special plans for Israel in the future. And those plans, as I have alluded to several times, are the promises given to Israel as a future nation in the millennium. But for pretribulational teachers like Ice and others to say there is a different and distinct program for Israel, and totally remove the church from the biblical equation, is not exegetically justified.

In chapter one, dispensationalism was defined how God worked in distinct historical time periods to fulfill His work under different covenants to specific people. Israel and the church, being central to the rapture debate, are considered by the pretribulation theory two totally distinct groups without any historical overlapping of each other while God fulfills His plan. Supposedly, God will deal specifically with the nation of Israel in the 70th week after He raptures the church; thus, this should be a different dispensation in itself, but Darby's dispensational chart does not acknowledge this- strange!

First, we need to get a basic understanding of this teaching and its effect on the rapture debate. The word dispensation appears four times in the Authorized Version of the King James Bible; therefore, we need to see how the Scripture uses this word in its proper context.

For though I preach the gospel, I have nothing to glory of: for necessity is laid upon me; yea, woe is unto me, if I preach not the gospel! For if I do this thing willingly, I have a reward: but if against my will, a **dispensation of the gospel** is committed unto me. (1 Cor. 9:16-17)

Having made known unto us the mystery of his will, according to his good pleasure which he hath purposed in himself: That in the **dispensation** of the fulness of times he might **gather together in one all things in Christ**, both which are in heaven, and which are on earth; **even in him**: (Eph. 1:9-10)

If ye have heard of the **dispensation** of the grace of God which is given me to you-ward: How that by revelation he made known unto me the mystery; (as I wrote afore in few words, (Eph. 3:2-3)

> Whereof I am made a minister, according to the **dispensation of God** which is given to me for you, to fulfil the word of God; Even the **mystery which hath been hid from ages and from generations**, but **now is made manifest** to his **saints**: To whom God would make known what is the riches of the glory of this **mystery among the Gentiles**; which is Christ in you, the hope of glory: (Col. 1:25-27)

Paul is the writer of all three New Testament books that reference the word dispensation. In two of the four times when he uses the word dispensation, it's used in context with his ministry of preaching the gospel. When these verses are seen in their full context, the emphasis is that the Gentiles are now "included" in the promises God gave to Israel. Part of the mystery Paul speaks of, is that Israel and the church have become "one" in Christ. The church became part of the covenant promises that God made specifically with Abraham (Romans 4:12-14). Note, the use of the word "saints" in Colossians 1:26 in reference to the mystery in the Old Testament. It did not say the dispensation of the "church." More on this thought later.

The true biblical definition of dispensation is tied directly with Gentiles becoming heirs to these promises. Ephesians and Colossians were written to show this. As an example, we see in chapter two of Ephesians.

> Wherefore remember, that ye being in time past **Gentiles** in the flesh, who are called Uncircumcision by that which is called the Circumcision in the flesh made by hands; That **at that time** ye were without Christ, **being aliens from the commonwealth of Israel, and strangers from the covenants of promise,** having no hope, and without God in the world: But **now in Christ Jesus** ye who sometimes were far off are made nigh by the blood of Christ. For he is our peace, **who hath made both one, and hath broken down the middle wall of partition between us;** Having abolished in his flesh the enmity, even the law of commandments contained in ordinances; for to make in himself of **twain one new man,** so making peace; (Eph. 2:11-15)

From these few verses, we can see how the Gentiles were originally separated from the promises of God given solely to Israel. Paul states that the Gentiles were *aliens* and *strangers*. Ultimately, Israel's promises and covenants were dependent on the person of Jesus Christ, which is what Daniel's seventy-week prophecy teaches. This was accomplished by Christ fulfilling our righteousness to the Father, by living a sinless life and giving his life on the cross of Calvary. This brings to light the emphasis on Genesis 3:15 how the *seed of the woman would bruise the head of the serpent.* Concluding then, God had in view from the beginning at the Garden of Eden that all people could come to a saving knowledge of the Messiah- Jesus Christ.

> And in that day there shall be a root of Jesse, which shall stand for an ensign of the people; to it **shall the Gentiles seek**: and his rest shall be glorious. (Isaiah 11:10)

> I the LORD have called thee in righteousness, and will hold thine hand, and will keep thee, and give thee for a covenant of the people, for a **light of the Gentiles**; (Isaiah 42:6)

> And he said, It is a light thing that thou shouldest be my servant to raise up the tribes of Jacob, and to restore the preserved of Israel: I will also give thee for a **light to the Gentiles,** that thou mayest be my salvation unto the end of the earth. Thus saith the LORD, the Redeemer of Israel, and his Holy One, to him whom man despiseth, to him whom the nation abhorreth, to a servant of rulers, Kings shall see and arise, princes also shall worship, **because of the LORD that is faithful, and the Holy One of Israel, a**nd he shall choose thee. Thus saith the LORD, In an acceptable time have I heard thee, and in a day of salvation have I helped thee: and I will preserve thee, and give thee **for a covenant of the people, to establish the earth**, to cause to inherit the desolate heritages;...Thus saith the Lord GOD, Behold, I will lift up mine hand to the **Gentiles**, and set up my standard to the people: and they shall bring thy sons in their arms, and thy daughters shall be carried upon their shoulders. (Isa. 49:6-8, 22)

> Blessed be the God and Father of our Lord Jesus Christ, who hath **blessed us** with all spiritual blessings in heavenly places **in Christ:** According as he hath chosen us in him before the **foundation of the world**, that we should be holy and without blame before him in love: (Eph. 1:3-4)

27. And he came by the Spirit into the temple: and when the parents brought in the child Jesus, to do for him after the custom of the law,

28. Then took he him up in his arms, and blessed God, and said,

29. Lord, now lettest thou thy servant depart in peace, according to thy word:

30. For mine eyes have seen thy salvation,

31. Which thou hast **prepared** before the face of **all people**;

32. A light to **lighten the Gentiles**, and the **glory of thy people Israel.** (Luke 2:27-32)

In Jeremiah 31:31-34, this passage teaches that God will make a new covenant with the House of Israel. Hebrews 10:16-17 is a reference to Jeremiah's prophecy, which was fulfilled by Christ at Calvary. Because of Israel's unbelief in Christ as Messiah, as we saw, they will not experience the fulfillment of this blessing until the millennium. The church in the meanwhile has become God's instrument of His will upon the earth in these last days. Let me state that prewrath teaching does not believe in a "replacement theology" doctrine. Replacement theology espouses that the church totally replaced Israel since they rejected Christ; therefore, all the promises were transferred to the church and Israel is no longer the benefactor. According to this teaching, Israel will not experience any type of national revival in the future. Jews simply become assimilated into the church and the nation of Israel is to never be heard from again. This is something that many pretrib believers accuse both prewrath and posttribulationist of. Their lack of understanding of the covenant promises in the Bible, along with forcing a pretrib rapture upon the Scriptures, leads pretribulationist to believe we teach replacement theology. I say, dogmatically, both Israel and the church will be dealt with during the final week.

Replacement theology was fairly popular in the late 1800s into the 1900s. However, due to World War I and with Israel becoming an independent nation in 1948, replacement theology faded. However, it's beginning to make a resurgence with the political environment vilifying Israel as a foreign invader in Palestine (a false name imposed on Israel by the Romans). Many religious denominations are beginning to embrace the political headwinds that are wanting to force Israel to give up much of her land in the ongoing Palestinian conflict.

Dispensationalism

Dispensationalism has falsely categorized "two systems" of salvation, one for the Jews and one for the church. The Bible teaches that a Jew under the Old Testament covenant participated in the ordinances and statutes of the law. We know they were never justified by the law, but partook in the Jewish ordinances with God, such as dietary laws, special cleansings of the body when exposed to dead animals or people. The sacrificial system was set up by God to establish in the lives among the people that sin must be paid for. Those who participated showed they had a faith and belief in God. We understand that salvation has always been by faith apart from works; however, our works show that we are saved, as the book of James testifies to this fact (James 2:17-18).

Many dispensational churches teach that a person today may be saved but not necessarily a true disciple of Christ. Not only does dispensationalism teach "two types" of Christians- disciples and non-disciples; but two "salvations," one for Israel and one for the church.

The major problem created by the pretribulation view of dispensationalism, is that by separating the church from Israel in the future 70th week, now they are forced to teach separation patterns in the historical record throughout the Old Testament.

As we begin to look at Darby's eight dispensations, we need to realize that dispensational teaching cannot afford any "overlapping" of each dispensation (ages) throughout the Bible, if so; why can't there be an overlapping of the church and Israel in the final week of time? This will be my main point of argument. Pretribulationist teaching unknowingly espouses that there is a mini-dispensation of seven-years coinciding within the 70th week of Daniel. This is the reason they're so adamant on excusing the church from being addressed in Matthew 24. However, we will see that there were overlapping of supposed dispensations in the Old Testament, and this will be the case in the final seven-years.

Prewrath teaching states we will still be in the church-age during the great tribulation, which is part of the final seven-years. At some unknown point during this time, God will supernaturally intervene and rapture His saints along with sealing the 1440,000 for protection from His wrath. After a time of judgment on the world during the day of the Lord, Christ will return to earth and establish the millennium. It will be at this time when

Israel enjoys the fulfillment of the covenant promises of God. True covenant fulfillment will be enjoyed by Israel in the millennium, not before then.

First, we need to look at the dispensations that Darby established and compare it to the Word of God. My intent here is not to break down every aspect of the dispensational belief system, but to build a case and show the reader the inconsistencies of dispensationalism from a pretribulation view.

Philip Hughes correctly wrote.

> But we fear that the dispensationalist method of interpretation does violence to the unity of the scriptures and to the Sovereign continuity of God's purposes, and cavalierly leaves out of account a major portion of the apostolic teaching- that, chiefly, of the Acts, and the Epistles- as unrelated to the perspective of the Old Testament authors.[35]

1. The Age of Innocence:

This dispensation is introduced when God created Adam where he was created in a state of innocence (lack of knowledge). Like a child who is innocent at birth, their innocence is presumably based upon their lack of knowledge of good and evil. Therefore, Adam and Eve's fellowship with God was based on innocence of not knowing what evil was. Their innocence was taken away when they sinned, and became "ashamed" of their nakedness. This dispensation-age supposedly ended with their expulsion from the garden.

If we look at this from the biblical narrative, we see from the beginning of the creation account in Genesis chapter 1, at the completion of each day, God said, *"it was good."* When God declared something good, it was not just innocent, but it was complete and pure. After the sixth day of creation the Bible says in Genesis 1:31 that everything God created was *"very good."* Man, could enjoy the intimate fellowship with God because he was perfect and holy (without sin), which allowed him to be in the presence of a holy God. When Adam was given the command by God *not to eat from the tree of knowledge of good and evil,* he was not in danger of losing his innocence, but his holiness. This would result in him losing his life, both spiritually and eventually physically (Gen. 2:17). Adam had no need to understand what evil was; he only needed to obey God's command, which established a righteous relationship with God.

Man was created a living soul with a conscience, which he was accountable to God by his actions. Unlike the animal world, man was created with a free-will to accept or reject what God had commanded. Throughout the Old Testament, people had this same free-will to believe in God or reject him. Today man has the same accountability to God, to accept or reject His command. The command for you and I is to believe upon Jesus Christ as Savior and Lord. And when we believe, it's not just a verbal acknowledgment of who Jesus is and what he did, but our actions testify as well. This command started with the ministry of John the Baptist, who introduced Jesus as the Messiah to Israel; and later instituted with the apostles at the great commission in Matthew 28, and will still be the same command through the 70th week (Rev. 14:12).

The true biblical word that described Adams relationship to God is "righteousness." Adam could stand in the presence of God because he was righteous, not innocent because he lacked knowledge of evil. Whether a person wants to split hairs and say that Adam was innocent, of course he is innocent, but do not invent categories that do not reflect what the Bible teaches, solely to beef-up your view. Adam was righteous, which described the proper biblical definition of his innocence.

The question that should be asked: is there an overlapping of this age with any other age? The answer to the question is, yes! When Adam sinned (a transgression of God's command) he became what the Bible called "unrighteous." We today have "inherited" his unrighteousness nature through human birth. Nowadays, we are still reaping the consequences of Adam's choice from the beginning of creation, which is sin and death.

> Wherefore, as by one man **sin** entered into the world, and death
> by sin; and so **death passed** upon all men, for that all have
> **sinned:** (Rom. 5:12)

When Adam and Eve sinned, they tried to cover up their unrighteousness (not innocence) by covering up their shame of nakedness with fig leaves. God ultimately had to kill an animal and cover them with a type of Christ's sacrifice; and this will become the theme throughout the Old Testament.

2. Age of Conscience and Moral Responsibility:

Here is an opening statement in a sermon on the dispensation of conscience.

Man's Responsibility to Do Good

Living under the circumstances described, there was **placed upon man a very real responsibility**. That's the reason this dispensation is called by some the *Dispensation of Moral Responsibility*. There are many ways that this responsibility could be described, but I prefer to draw your attention to a portion of the Word found in the epistle of James. Turn there, please, and notice chapter 4. You will recognize a passage of Scripture which is familiar to you because you have often turned to it and you have often used it. James 4:17

Therefore to him that knoweth to do good, and doeth it not, to him it is sin.

When man is faced with the knowledge of good and evil, he is faced with the responsibility of doing good instead of evil.[36]

My first question is: how is this dispensation different from any other time period? It's not! Is there not an overlap of these time periods? Was not Adam faced with the choice of good and evil even though he did not understand what evil entailed? Adam was responsible for his choices, just as the people who lived after the fall? Adam did have a moral responsibility to make the right choice. James 4:17 is just as real to Adam as it was to people after the fall, which includes you and I today. In this short section, we can see the nonsense of this dispensation of conscience.

For when the Gentiles, which have not the law, do by nature the things contained in the law, these, having not the law, are a law unto themselves: Which show the work of the law written in their hearts, their **conscience also bearing witness**, and **their thoughts** the mean while accusing or else excusing one another. (Rom. 2:14-15)

Paul was teaching that the Gentiles throughout the Old Testament, God was dealing with them in their hearts, even though, specifically, God was working through the nation of Israel. By God doing this, they understood what "moral conscience and responsibility" was, and became accountable to God for their choices. Romans 1:21 Paul explains man's accountability to

God: *Because that, when they knew God, they glorified him not as God.* These people "chose" to reject God, and for this they will come under the condemnation of God. The same is true today for every individual on earth.

3. <u>Human Government: After the Flood:</u>

> By **faith** Noah, being warned of God of things not seen as yet, moved with fear, prepared an ark to the saving of his house; by the which he condemned the world, and became **heir of the righteousness which is by faith**. (Heb. 11:7)

The first question that should be asked about this dispensation is: who was left after the flood? Just eight people, Noah and his wife, Shem, Ham, Japheth, and their wives. Through childbearing from Noah's sons and their wives is where all the nations on the earth would eventually stem from. The natural conclusion would be the establishment of human government within these nations. It would not be until tower of Babel when God supernaturally separated people into the nations (races) throughout the earth, along with installing a particular language for each nation. Today, the world is still separated by governments and languages, which is the natural result of this supernatural event at the tower of Babel.

4. <u>The Promise- Abraham:</u>

Now we come to one of the central figures in the Word of God, Abraham. Abraham is declared the father of the faith, and the result of his faith his seed will be blessed. Abraham would be the one chosen that would establish the nation of Israel for God's plan of redemption for mankind, which would also include Gentiles today.

Here is a statement in a sermon by a pretribulationist describing what this dispensation period is.

> **Introduction**: The dispensation of Human Government lasted long enough for the "world" to establish a false religion and build a "tower" to reach heaven apart from faith in God and His grace. After the Tower of Babel, God worked through the Patriarchs, highlighted by Abraham. **The Dispensation of Promise is the foundation of the nation of Israel.**[37]

How does this dispensation of Human Government end at the Tower of Babel? Were there not nations formed after the dispersion of the Tower of Babel? Also, this "promise" is not only for Israel, but the church as well. This is the beginning of the dispensational debate between the two groups (church and Israel); however, the apostle Paul clarified how God viewed the church in relation to Abraham.

> For the promise, that he should be the heir of the world, was not to **Abraham, or to his seed**, through the law, but through the **righteousness of faith.** For if they which are of the law be heirs, **faith is made void,** and the promise made of none effect: Because the law worketh wrath: for where no law is, there is no transgression. Therefore it is of **faith, that it might be by grace; to the end the promise might be sure to all the seed**; not to that only which is of the law, **but to that also which is of the faith of Abraham; who is the father of us all,** (Rom. 4:13-16)

Abraham is much as the father to the church saints as he is to Israel.

5.   The Law- Beginning with Moses up to the Church:

By God giving the law, He was establishing a system that would "continue" the separation from the nations that started with Abraham (Lev. 18:3-4). Israel, having come out of the bondage in Egypt, was about to enter the promise land that was inhabited by pagan nations that were rebellious towards God. For God to continue His plan for Israel to prosper spiritually, He commissioned Joshua to expel or destroy the peoples of the land (Duet. 7:4). Here is a later example in Israel's history, found in the book of Ezra, where Israel failed to honor God by mixing with the pagan people.

> Now when these things were done, the princes came to me, saying, **The people of Israel, and the priests, and the Levites, have not separated themselves from the people of the lands, doing according to their abominations,** even of the Canaanites, the Hittites, the Perizzites, the Jebusites, the Ammonites, the Moabites, the Egyptians, and the Amorites. For they have taken of their daughters for themselves, and for their sons: so that the **holy seed have mingled themselves with the people of those**

lands: yea, the hand of the princes and rulers hath been chief in this trespass. (Ezra 9:1-2)

I noted in chapter three where God even separated the tribe of Levi from the rest of the nation. Levites were to perform the oaths and ordinances of God, because the people were not allowed to enter the presence of God at the temple (Num. 18:19). This system was uniquely designed for the nation of Israel through the temple sacrificial system. Also, for landowners only, they were commanded to tithe the fruit from the land and of the livestock (not money) to the Levites -does your pretrib-dispensational church teach tithing? The covenant of circumcision God made with Abraham was grafted in by Israel. The other identifier for Israel was keeping of the Sabbath on the seventh-day (Saturday). However, the New Testament declares that these things done under the law were the school master to bring the individual to a saving relationship with God through Jesus (Gal. 3:24-26). These ordinances were done away when Christ died on the cross (Col. 2:13-17).

Righteous Acts

My question is: how were the people of Israel made righteous in the eyes of God during this time?

But Israel, which **followed after the law of righteousness**, hath not attained to the law of righteousness. Wherefore? Because **they sought it not by faith**, but as it were **by the works of the law**. For they stumbled at that stumblingstone; (Rom. 9:31-32)

In these few verses, we see that the law **never** justified or saved anyone in Israel.

Brethren, my heart's desire and prayer to God for Israel is, that **they might be saved**. For I bear them record that they have a zeal of God, but **not according to knowledge**. For they **being ignorant of God's righteousness**, and **going about to establish their own righteousness, have not submitted** themselves unto the righteousness of God. (Rom. 10:1-3)

We see in this dispensation pertaining to the law, Israel missed the plan and purpose of God.

> Which was a figure for the time then present, in which were offered both gifts and sacrifices, that could not make him that did the service perfect, as pertaining to the **conscience;** (Heb. 9:9)

> For the **law having a shadow of good things to come,** and not the very image of the things, can **never** with those sacrifices which they offered year by year continually **make the comers thereunto perfect.** (Heb. 10:10)

Just as Adam who was made perfect and later sinned; he could not have been declared perfect by any type of works system. Israel was in the same situation. This sacrificial system was only a "shadow" or "type" of the perfect sacrifice to come, which was Jesus Christ.

Here is a statement by a prominent dispensation teacher, C. I. Scofield.

> As a dispensation, grace begins with the death and resurrection of Christ…The point of **testing is no longer legal obedience as the condition of salvation,** but acceptance or rejection of Christ, with good works as fruits of salvation[38](bold letters mine)

Grace has always been the character trait of God, along with mercy throughout the Word of God. Romans 5:10 states, *But where sin abounded, grace did much more abound.* Adam, Noah, Abraham, Moses, Israel, even the pagan city of Nineveh experienced God's grace and mercy. Grace is not separated from the Old Testament and the New Testament. Grace and mercy will always be associated with salvation, which works on the heart of man, allowing him to understand his sinful condition in the sight of God. This will lead a person to repentance and asking for forgiveness and mercy through Christ. Good works in the Old and New Testaments always should reflect the decision in a person's life that they truly repented and understood the eternal judgment they will face. Darby, Scofield, or anyone else who teaches that Old Testament saints were under legal obedience of the law as a condition for salvation have missed God's intention for His law.

Darby's doctrine of pretrib-dispensationalism builds a straw man throughout the Bible, all the while trying to justify the pretribulation rapture theory. Here is a quote by John Macarthur, warning how dispensationalism can be carried to an extreme.

There is a tendency for dispensationalist to get carried away with compartmentalizing truth to the point they can make unbiblical distinctions. An almost obsessive desire to categorize everything neatly has led various dispensationalist interpreters to draw hard lines not only between the church and Israel, but also between salvation and discipleship, the church and the kingdom, Christ's preaching and the apostolic message, faith and repentance, and the age of the law and the age of grace.[39]

Macarthur identified the main fallacy of Darby's dispensational teaching when taken to its logical conclusion. He is correct in his assessment, identifying the "hyper-dispensationalist" who segments the New Testament into compartments by separating the Apostles who supposedly taught a Jewish conversion and the Apostle Paul who taught a Gentile conversion. Dispensationalism even takes the Sermon on the Mount away from having application to the church; it only applies to Israel. Here is a quote from John Darby about the baptism question.

> ...if Christianity were the new covenant, which it is not, the Holy Ghost is the seal of faith now as circumcision was then. Matthew 28 was never carried out. The mission to the Gentiles was given up to Paul explicitly (Gal. 2) who was not sent to baptize and the mission in Matthew was from the resurrection, not ascension, and did not apply to the Jews but Gentiles only...[40]

Even Darby believed that Paul was not sent to participate in the baptism ordinance of the New Testament church. Also, circumcision was not a seal of "faith," but is constituted as a work of the law which was a covenant in itself (John 7:23; Acts: 7:8; Romans 2:25-29: Rom. 4:10). These are just a few of the many ramifications from the pretrib-dispensational teaching when taken to its final conclusion. He also proves my claim that dispensationalist do not understand the new covenant.

6. The Church- Begins in Acts 2:

We agree the church-age begins in Acts 2 at Pentecost and will last up to the rapture of the church. For the pretrib this will be before the 70th week begins; and for prewrath teaching this will be sometime in the second half of the 70th week. Remember, according to pretrib teaching, there must be a total separation between Israel and the church during the 70th week.

When Paul, who was a Jew, writing his epistle of Romans to the Gentile church, stated in chapter 11:1.

> I say then, Hath God cast away his people? God forbid. For I also am an Israelite, of the seed of Abraham, of the tribe of Benjamin

Paul acknowledges here that God did not cast away his people Israel.

> **God hath not cast away his people which he foreknew.** Wot ye not what the scripture saith of Elias? how he maketh intercession to God against Israel, saying, Lord, they have killed thy prophets, and digged down thine altars; and I am left alone, and they seek my life. But what saith the answer of God unto him? **I have reserved to myself seven thousand men,** who have not bowed the knee to the image of Baal. (Rom. 11:2-4)

Paul used an Old Testament example, when Israel in Elijah's day had forsaken God because of the false worship of Baal; God told Elijah, who thought he was all alone, there were seven thousand men who did not bow their knee to this false god.

> Even so then at **this present time** also there is a **remnant** according to the election of grace. (Rom. 11:5)

Paul declares even now that God has a remnant from Israel preserved; and he included himself (a member of the New Testament church) in this remnant. This remnant consisted of Jews who had placed their faith and trust in the promised Messiah, Jesus the Christ. The remnant of saved Jews who were participants in the Old Testament system, are now placed in the New Testament church.

What's interesting is that the first New Testament Gentile church was made up of only "Jews." It was not until Acts chapter 10 that the first Gentile believer (Cornelius) came to faith in Christ, which was about eight years after Pentecost. Pretrib-dispensationalism does not address the early church being Jewish. In fact, I ask my pretrib friends to explain why the seven churches in Revelation (early historical churches) use Jewish language to describe each New Testament church (e.g. synagogues, say they are Jews, doctrine of Balaam, Jezebel, keys of David, I will write upon him my name and city which is new Jerusalem)?

Jesus established the foundation of the church with the choosing of the twelve apostles (Jews) during His ministry under the Old Testament system (the Gospels). They were instructed by Christ for about three-and-half years under His ministry before He went to the cross. Even though the church was born at the Jewish Feast of Pentecost, its foundation was formed in the Gospels.

As Paul develops Romans chapter 11, he gives some clues as to what was happening in God's plan of redemption.

> I say then, Have they stumbled that they should fall? God forbid: but rather through their fall **salvation is come unto the Gentiles, for to provoke them to jealousy.** (Rom. 11:11)

Like the jealous boy who has lost his girlfriend after he had her heart and attention; now he is faced with the task of doing the right thing to win her back. That is the position God placed Israel in so they can see they have lost God's favor and repent and return back to God. In this case, they rejected God's love expressed solely through the person of Jesus. God miraculously preserved and worked with Israel for two thousand years; but when the time came for the fulfillment of God's redemptive plan, they failed the test.

> Jesus saith unto them, Did ye never read in the scriptures, The stone which the builders rejected, the same is become the head of the corner: this is the Lord's doing, and it is marvellous in our eyes? Therefore say I unto you, **The kingdom of God shall be taken from you, and given to a nation bringing forth the fruits thereof.** And whosoever shall fall on this stone shall be broken: but on whomsoever it shall fall, it will grind him to powder. And when the **chief priests and Pharisees** had heard

his parables, **they perceived that he spake of them.** (Matt. 21:42-45)

Jesus used this illustration to help explain that God would replace Israel as servants in His vineyard in the world, and would use another people to fulfill His plan on earth. We understand this now to be the New Testament church. The phrase *the kingdom of God taken from you*, is not talking about their eternal kingdom, but the kingdom of God in relation to God's work here on earth. This is reinforced by the statement, *given to a nation bringing forth fruits.* The "church-age" is a continuation of Gods plan of redemption, which is to bring others to a saving knowledge of Christ. Moreover, Jesus said the kingdom would be taken and given to another. He did not say there would be another kingdom given, but the same one. Simply put, Israel was "before" the cross and the church is "after" the cross. In the Old Testaments it stated that Abraham would be the father of "many nations" (Genesis 17: 5-8); the same language Jesus uses here in Matthew 21. And another note, dispensationalist teach the church is not part of the "kingdom" teachings by Christ, this is solely designated for the nation of Israel; yet, they acknowledge this verse is foretelling the churches role after Calvary.

Paul said here in Romans that the fall of Israel meant that the peoples of the world now will be included in Gods reconciliation to Him.

> For if the casting away of them be the **reconciling of the world,** what shall the receiving of them be, but life from the dead? (Rom. 11:15)

Let's read from Romans chapter 9 how God purposed to bring in Gentiles in His plan.

> 24. Even us, whom he hath called, not of the Jews only, **but also of the Gentiles**?
> 25. As he saith also in Osee, **I will call them my people, which were not my people; and her beloved, which was not beloved.**
> 26. And it shall come to pass, *that* in the place where it was said unto them, **Ye *are* not my people; there shall they be called the children of the living God.**

Paul reminded his readers here he was quoting Hosea 1:10; and that Hosea (Osee) was commanded to go and take a wife who was a harlot (picture of Israel who departed from God). Yet, in the midst of their rebellion, the number of the children of God would actually multiply as the sand of the sea.

> **Yet the number of the children of Israel shall be as the sand of the sea,** which cannot be measured nor numbered; and it shall come to pass, *that* in the place where it was said unto them, **Ye *are* not my people,** *there* it shall be said unto them, *Ye are* **the sons of the living God.**

God is referencing Gentiles here as being part of Israel. New Testament believers are spiritually considered one with Israel, not replacing Israel in their future promises.

In Paul's epistle to the Ephesians, he dealt with the subject of the relationship between the church and Israel, which I have already touched on briefly, so let's turn our attention once again to Ephesians.

> 13: But now in Christ Jesus **ye** who sometimes were far off are **made nigh** by the blood of Christ.
> 14: For he is our peace, who hath **made both one**, and hath **broken down the middle wall of partition between us;**
> 15: Having abolished in his flesh the enmity, **even the law of commandments contained in ordinances**; for to make in **himself of twain one new man**, so making peace;
> 16: And that he might **reconcile both unto God in one body** by the cross, having slain the enmity thereby:
> 17: And came and preached peace to **you which were afar** off, and to **them that were nigh.**
> 18: For through him **we both** have **access by one Spirit unto the Father.**
> 19: Now therefore ye **are no more strangers** and foreigners, but **fellowcitizens with the saints, and of the household of God;** 20: And **are built upon the foundation of the apostles and prophets,** Jesus Christ himself being the chief corner stone;
> 21: In whom **all the building** fitly **framed together** groweth unto **an holy temple** in the Lord:

> 22: In whom ye also are **builded together** for an habitation of
> God through the Spirit. (Eph. 2:13-22)

These verses could not be any plainer by the fact that God enjoined both Israel and the Church together after the sacrifice of Jesus Christ. Verse 13 says that *ye* (Gentiles) are *made nigh* (not made separate). Verse 14 teaches that God *made both one* (Jew and Gentile) *and hath broken down the middle wall of partition* (law of the commandments contained in ordinances). Verse 15 is teaching that God *reconciled* (brought unity) in *one body.* Verse 18 confesses that by the *Spirit* (not the Old Testament sacrificial system) we have *access to the Father.* Verse 19 declares *we* (Gentiles) are *no longer strangers, but "fellow citizens with the saints* (Old Testament). Paul says that in verse 20 that the foundation was *both apostles* (New Testament) *and prophets* (Old Testament). In verse 21, Paul states *all the building* (not two buildings) are *framed together,* which will grow unto a (single) habitation.

After Lazarus was raised back to life, as recorded in John 11, there was an interesting prophecy given by Caiaphus the high priest about Jesus.

> 51. And this spake he not of himself: but being high priest that
> year, he prophesied that Jesus should die for that nation;
> 52. And not for that nation only, **but that also he should gather
> together in one the children of God** that were scattered abroad.

Here is Paul declaring in his closing remarks in the book of Romans chapter 15 after he had meticulously pointed out to the Christians in Rome that God has established one people both Jew and Gentile.

> For whatsoever things were written **aforetime were written
> for our learning,** that we through patience and comfort of
> the scriptures might have hope. Now the God of patience and
> consolation grant you to be **likeminded one toward another**
> according to Christ Jesus: That ye may with **one mind and one
> mouth glorify God,** even the Father of our Lord Jesus Christ.
> Wherefore receive ye one another, as Christ also received us to the
> glory of God. Now I say that **Jesus Christ was a minister of the
> circumcision for the truth of God, to confirm the promises
> made unto the fathers:** And that **the Gentiles might glorify
> God for his mercy**; as it is written, For this cause I will confess

to thee among **the Gentiles,** and sing unto thy name. And again he saith, **Rejoice, ye Gentiles, with his people.** And again, Praise the Lord, **all ye Gentiles**; and laud him, all ye people. And again, **Esaias saith, There shall be a root of Jesse, and he that shall rise to reign over the Gentiles; in him shall the Gentiles trust.** Now the God of hope fill you with all joy and peace in believing, that ye may abound in hope, through the power of the Holy Ghost. And I myself also am persuaded of you, my brethren, that ye also are full of goodness, filled with all knowledge, able also to **admonish one another.** Nevertheless, brethren, I have written the more boldly unto you in some sort, as putting you in mind, because of the grace that is given to me of God, **That I should be the minister of Jesus Christ to the Gentiles, ministering the gospel of God, that the offering up of the Gentiles might be acceptable, being sanctified by the Holy Ghost.** I have therefore whereof I may glory through Jesus Christ in those things which pertain to God. For **I will not dare to speak of any of those things** which Christ hath **not wrought by me, to make the Gentiles obedient, by word and deed,** (Rom. 15:4-18)

Paul, by the leading of the Holy Ghost, understood the relationship that Christ instituted between Israel and the church. He counted it a privilege to preach the gospel to the Gentiles, even though he was a Jew. He understood that he was not to teach anything to the Gentiles to make them obedient to any of the Jewish laws or ordinances, because they became obsolete through Christ. Paul "dared not" to put the yoke of bondage around the neck of New Testament believers!

Israel did not have a problem with a Messiah; they understood this truth even at the time of Jesus (John 4:25). Unfortunately, they missed the opportunity by not recognizing Christ as the promised Messiah, so now God is temporarily dealing with the Gentiles in this church-age. And at some point in the future (millennium), God will reestablish His promises to Israel and they will enjoy the benefits of the covenant.

According to Hebrews chapters 7 – 10, believers in Christ have entered into the New Covenant with God. This is the dispensational definition given in the Bible. Paul's use for the word dispensation four times in the New

Testament all reference the completed work of Christ, and that by grace all can be saved. Hebrews 1:1-3 captures this paradigm shift from the old to the new.

> God, who at sundry times and in divers manners spake in time past unto the fathers by the prophets, Hath in these last days spoken unto us by his Son, whom he hath appointed heir of all things, by whom also he made the worlds; Who being the brightness of his glory, and the express image of his person, and upholding all things by the word of his power, when he had by himself purged our sins, sat down on the right hand of the Majesty on high;

Dispensations according to the Bible should be before and after the cross, that's it. Before the cross, man waited for the fulfillment of the promised Messiah, and after the cross, this promise has been fulfilled in Christ (cf. Luke 24:44-45). This should be the only "progressive revelation" that pertains to dispensational teaching; not a contrived series of events attempting to categorize the Bible into different time periods for the sake of a pretrib rapture.

> Receiving the end of your faith, even the salvation of your souls. **Of which salvation the prophets have inquired and searched diligently, who prophesied of the grace that should come unto you**: Searching what, or what manner of time the Spirit of Christ was in them signify, when it testified beforehand the sufferings of Christ, and the glory that should follow. Unto whom it was revealed, that not unto themselves, but unto us they did minister the things, which are now reported unto you by them that have preached the gospel unto you with the Holy Ghost sent down from heaven; which things the angels desire to look into. Wherefore gird up the loins of your mind, be sober, and hope to the end for the grace that is to be brought unto you at the revelation of Jesus Christ; (1 Peter 1:9-13)

> So Christ was once offered to bear the sins of many; and unto them that look for him shall he appear the second time without sin unto salvation. (Heb. 9:28)

7. <u>Israel in the 70th week:</u>

I have already stated this is the dispensation that I have designated based on Darby's teaching to separate Israel and the church during the 70th week. Even though dispensationalist do not specifically define the 70th week as so. I will deal with the specific fallacies of this theory throughout the remainder of this book.

8. <u>The Kingdom- Revelation chapter 20:</u>

This last category on dispensation which relates more to the book of Revelation, I will deal specifically with this topic then.

I would like to conclude this chapter by observing some closing thoughts about dispensationalism.

Questions to Ponder Regarding Dispensationalism

1.) What is the significance of the church being born on the Feast of Pentecost, which is a Jewish holyday?

2.) What effect did other "Jewish" feasts in the Old Testament have on the New Testament church? The Passover feast, for example, Israel celebrates their deliverance from bondage in Egypt, and now is celebrated by the church because of the death, burial, and resurrection of Jesus.

3.) If the dispensation of grace started at Pentecost as Darby attested to, how were Jews saved in the gospels under the ministry of Jesus if they were still under the Old Testament?

> Wherefore I say unto thee, **Her sins, which are many, are forgiven;** for she loved much: but to whom little is forgiven, the same loveth little. And he said unto her, **Thy sins are forgiven.** And they that sat at meat with him began to say within themselves, **Who is this that forgiveth sins also?** And he said to the woman, **Thy faith hath saved thee; go in peace.** (Luke 7:47-50)

I find it ironic that pretribulation teachers such as J. Vernon McGee in his radio address **Thru the Bible** used Scriptures from the Old Testament to teach "types" of the rapture of the church; for example, Elijah being taken up in the fiery chariot-Elijah was a Jew! Furthermore, this event was not invisible, but visible which goes against pretrib typology. How do dispensational teachers justify their theology by mixing and matching the Scriptures when they want to? What about the time Abraham sent his servant to get a Gentile bride (Rebekah) for Isaac, who was a Jew? Again, pretribulation teachers teach this "Jewish" story is a picture of the rapture of the church where Christ comes to get His bride. I believe this story is more in line with Israel (Isaac) and the church (Rebekah) being joined together by Christ. I ask my pretrib friends: why would God separate this marriage, leaving Israel (Isaac) here to go through the tribulation and take the church (Rebekah) away when He comes back?

4.) When Israel was in captivity in the Old Testament (e.g. Babylonian captivity), how were the Jews justified by God if they could not participate in the sacrificial system according to the Law of Moses? Would this time in captivity be a different dispensation as well?

5.) If the early church possessed the ability to perform miracles (e.g. dead people raised back to life, blind seeing again, lame walking, etc.) would we be classified as a different dispensation today since there are no "recorded" miracles performed like those in the early church? Many pretrib believers hold to the doctrine of cessation (as I believe). They believe when the cannon of Scriptures was completed, which is approximately the same time all the apostles died; therefore, the sign-gifts given to the early church were done away with. There was a cessation of these "sign" gifts and all faith must be based upon the written Word of God. Where does the early church fit in with dispensation teaching?

I encourage the reader to read Hebrews chapter 11 to see how God worked throughout the Old Testament, and see if there is not continuity with each individual listed. Hebrews 11 emphasizes **faith,** which is the common component to each person listed. In this chapter the writer traverses through time, from after the fall of man, beginning with Abel, to later in the Old Testament. The writer has been expressing throughout the book of Hebrew to the new Jewish believers that Jesus Christ is the fulfillment of the Old Testament Scriptures, which is a "better way" than the sacrificial system of the law.

Again, my point of emphasis in this chapter on dispensation is that there is not a separation during the church-age, but a collating together. And this assembling will last well into the 70th week, not up to the 70th week as pretrib prescribes.

I closeout this chapter by reminding the reader that the Trojan horse of pretrib-dispensationalism was instituted only to excuse the church in the final week of history. Ending with that thought, I ask my pretrib friends: what benefit is dispensationalism (defined by pretrib) to the church outside the rapture debate? Does this doctrine serve any purpose other than the argument against the church being in the 70th week? I say a resounding, NO!

In the next chapter, we will look at the prophecy of the seventy-weeks of Daniel and see how it fits within the framework for both Israel and the church.

CHAPTER SIX

THE SEVENTY WEEKS OF DANIEL

We now turn our attention to Daniel's seventy-week prophecy and how it specifically relates to our rapture study. Daniel was one of the young Jews taken captive by Nebuchadnezzar after the fall of Jerusalem in 605 BC. In the year of 586 BC, Jerusalem would suffer total defeat by the Babylonian army.

As the children of Israel became assimilated into the Babylonian society, most gave into the demands of their captors; however, Daniel and a few others remained faithful to God (Daniel 1:12-15) in spite of the extreme pressure. Because of Daniel's faithfulness, God promoted him through the Babylonian ranks during the years of his captivity (Daniel 1:17-20).

After many years passed, and as Daniel was reading from the book of Jeremiah, he understood that the seventy-years of captivity were coming to a finality.

> In the first year of Darius the son of Ahasuerus, of the seed of the Medes, which was made king over the realm of the Chaldeans; In the first year of his reign I Daniel understood by books the number of the years, whereof the word of the LORD came to **Jeremiah the prophet, that he would accomplish seventy years** in the desolations of Jerusalem. (Dan. 9:1-2)

> For thus saith the LORD, **That after seventy years be accomplished at Babylon** I will visit you, and perform my good word toward you, in causing you to return to this place. (Jer. 29:10)

Daniel, knowing God was about to intervene for Israel, proceeded to pray to the Lord and confess for the nation their sin and rebellion. It was during this prayer the Lord sent the angel Gabriel to Daniel to verify the prophecy in Jeremiah.

> Yea, whiles I was speaking in prayer, even the man Gabriel, whom I had seen in the vision at the beginning, being caused to fly swiftly, touched me about the time of the evening oblation. (Dan.9:21)

In the following chapters, Daniel would have various dreams and visions, and with the help of the angel Gabriel, he would give Daniel understanding (vs.23). The next four verses in the Daniel 9 are perhaps the most studied and talked about verses in all the Word of God, certainly when discussing Bible prophecy.

> 24: **Seventy weeks** are determined upon thy people and upon thy holy city, to finish the transgression, and to make an end of sins, and to make reconciliation for iniquity, and to bring in everlasting righteousness, and to seal up the vision and prophecy, and to anoint the most Holy. 25: Know therefore and understand, that from the going forth of the commandment to restore and to build Jerusalem unto the Messiah the Prince shall be **seven weeks, and threescore and two we**eks: the street shall be built again, and the wall, even in troublous times.
>
> 26: And **after threescore and two weeks shall Messiah be cut off**, but not for himself: and the people of the prince that shall come shall destroy the city and the sanctuary; and the end thereof shall be with a flood, and unto the end of the war desolations are determined.
>
> 27: And **he shall confirm the covenant with many for one week**: and in the **midst of the week** he shall cause the sacrifice and the oblation to cease, and for the overspreading of **abominations he shall make it desolate**, even until the consummation, and that determined shall be poured upon the desolate. (Dan. 9:24-27)

We already defined that a week is equal to seven-years, where the totality of the seventy-weeks would equal 490 years. These years would be divided into three segments: 7 weeks (49 years), 62 weeks (434 years), and 1 week (7years), for a total of 490 years. At the completion of these 490 years the angel told Daniel that six things would be accomplished.

1. To finish the transgression
2. To make an end of sins
3. To make reconciliation for iniquity
4. To bring in everlasting righteousness
5. To seal up the vision and prophecy
6. To anoint the most Holy

Daniels's prayer consisted of his acknowledgment of the people's transgressions (vs. 11), their sins (vs. 5), and their iniquity (vs. 5). According to these three statements, the Lord responded to Daniel's confession by assuring him that He is a merciful and forgiving God. What God ultimately will fulfill would be to: (1) finish the transgression; (2) make an end of sins; (3) and make reconciliation for His people. When this is completed, God would eventually: (4) bring in everlasting righteousness; (5) seal up the vision; (6) anoint the most Holy. As Christians, today, we understand the first three events listed in verse 24 were accomplished by Christ at Calvary. These six events are a dual prophecy- a single prophecy split into two stages. The first three were with Christ's first coming, and the second three will be completed when Christ comes a second time.

Gabriel tells Daniel, this prophecy will begin at the giving of the commandment to restore and rebuild Jerusalem. This is not to be mistaken with the Persian King Cyrus, who gave a commandment in Ezra chapter 1 to rebuild the temple, not Jerusalem.

> Now in the first year of Cyrus king of Persia, that the word of the LORD by the mouth of Jeremiah might be fulfilled, the LORD stirred up the spirit of Cyrus king of Persia, that he made a proclamation throughout all his kingdom, and put it also in writing, saying, Thus saith Cyrus king of Persia, The LORD God of heaven hath given me all the kingdoms of the earth; and he hath charged me to **build him an house** at Jerusalem, which is in Judah. Who is there among you of all his people? his God be with him, and let him go up to Jerusalem, which is in Judah, and

build the house of the LORD God of Israel, (he is the God,) which is in Jerusalem. (Ezra 1:1-3)

This particular commandment came in 539 BC when Israel's seventy-years of captivity were completed. The commandment to restore and build Jerusalem is predicated upon rebuilding the wall and street (Dan. 9:25). This specific commandment, which is associated with the rebuilding in *troublous times,* is found in Nehemiah.

> And it came to pass in the month Nisan, in the twentieth year of Artaxerxes the king, that wine was before him: and I took up the wine, and gave it unto the king. Now I had not been beforetime sad in his presence....And I said unto the king, If it please the king, and if thy servant have found favour in thy sight, that thou wouldest send me unto Judah, unto the city of my fathers' sepulchres, that I may build it...And a letter unto Asaph the keeper of the king's forest, **that he may give me timber to make beams for the gates of the palace which appertained to the house, and for the wall of the city, and for the house that I shall enter into.** And the king granted me, according to the good hand of my God upon me. (Neh.2:1, 5, 8)

Here we have the first segment of the seventy-week prophecy. The commandment from Artaxerxes came in 445 BC, and the rebuilding lasted for forty-nine years. This rebuilding process was met with opposition, particularly by Sanballat and Tobiah (Nehemiah 2:19). The second segment would last 62 weeks or 434 years. The key to this is the double statement about Jesus Christ, *unto Messiah the Prince* (vs. 25) and after three score (60) and two weeks *shall Messiah be cut off* (vs. 26).

Sir Robert Anderson, in his book "The Coming Prince," is credited with calculating the time from the commandment to its fulfillment. He calculated the 69 weeks or 483 years, and more specifically- 173,880 days. He determined that from 14th March, 445 BC, and counting the days, this was fulfilled on April 6th, AD 33.[41] It is believed that this date coincided with Jesus's triumphal entry into Jerusalem; to which Luke's gospel makes a couple of interesting statements.

Saying, If thou hadst **known**, even thou, **at least in this thy day**, the things which belong unto thy peace! but now they are hid from thine eyes. For the days shall come upon thee, that thine enemies shall cast a trench about thee, and compass thee round, and keep thee in on every side, And shall lay thee even with the ground, and thy children within thee; and they shall not leave in thee one stone upon another; because **thou knewest not the time of thy visitation.** (Lk.19:42-44)

Jesus rebuked the leaders of Israel because of their denial of Him as their Messiah. After seeing and hearing about all the miracles and listening to His teachings, along with other Old Testament Scripture containing the prophecies of the coming Messiah, they were still steadfast in their rejection of Him. Instead of receiving Christ as savior, He was rejected by them, and in turn, Israel would receive its just punishment. Jesus had continually fought the leadership of Israel from the inception of His ministry. Christ was continually challenged due to their unbelief and their religious status among the people. And when the perfect opportunity arose, they accused Jesus of a crime against Caesar; then they seized upon it and persuaded the multitude to have him crucified.

Jesus's entry into Jerusalem before his crucifixion led him directly to the temple to chastise the priest for turning God's house into a money-making venture. It is not uncommon to compare what was taking place in Israel to our present day. In many churches, especially in America, the emphasis is on money and church growth in numbers (2 Peter 2:3) at the expense of spiritual growth. Sadly, many preachers on the religious channels on television continue to prostitute the gospel of Christ, as though God has blessed them and their ministry because of a financial gain. We might take a solemn warning by seeing how God's judgment was placed upon Israel for their thirst for money. Peter wrote in his epistle in 1 Peter 4:17-18, that before God brings judgment to this earth, He first will deal with His church. Also, I am not saying there aren't any large churches that are good gospel preaching churches, because there are.

Jesus's entry in Jerusalem ended the 69th week of Daniel's prophecy, when God said *unto Messiah the Prince* (Dan. 9:25). Notice in verse 26 of Daniel 9, the Messiah will be *cut off,* which pertains to the death of Christ that took place that same week He entered Jerusalem. There is no room for error as to the meaning of this prophecy. It also states in the same verse that He would be cut off, but *not for himself.* We know today, this prophetic statement is applied to the Gentiles, though the Lord was specifically addressing Israel. This is a beautiful description of Jesus who freely gave His life for mankind. Christ's death fulfilled the first three elements of Daniel 9:24, with the next three to come later. I'm reminded in Luke's gospel as Christ gave His first public sermon to His local hometown synagogue in Nazareth; He read from the book of Isaiah 61:1-2 (Luke 4:18-19). *The Spirit of the Lord is upon me, because he hath anointed me to preach the gospel to the poor; he hath sent me to heal the brokenhearted, to preach deliverance to the captives, and recovering of sight to the blind, to set at liberty them that are bruised, To preach the acceptable year of the Lord.*

What's interesting is that Jesus only read part of Isaiah 61:2, and left off the last phrase of the verse: *and the day of vengeance of our God; to comfort all that mourn.* We know today, as we look back upon the work of Christ, that the "day of vengeance" was not fulfilled at His first coming. If this were strictly read from Isaiah's view back in the Old Testament, I'm sure the people thought that verses 1 & 2 would be fulfilled the same time. Yet we realize today, almost two-thousand years and counting, that the day of vengeance has not occurred. When we study Scripture through the lens of Bible prophecy, we need to be aware of the potential dual prophecies that prophetic verses can contain. This is true with Daniel's seventy-week prophecy as we just seen. One more note, notice the Bible says that Christ's second coming is called the "day of vengeance," which entails that Jesus will exact retribution on those who caused others (saints) to mourn. Looks like there will be comfort and judgment at Christ's second coming. And this is exactly what we will see in our study.

Therefore, we are now left with the final week in God's prophetic time clock that will be played out, not in obscurity, but on the world stage.

The 70th week

With all this said, the debate rages whether the church will be present on earth for the 70th (final) week. This is why we have pre, mid, and posttribulation rapture positions taught in the church.

I mentioned in chapter one, the word tribulation is a name prescribed only by the pretribulation teaching; however, there is not a single verse that proves the 70th week is biblically called the tribulation. Here are a few of the leading pretribulation teachers attempting to justify their theory.

15. Where does the Bible teach a seven-year tribulation?
Belief that the tribulation will last for seven-years comes from the
prophetic calendar of Daniel 9:24-27.[42]

Thomas Ice and Timothy Demy

That's it! Two leading pretribulationist only cite one passage from the book of Daniel trying to prove that the final week is called the tribulation. And the passage they used says nothing about a seven-year tribulation. The "prophetic calendar" they cite in this passage is the complete seventy-week prophecy; surely, they are not saying the entire seventy-weeks is called the tribulation. They just make a blanked statement about the tribulation without a true definition and assume everyone is to believe them.

Here another example proving my point. Thomas Ice and Timothy Demy in their book "The Return," discusses the definition of the tribulation.

> While these 'terms and expressions' would 'seem' to indicate an eschatological time of fulfillment for the events they describe, and Jesus and the New Testament writers certainly understood the Tribulation as a future event.[43]

These terms and expressions they are referring to say nothing about the 70th week of Daniel being called the tribulation. Jesus most certainly understood the coming future events. Jesus was clear to the disciples that there would be a time of great tribulation beginning at the midpoint of the final seven-years, not before. I say pretrib teachers cannot produce one "literal" verse proving this theory.

H.A. Ironside (1876-1951), a pretribulationist, wrote numerous books and commentaries. One such book is related to our study, **Not Wrath but Rapture: Will the Church Participate in the Great Tribulation.** In his opening chapter "What is meant by the term, 'The Great Tribulation'" he stated what the great tribulation was.

> The careful student of the prophetic Scriptures cannot fail to observe that in both the Old and New Testament, the Spirit of God directs attention to a time of very special trial involving the pouring out of **divine wrath upon men, known as "the great tribulation,"** "the time of Jacob's trouble," "the coming hour of

temptation," the day of the Lord," and also designated by other striking terms.[44] (bold letters mine)

In this short book (37 pages) he never gives one Scripture saying that the great tribulation is equal to the 70th week. Yet, he uses the name "great tribulation" loosely as if its common knowledge the great tribulation is the70[th] week. Here is further proof of Ironside using the term "great tribulation" loosely.

> Practically all futurist interpreters are agreed that in chapters 6 to 19 of Revelation we have **the great tribulation period**. It is then that the wrath of the Lamb and the wrath of God will be poured upon the habitable earth, and Satan will be cast down from the heavenlies, having great wrath, knowing his time is short.[45]

Satan is cast out of heaven at the midpoint of the final week; so how does Satan's wrath compare to God's outpouring wrath on the world? According to Ironside, God punishes the world for three-and half-years before Satan even shows up.

John Walvoord sheds the true light of the pretrib dilemma when trying to define the tribulation.

> Though the **Bible does not give** a specific term covering this time period of more than seven years, frequently in eschatological literature it is referred to as the Tribulation, **though scriptures do not use the term in this sense**. (emphasis mine)[46]

The pretrib teachers are attempting to hijack the rapture discussion by arguing from their contrived perspective on how they want to define the debate. That is one reason they can make statements like, "You can go through the tribulation if you want to." This shows how they set up their straw-man argument based on a preconceived theory. Biblical definitions are extremely important in obtaining the proper meaning for Bible passages. We cannot afford to interject what we "perceive" a passage means to fit our view (called a pretext); we must let the Scriptures define the meaning.

What pretribulation teachers will emphasize in their argument to justify a pretribulation rapture; they say that even though the word "pretribulation" is not used in scripture, neither is the word trinity or second coming. That might be true; however, we know from Scripture the word trinity is used to define the godhead. 1 John 5:7 *"For there are **three** that bear record in heaven, the Father, the Word, and the Holy Ghost: and these **three are one**."* Three in one! As for the word "second coming," Jesus stated in John 14:6 *"I will come again."* He only came the first time, so adding up the math, coming again would be the second coming of Christ. Both pretribulationism and prewrath agree that the rapture is prewrath- before God's wrath. But scripture certainly does not teach a pretribulation rapture. There is no clear-cut scripture saying "before the tribulation Christ will come." But we do find, as an example, Christ's coming in Matthew 24, where Jesus said "after the tribulation."

Continuing our study with the final week from Daniel's prophecy, in verse 27 we see that the 70th week starts with an individual confirming a covenant; *He shall confirm the covenant with many for one week* (Isaiah 28:15). The word, *many,* is up for debate as to whether it is strictly Israel, or a confederate of nations. I believe it will be a multitude of nations headed by the U. N. in a final attempt to bring a halt to the embattled Middle East crises. The crises will eventually reach an apex that will have a major ripple effect throughout the world, where the U. N. will be forced to intervene, as history has already proved. Through these unfolding events, the "man of sin" (Antichrist) will rise to a position of power on the world stage.

The Seven Year Peace Treaty

There is peace treaty coming that will usher in the 70th week. In Daniel 9:27 it states that the Antichrist will *confirm the covenant for one week,* and in the midst of this week (3½ years) he will break the covenant and begin the great tribulation.

It is agreed upon, there will be a final seven-year time period and the ceasing of some type of sacrifices will occur during the middle of the week; however, I personally believe there will not be a specific seven-year peace treaty, or a seven-year agreement signed by world leaders. There will be a "confirmation or agreement" that attempts to finalize a treaty of some kind which is already in place; however, I believe it will not be stated or agreed upon as a "seven-year" treaty. These seven-years are on God's timetable, given to Daniel by the angel Gabriel. God will be controlling the unfolding events as He brings man's reign to an end. This agreement ultimately will only last three-and-half-years before it is broken. This peace treaty will be implemented by man as a final solution to the Middle East problems that will be intended to last a lot longer than seven-years. I believe this is one reason that we will not fully comprehend the 70th week when it commences. Remember, Jesus stated that when you see the abomination of desolation (Matt. 24:15), you will know His return is near, not when you see a seven-year peace treaty.

> When ye therefore shall see the **abomination of desolation, spoken of by Daniel the prophet**, stand in the holy place, (whoso readeth, let him understand:) (Matt. 24:15)

The angel Gabriel said in Daniel 9:24, the seventy-weeks are *determined*, which means they are set on God's time. When the seventy-weeks began, it was between two men, Nehemiah the cup bearer and the King Artaxerxes. God alone determined the status of the time frame of this prophecy- He is sovereign. Artaxerxes did not tell Nehemiah that you have exactly forty-nine years to complete your task. The sixty-nine weeks were fulfilled because it was God who determined when Christ's birth would take place and finally his death. At some unknown point in the future a particular generation will enter the final week, and when it does it will be God who determines when it begins.

Futurist prophecy teachers agree that in the middle of the 70th week, when the Antichrist causes the sacrifices to cease, this will be commenced by the abomination of desolations. Matthew 24:9-14 could very well be describing what is taking place during the great tribulation, which is identified in verse 15 (we will view these verses later). Daniel chapter 12 describes that *the wise* will understand and turn many to righteousness. It will be Christians, not the world, who understand the events as the 70th week unfolds and moves towards the revealing of the Antichrist and the start of the great tribulation.

See appendix: On the Feasts of Israel and the Abomination of Desolations.

Ceasing of the Sacrifice

Related to the 70th week, is a notable event that will take place regarding the man of sin causing the sacrifice and oblation to cease. I will present two options at this time that could possibly unfold in the final week. One will be the actual rebuilding of the end-time temple on the temple mount in Jerusalem where the literal animal sacrifices will have begun. Precisely at the midpoint of the final week, Antichrist will personally go into the temple and will cause the sacrifices to cease, and declare himself God. This is the common thought amongst prophecy teachers. Currently, this is my belief; however, I am not dissuaded to another view that teaches that there will not be a final temple and no animal sacrifices will be taking place; but the ceasing of the sacrifices and oblation will be directed toward the saints world-wide. Now, it's not my intention to get side-tracked on this subject, but I believe it's extremely pertinent to our rapture topic; especially since there is so much speculation about the final temple being rebuilt. Here are the verses pertaining to our discussion.

> And he shall confirm the covenant with many for one week: and in the midst of the week he shall cause the sacrifice and the oblation to cease, and for the overspreading of abominations he shall make *it* desolate, even until the consummation, and that determined shall be poured upon the desolate. (Daniel 9:27)

> And from the time *that* the daily *sacrifice* shall be taken away, and the abomination that maketh desolate set up, *there shall be* a thousand two hundred and ninety days. (Daniel 12:11)

These two verses are not to be mistaken with another prophecy in Daniel 11:31

> And arms shall stand on his part, and they shall pollute the sanctuary of strength, and shall take away the daily *sacrifice*, and they shall place the abomination that maketh desolate.

This event took place when Antiochus Epiphanies was returning back to Greece after attacking Egypt. As he passed through Jerusalem, he entered into the temple and sacrificed a pig on the altar for his god, Zeus. This was a precursor to the final abomination that will take place by Antichrist. You can read Antiochus Epiphanies in the book of Maccabees.

Here are scriptures from the New Testament related to this final event.

> When ye therefore shall see the abomination of desolation, spoken of by Daniel the prophet, stand in the holy place, (whoso readeth, let him understand:) (Matthew 24:15)

Who opposeth and exalteth himself above all that is called God, or that is worshipped; so that he as God sitteth in the temple of God, shewing himself that he is God. (2 Thess. 2:4)

Option One:

Solomon, David's son, built the first temple, which was destroyed in 586 BC. After Israel's captivity in Babylon, Cyrus allowed Israel to return to the land, and the temple construction began in 536 BC. Later, it would be Herod, the Roman governor, who expanded and magnified the temple to appease the Jews in Roman captivity around the time before Christ's birth. Eventually, the Romans would destroy the temple in AD 70, and the only remains today are the foundation walls and two Muslims shrines- the Dome of the Rock and the Al Aqsa Mosque- which were built hundreds of years after the fall of Jerusalem.

Option one therefore is that the Antichrist, precisely in the middle of the 70th week, will enter the rebuilt temple and cause the animal sacrifices taking place to cease.

Here is Thomas Ice of the Pretrib Research Center in his article, "Is it Time for the Temple," stating:

Conclusion

In spite of contemporary turmoil, Israel's Third Temple will one day be rebuilt as Dr. Price and I demonstrated in *Ready To Rebuild* from Daniel 9:24-27; Matthew 24:15; 2 Thessalonians 2:4; Revelation 11:1-2; 13:14-15. Few observers of world events ever thought Israel would become a nation again, but it did occur in 1948. **Yet, there will be a rebuilt temple by the middle of the seven-year tribulation in order to facilitate the fulfillment of Bible prophecy.**

I have often taught that the long-awaited permission for the Jews to rebuild their Temple will likely be part of the covenant between Antichrist and Israel that starts the seven-year tribulation after the rapture. **It appears to me that the Temple will be rebuilt and supervised supernaturally by the two witnesses during the first half of the tribulation.**"[47] (bold letters mine)

As I stated near the beginning of this book, the temple could be rebuilt **before** the rapture. Ultimately, we don't know if it will be built inside the 70th week or before.

It is often quoted by the pretrib teachers, "the next event in God's prophetic time clock is the rapture of the Church"- keeping their followers on the edge of their seat at all time. Since this statement is so prevalent among their teaching, it comes naturally then to disregard any other future prophesied event, because any major event before the rapture ruin's imminence. However, case in point: The pretrib followers had to accept the "prophesied fact" that Israel had to become a nation again for Daniel's 70th week could be fulfilled.

The rebuilding of the final temple will be on the same prophetic magnitude as Israel becoming a nation after almost two-thousand years of dispersion. I believe the pretrib teachers will go into PR mode to diffuse any discrepancy in their theology, or they should accept the fact "not all prophecies were fulfilled" up to our present day.

Here is a quote by pretrib teachers Ed Hindson and Tim LaHaye about the future temple.

> This new temple or the third temple will be constructed on the original site of the Temple Mount in Jerusalem. Its destiny is to be desecrated or destroyed by the Antichrist—an event that is prophetically referenced by Jesus in Matthew 24:15 and the apostle Paul in 2 Thessalonians 2:4. Although plans for the rebuilding the temple have been on hand for decades, the Jews must wait for the right political climate and must have control of the area before they can begin construction. **Many prophecy scholars believe these terms will be part of the seven-year agreement between the Jews and the Antichrist mentioned in Daniel 9:27.**[48] (bold letters mine)

To throw in my two-cents on the subject; I believe the rebuilding of the temple could be an economic boom for Israel. As Christians, we know that the final sacrifice for the sins of the world was laid on Christ at the cross, so there is no further need for a sacrificial system. However, for Israel, the Old Testament requires the males to appear in Jerusalem three times a year- along with this becoming a major tourist attraction- this will be an economic wind-fall for Israel. Also, the division in Israel will be more united with their religious identity restored. The re-gathering of Jewish families moving back to their rightful inheritance would be monumental for the nation of Israel. The land for peace mentality that permeates most of the current peace-process could entail that Israel receives a portion of the Temple Mount as part of the agreement. LaHaye and Hindson could be correct in their assumption about the Antichrist's seven-year agreement; however, with one stipulation-the church will be here to witness this.

Option Two

Here is the other scenario that could be played-out in the final days. As I stated, I still believe option one is probable; however, I could see this unfold as well. The subject of this book is about the rapture; however, equally important and having a direct impact on the rapture is Christ's and the apostle Paul's teaching about the man of sin declaring himself God. Maybe we have overlooked a fundamental characteristic of the real meaning of that great moment when the man of sin real nature is revealed at the middle of the 70th week. What I propose in option two is there will be no literal temple or animal sacrifices, but the temple spoken of is what the New Testament regards the temple today-the believer's body which houses the Holy Spirit where God now resides. The ceasing of the sacrifices could be that the Antichrist will outlaw Christianity by implementing the mark of the beast-total worship and full surrender to his authority. I could write endlessly about the two scenarios that could possibly, but I will attempt to get straight to the point. Here are Scripture verses applied to this option.

First, with the advent of Christ in the New Testament he compared himself greater than the physical temple that stood in Jerusalem.

> 6. But I say unto you, That in this place is *one* **greater than the temple**.
> 7. But if ye had known what *this* meaneth, I will have mercy, and not sacrifice, ye would not have condemned the guiltless. (Matt. 12:6-7)

This was said by Christ in response to the Pharisees who accused his disciples picking corn in the fields on Saturday and violating the Sabbath law. Jesus was plainly telling them that He was greater than the temple where the

Levites offered sacrifices for the Jews. There was mistaking this, Jesus later tells the Pharisees in John 2:

> 19. Jesus answered and said unto them, **Destroy this temple**, and in three days I will raise it up.
> 20. Then said the Jews, Forty and six years was this temple in building, and wilt thou rear it up in three days?
> 21. But he spake of the **temple of his body**.

We see that at the death of Christ, the temple and its system of sacrifices will be taken away.

> 50. Jesus, when he had cried again with a loud voice, yielded up the ghost.
> 51. And, behold, the **veil of the temple was rent in twain** from the top to the bottom; and the earth did quake, and the rocks rent; (Matt. 27:50-51)

This is obvious to the believer that the Jewish temple has been taken away by the sacrifice of Christ. Furthermore, we find in Scripture it is prophesied that God, who resided in the temple, will put His spirit in true believers.

> 26. A new heart also will I give you, and a **new spirit will I put within you**: and I will take away the stony heart out of your flesh, and I will give you an heart of flesh.
> 27. And I will put **my spirit within you**, and cause you to walk in my statutes, and ye shall keep my judgments, and do *them*. (Ezekiel 36:26-27)

> 16. Know ye not that **ye are the temple of God**, and *that* the Spirit of God dwelleth in you?
> 17. If any **man defile the temple of God**, him shall God destroy; for the **temple of God is holy, which *temple* ye are**. (I Cor. 3:16-17)

What? know ye not that your body is the temple of the **Holy Ghost *which is* in you**, which ye have of God, and ye are not your own? (1 Cor. 6:19)

This is emphasized in the book of Hebrews with the narrative of "better things" (new way of worship with God) has replaced the ordinances and laws of the Old Testament.

> For the law having a shadow of good things to come, *and* not the very image of the things, can never with those sacrifices which they offered year by year continually make the comers thereunto perfect. (Hebrews 10:1)

There's an interesting prophecy given by Haggai pertaining to a future temple.

> The glory of this latter house shall be greater than of the former, saith the LORD of hosts: and in this place will I give peace, saith the LORD of hosts. (Haggai 2:9)

Now notice what the prophet Zechariah said about the temple.

> 12. And speak unto him, saying, Thus speaketh the LORD of hosts, saying, Behold the man whose name *is* The BRANCH; and he shall grow up out of his place, **and he shall build the temple of the LORD:**
> 13. Even he shall **build the temple of the LORD**; and he shall bear the glory, and shall sit and rule upon his throne; and he shall be a priest upon his throne: and the counsel of peace shall be between them both. (Zech. 6:12-13)

> And are built upon the foundation of the apostles and prophets, Jesus Christ himself being the chief corner *stone*;

> 21. In whom all the building fitly framed together groweth unto an **holy temple** in the Lord:
> 22 In whom ye also are **builded together for an habitation of God** through the Spirit. (Ephesians 2:20-22)

Does not Christ reign and rule in the heart and life of a believer? It's plain to see the New Testament temple is the body of a believer where the Spirit of God resides. As we looked earlier regarding Israel and the Gentile believer's relationship in the New Covenant, let's look again, now, with the believer in view pertaining to sacrifices to the Lord.

> How much more shall the blood of Christ, who through the eternal Spirit offered himself without spot to God, purge your conscience from dead works **to serve the living God**? (Heb. 9:14)

> 19. Having therefore, brethren, boldness to enter into the holiest by the blood of Jesus,
> 20. By a **new and living way**, which he hath consecrated for us, through the veil, that is to say, his flesh;
> 21. And *having* an high priest over the **house of God**; (Heb. 10:19-21)

Just as Israel identified with their temple where God dwelt, there they offered continual sacrifices and offerings to Him. As we have just read, those sacrifices in this earthly temple never took away sin, but were a shadow of the true offering to come, which was the person of Christ. However, as believers today, we identify, worship, and offer sacrifices to/in, not a building, but the person of Christ- he is our Lord and God.

> 1. I beseech you therefore, brethren, by the mercies of God, that ye present your bodies **a living sacrifice**, holy, acceptable unto God, *which is* **your reasonable service**.
> 2. And **be not conformed** to this world: but be ye transformed by the renewing of your mind, that ye may **prove** what *is* that good, and acceptable, and perfect, **will of God**. (Romans 12:1-2)

It's not that our sacrifices make us perfect, only the righteousness of Christ makes us perfect. However, by us becoming a "living sacrifice" we are testifying (prove, as the verse says) to a lost world that Christ is the way, truth, and the life. And our actions and beliefs reflect that we are truly His disciples which agrees to the "will of God." Therefore, would it not stand to reason that when the man of sin comes on the scene, and demands total worship and obedience that he forces Christianity to stop serving Christ and following him? I believe it will be at this time our "faith" in Christ will stand the greatest test that we do trust him, even in the face of death. And as the Bible warns, those believers who accept the mark of Antichrist will cast-off their faith and will fall away. Those who accept the mark will not be done in ignorance, but a conscience decision under extreme pressure to reject Jesus as the only Lord.

Here is the reason why I suggest that the Antichrist and the ceasing of the sacrifices could be aimed at Christianity and not particularly at Israel and their rebuilt temple. Paul warned the Thessalonians what Christ spoke of in Matthew 24, that there will be a great falling away (apostasy) when the man of sin declares himself God. It will not be Israel who apostatizes, because they are already in unbelief, but professing Christians who "say" they are believers, yet, turn from Christ and make a fateful decision to receive Antichrist's mark. Israel is told flee when this event occurs.

We will deal with the Olivet Discourse in Matthew 24 in a later chapter, but I will state for now that verses 9-14 are related to the event in verse 15, which is when Antichrist is seen "standing in the holy place." Matthew 24:9-14 is not speaking of Israel, but the followers of Christ in the last days. When Jesus referred to Daniel chapter 9 seventy-week prophecy, more specifically, in verse 27, it does not mention the temple, but only that the "sacrifice and oblation will cease." And if the weight of Scripture teaches that the final week occurs well after the 69th week has ended, then the intent of the 70th week is in the "latter times" after the church has been commissioned to go and proclaim the gospel of the coming kingdom. My question(s) is based on the New Testament teaching about the temple pertaining to the believer and the "perfect sacrifice" of Jesus on the cross. How can Christ be referring to the literal temple in Jerusalem as the "holy place" in verse 15 when he just told the disciples in verse 2 that the temple would be destroyed? And even more so, how could he be referring to the Jerusalem temple as "holy place" when he knows that it would no longer be the building that housed God, but the believer houses the Holy Spirit? (c.f. Eph. 2:20-22; 1 Pet 2:5-9) Finally, how can a temple that has reinstituted animal sacrifices be called "holy," by Christ after Christ's atonement for sin?

When we look at this more closely in Revelation chapters 12-14 we see more clearly how and what Satan does when he comes on the scene. These three chapters are parenthetical, which means there is a pause in the unfolding of the storyline from the previous chapters to help explain more precisely the events just described. These chapters surround the unveiling of the Antichrist at the midpoint of the 70th week, yet, no temple is mentioned at all. Only the stated warning to the inhabitants of the earth is that Satan will be among them causing great wrath, and professing believers and Israel will be in his cross-hair. And those who end up following him will doom their soul for eternity. Satan's ultimate desire to be worshipped by God's creation (humanity) will finally be allowed by God, which is what he wanted when he rebelled while he was still Lucifer. This will be the true test for professing believers. If you recall, it was Job whom God allowed Satan to persecute him, proving Job's faithfulness to worship God despite his painful affliction. It was Job's wife who told him plainly, "curse God, and die" (Job 2:9).

The problem verse that I am struggling with for a case of there not being a literal temple comes from Paul's explanation to the believers at Thessalonica in 2 Thessalonians 2:4. He is referencing Christ's teaching in Matthew 24:15 about the abomination of desolation. Paul, however, says that the man of sin will "'set' in the temple of God, showing himself that he is God." Therefore, if Paul was referring to the literal temple in Jerusalem, then a literal temple will need to be in place when this occurs; or is Paul making a symbolic remark about setting in the midst of the holy people- the church? The meaning "to set" can mean a place of authority.

It was Paul who taught in the epistles about the believer being the true temple of the Lord today. So how could Paul be referencing two different thoughts on the same subject? Another problem I have in being able to not reconcile the literal temple theory is I understand how important the city of Jerusalem is to God (Matt. 5:34-35). Therefore, I can see how Satan would love to mimic God in Jerusalem by being worshiped among the people in a temple. We also see that when this event does occur, those dwelling in Israel are told to flee immediately. Why? Because this event about the man of sin will take place in Jerusalem. So, does Antichrist go into a literal temple, or does he just go to Jerusalem and proclaim himself God and from there begin to demand full worship?

Jesus did not give an end-time sign that the temple would be rebuilt after he stated it would be destroyed; albeit, he doesn't have to. But the indication in Revelations chapters 12-14 does not involve the temple, but the installment of the image of the beast that the world is told to worship. I believe the image of the beast is the same as the abomination that maketh desolate that is set up (Daniel 12:11). What makes something desolate could very well be the same as causing all to receive the mark of the beast. In other words, the desolation is caused by forcing everyone to worship the Antichrist.

One more thought about the temple. In Revelation 13:6, Satan is seen, *And he opened his mouth in blasphemy against God, to blaspheme his name, and **his tabernacle**, and them that dwell in heaven.* Satan blasphemes God, and them that dwell in heaven. What's specifically noticeable is that Satan calls out God's tabernacle. The word tabernacle can be used interchangeably with the temple. The tabernacle was the temporary structure used by Israel in their journey in the wilderness and for a while in Israel. The temple is the permanent structure that replaced the tabernacle. As I have just previously laid out that the temple today for God is the Christian's body. Therefore, I believe Satan is blaspheming believers on earth at the time of his arrival which is the midpoint of the 70th week. If you recall, Satan is up in heaven presently accusing believers on earth to God (Rev. 12:10). Also, the Feast of Tabernacles references that God dwelt among Israel in the Old Testament. Jesus fulfilled the Feast of Tabernacles in the New Testament by "dwelling" among us as well. So today, Jesus tabernacles with His saints.

One last thought is that Islam is totally opposed to anything positive about Israel. Therefore, Antichrist going into a Jewish temple and declaring himself God in a Jewish temple would seem offensive to Islam, not something they would embrace. I can picture Islam embracing Antichrist if he were seen in their place of worship; this would in their eyes validate their religion as the true faith because it vehemently opposes Christ. I believe Islam to be Satan's ultimate religion.

In the end, this is something we can all speculate and ponder as we lead up to the final days. But I caution, if we are all looking for a temple and animal sacrifices to be taking place as an end-time sign and this is not taking place, just think how many people could reject Christ when the man of sin does declare himself God, because they were told this would happen in a rebuilt temple. The belief in a last-days rebuilt temple could be something that leads to deception.

Final thoughts

With the current atmosphere in the geo-political world around the globe, the Middle East continues to be the hotbed for international government involvement. The future prospect that this region of the world could erupt at any time seems to be daily headline news. We really don't know how things will go for Israel and the Middle East, but we do see how a political covenant could take place to restore some type of order amid this chaos. Israel is continually castigated in the media and the U N for their "occupation" of the supposed Palestinian land.

The 70th week will certainly be an interesting development, not only as it unfolds, but even leading up to it as foretold in Scripture. In our study, we will look at several other aspects of this final week as they relate to the rapture debate. However, as Christians, whether pretrib, prewrath, or another persuasion, we need to be walking faithfully with the Lord in this culture of uncertainty. It will be our testimony as Christians the world will be observing, as people look for real answers when world conditions deteriorate. As the antichrist (anti-Christian) spirit continues to take hold on societies throughout the world, it is imperative as believers, we maintain a proper testimony as light- bearers in a dark sinful world.

Satan surely understands the Scriptures regarding his demise. He now knows, for example, the prophecies about Nebuchadnezzar's vision of the beasts that represented the four future empires (Babylon, Media-Persia, Greece, and finally Roman) all have come and gone as God stated in His word. Satan knows now that he lost the head-to-head battle with Christ while Jesus was here on earth (the resurrection proved this). Satan knows his days of evil influence are numbered; and as I have been pointing out, the intensity of his influence upon this world will only get worse, especially as we approach the final-week of Daniel's prophecy. The final-week itself will certainly be the culmination of Satan's abilities to deceive the world before his doom by the return of Christ. But I ask again the question, when Christ returns will he find faith on the earth? How is your faith in these last days?

CHAPTER SEVEN

IMMINENCE PART ONE

We now are beginning to enter to the heart-beat of the rapture debate. Most of the material presented so far has been designed as a needed background for the rapture topic. We just looked at the 70ᵗʰ week and previously noted that pretribulationist taught the next event on God's calendar is the rapture, therefore, advocating imminence. Contrast to this teaching, the prewrath belief states there will be signs (prophesied events) before Christ will return. Let's now look at some quotes from the pretribulational teaching as they relate to the topic of signs.

Signs, Signs, Everywhere Signs?

Christ can return for His Church *at any moment* and that **no predicted event** will intervene before that return.[49] (bold letters mine)

John A. Sproule

If Christ can return at any-moment, **without the necessity of intervening signs or events,** then it renders pretribulationism most likely and posttribulationism impossible.[50] (bold letters mine)

Thomas Ice

Jesus said: "**When you see these signs**, lift up your head and rejoice. Your redemption draweth nigh." Simply stated: The King is coming! Get ready! Planet earth is about to become the playground for the Anti-Christ and his New World Order. The church will be raptured before the Anti-Christ appears; and I believe he could be introduced in Europe at any time. Pray up! Pack up! We're going up and very soon. I'll chat with you next week![51] (bold letters mine)

Pastor John Hagee

The certainty that He may come at any moment, the uncertainty of the time of that arrival, and **the fact that no prophesied event** stands between the believer and that hour.[52] (bold letters mine)

Gerald B. Stanton

The Bible teaches that **no prophesied events** must take place before Christ comes to rapture His bride.[53] (bold letters mine)

Ed Hindson

No less a prophet than Jesus Christ made it clear that **the generation that witnessed the return of the Jews to the promise land would live the see Him return to earth**. The modern state of Israel was born in 1948, **which means that you and I are part of the last-days generation** (see Matthew 24: 32-34). However, the Temple must once again occupy its place on the Temple Mount **before the major prophesied events of the last days can take place**.[54] (bold letters mine)

Grant Jeffrey

The rebuilding of the Temple has profound prophetic significance equal to the appearance of the Antichrist or the forming of the pagan armies to invade Israel in the coming Battle of Gog and Magog. Many students of biblical prophecy have debated the role that will be played by the Third Temple in end-times developments. **But the scriptures make it clear that just before Christ returns**, the Third Temple of God must stand once more on its original location on the Temple Mount.[55] (bold letters mine)

Grant Jeffery

What is the biblical definition of imminency? Four important elements contribute to a pretribulational understanding of imminency. First, imminency means that the rapture could take place at any moment. While other events *may* take place before the rapture, no event *must* precede it. If prior events are **required before the rapture**, then the rapture could not be described as imminent. **Thus, if any event were required to occur before the rapture, then the concept of imminency would be destroyed**.[56] (bold letters mine)

Thomas Ice

If we are indeed those end-times believers, that is, those who **see the signs of the times** of the Glorious Appearing of Christ to this earth, then we have reason to beware of deception, both from without and within. Satan, the master deceiver, does not want us to get excited about the fact that there are **more signs** of Christ's return today **than at any time in church history**.[57] (bold letters mine)

Tim LaHaye

In the twentieth century, **for the first time in history a world empire became a possibility.** A world government would require immediate communication such as radio, telephone, and television. **This is now an accomplished fact**. A world government would also require rapid transportation, which today is provided by planes. Control of business and finance contemplated in the world government (Rev. 13:16-17) would be provided by giant computers, already a feature in everyday life. The world rider would also have missile warfare as means of controlling the world. **Modern inventions have reduced the size of our world to where a world government is now mechanically possible.**[58] (bold letters mine)

John Walvoord

B. I believe that His coming is very soon.
1. I do not see how God can wait much longer.
2. The **signs** that the Bible **predicted for the last days before His return are all around us.**[59] (bold letters mine)

Chuck Smith

The variety of these quotes are emblematic of the contradictions among the view of the pretribulation teachers. Pretrib teaching pertaining to signs are extremely ambiguous in their defining signs. Are there signs or not that precede Christ's return? Reversing Thomas Ice's statement, if signs do indeed precede the rapture, then the "concept of imminence would be destroyed and render pretribulationism impossible?" Thomas Ice makes the contradictory statement, "while other events may occur before the rapture no event 'must' precede the rapture." However, if the Bible says certain events are to occur as signs to the church, then they "must" happen before the rapture- you can't have it both ways. Pretribulationist never define what "other events" are in relation to Bible prophecy and the rapture. Even in pretrib author and speaker Ed Hindson's book **Final Signs**, he documents the sign-events that precede the rapture.

H. A. Ironside states in his book, written in 1941, **Not Wrath but Rapture: Will the Church Participate in the Great Tribulation?**

> In recent years, particularly following the World War, there has been a recrudescence of Post-Tribulationism, brought about largely by the facts that so many stirring events have taken place **which seems to foreshadow the actual conditions** that will prevail during the time of Jacob's trouble. Already the Roman Empire seems in process of revival. The rise of dictatorships gives us to understand how readily the great world-ruler of the coming day will forge his way to the front and be acclaimed as the very representative of God Himself. **The return of thousands of Jews to Palestine, involving the rehabilitation of that land, is certainly preparing the way for the very events depicted in the prophets and by our Lord Himself, which are to take place in these last days...But the very fact that we see conditions shaping themselves for tribulation times should only lead us to realize the nearness of our Hope.**[60] (Bold letter mine)

Plain and simple, Ironside is saying the rapture is near (in 1941) because of the prophetic signs the church had witnessed.

On the weekly TV program **Christ in Prophecy**, David Reagan had on as his guest Ron Rhodes, a prominent Bible scholar and a pretribulationist as well. As he was being interviewed he was asked this question:

Nathan Jones: "Dr. Rhodes, do you believe we are in the "season" of our Lord's return? And if so, why?"

Dr. Rhodes: "Well I think we are. One, to begin with, let's recognize the really key **foundational prophecy of Israel becoming a nation and Jews streaming back to the Holy Land** ever since then. It's kind of interesting, because back in the 1800s I've looked at a couple of prophecy experts who were writing about this eventual rebirth of this nation, Israel; and everybody was saying no it will never happen, it's an impossibility, but then in 1948 it did happen. It's an amazing unfolding of events, but I think that kind of sets the stage for everything else. **If that one thing had not happened I have a problem in all other prophecy.** Because that's really the foundation you build from, but beyond that you have all kind of stuff (he list several events)...the way I look at it Dave, is this, you can imagine a bunch of lines intersecting each other, at some point in the near future, you know one of these lines is the Jewish temple, another of these lines is the rebirth of Israel, another line is **all these different prophecies are coming true** apparently intersecting at some point in the near future, and so it's the accumulative weight of all that we believe indeed we are living in the very end-time."

David Reagan: "It's seems like to me that you either have to be biblically ignorant or spiritually in a comatose state not to realize that God is really shouting from the heavens today that **Jesus is coming soon.**"

Dr. Rhodes: "That's right, you might remember Dave, Jesus chastised Jews of the day for **not being accurate observers of the time**. And today you have a lot of people who are naysayers about Bible prophecy..." (Parenthesis and bold letters mine)

You can observe from Dr. Rhodes statement that he agrees that the rebirth of Israel had to take place before other prophecies could come true; only after these, "then" the rapture was possible. Therefore, in the 1800s as Rhodes alludes to, those writers knew the rapture was impossible in their time; even at the same time while Darby was teaching about the imminent rapture.

As the questions and answers on the TV program progressed, David Reagan asked Dr. Rhodes "when is the rapture going to occur and what is the timing...?"

> Dr. Rhodes: Boy you could get me preaching on this (laughter), I'm a firm believer the rapture is going to happen before the tribulation there are number of reasons why I say."
>
> David Reagan: "What's the most important reason?"

It was at this time Dr. Rhodes gave several reasons why the tribulation was pretrib, mainly because the church has no business in the tribulation and a few other reasons. But David Reagan interrupted and said that he thought Dr. Rhodes was going to say the strongest argument for a pretribulation rapture was because of imminence. Here is Dr. Rhodes response:

> Dr. Rhodes: "Oh imminence is an absolute, that's an assumption that's always there."
>
> David Reagan: "Explain what it means."
>
> Dr. Rhodes: "There is nothing that needs to take place before the rapture of the church, it could happen any moment"

In the beginning of the program they talk about signs before the rapture; later in the program they say the rapture is imminent- signless. Finally, if you were observant, you would notice at the beginning of the interview the first question was framed with the intent that today we are in the "season" of the Lord's return. Was the first century church "in the season" for the rapture?

David Jeremiah attempts to answer the question of a little girl who was confused as to how signs are related to Christ's return:

...The given honest confusion deserves to be addressed because I believe she speaks for many who are simply puzzled about the events relating to the rapture.

> Most of the misunderstanding comes from confusing two events; the rapture and the second coming. **When we talk about signs that signal the return of Christ, we speak not of the**

Rapture, but of the ultimate return to the earth with all His Saints. According to the book of Revelation, this coming of Christ occurs after the Rapture and differs from it in at least two ways: First, the Rapture will be a "**stealth event**" in which Christ will be **witnessed by believers only.**

Secondly, all believers are raptured He will immediately take them back into heaven with Him. But when Christ returns to the earth seven years later in the 2nd coming, He is coming to stay. This return, usually referred to as "the 2nd advent", will take place at the end of the tribulation period and usher in the millennium- a thousand –year reign of Christ on this earth.

There is another important difference; there are no events that must take place before the rapture occurs. When I preached that signs are developing concerning the Lord's return, I referred to events that must yet occur before the return of Christ in the 2nd advent.

The prophecies I spoke of concerning the 2nd advent but that does not mean that the rapture doesn't figure into prophecy. **Future events "cast shadows" that are precursors to their coming.** Since the **Rapture takes place 7 years before the 2nd advent**, the signs that point to the advent "cast shadows" that clue us in to the **imminent Rapture**.[61] (bold letters mine)

Jeremiah's statement is nothing more than a convoluted explanation by falsely switching the true meaning of what Christ was teaching in the Olivet Discourse. Signs or shadows of the signs are still coming from the same source; which are ultimately the predictive Bible prophecies themselves? Changing the meaning by redefining the word does not justify a pretribulational rapture. And anyone who interprets any Bible passage to fit their belief system is walking on dangerous ground. Reread what Ironside said, he made the same declaration sixty-nine years before Jeremiah, calling signs, "foreshadows" of things to come.

Likewise, if all the signs Jeremiah is referring to are "inside" the seven-year tribulation, supposedly after the church is raptured, then why doesn't he or any pretrib teachers refer to the rapture itself as a sign before Christ's

Second Advent at the end of the tribulation? If the imminent rapture was possible at any time since the ascension of Christ before Pentecost, how could the signs within the seven-year tribulation "cast a shadow," let's say, three hundred years before the tribulation begins? Furthermore, the events within the seven-year tribulation are the seals, trumpets, and vials; these would be the actual events that would take place in the future: how could a real event "cast a shadow" if the event itself would not take place until a specified future time- the tribulation itself?

The precursors that Jeremiah is referring to are the signs and warnings Christ spoke of in Matthew 24, and other places, is to give understanding to the body of Christ the world condition and attitude of rebellion towards God and His people in the last days before Christ comes to judge them. These are signs leading up to and into the final week. This is the reason spiritually minded believers understand the "signs of the times," a phrase believers use all the time.

Grant Jeffery, a leading advocate in the pretrib movement, is now teaching that the temple "must" be built before the beginning of the 70th week and the rapture of the church; yet, in making this statement he nullifies the imminent return of Christ. He realizes the implications in his statement, so he covers his tracks with an unscriptural statement, "the temple will be built **'just before'** the tribulation." This supposedly lessens the impractical dilemma of a signless pretrib rapture.

Marvin Rosenthal in his book "The Pre-Wrath Rapture of the Church" gives an excellent explanation for the purpose of signs in the Bible.

> The word sign occurs 119 times in the Bible. The first usage is in Genesis in the context of God's creative acts and the beginning of human history. The sun, moon and stars were, in the divine scheme of things, intended to be "for signs, and for seasons" (Gen. 1:14). The final usage is in Revelation, the last book of the Bible, in the context of God's final judgment on the earth. "And I saw another sign in heaven, *great* and *marvelous*, seven angels having the seven last plagues, for in them is filled up the wrath of God" (Rev. 15:1). Signs were placed in heaven at creation and will be manifested in heaven at God's final judgment.
>
> It may appear obvious, but signs are for seeing. That is, men are called upon to see, look at, and behold signs. Signs are

intended to be conspicuous, not hidden, The Bible speaks of signs of appearing (Mark 24:30), being shown (Matt. 13:22), being accomplished before people (John 20:30), in the midst of people (Acts 2:22), and among people (2 Cor. 12:12). By their very nature signs are to be public."

Signs are more directional in natural than chronological. They tell men *which way* rather than *what time*. When the disciples inquired of the Lord, "What is the sign of the coming, and of the end of the age?" (Matt. 24:3), they were not so much asking *when* will it occur, but how will men recognize it when it does?[62]

Christ said his coming is in the "light" of signs, not something absent of signs. When He came the first time, it was based on various signs given in the Scriptures; where Christ would be born (Micah 5:2) and how He would be born (Isaiah 7:14). The Scriptures were even exact in stating He would be from the tribe of Judah. During the ministry of Christ there were numerous signs fulfilled from Old Testament prophecies; yet, with all what they witnessed He was still rejected by Israel's leadership. On one occasion, regarding signs, we see in Matthew 12:38-39 the Scribes and Pharisees asked Jesus for a sign, and in His response, He stated that an "evil and adulterous generation seeks after a sign." Within the context of this passage, Christ was accused by the Pharisees working for the devil by casting out a demon (vs. 23-24). Christ rebukes them sharply in His rebuttal by stating no kingdom can stand if it's divided, therefore advocating He was not of Satan. He then went on and gave the fiercest statement to them about the unpardonable sin of unbelief, because they had already disbelieved who He was after witnessing His acts of miracles. Christ exposed what was really taking place in their hearts- envy and jealousy.

The Scriptures give a detailed account of the crucifixion of Christ; even the betrayal of Christ by Judas as he received the thirty pieces of silver for his dirty work (Zechariah 11:12-13). The resurrection of Christ is what sealed the truth for the disciples and for you and me as well. James, the half-brother of Jesus, rejected Christ until he witnessed His resurrection. These were signs for believers to attest to the fact that Christ was who He said He was, and validated the truth of the Bible.

Signs themselves are not taboo concerning Christ's second coming. We do know that trying to force current-events as if Bible prophecy is being fulfilled is taboo. Back in chapter four when we saw the cult explosion in the 1800s, the French Revolution was one of the primary events at the time that fueled much of the speculation about Christ's return.

Some prophecy teachers try to fit the coming blood moon events as biblical sign events- which are not. When a violent hurricane struck one of the Southern States in the early 1990s, I recall listening to Hal Lindsey as he quoted Luke 21:26 over his radio broadcast:

> Men's hearts failing them for fear, and for looking after those things which are coming on the earth: for the powers of heaven shall be shaken.

This verse has absolutely nothing to do with a hurricane hitting the shores of America and striking fear in the hearts of men; nevertheless, it makes for spectacular prophecy teaching. This stirs up the psyche of folks making them believe they are participants of actual Bible prophecy taking place.

Posttribulationist teacher Irvin Baxter, director of the **End Times Ministry,** has, and continues to play, "pin-the-tail on the Antichrist." He forces all kinds of world events as though these signify biblical prophecy being fulfilled. One such example, he teaches the fifth trumpet in Revelation was fulfilled when Saddam Hussein blew up the oil wells in Kuwait. Read for yourselves Revelation 9:1-5 about the fifth trumpet, and determine whether this is what it says? The past and current activity in the Middle East has continued to be a hotbed for much speculation. How many prophecy teachers have you personally heard that made some statement about certain individuals being the Antichrist? We need to be wise in our discernment when comparing the Word of God with current events.

Stanley Ellisen of the **Pre-Trib Research Center** makes a good obervation about signs:

> ...The place of signs today: This being so, we are prone to scan the horizon for signals of that next prophetic event, the coming of Christ for the Church. Christian "astrology" has frankly blossomed into something of an art form in our time. Catering to this appetite for the sensational, a rash of prophetic seers has surfaced in the past half-century to almost pinpoint the day of the rapture, if not the hour...[63]

Stanley Ellisen

Ellisen is correct to throw caution-to-the-wind when trying to make current events fit into Bible prophecy. However, he does the typical pretrib dance with the question, whether or not these signs are precursors to Christ's return. Here's his statement.

> Jesus stressed the need for all believers to be alert to **prophetic seasons** (Mark 13:29). The writer of Hebrews also emphasized this point, saying that an alert Church will be able to *see the day drawing near* (Heb. 10:25).[64]

Ellisen references Mark 13:29 (budding of the fig three) and Hebrews 10:25, teaching that the church needs to be alert to the "prophetic seasons." However, when all the smoke clears, he is advocating signs do precede the rapture. After all, how can the church be alert to Christ's drawing near if there are no predicted signs before He comes?

Pretrib teachers like to quote additional Scriptures that say Christ could have come during Paul's lifetime, yet he died 35 years before the book of Revelation was written. This would have been impossible for the rapture because Revelation contained biblical truth relevant to the church. Also, Paul wrote in Philippians 1:23 that his desire was that he would "depart" so "he" could be with Christ in heaven. Furthermore, if the rapture was enveloped in his use of the word departure, how could he separate himself from the church here? He also stated in 2 Timothy 4:6-7 while in prison, that his "departure" was at hand, not that Christ's arrival was near.

2018

I would like to throw out a prediction (food-for-thought) based on the prophecy carousel of many pretrib authors who like seize the moment when it comes to potential notable events based on calendar dates. We discussed earlier how 1948 became an important date in relation to Israel becoming a nation again. And I do agree that Israel becoming a nation was significant regarding end-time events. It's my prediction that the year 2018 will be a big-time marketing year for prophecy teachers. There was so much hoopla about "forty-years" after Israel's rebirth to the point where we saw the explosion of prognosticators making bold predictions that brought so much excitement within evangelical Christianity and the sales of prophecy books to an all-time high. In 2018, it will be seventy-years since Israel will have become a nation and I can't imagine that pretribulation prophecy teachers will not miss the opportunity to build up the significance of 2018 with their advertisement of end-time marketing. Seventy is a very important number throughout the Bible. Here's a small list: Seventy is considered by many as a generation; seventy elders appointed in Israel; seventy-years of captivity in Babylon; seventy sevens in Daniel's prophetic calendar; Luke 10 records that Jesus sent out seventy disciples; Exodus 1:5 records that there were seventy souls from the loins of Jacob that began the nation of Israel while in Egypt. Jesus said that as believers we should forgive seventy times seven. Anyway, my prediction is that 2018 will not be a significant year spite pretribulationist rhetoric.

Feast of Trumpets

As I close out this section on imminence, I would like to bring to your attention that I have read and heard pretribulation teachers teach that the Feast of Trumpets has a significant bearing on the timing of the rapture. Many believe that the rapture could very well coincide with the Feast of Trumpets. Since Christ fulfilled the other feasts exactly (e.g. Passover, Pentecost, Tabernacles), He could easily fulfill this feast as well with the rapture of the church. This could very well be the case; however, there should immediately be a red flag raised in your thinking that this conflicts with the any-moment return of Christ. If the Feast of Trumpets were to take place in October in a given year, and let's say it is now January, how do the pretribulationist resolve this conflict with imminence? There's a nine-month difference between the two.

CHAPTER EIGHT

IMMINENCE PART TWO

Verses on Imminence

Previously, we saw the discrepancies from the pretribulation teachers, whether signs do or do not precede the rapture. Here in this chapter we will look at some verses from the John Darby's Bible as they pertain to the return of Christ. Then we will close out our study on imminence by looking at some biblical prophecies that must precede the rapture.

The John Darby Bible

As Christians debate any doctrinal topic, an even playing field is necessary to maintain a balance of consistency between the parties involved. And changing the rules to manipulate the discussion by one party is a characteristic that patently shows they really have no truth to stand on, or weak at best. And if, again, this were a court case, tampering with the evidence would be a criminal act. I would like to show you some verses from the John Darby Bible, how he purposely changed the meaning of the verses to make them sound as though Christ's return is imminent. A person's theology should stand alone on the merits of the Word of God without trying to create an advantage to mislead people. It was Darby who crisscrossed across America and was the first person that promulgated the pretrib rapture theory. And if pretribulationism is so basic to eschatology, as many pretribulationist claim, then why change the Scripture verses to make the pretrib rapture sound more viable?

We as Christians know how the Watchtower cult wrote their own Bible to keep millions in bondage to their false religion. Mormonism has done the same by creating their own Bible, "The Book of Mormon," which is completely heterodox. If there were any fundamental truth in the Bible to their belief system, then they would not need an outside source to present their case for biblical truth. However, because the Bible disproves what they believe, to solve their dilemma, they just create another Bible and call it "Another Testament" from God. (Look up the Mormon definition of dispensationalism- they define it the same as pretrib teaching, which espouses "progressive revelation"). Islam will only agree to "parts" of the Bible, while rejecting those Scriptures that contradict with their teachings. Their rebuttal to the conflicting verses about their doctrine they say the Bible has been "corrupted" by false teachers- How convenient!

While I cannot speak for all of John Darby's teachings, as well as his personal motives, I would like to expose his translation of the Bible. While the Darby translation is seldom quoted, I believe it is important to understand the background of this man's theological profanation. Darby is a major player in the pretribulation position, having been on the ground floor for this new doctrine. With that said, here are some verses showing that the instigator of the pretribulation rapture, John Darby, changed the Word of God to reflect his view of imminence of a pretribulation rapture.

King James Bible	John Darby Bible:
I Peter 5:1	
The elders which are among you I exhort, who am also an elder, and a witness of the sufferings of Christ, and also a partaker of the glory that **shall** be revealed:	The elders which [are] among you I exhort, who [am their] fellow-elder and witness of the sufferings of the Christ, who also [am] partaker of the glory **about** to be revealed:
Luke 21:36	
Watch ye therefore, and pray always, that ye may be accounted worthy to escape all these things that **shall** come to pass, and to stand before the Son of man.	Watch therefore, praying at every season, that ye may be accounted worthy to escape all these things which are **about** to come to pass, and to stand before the Son of man.

2 Timothy 4:1

I charge thee therefore before God, and the Lord Jesus Christ, who **shall** judge the quick and the dead at his appearing and his kingdom;

I testify before God and Christ Jesus, who is **about** to judge living and dead, and by his appearing and his kingdom,

Matthew 16:27

For the Son of man **shall** come in the glory of his Father with his angels; and then he shall reward every man according to his works.

For the Son of man is **about** to come in the glory of his Father with his angels, and then he will render to each according to his doings.

Acts 24:25

And as he reasoned of righteousness, temperance, and **judgment to come**, Felix trembled, and answered, Go thy way for this time; when I have a convenient season, I will call for thee.

And as he reasoned concerning righteousness, and temperance, and the **judgment about to come**, Felix, being filled with fear, answered, Go for the present, and when I get an opportunity I will send for thee;

1 Thessalonians 3:4

For verily, when we were with you, we told you before that **we should suffer tribulation**; even as it came to pass, and ye know.

for also, when we were with you, we told you beforehand we **are about to be in tribulation**, even as also it came to pass, and ye know.)

Hebrews 10:27

But a certain fearful looking for of judgment and fiery indignation, **which shall** devour the adversaries.

but a certain fearful expectation of judgment, and heat of fire **about** to devour the adversaries

Revelation 1:19

Write the things which thou hast seen, and the things which are, and the things **which shall** be hereafter

Write therefore what thou hast seen, and the things that are, and the things that are **about** to be after these.

Billy Broadwater

Revelation 3:10

Because thou hast kept the word of my patience, I also will keep thee from the hour of temptation, which **shall** come upon all the world, to try them that dwell upon the earth.

Because thou hast kept the word of my patience, I also will keep thee out of the hour of trial, which is **about** to come upon the whole habitable world, to try them that dwell upon the earth.

Revelation 3:16

So then because thou art lukewarm, and neither cold nor hot, I **will** spue thee out of my mouth.

Thus because thou art lukewarm, and neither cold nor hot, I am **about** to spue thee out of my mouth.

Revelation 6:11

And white robes were given unto every one of them; and it was said unto them, that they should rest yet for a little season, until their fellowservants also and their brethren, that **should** be killed as they were, should be fulfilled.

And there was given to them, to each one a white robe; and it was said to them that they should rest yet a little while, until both their fellow-bondmen and their brethren, who were **about** to be killed as they, should be fulfilled.

You noticed the verses I chose had to do with two words- shall and about. The word "shall" give's the meaning of something being absolute or certain with no specific timing. Whereas, the word, "about" adds the idea of something that will not only happen for certain, but it will happen soon or at any moment. For someone to introduce a new doctrine is one thing if provable within the Bible; but to change the words in a Bible in order to make their doctrine sound legitimate is outright dishonest. Here's an example of Darby's biased slant, which is taken from Matthew 16:27. Darby uses the word "about" in Matthew 16:27 instead of "shall;" however, in verses 25, 26, and 28, he retained the word "shall" as found in the King James Bible. He only changed the word from "shall" to "about" in the verse (27) to make his doctrine of the pretrib rapture tenable. I compared all these verses with several Bible translations (i.e. Webster's Bible; English Standard Version; Tyndale Bible; American Standard Version) and not one of these highly-recognized versions uses the word "about" as the Darby Bible did.

Here is Tim LaHaye praising Darby as a spiritual teacher in his book "Rapture Under Attack."

I am firmly convinced that Darby was influenced by the new wave of prophetic awareness in his day; **the godly influence** of his teachers at Trinity College, who were biblical literalist; the **leading of the Holy Spirit**, who wanted to bring that **truth to light for these last days** in preparation for the event; and from his "intense personal study" of the Word of God. **The character of the man** impels us to take him at his word when he says that he derived the concept from the study of the Word of God.

Thus very early in his life, by the time he was twenty-seven years old, he had formulated the basic elements of those principles upon which **he would build his entire system of thought**. **Today it is called *dispensationalism*, and it automatically assumes pre-tribulationalism**.[65] (bold letters mine)

While I affirm that I do not have knowledge of the godly character of Darby, I still question his motives for translating these verses in the consistent manner that he did, specifically, as they pertained to the Lord's return. When we hear the word, Bible, we should associate it with being God's Word, which is truth articulated in written form. A person's eternal destiny is dependent on the truth of God's word. Needless to say, I hold the Bible in the utmost highest standard of truth. However, to be honest, when I see the blatant changing of verses to fit a belief system, I have no respect for anyone or group who would stoop to this level of manipulation.

I would also like to point out that LaHaye acknowledges in his statement the entire system of dispensationalism is to prove the pretrib rapture; and, yet, the pretrib rapture is what proves dispensationalism. However, if you can disprove one theory, the other automatically falls. In short, LaHaye acknowledges that dispensationalism and the pretribulation rapture were created to complement each other.

Events That Precede Christ's Return

I now would like to introduce more evidence from the Scriptures and prove the pretribulation rapture cannot be imminent. Pretribulation teaching blares out that Christ could come back at any time, without, I believe, logically and biblically thinking through their reasoning. Two examples they continually make are: "Christ can come back at any moment;" and "the Bible says the next prophetic event to happen is the rapture of the church." The only ones saying Christ can come back any moment comes from the pretribulation camp.

There are, in fact, a number of prophecies that must take place first before the return of Christ can occur. The question I like to ask my pretrib friends is: At what time in history, since the ascension of Christ into heaven before Pentecost in Acts chapter 1, could Christ of have come back and raptured the church saints? Most pretribulational teaching identifies the signs of the times, reference in the events of Matthew 24 (e.g. wars, rumors of wars, earthquakes, famine, pestilences, etc.) as general signs relating to Christ's return before the 70th week begins. Matthew 24, as we will see later, is Christ's answer to the disciple's question about the unambiguous timing of his return; therefore, Christ spoke about events that "must" occur before His return. Here is a secondary list of events that fit within the framework of Christ coming back.

The Destruction of the Temple

In Matthew 24, Christ's teaching in the Olivet Discourse, Christ prophesied that the temple would be destroyed (v.2). This prophecy came true in AD 70 when the Romans came to Jerusalem to put down a rebellion, and destroyed the temple in the process. The Romans were attempting to erase Israel's common identity among the people that united their community, which was their temple. It would not be until AD 132 that Israel would be finally driven from their land and dispersed (the Diaspora) among the nations around the known-world. It was impossible for Christ to return before the prophecy of the temple destruction was fulfilled.

Peter

Peter was probably the most notable of all the disciples. He was very vocal with what he wanted to say, which frequently led to him being corrected and occasionally rebuked by the Lord. After Christ's resurrection, in John chapter 21, Christ made an astonishing statement related to Peter's life and ultimately his death:

> Verily, verily, I say unto thee, When thou wast young, thou girdedst
> thyself, and walkedst whither thou wouldest: **but when thou**

shalt be old, thou shalt stretch forth thy hands, and another shall gird thee, and carry thee whither thou wouldest not. (John 21:18)

The Lord gives the purpose of this prophecy in the next verse:

This spake he, signifying by **what death he should glorify God.** And when he had spoken this, he saith unto him, Follow me. (v.19)

Jesus told Peter point-bank he was going to die as an old man, and not only the time of his death, but, also by the manner of his death- he would stretch forth his hands, signifying crucifixion. And in his later years, Peter acknowledged this in his epistle.

Yea, I think it meet, as long as I am in this tabernacle, to stir you up by putting you in remembrance; Knowing that **shortly I must put off this my tabernacle, even as our Lord Jesus Christ hath showed me.** (2 Peter 1:13-14)

Peter, who stumbled and fumbled during the Lord's earthly ministry, became the pillar of the early church. Church history teaches that Peter chose to be crucified upside down; not counting himself worthy to be crucified as our Lord had been.

Here is my first question: Was it possible for Peter to have been raptured without the prophecy of his death being fulfilled? The answer is absolutely, no! Many times, in the New Testament the phrase is said, *that it might be fulfilled.* This is a clear-cut statement that God's word is without error, and what is spoken will take place as God promised. And this specific prophecy concerning Peter's death was no different. Church history records Peter's death about the same time as Paul's, around AD 64. Therefore, according to Christ's statement, his return was not possible in Peter's lifetime.

Allow me to make one more observation regarding Jesus's announcement about Peter in John 21. At the same time when Jesus told Peter that he would grow old; Peter made a comment about John and asked what will happen to him? Jesus's response to Peter was basically that Peter need not worry or concern himself with John's future. Jesus went on to say that even if He returned before John died, it shouldn't matter to Peter. Now notice what transpired between the other disciples regarding Jesus's remark.

22.Jesus saith unto him, **If I will that he tarry till I come**, what *is that* to thee? follow thou me.

23.Then went this saying abroad among the brethren, that that disciple **should not die**: yet Jesus said not unto him, He shall not die; but, **If I will that he tarry till I come, what** *is that* **to thee?**

The other disciples misunderstood Jesus and thought John would still be alive when He returns. In fact, this error was spread abroad (v. 23), which shows how easily things can get misapplied about Christ's second coming, even in the early church.

The Gospel

My next example is found in the book of Acts 1, where we read about the ascension of Christ into heaven.

When they therefore were come together, they asked of him, saying, Lord, **wilt thou at this time restore again the kingdom to Israel?** And he said unto them, **It is not for you to know the times or the seasons**, which the Father hath put in his own power. But ye shall receive power, after that the Holy Ghost is come upon you: **and ye shall be witnesses unto me both in Jerusalem, and in all Judaea, and in Samaria, and unto the uttermost part of the earth.** (Acts 1:6-8)

With the account of Christ's ascension into heaven, the disciples asked the obvious question to Jesus: *when will you restore the kingdom?* If Christ was going away as he said in John 14:1-3; when would he return according to his promise? Christ gives us insight to this event by saying *ye shall be witnesses unto the uttermost part of the earth.*

Christ was not saying if time allows before I return, go to the uttermost part of the earth. He was making the clear statement that this prophecy of the gospel being preached around the world would be fulfilled before he returns. I will list several points as follows:

1. This is the same statement that Christ made to the disciples in Matthew 24:14: *and this **gospel of the kingdom** shall be preached in **all the world** for*

a witness unto all nations; and then shall the end come. The Lord was making it perfectly clear, the gospel would be preached in the entire world before he returned; even though they would still have a difficult time understanding the ultimate plan of God for the Gentiles. The Gentiles would become part of the kingdom of God, and that is the reason Christ gave the Great Commission to the church (apostles) for the gospel to be preached throughout the world (Gentile nations).

> Go ye therefore, and teach all nations, baptizing them in the name of the Father, and of the Son, and of the Holy Ghost: Teaching them to observe all things whatsoever I have commanded you: and, lo, I am with you alway, **even unto the end of the world.** Amen. (Matt. 28:19-20)

2. The gospel according to Christ will go not only "to the ends of the earth," but **up to the end** of the world as well. How many times have you heard from pretrib teaching: the person you witness today about Christ could be the last person to get saved before the rapture occurs; as though we are somehow responsible for the return of Christ? Clarence Larkin, a very well-known pretribulational dispensational author and teacher in the early 1900s, confirms this particular belief.

> It is my firm conviction of the writer that there has been **unnecessary delay** in the Return of the Lord, **caused by the failure of the Church** to obey the 'Divine Commission' to evangelize the world (Matt. 28:19-20), **and it is past the time when He should have returned.**[66]

In the context of our discussion the pretribulation teachers are faced with a dilemma; the context of the gospel is preached well into the 70th week, which leads up to the end of the world. Larkin was advocating the rapture of the church years before Israel was a nation again.

> And I saw another angel fly in the midst of heaven, having the **everlasting gospel** to preach unto them that dwell on the earth, and to every nation, and kindred, and tongue, and people. (Rev. 14:6)

3. If the rapture occurs years before the 70th week, what happens to those folks who get saved during this time; yet, "before" the final week? The pretribulation theory has just created another group of Christians who are not part of the church or Israel! The pretribulation teachers cannot say that they become part of Israel, because dispensational teaching says Israel will not be dealt with until the beginning of the 70th week prophecy of Daniel, not before. Also, If the rapture takes place years before the 70th week begins, then dispensationalism itself is completely destroyed, because they teach that the "times of the Gentiles" is supposed to be the interim period **until** (not before) the 70th week of Daniel. And remember, the 70th week is exactly 2,520 days long. If the rapture occurs, let's say, twenty years before the final week, what dispensation would these believers be part of?

Here is a statement by the Rapture Ready website responding to a statement by those who reject the pretribulation rapture.

> **Nowhere in the Bible does it directly say the church will be raptured before the tribulation.**
>
> **Response:** "Pre-trib opponents should have thought this one through because any pre-tribulationist has the same right to say, "Nowhere in the Bible does it directly say the Church will go through the tribulation."
>
> Jesus did say, "Therefore be ye also ready: for in such an hour as ye think not the Son of man cometh" (Matthew 24:44). The only time frame I can think of when we believers would not be expecting Jesus to return would have to be before the tribulation.[67] (bold letters mine)

Again, in their zeal to protect the pretribulation rapture at any cost, they skirt the real issue. The pretribulation teachers must prove their theory of the rapture before the tribulation, not the other way around. In other words, if I were to make the outrageous claim "Mars is inhabited by green men;" would it be up to you to prove me wrong or would the burden of proof be upon me to prove my belief?

The Mustard Seed

> And he said, So is the kingdom of God, as if a man should cast
> seed into the ground; And should sleep, and rise night and day,
> and the seed should spring and grow up, he knoweth not how.
> For the earth bringeth forth fruit of herself; first the blade, then
> the ear, after that the full corn in the ear. But when the fruit
> is brought forth, immediately he putteth in the sickle, because
> the harvest is come. And he said, Whereunto shall we liken the
> kingdom of God? or with what comparison shall we compare it?
> It is like a grain of mustard seed, which, when it is sown in the
> earth, is less than all the seeds that be in the earth: But when it is
> sown, it **groweth up,** and becometh greater than all herbs, and
> shooteth out great branches; so that the fowls of the air may lodge
> under the shadow of it. (Mark 4:26-32)

On the heels of my previous statement about the gospel going throughout the world, is Christ's teaching in this passage in Mark that compares the end of the age (harvest) to the planting and growth of seeds. First, Christ teaches the harvest of the children of God are those identified by the fruit of the seed that sprang out of the good ground. If you go back to the beginning of the chapter in Mark 4, you will see that Christ taught that the seed represents the Word of God. It is from the Word of God that the children of God are brought into the kingdom of God. This is why Satan has always hated God's word (cf. Mark 4:14-15; Matt. 13:18-19; Luke 8:11-12). Satan's first attack upon mankind was his lie about Gods word in Genesis 3:1 to Eve, "Yeah hath God said?"

Second, Christ is teaching that the mustard seed represents the birth of Christianity with an inconspicuous beginning. However, over time, Christianity will grow into a very large tree, which shows how vast Christianity will grow throughout the world. As Christianity grows, our Lord teaches that the fowls of the air – false religions and unsaved religious people – will attach themselves to true Christianity (like the wheat and tares growing together). Christ is teaching about the kingdom of God, beginning with Himself; yet, the fowls are not attaching themselves to Israel, but the church.

What I would like to bring to your attention is the time that it takes for the mustard seed to grow into this enormous tree. Part of the analogy of this parable, Christ is teaching this tree (Christianity) will grow over a very long period throughout the earth. This is the same teaching by Christ as the gospel going throughout the world and converting sinners to the kingdom of God, which will take a very long time that leads up to the end of the harvest.

Modern Technology

This one should be obvious to everyone, regardless of which rapture position you believe. Most agree that there will be an Antichrist that will have unprecedented power and authority on the earth; and combined with his own supernatural power, he will use this to totally control the masses (2 Thessalonians 2:9). He will have at his disposal the means of the technology to force people to receive his mark. It will require modern technology, especially in the limited time, as a tool used by the followers of the Antichrist. In Revelation 13:16-17 it describes that unless an individual has the *mark of the beast or the number of his mark*, they will not be able to *buy or sell*. In other words, they will not have the ability to do the basic things in life to survive. The means of technology will be in place to cause all people to be under an advance system of control. In Daniel chapter 8 we have more insight to this world ruler whom the Bible dubs the "Antichrist."

> And in the **latter time of their kingdom**, when the transgressors are come to the full, **a king of fierce countenance**, and understanding dark sentences, shall stand up. **And his power shall be mighty, but not by his own power**: and he shall destroy wonderfully, and shall prosper, and practice, and shall destroy the mighty and the holy people. **And through his policy also he shall cause craft to prosper in his hand**; and he shall magnify himself in his heart, **and by peace shall destroy many**: he shall also **stand up against the Prince** of princes; but he shall be broken without hand. (Dan. 8:23-25)

The Antichrist will have the ability to control the daily life of mankind, and his policy will cause people who follow him to prosper. The opposite of this is that he will be able to force hardship upon his opposition. The major prophecy buzz that has been talked about for many years now is the prospect of a worldwide cashless society. Most prophecy teachers agree that this is one sign of the last days, especially with the implementation of an electronic system that uses bar codes and most recently, RFID chips (who knows what future technology will be in place). Many people now only buy and sell through credit or debit cards, and hardly use cash for purchases. A cashless system would certainly be a means by which the Antichrist could have unlimited power, and it seems that we are headed in this direction.

In another important aspect related to finances, I find it amazing how the stock market in most nations affect the everyday life of people around the world. The markets can create or dissolve whole economies in an instant. We saw how the collapse of the market in the 1920s caused a worldwide depression. The consequence of this event was the rise of Hitler and other dictators, which led to World War II.

People in Germany knew there were problems with Hitler, especially his vehement hatred of Jews; but because he promised a golden era and national pride, the people ended up electing the madman to bring them prosperity. Most world rulers are elected on the promises of security and economic prosperity they make for the public regardless of their moral position. The Antichrist will offer the same deceptive promises with one major difference; sell your soul to the devil for eternity for temporal survival.

It says in Daniel 8:25; *by peace, he* (Antichrist) *will destroy many.* It is believed by many prophecy teachers, in Revelation 6 when the first seal is broken, this is portraying the Antichrist on a white horse (symbol of peace). The question is: What will people do for peace, and not only peace from war and terror, but peace of mind for financial security? Faced with the possibility of losing all that a person has saved up, what are the prospects of people giving in to a system that becomes anti-God?

Jesus told His disciple's in Matthew 20, after His encounter with the rich man who walked away from Christ; *it is easier for a camel to go through the eye of a needle than for a rich man to enter into heaven.* This is a great illustration of what will take place when multitudes are forced to make a decision (Joel 3:14) during the great tribulation. The falling away in 2 Thessalonians is going to be the most tragic event ever, where many professing believers reject God and choose the Antichrist.

Another aspect regarding the pretrib teaching that parallels the revelation of the Antichrist, is many teachers claim that the man of sin is already present here on earth. If you have listened to much prophecy teaching or sermons, chances are you have heard this taught. I remind the reader this goes against the teaching on imminence, because it would have been impossible for the rapture to occur throughout church history if the Antichrist weren't present.

With that said, I refer back to John Walvoord's words as he acknowledges the ability of Antichrist to control mankind would have been impossible a hundred years ago.

Daniel 12

> But thou, O Daniel, shut up the words, and seal the book, even to the time of the end: **many shall run to and fro, and knowledge shall be increased**. (Dan. 12:4)

Pretribulation teachers commonly mention this verse as a reference to the technological explosion of the last days. After all, look how far we have advanced in the sciences and technology. Crossing the Atlantic Ocean a hundred years ago took several weeks, now it takes only a few hours. Our space exploration today, and our modern technology has skyrocketed; a seventy years ago, this would have been deemed impossible- science fiction. The computer has advanced modern technology at a frightening rate. Here is a quote by John Hagee advocating the pretrib teaching in Daniel 12:4

> In the last two generations, we have put men on the moon and redefined life and death. Medical science has the ability to keep a corpse breathing for months on life support. Tiny babies weighing less than one pound can survive outside the womb, and unborn babies can undergo surgery before birth. We can repair DNA before a child is conceived; we can clone sheep, mice, and cattle. We have the technology to clone humans, and before too long, I'm sure someone will.[68]

It sounds spectacular that Daniel 12:4 is a reference to these things; however, this passage in Daniel has absolutely nothing to do with the advancement of modern technology or mankind's knowledge. In the context of this passage, it is teaching that the time leading up to the Antichrist, Christians will become more conscious of the dangerous situation they are facing. In the previous verse (3) it states that the *wise* [Christians] *will turn many to righteousness.*

> Many shall be purified, and made white, and tried; but the **wicked shall do wickedly**: and **none of the wicked shall understand; but the wise shall understand. And from the time that the daily sacrifice shall be taken away, and the abomination that maketh desolate set up,** there shall be a thousand two hundred and ninety days. (Dan. 12:10-11)

These verses are mentioned in the same context as verse 3; the context is that the wise (saved) will understand and the wicked (lost) will not when these events unfold. This is what Christ was teaching about in the parable of the wise and foolish virgins in Matthew 25. The wise virgins understood and were ready; the foolish were not. Notice the timing of verse 3, it's centered around the midpoint of the 70th week. The pretribulation hyper-bandwagon on spectacular teaching such as Daniel 12:4 needs to be corralled by the truth, which can only be done through honest and thorough study by examining the Scriptures.

Revived Roman Empire

Another hot-topic among prophecy teaching relating to prophetic events that must occur in the last days is the image from Nebuchadnezzar's dream found in Daniel chapter 2. Nebuchadnezzar was initially troubled by the great image revealed to him by God in his dream. It would be Daniel who would eventually interpret the meaning of this great image (vv. 27-47). The key to understanding this prophecy, which applies to us today, is found in verses 41-45 that speak of the ten toes of the great image. Prophecy teaching has been very speculative for years as to the meaning and application of the ten toes. The standard teaching is that the ten toes represent some portion of the revived Roman Empire in the future. I recall reading and hearing in the 1970s and 80s, there would be a restructuring of the European Common Market that would be identified by the make-up of a ten-nation Confederation. Now, fast-forward to today, we see that there are over twenty nations that are part of the Common Market. What prophecy teachers are now saying is that there will be a confederation of ten world-wide regions around the globe. These confederations would engulf the entire nations of the world into a ten-region system controlled by the Antichrist. My argument is not against this theory; however, this fly's in the face of the pretribulationism teaching on the imminent return of Christ. Listen to their teaching and you will hear them say this prophecy needs to be in place for the rise of the Antichrist to have control. This would not of have been possible one hundred years ago, again, denying the possibility of an imminent return by Christ.

Also, read through the book of Daniel, mainly the chapters that deal with prophecy, and note how some of these prophecies pertain to the latter-days. The particular kingdoms referenced in those chapters will have to been in place for the set-up of the final events foretold. (cf. Dan. 7:1-14, 19-27; 8:19, 23-26; 11:31-35, 39-40)

The Seven Churches of Revelation

The description of the seven churches in Asia Minor, according to many in their prophetic studies of end-times, teach that these seven churches are an overall historical account of church history.

Clarence Larkin writes in his book "The Second Coming of Christ."

> We are now living in the 'Laodicean' or **'Last Stage' of the Church's History** in this dispensation, which reveals the fact that the next 'Event' is the 'Return of the Lord,' who will **'SPUE'** the '**Lukewarm**' Church out of His mouth. Rev. 3:14-16[69] (bold letters mine)

Remember, this explanation by Larkin was written over one hundred years ago. He also admits that the rapture of the church was not possible (next event) until the Laodicean Church existed. No possible rapture for 1900 years!

Here is Tim LaHaye's Prophecy Study Bible explaining the prophetic meaning of the seven churches.

> Many dispensational scholars believe Christ selected these seven churches in this particular order to prophetically suggest the major trends in church history, but this is not a universal belief. A study of history reveals that the Church has gone through seven basic periods or stages:
>
> 1. Ephesus- Apostolic church (Pentecost, A. D. 100)
> 2. Smyrna-Persecuted church (A. D. 100-316)
> 3. Pergamos-World church (A. D. 316-800)
> 4. Thyatira-Medieval church (A. D.800-1517)

5. Sardis- Rise of the state church (A. D. 1517-1750)
6. Philadelphia- Missionary church (A. D. 1750-1900)
7. Laodicea- Apostate church (A. D.1900-?)

As one surveys the history of the last two millennia, it is possible to see how these prophetic allusions may have been fulfilled. **One sign of Christ's soon return is the fact** that we are at the end of the age according to these two passages (Kingdom parables Matt. 13 and the **seven churches** Rev. 2-3). **The rapture of the Church and God's final judgment are the only prophetic events that remain to be fulfilled in this age.**[70] (bold letters mine)

My question to the pretribulation teachers who believe these seven churches represent seven different church-periods in history: would these be different dispensations within the church-age themselves? Larkin, acknowledges by his statement that the rapture could not have taken place prior to the Laodicean age. He even goes as far as stating that the four watches described in the gospels represent four periods of church history.

Watch ye therefore: for ye know not when the 'Master of the House' cometh, at EVEN, or at MIDNIGHT, or at the COCK-CROWING, or in the MORNING.' Mark 13:35.

FIRST WATCH:- 'Evening.' From 6-9 P.M. Corresponding to the 'Apostolic Times.'

SECOND WATCH:- 'Midnight.' From 9-12 A.M. Corresponding to the 'Dark Ages.'

THIRD WATCH:- 'Cock-crowing.' From 12-3 A.M. Corresponding to the 'Period of the Reformation.'

FOURTH WATCH:- 'Morning.' From 3-6 A.M. We are living in the 'MORNING WATCH.'[71]

Larkin did not realize he had conflicting statements within his book "The Second Coming of Christ," when he stated it is the churches fault for Christ's delay in his return for failing to evangelize the world. Conversely, he states that the different church ages/watches needed to be fulfilled according to the prophecy given by Christ in the gospels and in the book of Revelation.

I do not hold this view of church-ages representing the seven churches, because the context of the book of Revelation is centered on the time of Christ's second coming. I believe these seven churches give an overall picture of the condition of the church before the time of Christ's return in the last days.

Question: How could the rapture be imminent throughout church history if each church period were already prophesied to take place? In other words, if the rapture could have taken place in Sardis era (Rev 3:1), then how could the following church period (Philadelphia) have been fulfilled (Rev.3:7)? Also, if the church of Philadelphian represents the raptured church before the tribulation (Rev.3:10) as pretrib teaches; how can the return of Christ occur before the last church-age, which is the Laodicea church? The Laodicea church will not exist at this time according to pretrib theology. Also, why would Christ even be knocking on the door of the Church of Laodicea if the rapture occurred during the Philadelphia church-age? We would already be in heaven!

The 7ᵗʰ and 8ᵗʰ Kingdom

> And there are seven kings: five are fallen, and one is, and the other is not yet come; and when he cometh, he must continue a short space. And the beast that was, and is not, even he is the eighth, and is of the seven, and goeth into perdition. (Rev. 17:10-11)

This Scripture text deals with past, present, and future events. The past are the five fallen kings; it is commonly believed these would-be, Egypt, Assyria, Babylon, Medo-Persia, and Greece. Each of these kings (kingdoms) have something in common- they persecuted God's people. The one king that "is," would be Rome at the current time John was writing that suppressed Israel by its might. However, not only was Israel under the bondage of the Roman, but another group of people became subjected to Rome's wrath as well- Christians.

Christianity steadily grew throughout the Roman Empire. The Christian's rejection of calling Caesar their lord caused many to be driven to the catacombs, and eventually to the Roman coliseums to face a horrible death by unimaginable means as the spectators cheered. (Remember, according to many pretribulation teachers, these early Christians probably wanted to go through persecution). For the most part, all someone had to do was to burn incense to Caesar once a year in a Roman temple, and then they were free to worship any deity they chose. However, for the Christian to call anyone but Christ their Lord was in truth rejecting Jesus as their Lord.

The Roman dynasty was the sixth kingdom mentioned in this passage. The next king prophesied to come, which will be the seventh kingdom, will continue only a *short space*. I personally believe this was Germany under the rule of Hitler and his Nazi regime. This embellished thousand-year reign only lasted twelve years, which was the shortest reign of the empires within the context of this prophecy; yet it was perhaps the most destructive.

The holocaust was certainly a notable event in World War II; still, you must recognize there were Christian leaders who stood up against Hitler-Dietrich Bonhoeffer being a prime example. Eventually, all true believers under this satanic regime would have been targeted. Just as the Roman citizens had to burn incense on an altar dedicated to Caesar, folks in Germany had to greet each other in public with the right-hand salute and pronounce heil Hitler. This helped expose those who were not fully supportive of their leader. Christians were put in a predicament, because they knew they were pledging allegiance to a type of the Antichrist, and sadly most followed. The coming mark of the beast will most definitely separate the lost from the saved.

History has taught us when communism takes over a country, the first one thrown out of their society is God himself. Christians have been persecuted as much as the Jews, and Scripture teaches that both groups will be persecuted in the great tribulation. I think of Richard and Sabina Wurmbrand, who founded the **Voice of the Martyr's** ministry, how they suffered greatly in Romania under Russian suppression in the late 1940s into the 50s for simply being Christians. Christianity will be under immense pressure as the world becomes more anti-God.

The Final Kingdom

The eighth kingdom is identified in verse 11, and 12:

> And the **ten horns** which thou sawest are ten kings, which have received no kingdom as yet; **but receive power as kings one hour with the beast.** These have **one mind,** and **shall give their power and strength unto the beast.** (vv.11-12)

This prophecy given in Revelation 17 is what Daniel prophesied in chapter 2 while interpreting Nebuchadnezzar's dream. Here is John Walvoord explanation on the subject.

The Place of the Ten-Nation Kingdom in the End Time

The **prediction** that there will be a ten-kingdom stage of the revival of the Roman Empire is **one of the important descriptive prophecies of the end time.** This prophecy anticipates that there will be ten countries originally related to the Roman Empire the names of these countries are not given, but it can be presumed that Italy, the capitol country, would be included along major countries in southern Europe and possibly some countries of western Asia and northern Africa which were included in the ancient Roman Empire. Since the names of the countries are not given and there are many more than ten countries in the ancient Roman Empire, it leaves some flexibility in the fulfillment. The prediction, however, requires a political union and then a dictator over the ten countries. With the coming of the Common Market of Europe, now embracing twelve countries, a measure of unity has been achieved in Europe. With the thawing of the Cold War in eastern Europe, the breakdown of Communism, and the unification of East and West Germany, **the climate is more favorable now than ever before for the formation of such a ten-nation group.** Though the possibility of such a fulfilled prophecy was often scorned in preceding generations, **it now becomes a very likely possibility**, and even the secular world is predicting some sort of a United States of Europe. From a prophetic standpoint, **the importance is that this is a major step in end-time events** leading up to the second coming of Christ.[72] (bold letters mine)

I believe this assessment by Walvoord, stating that the formation of this coalition was only possible after the seventh kingdom had come and gone is accurate. I agree with Walvoord: the conditions are right for this fulfillment, which is coming true right before our eyes. I am glad to see that Walvoord realizes this as an important major event **before** the return of Christ. However, his statement nullifies the imminent return of Christ.

The Re-Gathering of Israel

And it shall come to pass in that day, that the Lord shall set his hand again the **second time** to recover the remnant of his people, which shall be left, from Assyria, and from Egypt, and from Pathros, and from Cush, and from Elam, and from Shinar, and from Hamath, and from the islands of the sea. And he shall set up an ensign for the nations, **and shall assemble the outcasts of Israel, and gather together the dispersed of Judah from the four corners of the earth**. (Isaiah 11:11-12)

Therefore say, Thus saith the Lord GOD; Although I have cast them far off among the heathen, and although I have **scattered them among the countries**, yet will I be to them as a little sanctuary in the countries where they shall come. Therefore say, Thus saith the Lord GOD; I will even **gather you** from the people, and **assemble you out of the countries** where ye have been scattered, **and I will give you the land of Israel**. (Ezek. 11:16-17)

By far, this is the most intriguing Bible prophecy related to end-time events. This is the sign that has set the stage for other prophecies to be fulfilled. The re-gathering of Israel back into the land is certainly the key to Bible prophecy, and the leading pretribulation scholars agree.

What is significant, here is this **"super sign."** As the editor of this book, prophecy scholar Tommy Ice, terms it. **It all started in 1917, with the fulfillment of the sign our Lord gave His disciples in Matthew 24:6-7: World War I,** followed by unprecedented "famines, pestilences, and earthquakes in various places." Notice, "wars and rumors of wars" were not the sign. Man's history is filled with war after war, but Jesus said, "See that you are not troubled; for all these things mist come to pass, but the end is not yet." **The sign was not wars, but a most significant war, which was World War I, with its accompanying phenomena of famines, pestilences, and earthquakes. Out of the fulfillment of this sign, Israel started going back into the land, leading many prophecy scholars to conclude the God's prophetic clock began ticking again. Personally, I look on**

that period, 1917-1948, as God winding His clock.[73]
(bold letters mine)

Tim LaHaye

If God's prophetic time clock started ticking with the return of the Jews to Israel, as stated by pretribulation teachers; does this mean that the rapture was not imminent before this time? Yes, it does! Pretribulationist Ron Rhodes even admits to this fact.

The Valley of Dry Bones

In the same context as Ezekiel's prophecy related to the Jew's return to the Promise Land is Ezekiel's prophecy about the dry bones of Israel (Ezekiel 37:1-5, 11-14).

> 1: The hand of the LORD was upon me, and carried me out in the spirit of the LORD, and set me down in the midst of the valley which was full of bones,
>
> 2: And caused me to pass by them round about: and, behold, there were very many in the open valley; and, lo, they were very dry.
>
> 3: And he said unto me, Son of man, can these bones live? And I answered, O Lord GOD, thou knowest.
>
> 4: Again he said unto me, Prophesy upon these bones, and say unto them, O ye dry bones, hear the word of the LORD.
>
> 5: Thus saith the Lord GOD unto these bones; Behold, I will cause breath to enter into you, and ye shall live:
>
> 11: Then he said unto me, Son of man, these bones are the whole house of Israel: behold, they say, Our bones are dried, and our hope is lost: we are cut off for our parts.
>
> 12: Therefore prophesy and say unto them, Thus saith the Lord GOD; Behold, O my people, I will open your graves, and cause you to come up out of your graves, and bring you into the land of Israel.
>
> 13: And ye shall know that I am the LORD, when I have opened your graves, O my people, and brought you up out of your graves,

14: And shall put my spirit in you, and ye shall live, and I shall
place you in your own land: then shall ye know that I the
LORD have spoken it, and performed it, saith the LORD.

Here we have the portion of Scripture that LaHaye called the "super
sign" as it's related to Israel's return to the promise land. This is referred
to by Christians as the "valley of dry bones." This depicts the harsh reality
of what Israel would witness as a nation. Israel would be viewed among the
nations in each time period as a "dead historical nation" never to be revived.
Israel was dead for about two thousand years from the time of their Roman
defeat to 1948. Ezekiel's prophecy was given about five hundred years before
Rome finally drove them from the land in AD 132. This prophecy in of itself
nullified the pretribulation rapture theory for over two-thousand years. I
would like to draw your attention to the last verse listed (14) that Israel still
does not know the Lord, so even this portion is still future. (See the first
appendix)

Ezekiel 38

Ezekiel chapter 38 is a prominent reference in prophecy teaching, particularly,
since we just saw where Israel had to be a nation again in their own land. It is
recorded that there will be an invasion from the north (probably led by Russia
or Turkey) that will attack Israel. The question is, when does this event take
place? Here is a quote by Thomas Ice of the pretrib research center:

Is America Referenced in Ezekiel 38?

These two chapters refer to the Battle of Gog and Magog and
speak of their invasion of Israel. Ezekiel says this will occur
"in the latter years" (38:8) and **"in the last days"** (38:16).
The invasion involves a coalition headed by "Gog of the land of
Magog, the prince of Rosh, Meshech, and Tubal" (38:2). Magog
has been identified as ancient terminology for the area including
modern day Russia, The Ukraine, and Kazakhstan.[2] Ezekiel
further identifies Magog as coming from "the remote parts of
the north (38:6).

Gog will lead the invasion of Israel, but Ezekiel 38:5,6 says that other nations will join with him. Persia (Iran), Ethiopia or Cush (Sudan), Put (Libya), Gomer and Beth-togarmah (Turkey).[3] All the allies of Magog are reasonably well identified and they are all presently Muslim. **Interestingly, such an alignment of nations is already configured on the world scene in our own day.**

I believe the invasion will most likely take place **before the tribulation officially begins, but after the rapture**.[4] Such a view would help to explain a vacuum on the world political scene at the beginning of the tribulations left by the removal of the influence of Russia and her Muslim allies, and possibly even the United States due to the conflict. This would then prepare the way for the Revived Roman Empire (Western Europe) and the Antichrist to sign the covenant with Israel (Daniel 9:2427).[74] (bold letters mine)

Ice acknowledges this prophecy is being fulfilled in our very day. However, Ice's realization of the possible discrepancy about imminence in his statement, he makes sure that he clarifies that the rapture takes place first. Remember, other pretribulation teachers say that the rapture inaugurates the beginning of the 70th week. Ice also claims there is a gap between the rapture and the invasion in Ezekiel's prophecy, which all happens before the 70th week begins. How long does this period of time last; and what dispensation would this be a part of?

Two Days

Hosea 6:1-3

1: Come, and let us return unto the LORD: for he hath torn, and he will heal us; he hath smitten, and he will bind us up.

2: **After two days** will he revive us: **in the third day** he will raise us up, and we shall live in his sight.

3: Then shall we know, if we follow on to know the LORD: his going forth is prepared as the morning; and he shall come unto us as the rain, as the latter and former rain unto the earth.

Some pretrib teachers use this prophecy of the two days to teach that each day represents a thousand years. Supposedly, after the second day (two thousand years), Israel would experience a revival. Since it has been two thousand years after Christ's first coming, according to the pretribulationism, the rapture can happen any day now.

Looking a little deeper into verse 1 of this passage, it states that Israel will need to return to the Lord. The question that should be asked: when did Israel reject the Lord? It was during the final week leading up to the crucifixion of Christ. Therefore, to be correct about this prophecy, we should not be counting two thousand years from Christ's birth, but from His death. If Christ was born around 3-4 BC (according to the scholars), then add about thirty-three years, this would put his death at around AD 30. This would still put us about sixteen years (from the time of this book) away from this prophecy being fulfilled. As a note, I do not hold to this belief of the two days' prophecy; however, when this time draws near, watch for the resurgence of prophecy literature soar from the pretrib camp about the imminent return of Christ. Of course, the year 2018 will come first, so let's see what happens then.

This concludes this section on imminence. You be the judge! There should be enough evidence here to convince the average Christian that there are many discrepancies among pretrib teaching pertaining to imminence. I ask you to weigh the evidence according to Scripture, and then verify the facts to determine if the pretrib rapture theory still holds water? If the different pretribulation teachers had to testify about their position on imminence in a court of law, would their conflicting interpretations be thrown out? I believe so!

I complete this section by stating the fact, if this was the year 1900, we certainly would not be having this conversation about imminence and a pretrib rapture.

CHAPTER NINE

THE GLORIOUS APPEARING

To Appear or not to Appear That is the Question

Looking for that blessed hope, and the **glorious appearing** of the great God and our Saviour Jesus Christ; (Titus 2:13).

As we just completed the discrepancies of pretrib teaching pertaining to imminence, now I need to address another fallacy, which has to do with the "glorious appearance" of Christ. The standard teaching within the pretrib theory is supposedly the glorious appearing takes place at the end of the tribulation, when Christ "appears" at His second coming; contrast to the rapture, when there is the disappearance of millions of Christians by the "invisible" return of Christ before the tribulation. Here are some quotes by leading pretrib teachers.

> The **Glorious Appearing**, on the other hand, is **not** for the Christians but for the remnant at the **end of the tribulation**.[75]
> (bold letters mine)
>
> Tim LaHaye

Tim LaHaye in his book "Rapture Under Attack," on page 69 states that the glorious appearing is at the **end** of the tribulation. However, in his same book on page 26, he contradicts himself by saying the signs of the glorious appearing are for the saints **before** the tribulation.

> The exhortation to look for 'the **glorious appearing**' of Christ to His own (Titus 2:13) loses its significance if the Tribulation

must intervene first. Believers in that case should look for signs.[76] (bold letters mine)

John Walvoord

Walvoord contradicts LaHaye by exhorting believers to look for the glorious appearance of Christ at the rapture "before" the tribulation. I also quoted Walvoord earlier about his belief that we are living in the last days. We read where he stated the signs proved that we are the generation that makes it possible for Christ to return. So, which is it; signs or no signs before the 70th week?

> This **glorious appearing of Christ** is described in Matthew 24:27, "As the lightning cometh out of the east and shineth unto the west, so also shall the coming of the Son of Man be." And when He comes, His feet will touch down upon the Mount of Olives in Jerusalem, Zachariah 14:4. (**At the end of the tribulation**) And He will then come regally and royally on that white horse, Revelation 19:11 and the armies in heaven follow Him.[77] (bold letters mine)
>
> Jack Van Impe

> Though the noun "appearing" (epiphaneia) can refer to the second coming of Jesus (2 Thess. 2:8), **twice it refers to the rapture** coming of our Lord (1 Tim. 6:14; Titus 2:13). As a verb, "to appear" is used twice in I John to **refer to the rapture** (2:28; 3:2), "when He appears."

> In Titus 2:13 Paul says "we" (us) are looking for this "appearing" of the glory of our great God and Savior, Jesus Christ. "The glory" is a descriptive genitive, translated as an adjective. Thus, "the glorious appearance," the "and" between the two phrases "is explanatory, introducing the definition of the character of the thing hoped for. Looking for the object of hope, even the appearing" of the glory. "The Greek connects 'the blessed hope and glorious appearing' under one article, suggesting that the reference is to one event viewed from two aspects." The reference to the Lord should read, "the great God even Savior, Christ Jesus."[78] (bold letters mine)
>
> Mal Couch

The Second Coming of Christ is a series of events fulfilling all end-time prophecies. These include predictions of Christ's coming for His Church and with His Church. Pretribulationists generally **divide the Second Coming into two main phases:** the Rapture of the Church and the **Glorious Appearing** of Christ.[79] (bold letters mine)

Ed Hindson

Some pretribulationists interpret this passage as referring to the second coming of Christ rather than the Rapture, because of Paul's use of the word ejpifavneia (appearing). However, all four uses of the term in the Pastoral Epistles (1 Tim. 6:14; 2 Tim. 4:1, 8; Titus 2:13) present the **appearing of Christ** as a joyous expectation apart from signs or tribulation and **thus refer to the Rapture**.

Others have related this event to Christ's posttribulational second coming because it states that Christ's appearing will be a "glorious appearing," which can only be the manifestation of an exalted and glorious Christ to the entire world (cf. Matt. 16:27; 19:28; 24:30; 25:31). **It must be noted, however, that although the world will not see Christ's glory until his second coming, the church will experience his glory when it meets him in the air** (Rom. 5:2; 8:18, 30; 1 Cor. 15:43; Phil. 3:21; Col. 1:27; 3:4; 1 Pet. 5:1; 1 John 3:2; Jude 1:24). This "glory" may be either an attributive genitive ("glorious appearing") or a subjective genitive (the glory "appears"). **Either way, there is nothing in the passage that restricts this appearing to Christ's second coming.**[80] (bold letters mine)

Wayne Bridle

These are some of the more prominent pretrib teachers, and they cannot build a consensus over a basic verse (Titus 2:13) about Christ's return. The discrepancy over a simple verse is exacerbated just because their melded interpretations are not reasoned from a hermeneutical approach to the Scriptures. Wayne Bridle believes he settled their dilemma by interjecting the secret rapture theory into the equation.

Consider the following versus and decide for yourself whether this is a reference to Christ's coming before the 70th week, or at the end.

> But thou, O man of God, flee these things; and follow after righteousness, godliness, faith, love, patience, meekness. Fight the good fight of faith, lay hold on eternal life, whereunto thou art also called, and hast professed a good profession before many witnesses. I give thee charge in the sight of God, who quickeneth all things, and before Christ Jesus, who before Pontius Pilate witnessed a good confession; That thou keep this commandment without spot, unrebukeable, until **the appearing of our Lord Jesus Christ:** (1 Tim. 6:11-14)

Paul is exhorting Timothy to follow godliness and to fight the good fight until the appearance of Christ. If the appearance of Christ is after the tribulation according to some pretrib interpretations, then Paul is plainly stating that Timothy would go through the tribulation. If the appearance is before the 70th week, then the glorious appearance is not invisible, which destroys the secret, invisible return of Christ.

The Holy Spirit commissioned Paul to write these words which were directed toward Timothy, but God's broader audience is the saints of Christ. He used illustrations and examples of people in the Bible to teach future generations what we need to know in our walk with Him.

> For I am now ready to be offered, and the time of **my departure is at hand**. I have fought a good fight, I have finished my course, I have kept the faith: Henceforth there is laid up for me a crown of righteousness, which the Lord, the righteous judge, shall give me at that day: and not to me only, but unto **all them also that love his appearing.** (2 Tim. 4:6-8)

Paul knows his time in this life is coming to an end. He speaks here of the future judgment, when he will receive the crown of righteousness. Paul references an appearance in verse one: *I charge thee therefore before God, and the Lord Jesus Christ, who shall judge the quick and the dead **at his appearing and his kingdom**.* Paul is not laying out a sequence of events here; he is simply stating a fact that there will be a time in the future when man will give an account to God. Just because this appearance is referenced at the judgment it does not mean that Christ is working secretly before this time. Christ will appear at the rapture, which is at the end of the tribulation; and He will appear at the end of the 70th week. The judgment of God's wrath during the set time on the final week will certainly not be done in secret, the world will know for sure it's from God.

> But ye shall receive power, after that the Holy Ghost is come upon you: and ye shall be witnesses unto me both in Jerusalem, and in all Judaea, and in Samaria, and unto the uttermost part of the earth. And when he had spoken these things, while they beheld, he was taken up; and a cloud received him out of their sight. And while they looked stedfastly toward heaven as he went up, behold, two men stood by them in white apparel; Which also said, Ye men of Galilee, why stand ye gazing up into heaven? this same Jesus, which is taken up from you into heaven, **shall so come in like manner as ye have seen** him go into heaven. (Acts 1:8-11)

The angels say to the disciples as Christ went up into heaven, He will come back the same way he left. His ascension was visible and His return will not be any different.

> And now, little children, abide in him; that, **when he shall appear,** we may have confidence, **and not be ashamed before him at his coming.** (1 John 2:28)

This is in the same context as the other verses that speak of Christ's appearance to believers, where His appearance will be visible to all at His coming. In this verse, John says we will "not be ashamed at His coming," also indicating a visible appearance to all, not just the saved. Jesus alluded to this in Luke 9 when He was teaching His disciples about what it means to be being a true Christian.

> 23: And he said to them all, If any man will come after me, let him deny himself, and take up his cross daily, and follow me.
> 24: For whosoever will save his life shall lose it: but whosoever will lose his life for my sake, the same shall save it.
> 25: For what is a man advantaged, if he gain the whole world, and lose himself, or be cast away?

26: For whosoever shall be **ashamed of me and of my words,** of
him **shall the Son of man be ashamed, when he shall come
in his own glory,** and in his Father's, and of the holy angels.

There is to be no mistaking the severity of not acknowledging the
Lordship of Christ in a person's life to those around them. A person's
religious beliefs will not only be exposed when they stand before God at the
final judgment, but also to those living at the time of Christ's return.

Beloved, now are we the sons of God, and it doth not yet appear
what we shall be: but we know that, **when he shall appear,** we
shall be like him; for we shall see him as he is. (1 John 3:2)

Again, is this before or after the rapture?

Now you see me and now you don't!

20: For our conversation is in heaven; **from whence
also we look for the Saviour,** the Lord Jesus Christ:
21: Who **shall change our vile body, that it may be
fashioned like unto his glorious body,** according to the
working whereby he is able even to subdue all things unto
himself. (Philippians 3:20-21)

Behold, I show you a mystery; We shall not all sleep, but we shall
all be changed, **In a moment, in the twinkling of an eye,** at
the last trump: for the trumpet shall sound, and the dead shall
be raised incorruptible, and we shall be changed. (1Cor. 15:51-52)

Because the pretribulation theory splits the return of Christ into two
events, rapture before the 70th week and the second coming at the end of the
70th week, they compound their fallacies by misinterpreting what Paul said.

The Lord shouts as He descends ("loud command" 1Thessalonians
4:16, NIV). **All this takes place** in the "twinkling of an eye" (1
Corinthians 15:52).[81] (bold letters, parenthesis mine)

Tim LaHaye

Through the years some have tried to discredit the pre-tribulation rapture theory by calling it the *secret rapture*. Of course, nowhere in Scripture is the term *secret* applied to this event. However, **anyone who does not participate in the Rapture will not actually see it** (secret), for it will occur in the 'twinkling of an eye.[82] (bold letters and parentheses mine)

Tim LaHaye

The "Secret" Rapture Myth

Included in the above tirade is an equation of the so-called "secret" rapture with pretribulationism. Sorry, but this is another mistake, another myth. In all my reading of pretribulationism and discussion with pretribulationists, **I have never, that I can recall, heard a pre-trib rapturist use the nomenclature of "secret" rapture to describe our view**. I have only heard the phrase "secret" rapture as a pejorative term used exclusively by anti-pretribulationists. Why? Apparently they enjoy fighting with a straw man.[83] (bold letters mine)

Thomas Ice

Ice's denial about never hearing a pretrib rapturist teaching a secret rapture is his straw man. Surely, Ice has seen the blockbuster hit movie by Tim LaHaye, "Left Behind," that overwhelmingly teaches a secret rapture; what other reasons would the world be at a loss due to the mysterious disappearance of millions of Christian's worldwide? (Maybe it was the space aliens who took us!).

There is no secret rapture" is the **beginning declaration** of a large percentage of messages **that attack the rapture**. Rarely is this statement backed by supporting Scriptural evidence. A few people will cite Revelation 1:17 "every eye shall see him" as proof that the rapture will not be a secret event. Of course, I would immediately note that "every eye shall see him" is the **second coming**.[84] (bold letters mine)

Todd Strandberg

I challenge Strandberg's use of "scriptural evidence" to support his belief in a secret rapture. Outside of pretrib miss-interpretation of 1 Corinthians 15, there is no evidence in the Bible for a secret rapture.

Here's a quote from a former pretribulationist, and an associate with John Darby, who once believed that the rapture was secret:

> When the theory of a **secret coming of Christ** was first brought forward (18oo's), it was adopted with eagerness; it suited certain preconceived opinions, and it was accepted by some at that which **harmonized** contradictory thoughts, whether such thoughts, or any of them, rested on the sure warrant of God; written Word.[85] (bold letters mine)
>
> S.P. Tregelles

Tregelles certainly understood what Darby and Irving were teaching in the early days as the pretrib rapture was being introduced to the church for the first time, since he was personally associated with their ministries.

> Rapture: **The Scriptures do not indicate that the lost of the world will see** His Rapture coming. (Makes it secret) Second Coming: The entire world will see the Son of Man coming. "All the tribes of the earth will mourn, and they will see the Son of Man coming on the clouds of the sky" (Matt. 24:30).[86] (bold letters and parentheses mine)
>
> Dwight Pentecost

> **In the twinkling of an eye,** Jesus is going to **step from His throne** in glory at the right hand of the Father in heaven and **make His way back to this earth.** First Thessalonians 4:16-17 says, "For the Lord Himself shall descend from heaven with a shout, with the voice of the archangel, and with the trump of God: and the dead in Christ shall rise first: Then we which are alive and remain shall be caught up together with them in the clouds, to meet the Lord in the air: and so shall we ever be with the Lord.[87] (bold letters mine)
>
> Adrian Rogers

I have great respect for the late Adrian Rogers and his preaching; however, on this point he is completely wrong. He teaches, along with many other pretribulationist, that Christ will come from heaven to earth, raise the dead, rapture the living, then go back to the throne in heaven, all in the twinkling of the eye is not biblical. The only aspect of the twinkling of an eye related to Christ's coming is the changing of the believer's body, nothing more.

> First, the Rapture will be a "stealth event" in which Christ will be **witnessed by believers only.**[88] (bold letters mine)
>
> David Jeremiah

Pretrib teachers like Jeremiah offer no biblical support for a "stealth" rapture.

> **How Will it Happen? On the day of the rapture, there will be a shout from heaven, with the voice of the** archangel and with the trumpet of God; in a moment, in a twinkling of an eye, the bodies of the Bride of Christ will suddenly be transformed to glorious heavenly bodies! From all four corners of the earth, people will start to rise up from the earth, floating right up through homes, buildings, cars or wherever this event finds them. They will go through right up into the clouds where they will meet Jesus in the air. *"Then there will be two men in the field; one will be taken and one will be left. Two women will be grinding at the mill; one will be taken and one will be left"* (Matthew 24:40). **This event will leave the whole world in a total shock as many people who are left behind will wake up to find out that some people have disappeared all over the world.** They will even be shocked more as they find out that all those who disappeared had one thing in common: they were committed Christians who fully followed Jesus. (bold letters mine)
>
> Unknown

Pretrib teachers need to produce the evidence of the world being in shock and disillusion by the disappearance of millions. You are probably familiar with the sketches showing planes and cars crashing because the pilot or driver were Christians; paralleled with the world in a frantic state because of the disappearance of their loved ones and children. The "Left Behind" movie completely falsifies the truth of the Scriptures. I have even heard in sermons from the pulpit that some airlines will not let two Christian pilots in the same plane because of the possibility of a pretrib rapture. All this hype makes for fanciful books, dramatic movies, and sensational preaching, but all these are ridiculous, nonetheless. Pretrib teaching states, as I have noted, that 1 Corinthians 15:51 says everything happens in a micro-second (twinkling of an eye). In covering up one problem, they continue to create more problems, which occur quite often in their teaching. Also, if the age of accountability (people who do not have the mental ability to understand their sinful condition related to salvation) is sometime before a child's teen years, then they will have to be raptured. That means there are no children in the entire world. Also, every pregnant woman will automatically become un-pregnant. You never hear this taught in pretrib teaching.

In another misleading attempt to try and explain an invisible rapture, some pretrib teachers cite John 10:27, *my sheep hear my voice, and I know them, and they follow me*, as a basis that only the saved will hear Christ's command "come up hither" at the rapture. As I have been saying, context, context, context, is how Bible verses need to be interpreted. If you read in the context of John 10, Jesus is teaching that the true sheep (believers) will not follow false teachers. This has nothing to do with hearing the voice of Christ at the rapture.

When the interpretation of the Scriptures is viewed from a presupposition, (i.e. the pretrib rapture) then they are forced to redefine for example, the meaning of signs, the glorious appearance, and the visible return of Christ. Prewrath teaching takes the common, literal, exegetical, biblical view that at the rapture, after the great tribulation is cut short, the entire world will see the glorious appearance of Christ. Many will be ashamed and try to hide from Christ's impending wrath, and the saved will rejoice and be taken back to heaven before the throne of God. We also believe before the rapture, we will witness the signs Christ spoke of that will make us aware of His soon return. In other words, we will not just disappear into thin air at any time.

CHAPTER TEN

WATCH AND BE READY

As we have dealt particularly with the teaching on imminence and the glorious appearing, another characteristic that parallels this is the word "watchfulness." The Word of God does teach that we are to be looking for Christ's return, since He promised that He is coming again to set up His literal kingdom where He will rule. As Christians, we are to be alert to His coming because the Word of God promulgates it. **Expectant**, should be the key word associated with the return of Christ; unfortunately, pretribulation teachers have (again) hijacked the discussion, this time verses pertaining to watchfulness and inserted imminence in their place. Here are some examples.

> **But of that day and that hour knoweth no man**, no, not the angels which are in heaven, neither the Son, but the Father. Take ye heed, **watch and pray: for ye know not when the time is.** For the Son of man is as a man taking a **far journey**, who left his house, and gave authority to his servants, and to every man his work, and commanded the porter to watch. **Watch ye therefore: for ye know not when the master of the house cometh,** at even, or at midnight, or at the cockcrowing, or in the morning: Lest coming suddenly he find you **sleeping**. And what I say unto you I say unto all, **Watch.** (Mark 13:32-37)

Mark 13 gives the same account of the Olivet Discourse as taught in Matthew 24-25. Based on the context, these servants are commanded to be watching for their master's return; with an emphasis on avoiding being caught asleep upon His arrival. Sleeping in this parable represents someone who is concerned more with the physical aspect of this temporal life than the eternal. Those who are not part of the master's household (non-Christian) will have no serious concern for His return. The meaning of, to watch, is for us as Christians not to be like the world and caught up in all its pretentious glamour, but to be living for the true master until Christ comes. All faithful servants know full well that the master is going to return (expectant); therefore, the servants need to be busy working for their master.

Refer to Luke 19:12-15, which is the account of the nobleman going into a far country (for a long time) to receive for himself a kingdom; however, the citizens of that country *would not have this man to reign over them.* This story depicts a rejection of Christ in the hearts of the people, and the Lord is warning His servants to "guard their hearts" by watching, because the nobleman will indeed return.

Watchfulness is about the servants living in such a way that they are doing what the master expects of them, regardless how long the master is away. Christ is not teaching about an imminent return, but an **expectant** return, because an accounting that must be given by those servants. Let's look at a perfect example of this in context of the rapture topic in 1 Thessalonians 5.

> But ye, brethren, are not in darkness, that **that day should overtake you as a thief.** Ye are all the **children of light**, and the children of the day: we are **not of the night,** nor of darkness. Therefore **let us not sleep**, as do others; but **let us watch and be sober.** For **they that sleep sleep** in the night; and **they that be drunken** are drunken in the **night.** But **let us, who are of the day, be sober**, putting on the breastplate of faith and love; and for an helmet, the **hope of salvation.** (1 Thess. 5:4-8)

These verses are the same as those taught by Jesus in the Olivet Discourse, to be watchful is to guard your heart and life against the unscrupulous pleasures of this life. First Thessalonians is talking about the night versus the day; the people of the night are those who sleep and are drunk, which depicts people who are only concerned with temporal things-unsaved. Those who are of the day are sober and watchful, depicting those who think about eternal things-saved. A drunken person depicts someone with no sense of direction and discernment; exposing the unspiritual nature of those who are not truly "born again."

The hope of salvation is based on a past decision that consistently shows resolution to follow the nobleman-Christ. As a believer, one will have a steadfast hope or assurance without wavering that Christ is coming back.

Those who profess a belief, but not truly born again, will end up like the five foolish virgins in Matthew 25 who had no oil in their lamps. These five virgins had knowledge of the bridegroom's return; however, they were not "watching" what was happening to the lamps, which pictures they were empty inside. The emphasis in the parable is to watch within your life, not necessarily watching for the Lord's immediate return. The foolish people will be both religious and non-religious; concluding, the Holy Spirit will not be indwelling them.

Watchfulness isn't teaching to be ready for an "any moment" appearance of Christ, but a guarding of something you possess - eternal salvation. Why? Because a genuine Christian knows the value of eternity compared to this life. For the lost, the rejection of God will result in the great "falling away" (2 Thessalonians 2:3), exposing the true nature of their heart. An example of the passages below demonstrates how pretribulation teachers distort a verse in their pursuit to teach imminence.

1: Forasmuch then as Christ hath suffered for us in the flesh, arm yourselves likewise with the same mind: for he that hath suffered in the flesh hath ceased from sin;

2: That he no longer should live the rest of his time in the flesh to the lusts of men, but to the will of God.

3: For the time past of our life may suffice us to have wrought the will of the Gentiles, **when we walked in lasciviousness, lusts, excess of wine, revellings, banquetings, and abominable idolatries:**

4: Wherein **they think it strange that ye run not with them to the same excess of riot,** speaking evil of you:

5: **Who shall give account to him** that is ready to judge the quick and the dead.

6: For for this cause was the gospel preached also to them that are dead, that they might be judged according to men in the flesh, but live according to God in the spirit.

7: But **the end of all things is at hand**: be ye therefore sober, and watch unto prayer. (1Pet. 4:1-7)

To separate the statement in verse 7 *the end of all things is at hand* (as though this is speaking of imminence) from the context of the other verses is an inaccurate teaching. These verses are teaching the following: in verses (1-2)

Christ ceased to live this life in the flesh; (3-4) we are now believers, but in the past, we walked as evil men, and evil men now judge us as strange; (5-6) however, there will be a judgment in which all men (living and dead) are accountable; (7) there is an end coming, and we as believers need to be living in this truth. Nowhere in this passage is this teaching that Christ's return is imminent.

We see in the news quite often how the world today cries for peace and safety (physical and monetary security); and as Christians, our "conversation" should be in "heaven" because this is what a Christian seeks (Mt. 6:33).

> But seek ye first the kingdom of God, and his righteousness; and
> all these things shall be added unto you.

How do we as Christians seek the kingdom of heaven first? If you look at the context of Christ's statement, we can get a glimpse into the meaning from the previous verses 21-25.

> 21: For where your treasure is, there will your heart be also.
> 22: The light of the body is the eye: if therefore thine eye be single,
> thy whole body shall be full of light.
> 23: But if thine eye be evil, thy whole body shall be full of
> darkness. If therefore the light that is in thee be darkness,
> how great is that darkness!
> 24: No man can serve two masters: for either he will hate the one,
> and love the other; or else he will hold to the one, and despise
> the other. Ye cannot serve God and mammon.
> 25: Therefore I say unto you, Take no thought for your life, what
> ye shall eat, or what ye shall drink; nor yet for your body, what
> ye shall put on. Is not the life more than meat, and the body
> than raiment?

How do we watch for Christ? As Christians, we are to keep our eye single (focused on what is right and true). This represents the Christian's perspective of life, that we seek (full hearted desire) the kingdom of God. This is the true nature (spiritual) of watching for the return of Christ. I would like to add one more thought about this passage, particularly verse 24 where it states, *for either he will HATE the one and LOVE the other.* This will be magnified during the great tribulation when the true test is given as to what a person sincerely holds dear in his or her life (Matt. 24:9-10). The darkness represented in this verse is the same as what Paul refers to in 1 Thessalonians 5: 4-8.

> 11: And that, **knowing the time, that now it is high time to awake out of sleep**: for **now is our salvation nearer than when we believed.**
> 12: The night is far spent, **the day is at hand**: let us therefore **cast off the works of darkness,** and let us put on the armour of light.
> 13: Let us **walk honestly, as in the day**; not in rioting and drunkenness, not in chambering and wantonness, not in strife and envying.
> 14: But put ye on the Lord Jesus Christ, and **make not provision for the flesh, to fulfill the lusts thereof.** (Rom. 13:11-14)

Like Peter in his epistle, Paul here warns the Christians at Rome to walk as honest Christians and *not to make provision for the flesh, to fulfill the lust* (vv. 13-14). We have the same warning as with Paul's letter to the Thessalonians. Note also, there is no mention of the return of Christ in these passages. The salvation referenced is speaking of a personal commitment to put on the armor of light and to cast off the darkness. Here is Paul's warning to the Philippians.

> 17: Brethren, be followers together of me, and mark them which walk so as ye have us for an ensample.
> 18: **(For many walk,** of whom I have told you often, and now tell you even weeping, that **they are the enemies of the cross of Christ:**
> 19: Whose **end is destruction, whose God is their belly,** and whose glory is in their shame, **who mind earthly things**.)
> 20: For **our conversation is in heaven**; from whence **also we look for the Saviour,** the Lord Jesus Christ:
> 21: **Who shall change our vile body,** that it may be fashioned like unto his glorious body, according to the working whereby **he is able even to subdue all things** unto himself.

The same point is made here: the saved are to live a different life than the lost people of this world. The phrase, *our conversation is in heaven* gives the same connotation that the lifestyles of both groups are very much in contrast to each other. Also, the phrase *we look for the Savior* is the natural statement that reflects that our conversation (testimony) is more concerned about eternal (heavenly) things than earthy. As I noted previously in Hebrews 11:10, the Bible records that Abraham *looked for a city whose builder and maker is God.* Abraham was not looking for a literal city of God, but spiritually indicated that Abraham's heart was directed where God would lead him.

There is nothing "imminent" about the return of Christ within these verses, only expectant. Paul concludes this passage by stating that Christ is able to- *subdue all things.* This should be the ultimate desire of all Christians who are waiting to live within the kingdom of God. As Christians, we pray the Lord's Prayer in Matthew 6:10 that our desire for this world to be like the kingdom of God.

> 5: That in everything ye are enriched by him, in all utterance, and in all knowledge;
>
> 6: Even as the **testimony of Christ was confirmed in you:**
>
> 7: So that **ye come behind in no gift; waiting for the coming of our Lord Jesus Christ:**
>
> 8: **Who shall also confirm you unto the end, that ye may be blameless in the day of our Lord Jesus Christ.**
>
> 9: God is faithful, by whom ye were called unto the fellowship of his Son Jesus Christ our Lord.
>
> 10: Now I beseech you, brethren, by the name of our Lord Jesus Christ, that ye all speak the same thing, and that there be no divisions among you; but that ye be perfectly joined together in the same mind and in the same judgment. (1 Cor. 1:5-10)

Paul's mention of the return of the Lord is reflective of their gift the believer receives from the Lord (v.7). The context of 1 Corinthians 1 is that there are divisions (unspiritual) within the church (v.9), and they were to work in unison by exercising their gifts. Their confirmation would come at the end (coming of Christ), which will be at the "day of Christ" when the rapture takes place (more on this later).

Paul reminds these professing believers by warning them in 1 Corinthians 10:6-8 how that Israel had just passed through the Red Sea, followed by Moses when he went up to the mount to meet with God. However, after a time, the people revolted against Aaron- thinking Moses would not return.

The story recalls how the people made a false idol, and began to commit fornication and rebelling against God. However, when Moses did return, the people were met with God's judgment and twenty-three thousand people died. The warning here is paralleled to the Lord coming back; as God's people, we need to guard our hearts from turning against God that we may be blameless in the final judgment.

> 7: **Be patient** therefore, brethren, **unto the coming of the Lord.** Behold, the husbandman **waiteth for the precious fruit** of the earth, and hath **long patience** for it, until he receive the early and latter rain.
>
> 8: Be ye also **patient**; stablish your hearts: **for the coming of the Lord draweth nigh.**
>
> 9: Grudge not one against another, brethren, lest ye be condemned: behold, **the judge standeth before the door.**
>
> 10: Take, my brethren, the prophets, who have spoken in the name of the Lord, for an **example of suffering affliction, and of patience.**
>
> 11: Behold, we count them happy which **endure. Ye have heard of the patience of Job,** and have seen the end of the Lord; that the Lord is very pitiful, and of tender mercy. (James 5:7-11)

God requires His people to have patience in order to reap the benefits. Patience is a virtue that is not passive, but is active and demands action on our part. The action however is that we as Christians maintain our faith in the one who will ultimately deliver us, which is Christ Jesus. Portrayed in this portion of Scripture is patience which is established over a long period of time, *"long patience"* (v.5). Just as Job was allowed to suffer the wrath of Satan by the sovereign hand of God, we are to have patience during our afflictions and trials. We are to trust God even if it seems like our oppressors are getting away with injustices. Why are we to wait: because the judge is coming from heaven to exact retribution on those who are troubling us.

> But after thy hardness and impenitent heart treasurest up unto thyself wrath against the day of wrath and revelation of the righteous judgment of God; **Who will render to every man according to his deeds:** To them who by **patient continuance**

in well doing seek for glory and honour and immortality, eternal
life: (Rom. 2:5-7)

This is the consistent theme by Paul that he exudes in his writings.
These believers must live for, and trust in God, the righteous judge who will
condemn the lost and justify the righteous. And this patient continuance is
over the long haul, not for a short period of time.

Luke 21:36

Watch ye therefore, and pray always, that ye may be accounted
worthy to escape all these things that shall come to pass, and to
stand before the Son of man.

Luke 21 is Luke's account of the Olivet Discourse in Matthew 24, and
verse 36 is cited by pretribulationist who attempt to prove the church will
be absent during the tribulation. They say, how can Christians "escape" the
things that are to come to pass if we are going through the tribulation? Like
all Scriptures, we need to discern what subject is being taught and how it
relates in the context. If you go back to verse 34, Christ warns His followers
to *take heed* with their lives and not to be overtaken by sinful passions. Again,
the emphasis is placed on the professing Christian to guard their life. Verse 34
ties in perfectly with verse 36 as it states *accounted to be worthy* as the emphasis.
"Worthy" is the operative word which necessitates action on the believer's
part to be faithful. This is speaking of self-responsibility on a person's part
on how they conduct themselves.

Added to the discussion, I would like to point out in verse 31 Jesus states:
when ye see these things come to pass, know ye that the kingdom of God is nigh at hand.
Jesus statement here emphasizes that believers living at this time would "see
these things come to pass" (be fulfilled). I ask my pretrib brethren: How
can the escape in verse 36 be from the tribulation, when Jesus told the same
people in verse 31 they would witness the events of the tribulation? What
Christ is teaching in verse 36 is not an escape from the events in the final
week, but to guard your heart from departing God so they would not be
condemned and be judged by His coming wrath. This is the consistent theme
with all other verses speaking about Christ's return.

One last point on this section of verses. Luke 21:28:

> And when **these things begin to come to pass, then look up**,
> and lift up your heads; for your redemption draweth nigh.

As Christ laid out the sequence of events in Luke 21, He said in verse 28, "then look up," which comes after they witness the previous events.

Why Imminence?

Now the question still remains: Why did Paul and other writers of the New Testament, by the inspiration of the Holy Spirit, use words that would seem to describe a "very near" return of Christ? It is not my intention to belabor this point, but I believe it is of utmost importance.

Looking at the overall theme of the Bible, from the beginning of the fall of man in the garden, man has conflicted with God. God in His holiness and perfect righteousness has no choice but to condemn mankind. However, the attributes of God are not limited that He cannot redeem humanity; He did so, ultimately through the person of Jesus Christ, the one to whom the topic of the rapture is centered around.

It is my firm belief that God intends for us to compare our short lifetime with eternity. At the beginning, up to the flood, mankind was allowed to live for hundreds of years. As I noted in the Old Testament overview, before the flood man became very wicked and one of the judgments that followed was that man's individual lifetime would be shortened. Psalms 90:10 states that man's years are threescore and ten (70), and if he was fortunate he could live to be fourscore (80). I believe God is allowing man to contemplate his own limited lifespan. The emphasis of many Bible verses used to teach the coming of Christ is to show man should focus on eternity than this temporal life.

> For he saith, I have heard thee in a time accepted, and in **the day of salvation** have I succoured thee: **behold, now is the accepted time**; behold, **now is the day of salvation**. (2 Cor. 6:2)

Many pretribulation teachers will use this verse in the context of the rapture, proclaiming that Christ's return is imminent. Are we to believe when Paul wrote this he was inferring that every (single) day Christ could come? No, he was teaching in light of eternity, that a person had better be saved, so when that day of reckoning does occur, they will be accepted of the Lord. James taught that a person's life was like a *vapor that appears for a short time then vanishes away* (James 4:14). Paul's statement in 1 Corinthians 5:30, *why stand ye in jeopardy every hour*; was not teaching that Christ could come back that vey hour. Paul was teaching that those who opposed the resurrection account of Jesus were in jeopardy of God's judgment. Compare 1 Corinthians 5:30 to Jesus's account of the rich man in Luke 12:16-21, whose life was completely built around himself. Christ calls this man a "fool" (v.20) because he died unexpectedly and his soul would be required (in judgment) "that very night." This man was not prepared to meet his maker, and he would suffer the immeasurable consequences for his attitude about the true meaning of life, which apparently was self-served.

The Pretrib Dilemma- Matthew 24:50-51

We will look at this portion of Scripture in Matthew 24 when we get to chapter thirteen; however, I would like to address two verses considering our study on watchfulness.

> The lord of that servant shall come in a **day when he looketh not for him, and in a hour he is not aware of,** And shall cut him asunder, and appoint him his portion with the hypocrites: there shall be weeping and gnashing of teeth.

If we were to interpret these verses according to the pretrib doctrine; then we would have to conclude that because this servant was not looking for the imminent return of his lord, he was found guilty and condemned. The pretrib teachers are forced to say that "anyone," pretrib believers included, will be left behind on the day of the rapture if they are doing something other than expecting Christ to come that very day and hour. According to pretribulation teaching, if a husband and a wife, both Christian, are having a major argument for whatever reason, will miss the rapture if it happens that very hour they are arguing. Pretrib teaching cannot deny this if this is how they interpret this passage that supposedly teach an imminent rapture. On the other hand, they have to interpret this passage, and "all others," accordingly, that there needs to be a watchfulness on the servant's part how they are conducting their life in light of the events, *an hour he is not aware* (v.50). For a person to be aware, is to be expecting (an unwavering heart belief) that Christ will return when events (hardship and tribulation) are taking place.

An Illustration from a Pretrib Perspective

Allow me to illustrate a thought that pretribulationist use quite often. As noted by their use of the word, watchfulness, based on the belief that if you do not allow an "any moment" rapture, then this would produce unfaithfulness in the life of a believer. You know, like the son, whose father who was leaving on Monday for an out of town trip, said to his son, "no playing ball until you cut the grass today!" The son says to himself, "I have all week to do this, because I know my father won't be home until Saturday." Yet, to the son's surprise, the Father returned home early only to find the grass was not cut. See, pretribulationist will say, any teaching other than a pretrib rapture produces disloyalty. I have heard numerous illustrations on this. But I have never heard their reasoning based on my next point, which goes like this.

Let me take this illustration a step further, again using the pretrib perspective of an any-moment and unannounced return. According to the pretribulationism, a husband should "never" tell his wife the time of his arrival from his business trip. If he does, the wife will not be faithful to her marriage vows because she knows how long he will be gone. Another way to say this; the only way for her to be faithful to him is for the husband to never tell her when he will arrive; making his return imminent. How about if the wife stays faithful simply for the reason she loves him, regardless of the time of his unknown arrival! As Christians, I say how about we stay faithful to Christ, not based on him coming back sudden and unexpected, but because we love him. If pretrib teachers want to reason the story of the son cutting grass, then they must agree to the story about the wife as well. Another way to put this; how sad it's been for so many men who have gone off to war, only have their wife or fiancé write him to say they have found another man. They did not stay faithful because their husband or fiancé was gone away and they become impatient and found someone else.

Final Thought

I would like to say God was not misleading the New Testament writers into thinking that Christ was coming back at any day, any more than he would mislead Abraham into thinking that Sarah was going to give birth to their son Isaac, soon following His announcement to Abraham; which actually didn't occur until twenty-five years later. God waited until the proper time, unfortunately for Abraham, Sarah, grew inpatient and persuaded Abraham to go into her handmaid, Hagar. Through this event, Ishmael was born and a conflict was birthed that is still ongoing today. Could this be a type of warning to us today, not to think that God will establish His kingdom "any day now?"

Is it coincidental that many passages in the Bible related to the return of the Lord, along with the establishment of His kingdom, are in the same context for Christians to be aware and watchful? This watchfulness can be used in one of two ways. One, watchfulness could be a general description for all Christians to maintain their testimony and witness. Two, it could be a description to a specific generation of Christians living at this particular-time in history that will be participants of the final seven-years of man's history. Given the special circumstances of this time-period in which intense persecution will be taking place, along with a worldwide rejection of God, these people need to maintain faithfulness to Christ. There will be no riding the fence during this time that's for sure.

We will see in 1 & 2 Thessalonians in our study how it will become apparent that when the thief comes the people will be saying *peace and safety*. Christians are not to feel safe in this world when it comes from the humanistic reasoning. This world has only known rebellion since the fall of man, and, unfortunately, mankind has forgotten their Creator. Now mankind believes they are running the show; and it's as if God is saying "go ahead and see what happens!"

In closing, we saw that pretribulation teachers have pulled out of context a few verses that seem to teach an "any moment" rapture; yet, they must bypass multiple verses that teach certain events will transpire first. And this includes taking out of context the true meaning of "watchfulness." The "expectant" return of Christ, even when signs are given, should not lessen the importance of Christ's return in a Christian's life. We expect all things to be fulfilled pertaining to God's plan. What cannot be denied is that almost two-thousand years has elapsed since the ascension of Christ into heaven. We need not to grow impatient, even though, as Romans 8:22 states, *we know that the whole creation groaneth and travaileth in pain until now.*

CHAPTER ELEVEN

THE DAY OF THE LORD

As we move through our study, we have already seen multiple discrepancies within the pretribulation rapture theory (i.e. dispensationalism, signs, imminence, glorious appearing, the secret rapture, and the meaning of watchful). In this chapter, we will look at the teaching in the Bible on the theme "day of the Lord." I want to bring to your attention the basic premise that this specific event is a day designated to destruction upon "lost people." The day of the Lord is when God supernaturally intervenes into the affairs of man. I will also prove that the day of the Lord will be an event "inside" the final seven-year period, and not in-and-of-itself the tribulation as prescribed by pretribulationist. This is paramount when you understand the timing and the purpose of the day of the Lord.

We are currently living in what the Bible terms "man's day" in contrast to "God's day." God is now allowing man to rule and reign even though God is sovereign (in control). However, there is a day coming in which God will "supernaturally" intervene directly in man's affairs.

Jesus spoke often in the gospels that he came to establish His kingdom. In the interim, until Christ returns to set up His millennial kingdom, the kingdom He talked about is spiritual in its makeup. When Pilot asked Jesus if he were a king in John 18:33, Jesus responded in verse 36: *My kingdom is not of this world: if my kingdom were of this world, then would my servants fight.* As Christians, it is not our responsibility to usher in the kingdom of God (kingdom now theology). But if you are a born-again Christian you will want to be living for Christ that glorifies Him and the Father contrary to this world's philosophies. We know with absolute truth Christ is coming back to establish the kingdom.

When the Lord revealed the mystery of the rapture to Paul in 1 Corinthians 15, he was revealing for the first time there would be people alive at a particular time in history who would not see death, which will occur at Christ's second coming. However, the day of the Lord was never a mystery, for it was talked about numerous times throughout the Old Testament.

> For **the day of the LORD** of hosts shall be upon every one that is **proud and lofty**, and upon every one that is lifted up; and he shall be brought low: (Isa. 2:12)

> Howl ye; for **the day of the LORD is at hand;** it shall come as **a destruction from the Almighty**. Therefore shall all hands be faint, and every man's heart shall melt: And they shall be afraid: pangs and sorrows shall take hold of them; they shall be in pain as a woman that travaileth: they shall be amazed one at another; their faces shall be as flames. Behold, **the day of the LORD cometh, cruel both with wrath and fierce anger,** to lay the land desolate: and he **shall destroy the sinners** thereof out of it. (Isa. 13:6-9)

> Sanctify ye a fast, call a solemn assembly, gather the elders and all the inhabitants of the land into the house of the LORD your God, and cry unto the LORD. Alas for the day! **for the day of the LORD is at hand,** and as **a destruction from the Almighty** shall it come. (Joel 1: 14-15)

The book of Joel was written around the ninth Century BC, uses the phrase "at hand" in conjunction to God's final judgment that will take place at the end of the world. In the New Testament, when verses speak of nearness as we have seen, they are viewed from God's eternal perspective.

> Blow ye the trumpet in Zion, and sound an alarm in my holy mountain: let all the inhabitants of the land tremble: for **the day of the LORD** cometh, for it is **nigh at hand**; A day of darkness and of gloominess, a day of clouds and of thick darkness, as the morning spread upon the mountains: a great people and a strong; there hath not been **ever the like**, neither shall be **any more after it, even to the years of many generations.** (Joel 2:1-2)

This is a perfect example where the Lord says *at hand* then qualifies it by saying, "after many generations." Imminence is implied; however, prophetically, it is future. Joel also makes the statement that the day of the

Lord is unlike any other day and nothing will match its intensity. In other words, this is not a general judgment. Here are some more Old Testament writers talking about the day of the Lord.

> Woe unto you that desire **the day of the LORD**! to what end is it for you? **the day of the LORD is darkness**, and not light. As if a man did flee from a lion, and a bear met him; or went into the house, and leaned his hand on the wall, and a serpent bit him. Shall not **the day of the LORD be darkness**, and not light? even very dark, and no brightness in it? (Amos 5:18-20)

> For **the day of the LORD is near upon all the heathen**: as thou hast done, it shall be done unto thee: thy reward shall return upon thine own head. For as ye have drunk upon my holy mountain, so shall all **the heathen** drink continually, yea, they shall drink, and they shall swallow down, and they shall be as though they had not been. (Obadiah 15-16)

> **The great day of the LORD is near**, it **is near**, and hasteth greatly, even the voice of **the day of the LORD:** the mighty man shall cry there bitterly. **That day is a day of wrath, a day of trouble and distress, a day of wasteness and desolation, a day of darkness and gloominess, a day of clouds and thick darkness, A day of the trumpet** and alarm against the fenced cities, and against the high towers. And I will bring **distress upon men,** that they shall **walk like blind men, because they have sinned against the LORD**: and their blood shall be poured out as dust, and their flesh as the dung. (Zeph. 1:14-17)

Here are a few interpretations by the pretribulation teachers about the day of the Lord being God's supernatural divine judgment. Then I will point out the "misuse" of their overall teaching on the day of the Lord, especially as it relates to the tribulation.

> Here is the first occurrence of Joel's theme (ch.1:15). The basic meaning of the term refers to any time when **God intervenes in history, usually in judgment**.[89] (bold letters mine)
>
> Tim LaHaye

We will see that this is not just "any time" when God intervenes in history, but a very special time in the future. And this is not something that is "usually in judgment," but a very **specific kind** of judgment.

The Scope of the "Day of the Lord"

> While Joel's prophecy increases in intensity and scope, the idiomatic (hyperbolic) language he uses of the "day of the Lord" is applicable **to any day of divine intervention** that has these elements, but ideally to that **future day** which completely fulfills and concludes the literal realities behind his figures.[90] (bold letters mine)
>
> Randall Price

The Day of the Lord in the Old Testament

> According to the Bible, **the day of the Lord is a time when God deals in direct judgment of the world in contrast to a time of grace when he does not.** There were frequent days of the Lord in the Old Testament when God dealt with Israel because of their straying and would bring in an invader or would introduce drought or famine or some other catastrophe.[91]
> (bold letters mine)
>
> John Walvoord

If you were to traverse through the writings of the pretribulation authors, you will see they (correctly) realize the day of the Lord is a time of divine judgment on earth, as noted by Price and Walvoord. However, Walvoord, like others, mistakenly adds that the day of the Lord was also a time of judgment in the Old Testament upon Israel. There were God's judgments throughout the Old Testament, but when the description of the day of the Lord is used, it speaks of a future time upon the lost. Only in Joel chapter 1 is the day of the Lord mentioned outside the context of a future judgment. However, even in Joel 1, it says that the day of the Lord is "at hand," which implies it has not occurred yet.

The necessity of this teaching by pretrib goes back to their pretribulational-dispensational teaching. If the tribulation is for Israel in the future, as pretribulation teaching states, then they must insert into their teaching that

Israel's judgments in the Old Testament were the day of the Lord as well. They must be consistent with their theory, or else it falls apart. The day of the Lord is always regarded as a future time. Look up all the passages where God brought judgment upon the earth (e.g. the flood, the plagues upon Pharaoh and Egypt, the walls of Jericho, etc.), and none of these catastrophic events are referenced specifically as the day of the Lord.

Pretrib teaching is correct that the church is not appointed unto wrath (1 Thess. 5:9); however, Israel is God's people as well and they are not appointed unto wrath either. God's anger was kindled many times with Israel and they were judged for their disobedience; however, they will not face the final judgment on this world as defined by the day of the Lord. Are not New Testament believers subject to God's discipline as well (Hebrews 12:5-7)?

The Tribulation and God's Wrath

We are now entering the heart of the rapture debate. I will show that pretribulational thinking is wrong to assume that **all** the 70th week is the wrath of God.

Since pretribulation teachers understand the day of the Lord is strictly God's wrath upon the lost, and believers are exempt from this wrath; they are now forced to make the entire 70th week God's wrath.

Here is pretribulationist John Hagee.

> First, the very nature of the Tribulation precludes the church from suffering any of it. **The Tribulation is a horrendous time of wrath,** judgment, indignation, darkness, destruction and death—and it leads to doomsday. Paul wrote, "There is therefore now no condemnation [judgment] to those who are in Christ Jesus (Rom. 8:1).[92]

In LaHaye's book "Rapture Under Attack" he cites fourteen reasons for the pretribulation rapture as the correct position on the rapture.

> 6.) *It is the only view that takes God at His Word and claims His promises literally to save us out of the wrath to come.*
> As the New King James Version phrases it, "I also will keep you from the hour of trial which shall come upon the whole world" (Revelation 3:10). See also 1 Thessalonians 1:10; 5:9; Romans 5:9.

The Tribulation which our Lord described in Matthew 24 is that period of trial.[93]

First, if LaHaye understands the prewrath positions, he should know prewrath "literally" believe we are exempt from God's wrath. He may disagree with our position, but he is incorrect as to what we believe. Second, the wrath to come is not the same typical judgment spoken of throughout the Old Testament. In fact, it says in 1 Peter 4:17 *that judgment must begin at the house of God, if it first begins at us, what shall the end be of them who do not obey the gospel of God?* Neither the church nor Israel is the recipient of God's future wrath, however, we are not immune to His discipline. It says in Hebrews 13 that the children of God are subject to God's discipline who need correcting for the wrong choices they make. Paul even taught in 1 Corinthians 11 that believers died prematurely because of the sin in their lives. Lastly, LaHaye's remark about Revelation 3:10 will be addressed in a later chapter.

Here is a portion of LaHaye's commentary on the day of the Lord.

> Here, 'the day of the Lord' specifically refers to an event that is now in the **past, as the context indicates**. The other instances in Joel refer to the future time often known as the **Tribulation.**[94] (bold letters mine)

As I have already stated, pretribulation teachers are required to make the day of the Lord a past event to justify their dispensational position.

> **2:1-11** "Having introduced a **past** "day of the lord" judgment in chapter 1, Joel's use of the term in this passage refers to the future time **often called "the seven-year Tribulation."**[95] (bold letters mine)
>
> Tim LaHaye

We have here the perfect example of pretribulation teaching manipulating the Scriptures. Joel is not referring to a seven-year tribulation, but to the day of the Lord. LaHaye makes the "seven-year tribulation" "the day of the Lord," which is an incorrect assessment.

> The judgment of the "day of the Lord" is **at hand**. This will be
> a universal judgment upon all human government. (Cf. Joel and
> 2 Thess. 1:7-2:12).[96]
>
> Tim LaHaye

LaHaye correctly acknowledges that the day of the Lord is the universal judgment of God, and a judgment upon "all" human governments, which will occur in the future even though it says "at hand."

Here are more examples of the pretribulation teachers saying the 70th is equated to the day of the Lord without biblical merit.

> C. **The scope of the seventh week**. "There can be no question
> that this period will see the wrath of God poured out on the
> whole earth. Revelation 3:10; Isaiah 34:2; 24:1; 4-5, 16-17, 18-21,
> and many other passages make this very clear. And yet, while the
> whole earth is in view, this period is particularly in relation to
> Israel. Jeremiah 30:7, which calls this period "the time of Jacob's
> trouble", makes this certain. The events of the **seventieth week
> are events of the "day of the Lord" or "Day of Jehovah."**[97]
>
> Dwight Pentecost

Dwight Pentecost, in his 670-page book "Things to Come," makes the statement that the day of the Lord (70th week) without citing one Bible verse to back up his theory. He falls in line with other pretrib teachers assuming the final 70th week is the day of the Lord.

Day of the Lord:

> This "day" is one of the major themes of Bible prophecy. When it
> occurs, it involves **God" direct intervention in human affairs**
> and human history. The phrase "the day of the Lord" is **one
> of numerous terms and phrase** used throughout the Bible to
> refer to both a time of judgment **(such as the tribulation)** and
> a time of blessing (such as the millennium). In other words, the
> day of the Lord will literally be a day or period of time in which
> Jesus will impose His presence or rule, whether in judgment
> **(the tribulation)** or in glorious display (the millennium). In the
> current state of affairs, the Lord is not exerting His rule in a

• 162 •

visible way. Of course, He could, if He were pleased to do so, but His plans calls for current time to be a temporary period in which He lets humanity go its own way (Romans 1:24-32).

We normally associate the day of the Lord with **the future seven-year tribulation** (see, for example, Zephaniah 1:14-15)[98] (bold letters mine)

Thomas Ice and Timothy Demy

Only through pretrib interpretation do they "associate" tribulation with the day of the Lord; it is certainly not spelled out in Scripture. Again, they are correct to say this day is God's intervention- it will be supernatural- however, to say that this phrase speaks of judgment "such as the tribulation" is inserting a pretrib interpretation. We will see that the great tribulation which occurs at the mid-point of the 70th week is not a time of judgment on the lost, but strictly persecution upon believers. Judgment is when someone receives correction, and persecution is when someone causes affliction, which Walvoord previously said.

Now read the passage that Ice and Demy cited in Zephaniah 1:14-15 and see if it refers to the seven-year tribulation:

The **great day of the LORD** is near, it is near, and hasteth greatly, even the voice of the day of the LORD: the mighty man shall cry there bitterly. That **day is a day of wrath**, a day of trouble and distress, a day of wasteness and desolation, a day of darkness and gloominess, a day of clouds and thick darkness,

This day of the Lord says nothing about a seven-year tribulation. The pretrib theory is nothing more than circular reasoning, which goes like this:

1. We believe the rapture of the church is pretribulational, because we are not subject to God's wrath.
2. Therefore, we believe the seven-year tribulation is God's wrath.
3. And since the day of the Lord is called God's wrath in the Old Testament.
4. Therefore, the day of the Lord must be the seven-year tribulation.

Here is a statement by pretribulationist Charles Ryrie which validates my line of reasoning used by pretrib teaching.

> Joel 2:1-11
> The locust army is regarded as a foretaste of an invading army in the **day of the Lord**; i.e. in the **tribulation period**.[99] (bold letters mine)
>
> Charles Ryrie

Charles Ryrie, without biblical support, compares the day of the Lord to the tribulation. The locust army he is referring to is mentioned in chapter 1:4, which has nothing to do with the day of the Lord mentioned in chapter two or the future tribulation.

Tommy Ice and Timothy Demy teach the same lesson from the use of Joel's teaching about the day of the Lord in Joel.

> The whole book of Joel is about the "day of the Lord" which is a synonym for "the tribulation.[100]

The synonym used here is only created by the pretrib teachers based on their subjective reasoning, the day of the Lord is an actual event apart from the tribulation period, and this would be the objective interpretation. Here is John Walvoord espousing pretrib doctrine in the rapture subject.

> THE PROPHECY IN JOEL
> The theme of the Book of Joel is the Day of the Lord (Yahweh), an expression found often in the Old Testament and also in the New Testament. The Day of the Lord refers to any period of time in which God deals directly with the human situation either in judgment or in mercy. The expression may refer to a specific day or to an extended period of time as in the **Day of the Lord eschatologically which stretches from the Rapture of the Church** to the end of the millennial kingdom (1 Thess. 5:1-9; 2 Peter 3:10-13).[101] (bold letters mine)

Walvoord is correct by saying the day of the Lord begins with the rapture of the church. He is wrong to state that the day of the Lord goes through the millennium. The day of the Lord (judgment) is what ushers in the millennium, but is not the millennium itself.

Here is another quote by John Walvoord describing the difference between the tribulation and the wrath of God.

> The tribulation is a time of wrath of Satan (Rev. 12:6), which is vented on believers of that time; whereas the wrath of God is vented on unbelievers,[102]

Correct! Therefore, as believers we are subject to Satan's wrath (i.e. the great tribulation), however, we will escape God's wrath (i.e. Day of the Lord) via the rapture.

In their pamphlet "The Tribulation" by Tommy Ice and Timothy Demy, they ask the question:

> **Why is the tribulation necessary?**
>
> God's basic purpose for the tribulation is that it be a time of judgment, while at the same time holding forth the grace of the gospel, which will precede Christ's glorious 1000- year reign in Jerusalem from David's throne.

As I pointed out already, some pretribulation teachers say that Israel will suffer God's wrath during the 70th week. Here is another statement by Thomas Ice with regard to the 70th week in the book of Daniel.

> **Daniel views the entire seventieth week as a time of wrath** (cf. Dan. 12:7). The exilic condition he suffers is understood as a punishment for transgression, sin and iniquity (Dan 9:24b-c), and this condition will continue as a **decree of divine wrath against Israel until the end**, when everlasting righteousness and the messianic consecration of the temple can take place (v.24d-f). The resolution of Daniel's concerns for his city and people (Dan. 9:2,24a) will not be realized until after the seventieth week has concluded and its events of deception and desecration have passed (Dan.9:27; 12:1).[103] (bold letters mine)

If the 70th week is a decree of "divine wrath" on Israel, was the exilic condition divine wrath as well? If Israel is God's people how can they be appointed unto wrath and the church "not" be appointed unto wrath? (1 Thessalonians 5:9). What about the holocaust: was it God's decree of "divine wrath" on Israel during Hitler's reign of terror in WWII? Maybe we as a nation should not have intervened in God's judgment on them during the holocaust while they were being punished? Of course, I am being sarcastic!

In Isaiah 26 in the context of the 70th week we peer into time regarding what is taking place.

> Thy dead men shall live, together with my dead body shall they arise. Awake and sing, ye that dwell in dust: for thy dew is as the dew of herbs, and the earth shall cast out the dead. Come, **my people, enter thou into thy chambers, and shut thy doors about thee: hide thyself as it were for a little moment, until the indignation be overpast.** For, behold, the LORD cometh out of his place **to punish the inhabitants of the earth for their iniquity**: the earth also shall disclose her blood, and shall no more cover **her slain**. (Isa. 26:19-21)

First, if the rapture is "before" the 70th week, then how can Israel suffer God's wrath if she is protected when told to come and hide from the indignation? Clearly, Israel is "not" suffering God's wrath at this time.

Second, if these verses are teaching a posttribulational rapture at the "end" of the 70th week, then why would God's people, Israel, be protected by the same God that punished them for seven-years of His wrath? Also, the 70th week would be over at this time, so why even come into the chambers and hide for "a little moment?" And one more important note needs to be made, this verse says "my people" (God's people) are to go and hide, "then" the Lord will come out to punish the earth for their iniquity. This verse teaches that God's punishment against those on the earth takes place after His people hide.

The indignation mentioned in verse 20 is clarified in verse 21, because the Lord refers to the earth disclosing her blood by those who are slain. The indignation must be God's retribution on the world for the offenses they committed against believers. This is the exact same reference to the fifth seal in Revelation 6 when those seen under the altar in heaven asking God: "when" would He avenge their blood? God responded that more of their fellow servants would be killed as they were, "then" He would come punish the world.

I believe there will be increasing pressure in the world upon Christianity in general, even before the unfolding seven-year time period. Inside the 70th week it will get worse for Christians, especially leading up to the middle of the 70th week when Antichrist breaks the covenant with Israel, and then he unleashes his full fury during the great tribulation. God will supernaturally protect many in Israel who will flee into the wilderness. Antichrist will attempt to force everyone to receive his mark, where true believers who follow Christ will refuse, and many will be killed. At an appointed time during the great tribulation, God will cut short the persecution by the Antichrist at the opening of the sixth seal. In Revelation 7 God seals the 144,000 (vv.2-3), then we witness the great multitude that come out of great tribulation, which are the church saints (vv.9-14) that are raptured at sixth seal in chapter 6 of Revelation. Starting in chapter 8 of Revelation at the opening of the seventh seal, this initiates the seven trumpet judgments- God's wrath at the day of the Lord. Isaiah 26 is referencing the same event when God will come out of His place (heaven) and punish the world.

We saw the same example in Joel 3:13-16 at the day of the Lord when God will be a hope to His people (rapture of the church) and strength to Israel (protection), until His indignation (wrath) is passed.

Paul taught in 1 Thessalonians 5 how the rapture is associated with the day of the Lord.

> For yourselves know perfectly that the **day of the Lord so cometh as a thief** in the night. For when **they shall say, Peace and safety; then sudden destruction cometh upon them,** as travail upon a woman with child; and they shall not escape. But **ye, brethren**, are not in darkness, **that that day should overtake you as a thief.** Ye are all the **children of light**, and the children of the day: **we are not of the night,** nor of darkness. Therefore let us not sleep, as do others; but let us watch and be sober. For they that sleep sleep in the night; and they that be drunken are drunken in the night. But let us, who are of the day, be sober, putting on the breastplate of faith and love; and for an helmet, **the hope of salvation.** For God hath not appointed us to wrath, but to obtain salvation by our Lord Jesus Christ, (1 Thess. 5:2-9)

First question to my pretrib friends is: where in this context about the rapture and God's wrath does it mention Israel being punished? Second, if this is the rapture "before" the 70th week, how do you reconcile the "sudden destruction" on the world? We see during the great tribulation the world is persecuting believers and Israel? As I said before, there is no sudden destruction at the beginning of the 70th week. Here is what John Walvoord says happens during the first part or three-and-half years of the 70th week.

> Earlier the question was raised as to what time frame chapter 6 (Revelation) and following falls in consideration that the last period preceding the Second Coming is divided into seven years, with the **first half a time of peace** and the **second half a time of persecution**.[104] (bold letters mine)

If there is peace in the first half of the 70th week, then 1 Thessalonians 5 cannot be a reference to the rapture before the 70th week begins. However, there cannot be God's wrath in the first half either, because the world does not cry out about God's wrath until the opening of the sixth seal, which takes place "after" the great tribulation begins. By the way, LaHaye states in his book **Rapture under Attack** that 75% of the world's population is killed in the first half,[105] where Walvoord says there is world peace. Remember, these pretrib teachers get together at the Pretrib Research Center for 3 days each year to defend their doctrine.

As discussed in Daniel's prophecy about the final week (70th), among the six things God will do to accomplish His goal does include a time of judgment on the world to bring in the 1000- year reign. Ice says that the basic purpose of the tribulation is to punish the world; however, when we compare Ice's teaching to the book of Revelation, we see the world is giving honor unto the Antichrist in the middle of the seven-years. So how is the world being punished at this time? Their punishment will not take place until God intervenes during the seven-years, which will occur at the day of the Lord.

Pretribulationist Dr. Arnold Fruchtenbaum, Director of Ariel Ministries, who himself is Jewish, divides God's purpose into three aspects."

To make an end of wickedness and wicked ones.

Isaiah 13:9- Behold, the day of the Lord is coming, cruel, with fury and burning anger, to make the land a desolation: and He will exterminate its sinners from it." (bold letters mine)

Isaiah 24: 19-20- "The earth is broken asunder, the earth is split through, the earth is shaken violently. The earth reels to and fro like a drunkard, and it totters like a shack, for its transgression is heavy upon it, and it will fall, never to rise again."

The **first purpose for the tribulation** is seen to be a punishment in history upon the whole world for its sins against God, in a way similar to that of the global flood in Noah's time (Matthew 24:37-39)[106] (bold letters mine)

In Fruchtenbaum's comparison of the tribulation to the global flood, we will see later, as I have been espousing, this will be the punishment at the day of the Lord and not the tribulation. The punishment of God will not take place until "after" the middle of the seven-years.

Here is a perfect example of this in Revelation 6 at the fifth seal, which is well inside the tribulation.

And when he had opened the fifth seal, I saw under the altar the souls of them that were **slain for the word of God, and for the testimony which they held:** And they cried with a loud voice, saying, **How long, O Lord, holy and true, dost thou not judge and avenge our blood on them that dwell on the earth?** And white robes were given unto every one of them; and it was said unto them, that they should rest yet for a little season, until their fellowservants also and **their brethren, that should be killed as they were,** should be fulfilled. (Rev. 6:9-11)

These people were slain for their testimony of the Lord; this is definitely not God's wrath upon the saved. The pretribulationist will counter and say that these were the ones left behind after the rapture and became saved during this time- which is incorrect. However, my point here is not essentially about the salvation of these people, but what they say at this time. They ask

God: **when** will he pour out His vengeance on those who persecuted them during the great tribulation? This is clearly teaching that the day of the Lord **has not** yet begun. I regress again, the day of the Lord is specifically a time when God punishes the world and the sinners in it. And another surprisingly tidbit of insight about this verse, the Lord's response to those killed is the vengeance of God will **NOT** happen until the remaining martyrs are killed.

Here is pretribulation teacher Renalde Showers, forcing the day of the Lord's wrath as though it's the tribulation period:

The Purposes of God for the Seventieth Week:

The crushing of the kingdom of Satan. From the fall of man to the seventieth week God has been allowing Satan to try every means possible to overthrow the kingdom of God. Although God has been preventing Satan from accomplishing his goal, **He has not begun to execute the sentence of judgment** upon him and his kingdom. Thus, Satan has been having his day. However, once the Antichrist is revealed and Satan begins his ultimate attempt of overthrow, **God finally will begin to close** in upon him to crush both him and his kingdom. Thus, God will **start** to have His day, and the seventieth week will begin a period of time called the day of the Lord (2 Thessalonians 2:1-3)

The seventieth week will be characterized by divine judgment, as God pours out His wrath upon godless people and domain of the earthly province of Satan's kingdom (Zephaniah 1:14-18).[107] (bold letters mine)

I am not sure who is copying who in the pretribulation writings, they all reference the same verses in Zephaniah 1, and say that this is the tribulation period. Moreover, Showers comments that the day of the Lord is a time of progression, getting worse and worse, which the Word of God does not teach. We will see that the day of the Lord will occur as a sudden, unforeseen event (1 Thess. 5:2). Also, if the entire 70th week is divine judgment; how is Satan "having his day" where he is worshipped by the world?

Showers says God has been allowing Satan to have his day up to the 70th week, but will begin to close in on him when the Antichrist is revealed. So, when is Antichrist revealed? Most pretrib believers say it's at the beginning of the 70th week. If this is true, how can God begin to punish Antichrist if he comes in and brings peace and is ultimately worshiped by the world at the midpoint of the 70th week? If pretrib teachers agree that Antichrist is revealed in the middle of the 70th week, which is what I believe, then Showers is admitting that God's wrath will not begin at the start of the 70th week; which destroys the pretrib reasoning for a pretrib rapture solely based on their argument "we are not appointed unto wrath." Showers, like other pretrib teachers, does not make the clear distinction in his statements, certainly when it comes to describing wrath or tribulation.

Tommy Ice and Timothy Demy are correct when they teach in their booklet "The Tribulation" (pages 25-26), that the day of the Lord is compared to the time of Noah and the flood when God poured out His wrath on the world for its sins. This is also what Arnold Fruchtenbaum stated earlier. Furthermore, we need to understand that in Noah's day, God's wrath was sudden, not progressive.

I conclude this chapter by stating that the day of the Lord is a future time of judgment on the world that is in total rebellion toward God. We saw the tribulation period defined by pretribulationism cannot be the wrath of God; no clear Scripture was given. Finally, by their subjective interpretation, pretribulational teachers gave no clear scriptural evidence that the tribulation is identical with the day of the Lord.

CHAPTER TWELVE

THE TIMING OF THE
DAY OF THE LORD

As prewrath believers, we have a consensus with the pretrib teaching that the day of the Lord is the wrath of God upon the lost. We also agree that this will be a special time when God intervenes supernaturally in the affairs of mankind. However, we disagree on the timing of the day of the Lord. Pretribulation teaching says it is the entire seven-years of the 70th week; prewrath teaches it to be a specific time inside the 70th week- so who's right? Personally, for me, when I understood the purpose and timing of the day of the Lord, this was the catalyst that convinced me that the rapture was prewrath.

We will now look at many more day of the Lord passages as they relate to the rapture debate; key passages in the Old Testament that are seen in the New Testament, especially 1 & 2 Thessalonians, Matthew 24, and Revelation.

The Seven Seals

In the book of Revelation chapter 6 it gives the outline of future events as they relate to the 70th week. Pretribulational teaching says that by this chapter the church is absent before the opening of the first seal. Their reasoning is that the seals are the wrath of God, concluding the church must be raptured before this. Prewrath teaches that the seals are not the wrath of God, and the church will still be here on earth during this time. However, there is a specific time **within** the opening of these seals that points to an event clearly teaching a "supernatural intervention" by God himself.

First, we need to look at the seven seals where they are located on the scroll. John recorded in chapter 5:1 *And I saw in the right hand of him that sat on the throne a book written within and on the **backside, sealed with seven seals**.*

What's significant about the location of the seals is that they are located on the "outside" of the scroll. Some pretribulationist will argue that the seals are positioned on the scroll where after each seal is removed then the scroll will unroll until the next seal, depicting events occurring from inside the scroll. And this supposedly occurs throughout the final seven-years. This view allows them to make their case that the seals are part of the events pertaining to the scroll which contains the wrath of God.

My rebuttal to this argument is that the seals are not contained within the scroll but located on the outside just as the verse describes. I ask the pretrib advocates, how can John know that there are "seven" seals if they are rolled up on the inside of the scroll? The seals are on the outside, and when the seventh seal is broken, only then does God's wrath ensue. There is no biblical substantiation by pretrib folks to make their argument valid.

Let's take a look at the seals in Revelation chapter 6.

> 1: And I saw when the Lamb opened **one of the seals**, and I heard, as it were the noise of thunder, one of the four beasts saying, **Come and see**.
>
> 2: And I saw, and behold a white horse: and **he that sat on him had a bow; and a crown was given unto him**: and he went forth conquering, and to conquer. 3: And when he had opened the **second seal**, I heard the second beast say, **Come and see**.
>
> 4: And there went out another horse that was red: and power was given to him that sat thereon **to take peace** from the earth, and that **they should kill one another**: and there was given unto him a **great sword**.
>
> 5: And when he had opened the **third seal**, I heard the third beast say, **Come and see**. And I beheld, and lo a black horse; and he that sat on him had a pair of balances in his hand.
>
> 6: And I heard a voice in the midst of the four beasts say, A measure of wheat for a penny, and three measures of barley for a penny; and see thou hurt not the oil and the wine.
>
> 7: And when he had opened the **fourth seal**, I heard the voice of the fourth beast say, **Come and see**.
>
> 8: And I looked, and behold a pale horse: and his name that sat on him was Death, and Hell followed with him. And **power**

was given unto them over the fourth part of the earth, **to kill with sword, and with hunger,** and with death, and with the beasts of the earth.

9: And when he had opened the **fifth seal**, I saw under the altar the **souls of them that were slain for the word of God, and for the testimony which they held**:

10: And they cried with a loud voice, saying, How long, O Lord, holy and true, dost thou not judge and avenge our blood on them that dwell on the earth?

11: And white robes were given unto every one of them; and it was said unto them, that they should rest yet for a little season, until their fellowservants also and their brethren, that should be killed as they were, should be fulfilled.

12: And I beheld when he had opened the **sixth seal**, and, lo, there was a **great earthquake**; and **the sun became black** as sackcloth of hair, and the **moon became as blood**;

13: And the **stars of heaven fell unto the earth,** even as a fig tree casteth her untimely figs, when she is shaken of a mighty wind.

14: And the **heaven departed as a scroll** when it is rolled together; and every mountain and island were moved out of their places.

15: And the kings of the earth, and the great men, and the rich men, and the chief captains, and the mighty men, and every bondman, and every free man, **hid themselves** in the dens and in the rocks of the mountains;

16: **And said to the mountains and rocks, Fall on us**, and **hide us from the face of him that sitteth on the throne, and from the wrath of the Lamb:** 17: For **the great day of his wrath is come;** and **who shall be able to stand?**

Allowing Scripture to interpret itself without any presupposition about the rapture of the church; did anyone of these seals standout that seem to acknowledge God's supernatural intervention?

In their booklet "The Tribulation," Ice and Demy state the typical pretrib position on the seals in Revelation chapter 6.

Events of the First Half of the Tribulation

1. *The seal judgments-* "Revelation 6 outlines the seven seal judgments (the seventh contains the trumpet judgments) **that kick off the tribulation.** The first four seals are also known as the four horsemen of the Apocalypse. **These judgments are the beginnings of the wrath of God** which is directed at the earth."[108] (bold letters mine)

Without proper support, both Ice and Demy read into the text in Revelation chapter 6 and interpret it from a non-literal approach. As a reminder, if there is "sudden destruction" as the Scripture states, how are the seal the "beginnings of the wrath of God"? Furthermore, what Scriptural support does Ice and Demy have the right to call the seals, "judgments"? Only God's wrath associated with the final week is judgment. Let's now look at each one of these in more detail and see if we can determine God's wrath.

1. The First Seal: (vv.1-2) the White Horse – Antichrist: Almost all prophecy students agree that this person identified by the first seal is the Antichrist. Most futurist prophecy teaching takes Daniel 9:27, where it states that the coming Antichrist will "confirm the covenant for a week," and say the confirmation in Daniel is the first seal here in Revelation 6. This could very well be true; however, but I personally do not necessarily believe this seal has to match the beginning of the 70th week. This seal could be opened well before the 70th week or it could specifically target a group already in the 70th week.

Notice this person receives a "bow" (no arrows) and "crown," which most likely represents power and authority gained through political and economic power. The rider on the white horse brings false peace of deception, because he still seen as one who goes forth to conquer. Who is he attempting to conquer? Is it various peoples of the earth, or could it be a select group of people solely targeted by Satan? We know that in Revelation 12- 14 we see that when the Antichrist takes power he goes forth to conquer, first Israel, then believers. I believe the means how this is accomplished is by the political power first given him, then he moves to the next phase of his diabolical plan which is total subjugation through economic and military strength.

2. The Second Seal: (vv.3-4) the Red Horse- War/Persecution: peace is taken from the earth by the Antichrist. He (not God) is given a "great sword" to use it as an instrument of destruction of millions of people on the earth. Man is the object of the Antichrist's wrath; it states, *they should kill one another;* this is not God punishing the inhabitants of the earth. Again, is this an overall military campaign for the Antichrist to fight nations who oppose him, or could this a persecution upon the saints and Israel? I believe it's both (Revelation 13:7).

There is a coming war foretold in Scripture what we call the Magog invasion against Israel. This can be found in the book of Ezekiel chapters 38-39. What is not known is the timing of this war in relation to the 70th week. There are two basic schools of thought that commonly teach this is an Islamic invasion either headed-up by Turkey or Russia. This war could begin before the 70th week and go into the first half of the week, or it could begin in the first half of the 70th week and go into part of the final half of the week. We are told by Jesus in Mathew 24:8 there is a time called the "beginning of sorrows," and one main feature is war. But there is no biblical proof when the beginning of sorrows (and this is important) begins in relation to the 70th week.

3. The Third Seal: (vv.5-6) the Black Horse- Balances: this is the natural result from the second seal, which is war and persecution. This will cause a great famine where wheat and barley becomes precious commodity along with the oil and wine. I would further add that if this is meant to picture a specific persecution upon believers, then the cost to procure the basic food to sustain daily life would cost someone on the black market a lot of money. I believe the saints who do not receive the mark of the beast, yet, survive until the rapture at the coming of the Lord before the day of the Lord, will have to pay under-the table exorbitant prices for basic food. (Rev. 13:17)

Still, my point so far is we see there has been no distinction between God's supernatural wrath and the Antichrist's wrath. What has been described so far has been played out numerous times over man's history. First, the promise of peace, then war and famine.

4. The Fourth Seal: (vv.7-8) the Pale Horse: a fourth part of mankind is killed by the sword, hunger, and the beast of the earth. Again, nothing is mentioned up to this point about God pouring out His wrath or judgment upon the lost. When it says the "fourth part of mankind," there is no distinction given as to whom is killed at this time-saved or unsaved people. This could be referencing the Magog invasion that could spiral out of control and cause a world war. Or, with the implementation of the mark of the beast on the world, those who reject following Antichrist will become killed by "sword, hunger, and the beast of the earth." The beast are not literal animals, but are symbolic of the nations that give their allegiance and power to Antichrist (Revelation 13:1-5; 17:11-14).

The combined deaths from World War I and II accounted for over sixty-million. With the rise of communism in China, Russia, North Korea, and Vietnam, it's estimated that another seventy-five million were killed, totaling 135,000,000 who died within a period of about sixty-years. During the final seven-years when Antichrist rises to power, and specifically at the midpoint of the 70th week according to Matthew 24, there will be "great tribulation" (vs. 21-22). Christ said that the great tribulation is instigated by the Antichrist which will cause the worst persecution in history. This persecution however, will be directed solely toward God's people. This is why I personally believe the opening of these seals could be more for warning the saints (Rev. 1:3).

5. The Fifth Seal: (vv.9-11) Martyrs: this is what I referred to earlier, these individuals have died for their testimony and the word of God. These individuals are saved because they follow Christ, not lost people who don't. Verse 9 stated these folks had a testimony that the "held" (remained). Revelation 14:12 states that these same folks are who "keep" the commandments of God. Look at what John wrote in Revelation chapter one.

> I John, who also am your brother, and companion in tribulation, and in the kingdom and patience of Jesus Christ, was in the isle that is called Patmos, **for the word of God, and for the testimony of Jesus Christ.** (Rev. 1:9)

The apostle John is not a "tribulation saint" as described by pretribulationism. He is a New Testament believer, just like you and me. This is certainly not a "special" requirement exclusively for those in the 70th week.

Continuing, it will be at the mid-point of the 70th week that the world will be required to receive the mark of the beast. And I believe that these individuals are those who refuse the mark and do not worship the Antichrist. This seal is what Christ spoke of in the Olivet Discourse, which is the great tribulation when Antichrist declares himself god, and either literally goes into the temple or/and causes true Christianity to cease from worshiping Christ. I would also like to ask this to my pretrib friends: why is it that these folks died for "the Word of God?" I believe that in the midst of total deception caused by the Antichrist deceiving the world, Christians will understand what is unfolding before their eyes (Dan. 12:3, 10) and will speak the truth of God's word. They will heed God's warning from the Scriptures about God's wrath upon those who receive the mark of the beast and reject the coming kingdom. These are the true witnesses during the tribulation, not the 144,000.

Could the opening of the seals be related to the revealing of Antichrist at the middle of the 70th week, which is directed against Israel and the church? If you read Daniel chapter 12, Daniel is told to "seal" those things revealed to him until the "time of the end." Daniel 12:9 *"And he said, Go thy way, Daniel: for the words* are *closed up and **sealed till the time of the end**."* When you read Daniel 12, you will see the context of Daniel's discussion with the Lord is taking place when the abomination of desolation occurs. (vv. 7, 11). The revealing of the Antichrist at the first seal could very well be the unsealing of Daniel's vision. I admit this is speculation on my part. The opening of the seals, like I mentioned, could be related to the beginning of sorrows, which most likely will begin well-before the 70th week begins. Either way this causes problems for the pretribulation rapture doctrine, because, one of their main arguments is that the seals are God's wrath. However, if the opening of the first seal does not begin with the 70th week, but, either at the midpoint or before the 70th week begins, their foundational argument for the church escaping God's wrath suffers a major crack. To reemphasize the point I am making, God's supernatural wrath is absent up to this point so far. And believers are not appointed unto wrath, and God's wrath has not been seen up to the opening of the 5th seal- no rapture, yet!

6.) The Sixth Seal: (vv.12-16) cosmic disturbances: we now have recorded for the first time a supernatural, cataclysmic event taking place. This event is not caused by man or the Antichrist, this comes directly from heaven. This is the benchmark event that identifies the sign Jesus told the disciples in Matthew 24 that would take place before His return.

First, there is an earthquake, along with cosmic disturbances in the heaven, and the sun being darkened and the moon as if it turned to blood (the real blood moon). Next, the stars that fall to the earth could very well be the angels that will gather the believer's world-wide. If we compare this to Revelation 12:4, the fallen angels that were cast to the earth are said to be stars; the stars here in chapter 6 could very well be the angels sent to gather God's elect (cf. Mat. 24:31; Rev. 7:1-2). Another possibility is that the stars, compared to the fig tree shaking violently in the midst of a mighty storm, could picture the astronomical calamity associated with the heavens being shaken due to the unfolding events.

The cosmic lights are turned off, which will amplify the events that are taking place for the earth dwellers to witness. As prewrath teaching states, the rapture is not going to be invisible; therefore, John's description teaches the world will witness the events that are unfolding. This is paralleled with heaven departing as a scroll as if God were rolling back the curtain on the stage for the grand finale. Associated with this, is a very great shaking in the earth which causes the mountains and islands to be moved out of their place. Then the people on the earth of all classes, including kings, chief people, along with both, free and bond, run and hide from Him who is on the throne and the lamb, which is none other than Jesus Christ. The people of the earth cry out for the first time; *the great day of His wrath has come; and who shall be able to stand.* This event my friend is the prelude to the "DAY OF THE LORD." The people cry out "the great day," which indicates a special day is about to unfold. Notice, the people say *"His wrath,"* understanding that this is coming from God Himself, not man. If you recall the verse in the Old Testament quoted by nearly every pretrib teacher, which was Zephaniah 1:14, *The great day of the LORD is near, it is near, and hasteth greatly, even the voice of the day of the LORD: the mighty man shall cry there bitterly.* Pretrib teaching states this is God's wrath; however, they attempt to make God's wrath beginning at the first seal, which is clearly not the case. The opening of the sixth seal is the "great day" spoken, not only by Zephaniah, but all the prophets in the Old Testament.

We have Christ being revealed for the first time; and now we have people acknowledging the wrath of God for the first time here at the sixth seal. Now is that time of revenge when the martyrs of the fifth seal cried out: "when will God avenge their blood." Folks, this could not be any plainer that this is the "day of God's wrath" about to be unleashed on the world.

I would like to address a subtle tainting of the evidence by some pretribulationist when dealing specifically with the sixth seal. Some attempt to say that phrase "God's wrath has come" is written in the aorist tense. This tense states that "has come" is actually part of the preceding events. The British Dictionary defines aorist as: ...*indicating past action without reference to whether the action involved was momentary or continuous.* In other words, pretribulationist are asserting the sixth seal is summation of the ongoing past events. However, in believing this they have just denied the chronological order of the seals. Instead of allowing the events to unfold in a successive order they are basically saying the world is really crying out "God's wrath has come" at the opening of the first seal without acknowledging the world saying this. We saw the first seal is "peace" not the world crying out and hiding from God's wrath. The pretrib only say this so they can justify all the seals as being part of God's wrath.

Conversely, the pretribulation teaching say's that **all** the seals in Revelation are the wrath of God; however, notice when they teach specifically about God's wrath, they reference this event (sixth seal) and not any of the seals prior to this. Here is pretribulationist David Reagan of the "Lamb and Lion Ministries," explaining God's wrath.

The Coming Wrath

God's wrath will fall when Jesus returns (Jude 14-15). The passage in Revelation which pictures the return of Jesus says that He will return in righteousness to "judge and wage war" (Revelation 19:11).

The first time Jesus came, He came in loving compassion with eyes filled with tears. **But when He returns, He will come in vengeance (Revelation 6:12-17)**, with eyes like a flame of fire (Revelation 19:12). He will come to destroy the enemies of God (Revelation 19:11).

The presidents and kings and prime ministers of the world will get on their knees and cry out for the rocks and mountains to fall upon them, so great will be the terror of the Lord (Revelation 6:15-17). The unrighteous will stumble about like blind men, and their blood will be poured out like dust (Zephaniah 1:17).[109] (bold letters mine)

David Reagan identifies God's wrath with the sixth seal, because God's wrath cannot be identified in the previous five seals! He cites Zephaniah 1:17 as the identifier of the wrath of God, same as other pretribulation teachers. Reagan also says God's wrath will fall when Christ returns (correct!); however, where does Reagan place this event in the context of the final week? Reagan compares Rev 19:11, which is Christ's coming at the "end" of the 70th week at the battle of Armageddon to the sixth-seal in Revelation 6. So where does he place the wrath of God at during the tribulation? Is he saying that the sixth seal is the second coming event at the end of the tribulation? If so, he has just become a posttribulationist. Contextually, and sequentially, the sixth seal cannot be equated to Christ's return at the end of the 70th week.

Ten Reasons for a Pretribulational Rapture

2.) *Tribulation judgments are the "wrath of the Lamb."* **Revelation 6:16** depicts the cataclysmic judgments of the end times as the **wrath of Christ**. Revelation 19:7-9 depicts the church as the bride of the Lamb. She is not the object of His wrath, **which is poured out on the unbelieving world**.[110] (bold letters mine)

Thomas Ice and Timothy Demy

Here, both Ice and Demy state the same thing as Reagan when identifying God's wrath at the sixth seal. They also make a subtle claim in their opening statement using the word "judgments," as plural, which they are silently suggesting all the seals are God's wrath. Prewrath places the rapture at the opening of the sixth seal and immediately the church can be seen in heaven in Rev. 7 before the trumpet (wrath in the day of the Lord) judgments begin in chapter 8.

Here is Tim LaHaye's interpretation of the sixth seal.

#8: Revelation 6:12-17. "The sixth seal exhibits the **wrath of God** poured out in the form of a mighty earthquake the like which has never been experienced. It was so severe that the people call on the rocks to fall on them.[111]

LaHaye is correct to acknowledge the sixth seal as God's wrath; however, his explanation is actually silly! He claims that the earthquake is so great and terrible that the people cry for the rocks to fall on them. If you have been in an earthquake, and I have not, I would think, normally folks would try to "avoid" from being struck by falling objects, not desiring to be wiped out. If you read the context of the verses, the people cry out because they "see the Lamb" and Him who sits on the throne, which LaHaye doesn't even acknowledge Christ's presence. The world cries out because of Christ impending wrath, not because of the earthquake.

You be the judge, does Revelation 1:7 match the 6th seal or the coming of Christ in Revelation chapter 19? Pretrib advocates say Revelation 1:7 is Christ's coming in chapter 19.

> 1:7 Behold, he cometh with clouds; and every eye shall see him, and they *also* which pierced him: and all kindreds of the earth shall wail because of him. Even so, Amen.

If you're honest, after you compare the two passages, this matches the 6th seal in chapter six.

Here is another explanation by John Hagee, who calls himself "Americas Pastor."

> The sixth seal- is a continuation of a series of global [environmental] catastrophes. The Sun will become black; "the moon will become (as) blood; a great earthquake will shake the earth violently that every mountain and island of the sea will be shaken out of its place."

> Every person on earth will be filled with mind-bending terror. The wealthy, the powerful presidents, prime ministers, senators, congressmen, and the mighty men of war will hide in caves and underground government chambers to escape the wrath of God.[112]

He follows the same line with other pretribulationist when talking about the sixth seal. They acknowledge this is God's wrath, but deny Christ presence which the Scripture plainly says the world "sees" Christ. Why don't they acknowledge Christ's presence? Because this destroys their theory about the invisible rapture before the 70th week along with Christ's "glorious appearance" at the end of the tribulation. I would like to state nowhere in the context of Revelation 6 and Matthew 24 is there a mentioning of "environmental" catastrophes. What is taking place prior to this time is caused by men, not God. Hagee purposely slips in the phrase, "this is a continuation of a series," to make his readers **think** that God's judgment has been ongoing: WRONG- it is just **starting**. In fact, what we would term "environmental catastrophes" only take place during the trumpet judgments during the day of the Lords vengeance beginning in Revelation chapter 8.

John Walvoord, the dean of pretribulationism, acknowledges the wrath of God in the 70th week; however, guess which seal he says is the wrath of God?

> Christians in the present age who are looking forward to the Rapture are assured that they will be delivered from the day of wrath (1 Thessalonians 5:9). In contrast, in the period preceding the Second Coming the **wrath of God will be poured out on the earth** and the great disasters that take place will overtake Christians as well as non-Christians **(Rev. 6:12-17). The Tribulation is a time of the wrath of Satan (Rev.12:6)**, which is vented on believers of that time; whereas **the wrath of God is vented on unbelievers,** but the resulting judgments affect the entire race.[113] (bold letters mine)

There is a subtle underlining that must be recognized in order to discern Walvoord's statement. First, he says Christians in this "present age" are not subject to God's wrath. Then he remarks that God's wrath will overtake Christians during the tribulation. He says this because pretribulationist believe these are the ones who get saved after the rapture. This is dispensationalism at work, segmenting different time periods to fit their doctrine. Walvoord turns right around and contradicts his own statement by accurately saying the tribulation is Satan's wrath on believers, and God's wrath on unbelievers. First Thessalonians 5:9 teaches that we (Christians) are not appointed to wrath, which applies for all the ages, not supposedly just the 70th week. Actually, if you were to read through the New Testament and read the verses pertaining to God's wrath you will see a pattern that they overwhelmingly reflect God's wrath on the lost for eternity, not just the final week.

As with his predecessors, why does Walvoord refer to Revelation 6:12-17 the sixth seal as God's wrath, and not the preceding seals? Answer- the preceding seals are not the wrath of God, but the sixth seal, which we will see occurs after the great tribulation is over and signals God's wrath is about to begin.

In his book "Rapture Under Attack," LaHaye quotes Dr. Gerald Stanton in his critical assessment of Marvin Rosenthal's book "The Pre-Wrath Rapture of the Church." Here is Stanton's claim that Rosenthal is wrong on the first five seals not being the wrath of God.

> It is serious error to claim, as Rosenthal does, that "the first three and one-half years are not part of the Tribulation period" (106-7) because God's wrath does not start until "considerably further" into the 70th week. In his words, the seals are not God's wrath; "they are God's promise of eternal protection during man's wrath." (145) Moreover, "the first five seals relate to man's activity under the controlling influence of Satan. God's wrath has not yet begun." (247) But this is not entirely true, for the seals also are broken by Christ, and the riders of the first four seals and their accompanying judgments are initiated by four "living creatures" who descend from the very presence of God (Revelation 4:6-8). They are responding to divine holiness when they command these riders, not to "come and see," but simply to come!"
>
> It is a denial of Scripture to declare the first four seals the activity of men rather than the judgment of God. And a rapture placed after the first six seals would certainly not be a "pre-wrath rapture.[114]

First, Stanton's straw man is to accuse someone of denying Scripture because it conflicts with his view. Stanton believes the pretribulation view that the tribulation is the entire seven-year time period without scriptural evidence. The only tribulation recorded in the Word of God that is associated with the seven-years is the "great tribulation" that begins in the middle of the week (Dan. 9:27; Mat. 24:15). Second, Stanton is very misleading in his statement about Rosenthal's quote, "the seals are not God's wrath, but God's eternal protection during man's wrath." Rosenthal qualified his statement before this by saying, "The significance of the Lord Jesus Christ opening the seals is, among other things, the assurance of eternal security for those believers **who may be martyred** for Christ sake."[115] Rosenthal is asserting what Christ taught, that if a person loses their life for Christ they will gain eternal life.

Rosenthal does believe that many Christians inside the tribulation will be protected by God's hand; however, this does not affect the context of the debate as to whether the seals are the wrath of God or not. The truth is that many will not be killed during the tribulation, but will be raptured before the day of the Lord or "God's wrath." Therefore, they are going to be protected by God in some way; but to say that Rosenthal believes the seals themselves are God's protection is a very inaccurate statement.

The main point to be made in regard to the seals is whether or not they are intended to be God's wrath. This is called into question, due to the fact that it is Christ who breaks these seals. Stanton's argument, along with all pretribulation teaching, is incorrect to say that the seals are God's wrath based on the fact the seals are broken by Christ. True, Christ does open the seals to allow the riders to go forth, but all this is saying is that "God is in control." God will determine when the first seal is broken along with all others. Also, worth noting, the angels who are Gods ministering spirits and ministers of flame of fire (Hebrews 1:7); when the seals are opened, only say *"come and see."* They are not participating in the seal events, just observing. However, we will see at the trumpet and bowl judgments, angels are active participants of God's wrath on the world.

The seals in Revelation are no more the wrath of God than God's wrath in the book of Job. Job endured Satan's wrath; however, it was God that allowed Satan to persecute him.

> 9. Then Satan answered the LORD, and said, Doth Job fear God for nought?
> 10. Hast not thou made an hedge about him, and about his house, and about all that he hath on every side? thou hast blessed the work of his hands, and his substance is increased in the land.
> 11. But **put forth thine hand now, and touch all that he hath,** and he will curse thee to thy face.
> 12. And the LORD said unto Satan, **Behold, all that he hath** *is* **in thy power; only upon himself put not forth thine hand**. So Satan went forth from the presence of the LORD. (Job 1:9-12)

This was only God's test to prove to Satan that Job would still trust Him, despite the hardships. Job suffered directly by the permission of God; however, it was Satan that ultimately put his hand on Job. Even in Job chapter 2, Job took a direct hit on his body from Satan by God's permission. If someone says that the seals are the wrath of God, then they would have to say that Job suffered the wrath of God as well.

If you recall the story of Judas's betrayal of Christ, who sold him out for thirty pieces of silver; you will realize that Jesus was in control of that situation the whole time. Judas had already gone to the Pharisees in secret before the last supper to make his dirty deal with them. When Christ revealed to His disciples that one of them would betray him, they all began to ask Jesus, "who?" Jesus said it would be the one who he gave the sop to, which he handed directly to Judas. Notice something interesting now as we read this account in John's gospel.

> He then lying on Jesus' breast saith unto him, Lord, who is it? Jesus answered, He it is, to whom I shall give a sop, when I have dipped it. And when he had dipped the sop, he gave it to Judas Iscariot, the son of Simon. And **after the sop Satan entered into him.** Then **said Jesus unto him, That thou doest, do quickly.** (John 13:25-27)

Satan was not able to enter Judas until Christ had allowed him to, which was **after** receiving the sop. Jesus even commanded Satan to do his work "quickly," in which Satan obeyed. Here we have a picture of Christ allowing these things to be fulfilled, yet, it was carried out by Satan, via Judas. Also, the Scriptures teach that man has a free will just like Judas; and many will exercise their will in agreement with the Antichrist to persecute Israel and Christians. The opening of the seals during the 70th week will only be fulfilled when God allows this to take place.

I find it interesting that Stanton, by his own doctrinal admission, only acknowledges the "first four seals" as God's wrath, but leaves out the fifth seal. He does this because these individuals are killed as a result of persecution, not by God's wrath. Stanton is wrong to declare that the first four seals are the wrath of God and then say the fifth seal is Satan's wrath- he cannot have it both ways.

Back to the Old Testament

When you let the Word of God interpret itself it is amazing what you learn. However, when you have predetermined beliefs you can really foul up the continuity of the Bible. Let us now revisit the Old Testament passages about the day of the Lord and determine at what point God's wrath is poured out on the world during the 70th week. As a reminder, pretribulational teaching says the seals are God's wrath; and we saw where they attempted to identify God's wrath with the sixth seal. (Isaiah 2:8-12)

> 8: Their **land also is full of idols; they worship the work of their own hands,** that which their own fingers have made:
>
> 9: And the mean man boweth down, and the great man humbleth himself: therefore forgive them not.
>
> 10: **Enter into the rock, and hide thee in the dust, for fear of the LORD,** and for the **glory of his majesty.**
>
> 11: The lofty looks of man shall be humbled, and the haughtiness of men shall be bowed down, and **the LORD alone shall be exalted in that d**ay.
>
> 12: For the **day of the LORD** of hosts shall be **upon every one that is proud and lofty,** and **upon every one that is lifted up;** and **he shall be brought low:**

We are back to the original verse that demonstrates the day of the Lord is strictly God's wrath upon the lost. We see that the proud and lofty man is extremely humbled by this event (vs.11). We also see that these people in verse 10 are going to *enter into the rock and hide in the dust*; and for what reason? For *the fear of the Lord* is now before them, which is caused by *the Lord and His glory of His majesty.* The deduction can be made that **before** this event there was no Godly fear in the lives of these people.

Let us continue further in Isaiah chapter 2 and see if we can gain some more insight as to what is happening. (Isa. 2:17-21)

> 17: And the **loftiness of man shall be bowed down,** and the **haughtiness of men shall be made low**: and the **LORD alone shall be exalted in that day.**
>
> 18: And the idols he shall utterly abolish.

19: And **they shall go into the holes of the rocks, and into the caves of the earth, for fear of the LORD, and for the glory of his majesty, when he ariseth to shake terribly the earth.**

20: In **that day a man shall cast his idols of silver, and his idols of gold,** which they made each one for himself to worship, to the moles and to the bats;

21: **To go into the clefts of the rocks,** and into the tops of the ragged rocks, for fear **of the LORD, and for the glory of his majesty, when he ariseth to shake terribly the earth.**

We now get the complete picture of this passage. The day of the Lord is His wrath poured out; now we are given insight as to when it takes place. Notice again that the sixth seal in Revelation 6:15-17.

15: And the kings of the earth, and the great men, and the rich men, and the chief captains, and the mighty men, and every bondman, and every free man, **hid themselves in the dens and in the rocks of the mountains;**

16: And said to the mountains and rocks, Fall on us, and **hide us from the face of him that sitteth on the throne, and from the wrath of the Lamb:**

17: **For the great day of his wrath is come; and who shall be able to stand?**

It is exceeding biased of the pretrib camp to deny that these events are one in the same. In both books, we see that this is a supernatural event originating from heaven, and we also see that haughty mankind will be humbled to the degree to where they want to hide from the presence of God. The world now knows that God is about to pour out His wrath upon them for first time during the 70th week.

Signs in the Heaven

We saw the signs in the heavens associated with the opening of the sixth seal in Revelation 6; now we can see the same events taught from the day of the Lord passages in the Old Testament. We saw at the sixth seal, the lost hide from the presence of the Lord in the caves and cast out their idols in fear of God's wrath that is about to occur. Let's read Isaiah 13.

Howl ye; for the day of the LORD is at hand; it shall come as a destruction from the Almighty. Therefore shall **all hands be faint, and every man's heart shall melt:** And they shall be afraid: pangs and sorrows shall take hold of them; they shall be in pain as a woman that travaileth: they shall be amazed one at another; their faces shall be as flames. Behold, **the day of the LORD cometh, cruel both with wrath and fierce anger,** to lay the land desolate: and he shall **destroy the sinners thereof** out of it **For the stars of heaven and the constellations thereof shall not give their light: the sun shall be darkened in his going forth, and the moon shall not cause her light to shine.** And I will **punish the world for their evil, and the wicked for their iniquity;** and **I will cause the arrogancy of the proud to cease,** and will lay low the haughtiness of the terrible. (Isa. 13:6-11)

This is the same event as recorded in Isaiah chapter 2 and in Revelation 6:12-17. It would seem as though the heavenly bodies turned off all their lights. This allows the inhabitants on the earth to see the full spectrum of the coming events from heaven. And what unfolds at the sixth seal is the appearance of Christ. I personally have heard pretrib teaching say that the world can view Christ due to the technology related to the television and computers. I don't believe God will need our televisions or computers to reveal His glory!

Here we have a vivid picture of the scene portraying the inhabitants on the earth when the Lord of hosts comes in His glory.

Fear, and the pit, and the snare, are upon thee, O **inhabitant of the earth** And it shall come to pass, that he who fleeth from the noise of the fear shall fall into the pit; and he that cometh up out of the midst of the pit shall be taken in the snare: for **the windows from on high are open, and the foundations of the earth do shake.** The earth is utterly broken down, the earth is clean dissolved, **the earth is moved exceedingly The earth shall reel to and fro like a drunkard,** and shall be removed like a cottage; and the **transgression thereof shall be heavy upon it;** and it shall fall, and not rise again **And it shall come to pass in that day, that the LORD shall punish the host of the high ones that are on high, and the kings of the earth**

upon the earth. And they shall be gathered together, as prisoners are gathered in the pit, and shall be shut up in the prison, and after many days shall they be visited. **Then the moon shall be confounded, and the sun ashamed,** when the LORD of hosts shall reign in mount Zion, and in Jerusalem, and before his ancients gloriously. (Isa. 24:17-23)

Here's another picture of the day of the Lord when Christ is revealed from heaven.

Come near, ye nations, to hear; and hearken, ye people: **let the earth hear, and all that is therein; the world,** and all things that come forth of it. **For the indignation of the LORD is upon all nations, and his fury upon all their armies: he hath utterly destroyed them, he hath delivered them to the slaughter.** Their slain also shall be cast out, and their stink shall come up out of their carcases, and the mountains shall be melted with their blood And all the host of heaven shall be dissolved, **and the heavens shall be rolled together as a scroll: and all their host shall fall down,** as the leaf falleth off from the vine, and as a falling fig from the fig tree....For it is the **day of the Lord's vengeance**, and the year of recompenses for the controversy of Zion. (Isa. 34:1-4, 8)

Blow ye the trumpet in Zion, and sound an alarm in my holy mountain: let all the inhabitants of the land tremble: **for the day of the LORD cometh,** for it is nigh at hand; A day of darkness and of gloominess, a day of clouds and of thick darkness, as the morning spread upon the mountains: a great people and a strong; there hath not been ever the like, neither shall be any more after it, even to the years of many generations...**The earth shall quake before them; the heavens shall tremble: the sun and the moon shall be dark, and the stars shall withdraw their shining:** And the **LORD shall utter his voice before his army**: for his camp is very great: for he is strong that executeth his word: for the **day of the LORD is great and very terrible; and who can abide it?** (Joel 2:1-4, 10-11)

Notice at the end of the phrase in verse 11: *who can abide it?* This is the same statement the people on the earth cry out at the sixth seal: *For the great day of his wrath is come; and **who shall be able to stand**?* We also see the association of the sun, moon, and stars darkened as the Lord is being revealed in the earth.

> **And I will show wonders in the heavens and in the earth,** blood, and fire, and pillars of smoke. **The sun shall be turned into darkness, and the moon into blood, <u>before</u> the great and the terrible day of the LORD come And it shall come to pass,** that whosoever shall call on the name of the LORD shall be delivered: for in mount Zion and in Jerusalem shall be deliverance, as the LORD hath said, and in the remnant whom the LORD shall call. (Joel 2:30-32)

This is more scriptural evidence supporting that the day of the Lord is associated with the cosmic events. The word **before** is underlined to emphasize the fact that the cosmic disturbances in the sun, moon, and stars will take place before the day of the Lord begins. This will add even more reinforcement to the timing of the rapture as we will see a little later. With all the factual evidence we just looked at, here is Thomas Ice stating the typical mindless pretrib position comparing God's wrath to the tribulation.

> It **appears** that "the time of God's wrath" and "the tribulation" encompass the same seven-year time period.[116] (bold letters mine)

Why does Ice make the comment that it "appears" that God's wrath and the tribulation take place at the same time? There's nothing factual about his statement, which is suspect at best. We also saw earlier where Ice makes the statement by comparing the tribulation with God's wrath by saying, "we normally associate" and a "synonym for." This is not very convincing language to support one's theory. This proves that Ice and other pretribulationist have abandoned the literal interpretation of Scriptures when they interject their interpretation to Scripture. Here's another quote by Ice:

> However, the world's persecution of the church in this age is not the wrath of God. The future tribulation will be a time of **God's wrath upon a Christ-rejecting world**- a time from which

the **church has been promised by our Lord to be exempted**
(Revelation 3:10; 1 Thessalonians 1:10; 5:9)[117] (bold letters mine)

The world's persecution during the church-age is included in Christ's teaching in Matthew 24, which is described as the "beginning of sorrows." What pretrib teachers fail to distinguish is the difference between sorrows and God's wrath. They have no proof that the sorrows spoken of by Christ in Matthew 24 are exclusively part of the final 70th week.

The Day of the Lord: Rev. 8

Revelation 8:1-4

> 1: And when he had opened the seventh seal, there was **silence in heaven** about the space of **half an hour.**
> 2: And I saw the seven angels which stood before God; and to them were given **seven trumpets**.
> 3: And another angel came and stood at the altar, having a golden censer; and there was given unto him much incense, that he should offer it with the **prayers of all saints** upon the golden altar which was before the throne.
> 4: And the smoke of the incense, which came with the **prayers of the saints,** ascended up before God out of the angel's hand.

Following the cosmic disturbances at the sixth seal in chapter six, when the world cries out that God's wrath has come, what follows is the sealing of the 144,000 for protection from God's wrath in Revelation 7. Also in Revelation 7 we see the great multitude in heaven that came out of the "great tribulation" shouting "salvation" and clothed in white robes (Rev. 7:9-10).

> 9. After this I beheld, and, lo, a great multitude, which no man could number, of all nations, and kindreds, and people, and tongues, stood before the throne, and before the Lamb, clothed with white robes, and palms in their hands;
> 9. And cried with a loud voice, saying, Salvation to our God which sitteth upon the throne, and unto the Lamb.

This is the rapture of the church, which occurred in conjunction with the opening of the sixth seal. This multitude is delivered from the wrath to come, which is set to begin in chapter 8 at the blowing of the trumpet judgments. Also, notice what is said about this multitude in chapter 7:13-16

> 13. And one of the elders answered, saying unto me, What are these which are arrayed in white robes? and whence came they?
> 14. And I said unto him, Sir, thou knowest. And he said to me, These are they which **came out of great tribulation**, and have washed their robes, and made them white in the blood of the Lamb.
> 15. Therefore are they before the throne of God, and serve him day and night in his temple: and he that sitteth on the throne shall dwell among them.
> 16. They shall **hunger** no more, neither **thirst** any more; neither shall the **sun light** on them, nor any **heat**.

These are the raptured saints (church) that come out of the great tribulation. The last verse suggests that they had suffered hunger, thirst, no dwelling place (living in the sun light), and heat. Death is not specifically mentioned, these are those raptured. Those who have died for Christ are seen under the altar, these are before the throne. This is what Paul referred to in 1 Thessalonians 3:1. Jude vv. 24-25.

> 24. Now unto him that is able to keep you from falling, and to **present *you* faultless before the presence of his glory** with exceeding joy,
> 25. To the only wise God our Saviour, *be* glory and majesty, dominion and power, both now and ever. Amen.

As we come to the blowing of these trumpets in Revelation 8, God will now unleash the fury of His wrath on the world. The Bible records that there is *silence* in heaven for about a half an hour. Just prior to this silence, in chapter 7, the multitude is *shouting* salvation in the presence of God. The Bible records that there is continual praise of God before His throne in heaven. We see this silence takes place because of the awesomeness of God's wrath which is about to be thrust upon the earth. I will show that from the opening of the sixth seal in Revelation 6, and the blowing of the first trumpet in Revelation 8, both events will occur on the very same day.

We see in Revelation 8:3-4 the phrase *the prayers of the saints*. I believe this is a reference to the saints back in chapter 6, the souls under the altar who died for Christ, ask God, "when" would He avenge their blood (death)? The day of the Lord will be that day, and it is about to begin here at the blowing of the first trumpet, and will last through the remaining trumpets and vials, up to the battle of Armageddon.

Here is a list of the trumpet judgments, and you discern if they are different than what the seals portrayed. (Revelation chapters 8 and 9).

1.) The first angel sounded, and there followed hail and fire mingled with blood, and they were cast upon the earth: and the third part of trees was burnt up, and all green grass was burnt up.

2.) And the second angel sounded, and as it were a great mountain burning with fire was cast into the sea: and the third part of the sea became blood;

And the third part of the creatures which were in the sea, and had life, died; and the third part of the ships were destroyed.

3.) And the third angel sounded, and there fell a great star from heaven, burning as it were a lamp, and it fell upon the third part of the rivers, and upon the fountains of waters;

And the name of the star is called Wormwood: and the third part of the waters became wormwood; and many men died of the waters, because they were made bitter.

4.) And the fourth angel sounded, and the third part of the sun was smitten, and the third part of the moon, and the third part of the stars; so as the third part of them was darkened, and the day shone not for a third part of it, and the night likewise.

5.) And the fifth angel sounded, and I saw a star fall from heaven unto the earth: and to him was given the key of the bottomless pit.

And he opened the bottomless pit; and there arose a smoke out of the pit, as the smoke of a great furnace; and the sun and the air were darkened by reason of the smoke of the pit.

And there came out of the smoke locusts upon the earth: and unto them was given power, as the scorpions of the earth have power.

And it was commanded them that they should not hurt the grass of the earth, neither any green thing, neither any tree; but only those men which have not the seal of God in their foreheads.

And to them it was given that they should not kill them, but that they should be tormented five months: and their torment *was* as the torment of a scorpion, when he striketh a man.

And in those days shall men seek death, and shall not find it; and shall desire to die, and death shall flee from them.

6.) And the sixth angel sounded, and I heard a voice from the four horns of the golden altar which is before God,

Saying to the sixth angel which had the trumpet, Loose the four angels which are bound in the great river Euphrates.

And the four angels were loosed, which were prepared for an hour, and a day, and a month, and a year, for to slay the third part of men.

And the number of the army of the horsemen *were* two hundred thousand thousand: and I heard the number of them.

And thus I saw the horses in the vision, and them that sat on them, having breastplates of fire, and of jacinth, and brimstone: and the heads of the horses *were* as the heads of lions; and out of their mouths issued fire and smoke and brimstone.

By these three was the third part of men killed, by the fire, and by the smoke, and by the brimstone, which issued out of their mouths.

For their power is in their mouth, and in their tails: for their tails *were* like unto serpents, and had heads, and with them they do hurt.

And the rest of the men which were not killed by these plagues yet repented not of the works of their hands, that they should not worship devils, and idols of gold, and silver, and brass, and stone, and of wood: which neither can see, nor hear, nor walk:

Neither repented they of their murders, nor of their sorceries, nor of their fornication, nor of their thefts.

7.) But in the days of the voice of the seventh angel, when he shall begin to sound, the mystery of God should be finished, as he hath declared to his servants the prophets.

This is a list of the seven trumpets and the reader would have to acknowledge these do not match in comparison to the seals? Obviously, there is a vast difference between the seals and the trumpets. Seals are instigated by man (Antichrist), where the trumpets come from the direct hand of God. Furthermore, read the bowel judgments (Rev. 16) which occur when the seventh trumpet sounds, these are vastly different than the seals as well. One final point. In chapter 19:1-2 we see the multitude rejoicing, and why?

1. **And after these things** I heard a great voice of much people in heaven, saying, Alleluia; Salvation, and glory, and honour, and power, unto the Lord our God:
2. For true and righteous *are* his judgments: **for he hath judged the great whore,** which did corrupt the earth with her fornication, and hath avenged the blood of his servants at her hand.

Chapter 19 is describing the scene after the trumpet and bowl judgments (day of the Lord) on the great whore (antichrist system), yet before the battle of Armageddon, which is the Lambs wrath on Antichrist and Satan.

The World's Attitude in the Middle of the 70th Week

We need to look at another Scripture passage to see the condition of the world's attitude and actions prior the opening of the sixth seal. This is in regard to the reign of the Antichrist and his relation to the world beginning from the midpoint of the 70th week.

And I stood upon the sand of the sea, and saw a beast rise up out of the sea, having seven heads and ten horns, and upon his horns ten crowns, and upon his heads the name of blasphemy And the beast which I saw was like unto a leopard, and his feet were as the feet of a bear, and his mouth as the mouth of a lion: and the dragon gave him his power, and his seat, and great authority. And I saw one of his heads as it were **wounded to death**; and his **deadly wound was healed**: and **all the world wondered after the beast.** And **they worshipped the dragon** which gave power unto the beast: and they **worshipped the beast,** saying, **Who is like unto the beast? who is able to make war with him?** And there was given unto him a mouth speaking great things and blasphemies; and power was given unto him to continue forty and two months. And he opened his mouth in blasphemy against

God, to blaspheme his name, and his tabernacle, and them that
dwell in heaven. (Rev. 13:1-6)

Revelation chapters 12 to 14 are parenthetical chapters, which breaks
from the narrative and gives more of an in-depth look at what is taking place
at the time describing the middle of the tribulation. Satan was kicked out
of Heaven in chapter 12, now he embodies the individual who ultimately
becomes the Antichrist. The events given in these verses, is we see that the
Antichrist is killed and becomes embodied by Satan and raised back to life
(see appendix). After he has risen from his deadly wound the world wonders
in amazement. Verse 5 says that after the Antichrist is raised back to life, he
will continue (live) for 42 months. This agrees with Daniel 9:27 where the
covenant is broken in the "midst of the week;" which begins the forty-two
months of the final week. It will be at this point in the 70th week that the
Antichrist will go into the temple in Jerusalem (literal view) and declare
himself as God (cf. 2 Thess. 2:3-4). The reaction of the world towards the
Antichrist is described in verse 4- that he is their savior.

This must be before the day of the Lord begins; because at the day of
the Lord the people realize that God's wrath has finally come and cry out
in anguish. In Revelation 13 the world is giving praise and honor to the
Antichrist, where at the day of the Lord the people are humbled from their
pride. Also, we read in Isaiah 2:17 that Christ alone is "exalted" that day, but
in Revelation 13:3 the Antichrist is "worshiped," which is the same as being
exalted. The day of the Lord cannot be happening at this time. Again, here
is another contradiction in the pretrib rapture theory, because they fail to
distinguish between God's wrath and the Antichrist's persecution in their
belief system.

Elijah

Further proof that the day of the Lord will not start at the beginning of
the seven-years can be found in the book of Malachi. In the final book of
the Old Testament, Malachi chapter 4, the Lord records He will send Elijah
before *the coming of the Day of the Lord.*

Behold, I will send you Elijah the prophet **before** the coming of
the **great and dreadful day of the LORD:** And he shall turn the
heart of the fathers to the children, and the heart of the children

to their fathers, **lest I come and smite the earth with a curse.**
(Mal. 4:5-6)

Now let's compare the ministry of the two witnesses recorded in Revelation 11.

> And there was given me a reed like unto a rod: and the angel stood, saying, Rise, and measure the temple of God, and the altar, and them that worship therein. But the court which is without the temple leave out, and measure it not; for it is given unto the Gentiles: and the holy city shall they tread under foot forty and two months. And I will give power unto my **two witnesses, and they shall prophesy a thousand two hundred and threescore days**, clothed in sackcloth These are the two olive trees, and the two candlesticks standing before the God of the earth. (vv. 1-4)

Gods' two witness will prophesy 1,260 days or three-and one-half-years during the 70th week. It is typically taught that these two men are Moses and Elijah; now let's look at the time of the beginning and end of their ministry during the final seven-years.

We are told that they will be killed at the second woe (Rev. 11:14), which is sandwiched between the sixth and seventh trumpet. Their bodies will then lie in the streets for three-and-one-half days, and afterwards, be caught up to heaven (Rev. 11:7-12). They are killed by the *beast that ascends out of the bottomless pit.* These two witnesses die towards the end of the final seven-years, meaning their ministry started sometime around the middle of the week. They come on the scene approximately about the same time the Antichrist causes the abomination of desolation. This matches perfectly with Malachi's prophecy that Elijah will appear *before the day of the Lord*, indicating that the day of the Lord cannot take place before the mid-point of the tribulation and certainly not at the beginning of the 70th week. Again, this aligns with prewrath teaching, but conflicts with the pretrib theory.

Wrath in Revelation 11:18

Some pretrib teachers attempt to justify their "wrath theory" starting at the beginning of the 70th week by quoting Revelation 11:18: *And the nations were angry, and thy **wrath has come**.* This particular statement is made at the seventh trumpet. They compare this phrase with the statement made by those at the opening of the sixth seal, *"thy wrath has come."* Pretrib say, that at the sixth seal when the people cry out *thy wrath has come,* actually, God's wrath has been on going from the opening of the first seal as I explained with the aorist tense. They argue against prewrath teaching because, if at the sixth seal this is the "first occurrence" of God's wrath, then how does prewrath explain the same statement made in chapter 11, almost at the end of the 70th week. You can't have God's wrath just now occurring; it must have been already taking place. Here is the difference: The wrath to come at the sixth seal is God's wrath to be poured out on this earth for the first time once the great tribulation is cut short. Where the wrath in Revelation 11 is the final wrath to be experienced in hell for eternity (not the ongoing wrath on earth), and the people know it. Another proof of this is the next phrase in verse 18, *thy wrath has come, **and the time of the dead, that they should be judged.*** These people were warned not to take the mark of the beast (mid-point of 70th week), because they would suffer the consequences of their choice for all eternity (cf. Rev. 13:15-18; 14:9-11; 19:20; 20:4). Therefore, both statements are correct. The wrath at the sixth seal is about to occur for the first time during the 70th week. And the wrath mentioned in chapter 11 is speaking of the eternal wrath that is about to occur. Even Revelation 11:15 verifies this is eternal wrath to come by saying: *The kingdoms of this world are become the kingdoms of our Lord, and of his Christ; and he shall reign for ever and ever.*

Closing

Here are a few closing remarks pertaining to our study on the day of the Lord.

1.) Prewrath teaching: The day of the Lord is a future supernatural intervention by God in the affairs of mankind.
Pretrib teaching: Say that the day of the Lord is a time of judgment, past or future.

2.) Prewrath teaching: The opening of the sixth seal is what signifies the coming wrath of God on the world which begins with the trumpet judgments in Revelation chapter 8.
Pretrib teaching: The elite pretrib teachers acknowledges God's wrath by pointing to the sixth seal, but creating a discrepancy in their teaching that "all" the seals are God's wrath.

3.) Prewrath teaching: Beginning at the day of the Lord is when Christ is revealed, and at the sixth seal is where the world sees Christ.

Pretrib teaching: It cannot allow any revealing of Christ until the end of the 70th week, therefore, Christ is not in view in any of their teachings during the seals or trumpets. We saw some pretrib teachers identifying the sixth seal as though this was at the end of the 70th week. This is only to try to rectify the appearance of Christ at the sixth seal.

4.) Prewrath teaching: The seal judgments (first five) are solely that of Antichrist and men, where God's wrath is never mentioned before the sixth seal.

Pretrib teaching: The seals are the wrath of God, but say the fifth seal of the martyr saints is the wrath of men, not God.

The teaching on the day of the Lord should be an eye-opener for the pretrib adherents. To deny the timing and purpose of the day of the Lord will only expose the biasedness of this doctrine.

The Courtroom Witnesses

I will now like to finalize my conclusions pertaining to the legitimacy of God's wrath by introducing witnesses as in a courtroom setting. It's the testimony of a witness that can sway the final verdict of a jury when determining a trial. With that said, here are my (eye) witnesses proving God's wrath is not contained in the seals starting in Revelation chapter 6.

1. Martyred saints at the 5th seal in verse 10 ask: *And they cried with a loud voice, saying,* **How long,** *O Lord, holy and true,* **dost thou not judge and avenge our blood on them** *that dwell on the earth?* These martyred saints ask Christ: "when" will he avenge their deaths? Obviously, these saints are the eye-witnesses to the events taking place on earth, and surely, they would know whether God's wrath was taking place or not.

2. Christ's answer to the martyred saint's request in verse 11: "*and it was said unto them, that they should rest yet for a little season,* **until** *their fellowservants also and their brethren, that should be killed as they* were, **should be fulfilled.**" The witness of Jesus says that the martyrs would have to wait awhile longer until the persecution of other believers is completed. Christ is saying His wrath has "not" taken place yet.

3. The World at the 6th seal: For the first time these inhabitants of earth cry out that "God's wrath has come" (v.17). These witnesses are testifying that God's wrath is now about to occur, and we know this because they go and try to hide from the "great day of His wrath." This wrath will come shortly in the form of the trumpet and bowl judgments.

4. The Sealing of the 144,000 in Chapter 7: We see that these Jews are sealed for protection from God's wrath. If God's wrath has been occurring, then why just now seal them for protection from God's wrath?

5. The Multitude in chapter 7:14 are the ones that have come out of "great tribulation." These saints make up the completed church which were raptured by Christ's coming at the sixth seal.

6. Silence in Heaven: Chapter 8:1 records silence in heave for thirty minutes. This is the direct result from the prayers of the saints that ask God to avenge their death.

7. Trumpet Judgments: Just go back and read the results of the trumpet blasts. The judgment originates from heaven, where the seals were a result of coming from the earth. The trumpets are only blown when all the seals have been broken on the outside of the scroll, which is now opened for the first time. If you compare the scene in chapter 7 of multitude shouting "salvation" to the heavenly scene in chapter 19 you will see that the multitude in chapter 19:1-3 rejoices that the judgment" was done," yet, here in chapter 8, the silence recognizes that God's wrath is "about" to begin.

8. Matthew 24: The Olivet Discourse is the contemporary passage to the seals in Revelation 6. And when you read through Jesus's teaching, which we will see, there is nothing mentioned in the entire chapter pertaining to God's wrath.

This are eight powerful witnesses that are all in agreement with each other that God's wrath is certainly absent pertaining to the first five seals. Pretribulationist can say what they "think" to be God's wrath to bolster their case, but these witnesses alone should render a verdict disproving pretribulationism.

CHAPTER THIRTEEN

MATTHEW 24

As we discussed dispensationalism in chapter 5, we saw that there were overlapping of different so-called dispensations prescribed by pretribulationist. We noted the importance of this, because the pretribulation teaching says that there will be a direct cut-off between church and Israel at the rapture. This will theoretically usher in a new dispensation: the 70th week of Daniel. Strangely, Darby's dispensational formula does not include the 70th week as being part of the final dispensation (actually, none). They teach that the final dispensation is the millennium itself, consequently, they mistakenly created a gap in their dispensation time-table. To correct their problem, they caused one of the most tragic cases of Bible hermeneutics (interpretation of Scriptures). They simply dismiss the Olivet Discourse in Matthew 24 pertaining to the New Testament Church, and say Jesus is addressing only Israel. Like Houdini waving his magical wand in his disappearing act, pretribulational teachers by the leading of Darby and others, give the illusion that the church "disappears" before the events in Matthew 24 take place.

Jesus is explaining to His disciples (members of the church) His second coming. In Christ's discourse, he taught and warned His disciples that there will be certain events that would precede His coming (this is what the imminence debate is all about). Later in the chapter, Jesus poignantly said that there would be great tribulation before His coming. This statement alone destroys a pretribulational rapture. Consequently, for the pretribulation camp, the only viable argument for their theory is for them to excuse the church here in Matthew 24, so presto- we disappear! The pretribulation set-up is that Matthew is supposed to be the "Jewish" gospel, because throughout the book of Matthew Jesus is emphasized as the King and he teaches truths about the kingdom. In doing so, pretribulationist not only dismiss the church being addressed in chapter 24, but the kingdom teachings as well.

If one does a word search in the four Gospels, you might find it interesting that the word "church" is only used in the gospel of Matthew and not the other three gospels.

> And I say also unto thee, That thou art Peter, and upon this rock I will build my **church**; and the gates of hell shall not prevail against it. (Matt. 16:18)

> Moreover if thy brother shall trespass against thee, go and tell him his fault between thee and him alone: if he shall hear thee, thou hast gained thy brother. But if he will not hear thee, then take with thee one or two more, that in the mouth of two or three witnesses every word may be established. And if he shall neglect to hear them, tell it unto the **church**: but if he neglect to hear the **church**, let him be unto thee as a heathen man and a publican. (Matt. 18:15-17)

There are no more references in the gospels where the church is mentioned; but we know there are multiple passages in the gospels where Christ addressed the church. In Christ's Sermon on the Mount, which came after His baptism by John and His wilderness temptations, He was preaching tenants of New Testament Christianity to the Jews who were technically still under the Old Testament Jewish commandments and ordinances.

I find it strange that many dispensationalists teach that Christ's coming in Matthew 24, when He addressed the "church apostles," was only referring to Israel. Yet, in the previous chapter in Matthew 23, when Jesus was addressing the "Jewish Scribes and Pharisees" about their unbalanced life of hypocrisy pertaining to "tithing;" many dispensationalists will use this passage to say Jesus was teaching that Christians in the church-age should tithe according to this Jewish ordinance.

Two more examples in comparing Jesus's instructions to the apostles that we hold as "church" instructions are John 14, the "upper room discourse", and Matthew 28, the "great commission." John 14 was given by Christ only two days after the Olivet Discourse; yet, we acknowledge this is referring to the rapture in the first few verses. The great commission was forty days after His resurrection and the apostles were to go and teach the church everything Jesus taught them, including the Olivet Discourse. There needs to be a consistent biblical exegesis applied to one's theology.

The Olivet Discourse

I must ask the question now as we begin our study on the Olivet Discourse; if the timing of the rapture isn't important, why will Jesus spend so much time and detail in answering the disciples question "when" would Christ come again?

(Matthew 24:1-31)

1. And Jesus went out, and departed from the temple: and his disciples came to him for to shew him the buildings of the temple.
2. And Jesus said unto them, See ye not all these things? verily I say unto you, There shall not be left here one stone upon another, that shall not be thrown down.
3. And as he sat upon the mount of Olives, the disciples came unto him privately, saying, Tell us, when shall these things be? and what *shall be* the sign of thy coming, and of the end of the world?

#1) vv. 1-3: The disciples asked two questions (the second had two parts) in response to His comments about the temple being destroyed and Christ's return.

1. When shall these things be?
2. What shall be the sign of your coming and the end of the world?

I believe the last question was probably based on the previous conversation in chapter 23 between Jesus and the Jewish leadership where He scathingly rebuked them and pronounced judgment on Israel.

37. O Jerusalem, Jerusalem, *thou* that killest the prophets, and stonest them which are sent unto thee, how often would I have gathered thy children together, even as a hen gathereth her chickens under *her* wings, and ye would not!
38. **Behold, your house is left unto you desolate.**

39. For I say unto you, **Ye shall not see me henceforth, till ye shall say, Blessed *is* he that cometh in the name of the Lord.**

The disciple had to have heard Jesus's prior teaching about "the end of the world" to ask this specific question. As an example, Jesus taught:

The enemy that sowed them is the devil; the harvest is the **end of the world**; and the reapers are the angels.

As therefore the tares are gathered and burned in the fire; so shall it be in the **end of this world**. (Matthew 13:39-40)

Let me make a quick comment about Jesus's statement pertaining to the temple. Jesus taught in verse 2: *And Jesus said unto them, See ye not all these things? verily I say unto you, There shall not be left here one stone upon another, that shall not be thrown down.* The significance of this statement is two-fold. One, with Christ completing the redemption for man's sin through His death, burial, and resurrection; therefore, no longer would the sacrificial system be necessary. If you read the book of Hebrews, you can still see the struggle many Jews had leaving the temple ordinances after they came to a saving faith in Christ. Second, the temple destruction will validate Christ's far-distance prophecies by an earlier prophetic event that comes to pass. Therefore, Jesus's prediction about the temple being cast down will verify to everyone (present at that time and future believers) the things predicted (i.e. 70th week) will come to pass as well. This prophecy is not as the preterits would have you believe, that "all" what Christ was predicting would occur in AD 70. This was only a foretaste of the ultimate conclusion of the end of the age when Christ would set up His kingdom.

4. And Jesus answered and said unto them, Take heed that no man deceive you.
5. For many shall come in my name, saying, I am Christ; and shall deceive many.

#2) vv. 4-5: As Christ begins to lay a foundation for His discourse, the cornerstone He sets first which comes in the form of a stern warning. He tells the disciples to *"take heed that no man deceive you."* Watch out for the deceptions of false Christ's. Many will claim, not only are they supposedly the very Christ, but will also claim to be speaking as the authority for Christ. One example of such deception is what we noted in chapter four, how some false religions sprang up declaring they are speaking for God. Perhaps the main method of deception is for someone to claim some unknown truth not previously revealed that gives their followers that sense of being part of something special. That's how Satan made Eve feel-special! I cannot bypass this opportunity to mention the false spiritual prophesying being claimed in the name of Jesus. Numerous people claiming they are receiving special revelation from God; and are potentially more destructive than well-known false cults. The word of Faith movement is stripping the fundamental truth of God's word and degrading the Scriptures to an extremely dangerous level.

> 6. And ye shall hear of wars and rumours of wars: see that ye be not troubled: for all *these things* must come to pass, but the end is not yet.
> 7. For nation shall rise against nation, and kingdom against kingdom: and there shall be famines, and pestilences, and earthquakes, in divers places.
> 8. All these *are* the beginning of sorrows.

#3) vv. 6-8: Christ now moves from individual spiritual deception to world-wide physical calamities. Everything mentioned in verses 6-8, except for earthquakes, are manmade. Christ comments that these are just the "beginning of sorrows." What we know for certain, all the events described by Christ so far to the disciples have been part of mankind since Christ. History of national violence and upheavals even go back to the time of Noah, as we saw in our short Old Testament overview. On that note, we can safely say that verses 4-8 could be referencing the general time period building up to the 70th week of Daniel. What will transpire is that the beginning of sorrows will intensify to the "birth pangs" spoken by Christ. What ensues from this is the birth pangs will turn into hard labor. I believe the hard labor is identified with the abomination of desolation when intense persecution upon believers will be taking place.

One major observation needs to be noted here is that there is "no" mention of specific wrath on the lost, which is what pretribulationist say is the entire 70th week and why the church is supposedly absent here in Matthew

24. What is not seen, is that these events are biased as to who is suffering the effects. In other words, both lost and saved are feeling the effects.

The common outline which most prophecy students hold to is that the events described so far in Matthew 24 are the same first four seals described in Revelation chapter 6.

Matthew 24 Revelation 6

1.) Verses 4-5: False Christ White Horse- Antichrist
2.) Verse 6: War Red Horse- War
3.) Verse 7: Famines Black Horse- (High Price of food) Famines
4.) Verse 8: Death Pale Horse- Hunger and Death

I believe to match these is stretching it a little far. As I stated in our study in Revelation 6, I beg to differ that the first four seals are the contained within the first-half of the 70th week- it's a guess, at best. What Christ is laying out here is that the beginning of sorrows would start well before the 70th week begins (i.e. false religions, WWI, WWII, African famines, recorded major earthquakes that has killed hundreds of thousands, etc.). However, these sorrows will certainly go well into the 70th week.

9. Then shall they deliver you up to be afflicted, and shall kill you: and ye shall be hated of all nations for my name's sake.
10. And then shall many be offended, and shall betray one another, and shall hate one another.
11. And many false prophets shall rise, and shall deceive many.

#4) vv. 9-11: Christ begins His statement here starting in verse 9 with the word "then," which indicates there is a transition in the timing of the sequence of events. The word, "then" has the same meaning as the word, "afterwards." Christ states there will be affliction upon a specific group of people which results in death, where previously, disastrous events were broad in scope (e. g. wars, famines, nations, kingdoms, etc.).

The affliction or persecution comes upon people who are targeted for a specific reason- hatred against Christ. Believers will be hated for their commitment to Jesus. What's telling, is that Jesus said many will be "offended." I looked up the word offend in the Strong's Concordance and interestingly this word is used in connection with stumbling or to fall away. Therefore, the meaning of Christ's statement is that when persecution comes upon those who follow Christ, many who are claiming to be following Jesus will turn from Him and worship Him no longer. Their rejection is amplified by Christ saying they will betray and hate those who aren't offended, or fall away (v.10). And what fuels the hatred of the folks is that false prophets will deceive them into believing they made the right choice (v.11). Sadly, the only other option is to follow Antichrist and receive his mark. Many false teachers will go against the clear teaching of Scripture and tell others it will be ok to accept the mark of the Antichrist.

Another frightening means of submission by many Christians is that many will reject God's truth because they were told they would never have to face such a decision. Many will believe they were exempt from the tribulation because they were supposed to be raptured already. And I'm afraid what will ensue in this perplexing time is the reasoning of many believers who will believe the false premise that they can justify taking the Antichrist's mark based on believing they have "Jesus in their heart." Yet, Scripture is clear, anyone who takes the mark will damn their soul (Rev. 14:9-10; 19:20; 20:4)

There's another important understanding that I need to bring to the reader's attention about the saints in verses 9-13. These saints cannot be the ones who were lost before the great tribulation began then became saved during the great tribulation. There is nothing in Jesus's teaching that would indicate these saints had a conversion experience. Christ's warning here is about rejection of Him, not acceptance for salvation. Christ's teaching is for a believer's "continuing" of their faith, which is the common theme in Christ's warning about the 70th week. Even Christ warned the "church" at Thyatira in Revelation 2:26 "and keepeth my works unto the end."

The timing of this could not be any clearer, this will occur in conjunction with the great tribulation when Antichrist becomes the beast that he really is. But what's certainly not speculation is that this affliction is forced upon believers. Jesus uses the personal pronoun "you" (vv. 4, 6, 9, 15, 20, 23) in describing those who will be afflicted. This is certainly not describing Israel. These verses and the remaining chapter are unquestionably applied to the events taking place during the final week.

> 12. And because iniquity shall abound, the love of many shall wax cold.
> 13. But he that shall endure unto the end, the same shall be saved.

#5) vv. 12-13: One major end-time sign is the prevalence of sin. Isaiah recorded a solemn warning: *"O my people, they which lead thee cause thee to err, and destroy thy paths"* (Isaiah 3:12). Perhaps Isaiah 5: 20-21 sum it up the best. *"Woe unto them that call evil good, and good evil; that put darkness for light, and light for darkness; that put bitter for sweet, and sweet for bitter! Woe unto them that are wise in their own eyes."* We will read later in our study the warning from the Lord to the church of Laodicea pertaining to their complacency about spiritual things. The redefining of what constitutes sin will be attacked, as we have been witnessing in the last days. Abortion, homosexuality, immorality, drunkenness, pleasures and pride are leading the way across this globe. And it will only get worse, particularly homosexuality as it forces itself upon society in an unprecedented manner. Sadly, as the pressure to submit to this hellish social-political agenda, most churches and religions will only redefine their beliefs so they can "stay in business;" and "in the name of love," will be their motto to excuse sodomy in their church.

Love and hate are contrasted by many turning cold and not enduring (remaining) to the end. As I just stated, love, will be the battle cry of many religious people, but love in the wrong way. But love will also grow cold toward Jesus as Christianity becomes more infiltrated with unsaved people that run their individual churches. But the individual warning remains the same for each person. This ties in perfectly with the emphasis of "watching," which has to do with the individual continuing his or her belief in Christ. In verse 13 it talks about endurance. Sadly, much of Christian teaching is that if you once made a commitment, expressed faith, or made a decision to follow Christ, then you are eternally secured. This could not be further from the truth (Rev. 14:9-10). The Bible is very clear, even within the context of our study, that a person can freely choose Christ, they can freely reject Christ. I am not advocating a sinless-perfection that is taught by some religions, but I am saying what Christ is warning believers over- you can fall away (reject Christ). You can turn away from a belief once held.

> 14. And this gospel of the kingdom shall be preached in all the
> world for a witness unto all nations; and then shall the end
> come.

#6) v. 14: The gospel, which is the truth about the coming kingdom of Christ and delivering a person from God's wrath and judgment, will be spread throughout the world during the great tribulation. This is another reason why pretrib-dispensationalism is so dangerous, it's teaches another gospel. As we saw earlier, dispensational teaching says there is a gospel of salvation (Church) and a gospel of the kingdom (Israel). We also see for the first-time Christ gives His response to the disciple question- when is the end of the age? The end of the age will not come until the gospel has been proclaimed in a final effort during the great tribulation (c.f. Rev. 14:6)

15. When ye therefore shall see the abomination of desolation, spoken of by Daniel the prophet, stand in the holy place, (whoso readeth, let him understand:)
16. Then let them which be in Judaea flee into the mountains:
17. Let him which is on the housetop not come down to take any thing out of his house:
18. Neither let him which is in the field return back to take his clothes.
19. And woe unto them that are with child, and to them that give suck in those days!
20. But pray ye that your flight be not in the winter, neither on the sabbath day:
21. For then shall be great tribulation, such as was not since the beginning of the world to this time, no, nor ever shall be.

#7) vv. 15-21: Now Christ identifies the abomination of desolation, which marks the beginning of "great tribulation." Verse 15 does not begin with the word, "then," but, "when." I believe the "when" is describing the events starting back in verse 9 when saints will be delivered up to be afflicted (killed). I believe this is what Christ was referring to when He said many false prophets will arise during this time (v. 11). There will be many preachers and religions who will tell their members that it will be OK to receive the mark of the beast. The "abomination of desolation" (Dan.9:27) is described as occurring at the midpoint of the 70th week. This is the only tribulation associated with the 70th week; and notice, most importantly, there has been no specific reference to God's wrath on the world in these verses so far. For pretribulationist, they will use this event to bolster their belief that the Olivet Discourse is specifically written to the nation of Israel, after all, the events here certainly describe what is taking place in Israel. What should be noted is that the only importance about Israel in Christ's teaching here is the geographical location in the last days. There has been nothing specific about

Israel before now; it's been about the world and followers of Jesus, which excludes Israel because they are still in unbelief at this point in history. Jesus had already stated in chapter 23 that Israel as a nation does not see the errors of their way until Christ's return.

> 22. And except those days should be shortened, there should no flesh be saved: but for the elect's sake those days shall be shortened.

#8) v. 22: There are only two possible options why the "days are shortened."

1.) This is the 70th week of Daniel itself.
2.) This is the great tribulation.

The first option is held by the pretribulationist. They say the seven-year tribulation is so awful that there would not be anyone left alive; concluding, God must cut short the 70th week. Here is a response to Rosenthal's Pre-Wrath Rapture book, by Tommy Ice and Timothy Demy dealing with this particular question.

> Here one must **think theologically**. If according to Acts 17:26, God has marked out the times for the nations, His sovereignty would include the length of time of the Great Tribulation. Another passage says the very day of entering God's rest has been determined (Heb. 4:7). Certainly, the shortening of the days is fixed. Who is to deny that the three-and-a- half years have already been amputated from what may have been? **Certainly the world and Israel deserve more than seven years of tribulation! This shortening to seven years** is an evidence of God's grace.[118] (bold letters mine)

This will be a terrible time, there's no denying this; however, Ice and Demy's commentary does not fit Scripture. First, in the sequence of events described during the great tribulation, the Antichrist's persecution is geared toward believers, not God's wrath on the world and Israel. This is clearly stated in Revelation 12:7-14, along with the numerous verses I have referenced so far.

Also, their statement that the world and Israel deserve more than seven-years of tribulation is pure speculation (not thinking theologically!). The world through the Antichrist is "causing" the great tribulation; they are not the recipients of it.

I mentioned in chapter six "The Seventy Weeks of Daniel," this is God's time because it has been "determined" or set. The seventy-weeks will come to pass perfectly as God said they would, confirming that the shortening spoken of cannot be the 70th week itself. When Christ was teaching the Olivet Discourse to His disciples, He gave two specific events that would identify His return: the "abomination of desolation" and "cosmic disturbances." What the "shortening" of those days must refer to is the second option- the great tribulation. The great tribulation will be started by the abomination of desolations when the Antichrist declares that he is god. The phrase "no flesh would be saved," is in line with the Antichrist persecution on "believers," not on the entire world. The Antichrist is going to persecute those who call themselves Christians, along with Israel because they are God's chosen people. This attempt by the Antichrist to kill all believers and Jews, is so he can prevent Jesus from returning and establishing His millennial reign, which somehow, Satan must believe will delay his eternal punishment. This would fall in line with the Genesis 3:15 prophecy Satan knows his soon demise (Rev. 12: 12).

The only tribulation in view within the context of the Olivet Discourse is the great tribulation spoken previously in verse 21. And verse 21, the great tribulation, is a reference to verse 15, which identifies the "abomination of desolation." This can be verified in Revelation 13 when the Antichrist is killed and raised back to life, which is followed by the whole world wondering after the beast. We are told in Revelation 13:5 the Antichrist will continue for forty-two months, or three-and-half years. However, the Antichrist's persecution on the believers will be "cut short." To cut short, comes from the meaning to amputate. Revelation chapter 13 is in agreement with Matthew 24:15, 21.

The Antichrist

Let's look at the persecution by the Antichrist as it applies to the great tribulation.

> And there was war in heaven: Michael and his angels fought against the dragon; and the dragon fought and his angels, And prevailed not; neither was their place found any more in heaven. And the great dragon was cast out, that old serpent, called the Devil, and Satan, which deceiveth the whole world: he was cast out into the earth, and his angels were cast out with him. And I heard a loud voice saying in heaven, Now is come salvation, and strength, and the kingdom of our God, and the power of his Christ: for the accuser of our brethren is cast down, which accused them before our God day and night. And they **overcame him by the blood of the Lamb, and by the word of their testimony; and they loved not their lives unto the death.** Therefore rejoice, ye heavens, and ye that dwell in them. Woe to the inhabiters of the earth and of the sea! **for the devil is come down unto you, having great wrath,** because **he knoweth that he hath but a short time**. And when the dragon saw that he was cast unto the earth, **he persecuted the woman** which brought forth the man child. And to the **woman were given two wings of a great eagle, that she might fly into the wilderness, into her place, where she is nourished for a time, and times, and half a time,** from the face of the serpent. And the serpent cast out of his mouth water as a flood after the woman, that he might cause her to be carried away of the flood. And the earth helped the woman, and the earth opened her mouth, and swallowed up the flood which the dragon cast out of his mouth. And the dragon was wroth with the woman, **and went to make war with the remnant of her seed, which keep the commandments of God, and have the testimony of Jesus Christ.** (Rev. 12:7-17)

These verses are teaching that Satan is kicked out of heaven at the mid-point of the final seven-years, and immediately he goes to persecute the woman (Israel). Jesus warned that this would happen in Mt.24:15-21. However, we see in verse 17 after Israel flees into the wilderness, God intervenes to help Israel (not persecute with His wrath as the pretrib teachers teach). They will be kept safe for the remaining three-and-half-years. When the Antichrist sees that he cannot persecute the woman because of God's protection, he turns his attention to the remnant of her "seed"- the church/ saints (Rom 4:16; Gal. 3:29). How do we know this? Because, it is those who keep the commandments (obedience to God), and "have the testimony of Jesus Christ" that are persecuted. This is the exact same event as the fifth seal, when we saw the souls under the altar who were slain for their "testimony and the word of God" (Rev. 6:9-11).

> And **he causeth all**, both small and great, rich and poor, free and bond, **to receive a mark** in their right hand, or in their foreheads: And that **no man** might buy or sell, save he that had the mark, or the name of the beast, or the number of his name. Here is wisdom. Let him that hath understanding count the number of the beast: for it is the number of a man; and his number is Six hundred threescore and six. *(*Rev. 13:16-18)

> And the third angel followed them, saying with a loud voice, **If any man worship the beast and his image**, and receive his mark in his forehead, or in his hand, The same **shall drink of the wine of the wrath of God,** which is poured out without mixture into the cup of his indignation; and he **shall be tormented with fire and brimstone** in the presence of the holy angels, and in the presence of the Lamb: (Rev. 14:9-10)

> And the beast was taken, and with him the false prophet that wrought miracles before him, with **which he deceived them that had received the mark of the beast, and them that worshipped his image**. These both were cast alive into a lake of fire burning with brimstone. (Rev. 19:20)

> And I saw thrones, and they sat upon them, and judgment was given unto them: and *I saw* **the souls of them that were beheaded for the witness of Jesus, and for the word of God, and which had not worshipped the beast, neither his image, neither had received *his* mark** upon their foreheads, or in their

hands; and they lived and reigned with Christ a thousand years. (Rev. 20:4)

Again, the pretribulational rapture theory has a problem reconciling the teaching about God's wrath in the final week. Here in Revelation 14: 9 it says, *shall drink* (wrath) if you receive the mark, which taking the mark is only possible at the beginning in the middle of the week, not before then. When Antichrist comes on the scene at the beginning of the 70th week (not revealed yet), and as the week unfolds, many Christians will become aware of what's taking place and begin to warn others (Dan. 12:3-4, 10-11). However, when the Antichrist is revealed for who he really is in the middle of the week he will begin his wrath (vv.9-10). Simply, God's wrath has **not** occurred before now. The wrath of God will not happen until sometime after the mark of the beast in the middle of the tribulation has taken place. This is what Paul taught in 2 Thessalonians 2 regarding the falling away and the man of sin being revealed first. The argument by pretrib teaching that the church must be raptured before the tribulation, because it is all God's wrath, falls flat on its face.

What we have seen so far, in Jesus's teaching in the Olivet Discourse, is the persecution by the Antichrist on believers will be cut short by God's wrath; therefore, advocating the prewrath rapture of the church. Now you can see calling the 70th week "the tribulation" by pretrib definitions has clouded this simple description of Christ's discourse about His return.

23. Then if any man shall say unto you, Lo, here *is* Christ, or there; believe *it* not.

24. For there shall arise false Christs, and false prophets, and shall shew great signs and wonders; insomuch that, if *it were* possible, they shall deceive the very elect.

25. Behold, I have told you before.

#9) vv. 23-25: Christ said "behold I have told you before," which is reference to the time during the final seven-years where false Christ and deceivers will flourish. The great signs and wonders that bring deception is referring to Revelation 13:13-14 "*And he doeth great wonders, so that he maketh fire come down from heaven on the earth in the sight of men. And deceiveth them that dwell on the earth by the means of those miracles which he had power to do in the sight of the beast;*"

26. Wherefore if they shall say unto you, Behold, he is in the desert; go not forth: behold, *he is* in the secret chambers; believe *it* not.
27. For as the lightning cometh out of the east, and shineth even unto the west; so shall also the coming of the Son of man be.

#10) vv. 26-27: Christ said false prophets will say that he was in the desert place or somewhere hidden. The desert is implied that Christ won't be returning in some far away obscure place. He countered this by saying that His coming would be like lightening as it lights up a night sky. My question is: when does lightning occur? Answer: only when a storm is taking place. The great tribulation will be the greatest storm in human history just as Christ said in verse 21. The lives of inhabitants on the earth will be in complete total chaos due to the false signs and miracles, along with forcing mankind to follow the Antichrist. The Antichrist's proclamation as God will drive men to do unspeakable things. Furthermore, lightning in a storm is "visible;" there's nothing secret about it. Clearly, Jesus is stressing the point not to be deceived about His return- it will not be signless.

Behold, I come quickly: blessed is *he that keepeth the sayings of the prophecy of this book* (Rev. 22:7). When Jesus stated this, he was not saying His coming was imminent (quickly), but it would be sudden when certain things begin to unfold. His coming will be like the lightening as He taught here in verse 27. When he came the first time it was not until He thirty years old when He revealed himself; this will not be the case when He comes again the second time. There will not be a Sermon on the Mount or an Olivet Discourse, or even a Last Supper. He won't be teaching in the synagogues or the temple persuading folks to follow Him. No, when He comes again we need to already be prepared; there will be no choices, you will be either in or out when He arrives.

As stated previously, pretribulation teaches the rapture is secret so the world is at a loss to what happened to millions of people. I say, if you accept an invisible rapture, then do not argue with a Jehovah Witnesses claim that Christ's invisible return occurred in 1914. Same can be said with the Seventh-day Adventist, who claims the heavenly temple was invisibly cleansed in 1843 when William Millers prophecy failed.

Next, Christ's appearance will cut short the great tribulation. For the saved, it will be a day of the blessed hope; for the lost, a day of sadness and anguish. This is not the second coming as defined by the pretrib teachers, but the rapture, which is a visible event associated with Christ's second coming before God's wrath.

> 28. For wheresoever the carcase is, there will the eagles be gathered together.

#11) v. 28: Christ interjects a description which is going to parallel His return. He is describing the severity of His coming judgment. Carcass in the passage describes death. This symbolism describes birds feasting on those who rejected God's truth about Christ's coming kingdom. Isaiah 34: 1-15 gives a vivid description matching this time when God brings forth His judgment upon the earth, which occurs at the day of the Lord.

#12) vv. 29-30   Day of the Lord in the Olivet Discourse

> 29. Immediately **after the tribulation** of those days shall the sun be darkened, and the moon shall not give her light, and the stars shall fall from heaven, and the powers of the heavens shall be shaken:
> 30. And then shall appear the sign of the Son of man in heaven: and then shall all the tribes of the earth mourn, and they shall see the Son of man coming in the clouds of heaven with power and great glory.

Christ has been describing the first part of the disciple's question from verse two: "when shall these things be?" Next, they asked: "What shall be the sign of your coming and the end of the age?" Christ is now about to answer these two questions. We have already noted that the gospel must be preached before the end. And we saw that the gospel was preached in Revelation 14 which was during the time of Antichrist's reign.

These verses provide the same content as that of the Old Testament with regard to the day of the Lord. The sign given that the sun, moon, and stars going dark are the identical reference to the verses found in the Old Testament. What the pretribulation rapture teaches is that these verses in Matthew 24 are at the "end" of the 70th week of Daniel; supposedly after the rapture has already mysteriously occurred. Several aspects of this passage that drives their thinking are: The Antichrist has already been revealed in the middle of the 70th week (vs.15), as well as the statement *after the tribulation of those days* (vs. 29). Since believers are not supposed to encounter the Antichrist, and more telling, the tribulation, therefore we should have been raptured already. However, when you compare Scripture with Scripture this presents a problem for the pretrib theory, because this passage parallels the sixth seal in Revelation 6. *After the tribulation* is a reference to the great tribulation in verse 15 and 21, which will be "cut short" (v.22) by Christ's intervention at the day of the Lord to rapture His followers. Therefore, this cannot be at the end of the 70th week.

Another reason this is not at the end of the 70th week, is that the trumpet and bowl judgments, as well as the battle of Armageddon, are not even referenced here in Matthew 24. If Christ were giving a sequence of events that pertained to His coming at the end of the 70th week there would be other signs given, which would certainly include the trumpet and bowl judgments of His wrath before He returned.

Not only is the sign of the sun, moon and stars given, but also notice that the world will *see the Son of man* coming in the clouds of heaven and with great glory. This is a perfect match for the sixth seal in Revelation chapter 6. When the people of the earth witness Christ coming, they *mourn*, not in repentance, but in agony, because they know that God's wrath and anger is about to be poured out on them (cf. Rev. 1:7).

The phrase in verse 29, *powers of the heavens shall be shaken,* can be understood in comparison to Hebrews 1:3, that Christ is *upholding all things by the word of His power.* We know from Scripture that Christ made or created all things (cf. Colossians 1:16; John 1:3). The powers that are shaken are caused by the unfolding of the heavens and the revealing of the Lord's at the sixth seal. This is certainly a supernatural event brought about by the Lord himself.

In Luke's account of the Olivet Discourse in chapter 21 it states in verses 25-27:

> And there shall be **signs in the sun, and in the moon, and in the stars;** and upon the earth distress of nations, with perplexity; the sea and the waves roaring; **Men's hearts failing them for fear,** and for looking after those things which are coming on the earth: for the **powers of heaven shall be shaken**. And then shall they see the Son of man coming in a cloud with power and great glory.

Luke's account is exactly the same as Isaiah 13:6-9 and Revelation 6. Men's hearts fail them, **not at the beginning of the 70th week**, but at the day of the Lord at the sixth seal- well into the 70th week. The world will know full well the fury and vengeance of the coming wrath of God upon them. Here's Isaiah 34 description of this event in the Olivet Discourse.

1. Come near, ye nations, to hear; and hearken, ye people: let the earth hear, and all that is therein; the world, and all things that come forth of it.

2. For the **indignation of the LORD *is* upon all nations**, and *his* fury upon all their armies: he hath utterly destroyed them, he hath delivered them to the slaughter.

3. Their slain also shall be cast out, and their stink shall come up out of their carcases, and the mountains shall be melted with their blood.

4. And all the host of heaven shall be dissolved, and the heavens shall be rolled together as a scroll: and all their host shall fall down, as the leaf falleth off from the vine, and as a falling *fig* from the fig tree.

5. **For my sword shall be bathed in heaven: behold, it shall come down upon Idumea, and upon the people of my curse, to judgment.**

6. The sword of the LORD is filled with blood, it is made fat with fatness, *and* with the blood of lambs and goats, with the fat of the kidneys of rams: for the LORD hath a sacrifice in Bozrah, and a great slaughter in the land of Idumea.

7. And the unicorns shall come down with them, and the bullocks with the bulls; and their land shall be soaked with blood, and their dust made fat with fatness.

8. For *it is* the day of the LORD'S vengeance, *and* the year of recompences for the controversy of Zion.

#13) v. 31   The Rapture / Resurrection

31. And he shall send his angels with a great sound of a trumpet, and they shall gather together his elect from the four winds, from one end of heaven to the other.

In verse 31 it states that the angels, at the *sound of the trumpet*, will gather His "elect" from the *four corners* of the earth. This is the rapture Paul speaks of in I Thessalonians 4:14-18. This is also in agreement with Revelation chapter 7, which immediately follows the sixth seal that is opened in chapter 6.

> And after these things I saw **four angels standing on the four corners of the earth**, holding the four winds of the earth, that the wind should not blow on the earth, nor on the sea, nor on any tree. (Rev. 7:1)

These four angels will seal the 144,000 from God's wrath. Why is that? Because, God is about to pour out wrath on the earth to punish them for their rejection of Christ and the acceptance of the Antichrist! The question I ask the pretribulationist is: If God's wrath is being poured out at the beginning of the tribulation, then why is God just now sealing the 144,000 from His wrath? Simply stated, God's wrath has not begun until now! Furthermore, this matches Isaiah 26 where God will hide Israel for a short time until the indignation (wrath) is over. Israel will be supernaturally protected just like they were in Egypt when God sent the plagues on the Egyptians- Israel was unharmed.

The 144,000 are Witnesses in the Tribulation:

Pretribulationism teaches that since the rapture occurs at the beginning of the tribulation, then the 144,000 (Jews) become the tribulation witnesses; supposedly, due to the great multitude saved during the tribulation (Rev.7:9).

Here is pretribulationist Mark Hitchcock expounding the pretribulation view.

> There **appears** to be a cause-and-effect relationship in Revelation 7 between the 144,000 in verses 1-8 and the innumerable crowd of believers in verses 9-17. The ministry of the 144,000 is the cause that leads to effect of salvation for millions of people.[119] (bold letters mine)

There is no scriptural proof for the 144,000 to be witnesses during the 70th week, only assumptions. Hitchcock follows the typical usage of words by saying "appears," for his explanation for the 144,000 - nothing literal is mentioned. This is hardly provable evidence if this were a court of law! Prewrath teaches the ones saved are the same ones who entered the great tribulation to begin with - the church saints. The Bible teaches that the 144,000 go into the wilderness for the full three-and-half years when the great tribulation begins. Then they are eventually sealed at the beginning of the day of the Lord for protection from God's wrath during the trumpet and bowl judgments.

Next, we see in Revelation 7 after the sealing of the 144,000, the great multitude in verse 14 that have washed their robes and made them white in the blood of the Lamb. This multitude are the ones recognized as having come out of the great tribulation. This is the rapture of the church before God pours out His wrath on the earth, which starts in chapter 8 of Revelation. This is the gathering that Christ says takes place in Matthew 24:31.

The negative impact of the day of the Lord is that for the unrepentant sinner God's day of wrath will be an unmerciful time of judgment, which there will be no hope of deliverance for those individuals. When we see the sixth seal opened in Revelation 6, the world cries out in anguish, even to the point of wishing for death, knowing they rejected God's truth.

The positive impact of this event is believers will be the raptured and delivered from God's wrath. We see this taught in the Old Testament book of Joel.

> Put ye in the sickle, for the harvest is ripe: come, get you down; for the press is full, the vats overflow; for their wickedness is great. **Multitudes, multitudes in the valley of decision: for the day of the LORD is "near" in the valley of decision. The sun and the moon shall be darkened, and the stars shall withdraw their shining.** The LORD also shall roar out of Zion, and utter his voice from Jerusalem; and the heavens and the earth shall shake: **but the LORD will be the hope of his people, and the strength of the children of Israel.** (Joel 3:13-16)

The reference to the *multitudes in the valley of decision* is the world will be at a crossroad when the Antichrist is revealed. They will have to accept the Antichrist and his mark, or reject him and suffer the consequences. Again, this matches perfectly with what we discussed previously. Many (professing Christians) will be "offended" and turn from God (Matt. 24:9-13).

Jesus made reference to this event in Luke 9:26.

> For whosoever shall be **ashamed** of me and of my words, of him shall the Son of man be **ashamed, when he shall come in his own glory**, and in his Father's, and of the holy angels.

This will happen at the rapture of the church, not at the end of the 70th week. Those who fell away are ashamed of Christ and followed the Antichrist, and those not ashamed are the ones who remain faithful to Christ.

The Fullness of the Gentiles

Back in chapter five when we were looking at the doctrine of dispensationalism, I briefly mentioned in Romans 11 how the church has been "grafted into" the olive tree (Israel), until the "fullness of the Gentiles" be brought in.

> For I would not, brethren, that ye should be ignorant of this mystery, lest ye should be wise in your own conceits; that blindness in part is happened to Israel, **until the fulness of the Gentiles** be come in. And **so "all" Israel shall be saved**: as it is written, There shall come out of Sion the Deliverer, and shall turn away ungodliness from Jacob: (Rom. 11:25-26)

The rapture will not occur until every Gentile gets saved in this church-age, which will end with the fulfillment of this prophecy. This is perfect in comparing the days of Noah and Lot to this prophecy, which we will see shortly. When the rapture takes place, which occurs on the same day as the day of the Lord begins, Israel will had been hiding in the wilderness since the unfolding of the great tribulation. They will now be sealed for protection from God's wrath, as we have already seen. It is interesting to see the phrase *so shall all Israel be saved*, tied to, not separate from, the prophecy of the fullness of the Gentiles, which is speaking to Israel as a nation. As Zechariah 12:10 says *"And I will pour upon the hose of David, and upon the inhabitants of Jerusalem, **the spirit of grace** and of supplications: and they shall look upon me whom they pierced, and they shall mourn for him, as one mourneth for his only son, and shall be in bitterness for him, one that is in bitterness for his firstborn."* Israel's salvation back to God as a nation will not happen until the latter end of the 70th week. It's interesting that God will extend "grace" to Israel, after the pretrib-dispensation of grace has supposedly already ended with the rapture of the church? Just a thought!

Let's turn our attention now to another important passage in the Scriptures that will tie-in beautifully with Romans 11.

The Sermon at Pentecost

> But Peter, standing up with the eleven, lifted up his voice, and said unto them, Ye men of Judaea, and all ye that dwell at Jerusalem, be this known unto you, and hearken to my words: For these are not drunken, as ye suppose, seeing it is but the third hour of the day. But this is that which was **spoken by the prophet Joel;** And **it shall come to pass in the last days,** saith God, I will pour out of my Spirit upon all flesh: and your sons and your daughters shall prophesy, and your young men shall see visions, and your old men shall dream dreams: And on my servants and on my handmaidens I will pour out in those days of my Spirit; and they shall prophesy: And **I will show wonders in heaven above, and signs in the earth beneath; blood, and fire, and vapour of smoke The sun shall be turned into darkness, and the moon into blood, before that great and notable day of the Lord come:** And **it shall come to pass,** that whosoever shall call on the name of the Lord shall be saved. (Acts 2:14-21)

Here in Acts 2 we have the birth of the church; though the foundation was laid in the Gospels with the choosing of the apostles. Peter is standing and preaching to Israel at the Feast of Pentecost, essentially the message is that Christ fulfilled God's plan of redemption for mankind. Therefore, the sacrificial system has now become obsolete. Because of Israel's unbelief, mainly instigated by the rulers, Israel as a nation had rejected their only hope of reconciliation with God, which was Jesus the Messiah.

Peter's sermon eventually cut through their hearts, and many repented by calling upon Christ as Lord and Savior, and the church was established. In his sermon, Peter started off by quoting the prophecy in Joel that pertained to the subject of the day of the Lord. Peter said that this event, where the apostles were speaking in tongues (human languages), was related to Joel's prophecy about the day of the Lord.

We need to recall what Christ said to the nation of Israel at His triumphal entry; he stated that Israel had fallen under the judgment of God. Because they rejected Him as the Messiah, God would now turn to the Gentiles to bring others to Christ. The fact that many Jews called on Christ here at Pentecost did not negate Christ's statement to Israel that God would be establishing the Gentile church.

What we do see by this prophecy in Joel is that there will be a future time when Israel sees these cosmic-events take place- this would be the sign that God will revisit Israel, even though Israel will not be occupying the land at this time, they will have fled to the wilderness (probably Petra). My friend, this will happen at the rapture of the church when the day of the Lord occurs. This will be when the "times of the Gentiles" is completed at the rapture just before the day of the Lord. Israel will see Christ coming while they are in the wilderness, and once God's judgment on the world has passed Israel will mourn over their sin of rejecting Christ and will repent; completely opposite of the world who mourns over the impending wrath of God.

Again, I must note that pretribulational teaching says the dispensation of the Gentile church will end before the 70th week with the rapture, and then God deals directly with Israel again; yet, they say Gentiles are saved in the 70th week. They fail to explain the "fullness of the Gentiles" in the context of the Scriptures. And as I have already said, according to pretrib teaching, the rapture "must" occur on the "very day" the final week starts (2,520 days) or this destroys their belief that the seventy-weeks is only for Israel.

#14) vv. 22, 24, 31   God's Elect:

22. And except those days should be shortened, there should no flesh be saved: but for the elect's sake those days shall be shortened.
24. For there shall arise false Christs, and false prophets, and shall shew great signs and wonders; insomuch that, if *it were* possible, they shall deceive the very elect.
31. And he shall send his angels with a great sound of a trumpet, and they shall gather together his elect from the four winds, from one end of heaven to the other.

Another key word we need to look at regarding the context of this chapter is the word "elect." Some pretribulational teachers argue that the word elect is referring to Israel, since the context is supposedly for Israel and not the church. If you do a study throughout the New Testament, we see that the word elect is used regarding Christians. I believe Colossians 3:11-12 sums up whom the elect is very well.

> Where there is neither Greek nor Jew, circumcision nor uncircumcision, Barbarian, Scythian, bond nor free: but Christ is all, and in all. Put on therefore, as the **elect of God**, holy and beloved, bowels of mercy, kindness, humbleness of mind, meekness, longsuffering:

Paul is teaching here that the elect are all groups of people who are Christian, not just Israel.

> Romans 8:33 Who shall lay any thing to the charge of God's elect? It is God that justifieth.

> 2 John 1:1 The elder unto the elect lady and her children, whom I love in the truth; and not I only, but also all they that have known the truth;

In verse 24 of Matthew 24 it says *if it were possible, they should deceive the very elect*. The elect here cannot be a reference to Israel, simply, because Israel is still in blindness during the 70th week. This is speaking of many false prophets during the final week, leading up to rapture, that will be attempting to persuade countless religious people to follow the false messiah during the great tribulation. The majority of the teaching about the final seven-years is spiritual in context.

#15) vv. 32-33   Budding of the Fig Tree

> 32. Now learn a parable of the fig tree; When his branch is yet tender, and putteth forth leaves, ye know that summer *is* nigh:
> 33. So likewise ye, when ye shall see all these things, know that it is near, *even* at the doors.

It is commonly taught by pretribulation teachers that the budding of the fig tree represents the nation of Israel, because fig trees are used in some of Christ's teaching in the gospels, as well as a common sight in Israel. We saw several quotes by pretrib teachers alluding to this fact.

First, as a reminder, the emphasis on the generation that sees all these things reflects what is mainly happening **inside** the 70th week, not necessarily before. Second, when you read Luke's account of the Olivet Discourse he adds to the discussion, *all the trees*, not just the fig tree. The fig tree is not Israel. The symbolism of the fig tree in the context of Christ's teaching He is paralleling the events that are taking place in the 70th week prior to His return. The budding of the fig tree is simply teaching that Christ's return (rapture of the church) is near. We know this because we see the leaves starting to bud, which indicates a change is about to take place by the bearing of fruit. The fig tree is just speaking of all the signs given in His discourse.

This is also reflective of Daniel 12:4, which we studied already, showing the increase of knowledge and the running to and fro by the wise. They will understand the unfolding of the events during the final week.

#16) vv. 34-35   The Generation

> 34. Verily I say unto you, This generation shall not pass, till all these things be fulfilled.
> 35. Heaven and earth shall pass away, but my words shall not pass away.

There has been much discussion in the prophecy world as to what constitutes a generation. I will not argue here the length of a generation, if it is forty, seventy, or if it is one-hundred-twenty years. What I want to emphasize is the Scriptures teach the generation that is living at the time matches the budding of the fig tree, which was just referenced by Christ. The generation (people) living when these events unfold should not be deceived by what is all taking place, but should be alert and watching. Christ is simply stating that His return will not be secret or an unknown event, because of the signs spoken of in the Olivet Discourse.

#17)   Rapture or Second Coming?

> **Matthew 24:32** Now learn a parable of the fig tree; When his branch is yet tender, and putteth forth leaves, ye know that summer is nigh:

Matthew 24:33 So likewise ye, when ye shall see all these things, know that it is near, even at the doors.

Matthew 24:34 Verily I say unto you, This generation shall not pass, till all these things be fulfilled.

Matthew 24:36 But of that day and hour knoweth no man, no, not the angels of heaven, but my Father only.

Matthew 24: 42 Watch therefore: for ye know not what hour your Lord doth come.

Matthew 24: 44 Therefore be ye also ready: for in such an hour as ye think not the Son of man cometh.

Matthew 24:50 The lord of that servant shall come in a day when he looketh not for him, and in an hour that he is not aware.

Matthew 25: 13 Watch therefore, for ye know neither the day nor the hour wherein the Son of man cometh.

These eight verses are often cited in regard for not knowing when the rapture will happen, and rightly so. I have already listed several "failed" predictions of Christ's return by pretribulationist, and could have listed many more. Five of these verses listed are some of the foundational verses pretribulation teachers use to teach their doctrine of imminence (36, 42, 44, 50; 25:13) - Christ can come back at any moment!

As I have already stated, Marvin Rosenthal's book "The PreWrath Rapture of the Church," was the catalyst that helped to deepen my understanding that the pretrib rapture was in serious error. I was always taught that the context of the Olivet Discourse was for Israel during the tribulation. And particularly, when Christ compared His coming to the days of Noah (vv.37-41) was speaking of His coming at the "end" of the tribulation, not the rapture before the 70th week.

However, the pretrib interpretation about these eight verses has nullified their belief that the Olivet Discourse is strictly for Israel and not applied to the church. They cannot exclude the church throughout this chapter and turn-around and teach these specific verses at the end of the chapter are referencing the raptured church before the 70ᵗʰ week. Stanley Ellison emphasize that "an alert church will be able to see the day drawing near." He used the illustration about the budding of the fig tree as a sign that Christ's return is near. Yet, according to the pretrib theory this sign is supposedly for those after the rapture during the tribulation. Also, why isn't the rapture/resurrection a sign pertaining to the budding of the fig tree? Pretrib teachers try to make the disappearance of millions in the rapture a secret; however, the empty graves of all the saints in and the children missing will not be a mystery. I have not seen any pretrib literature or teachers addressing this issue.

Hal Lindsey in his popular book "The Late Great Planet Earth" tries to say that the budding of the fig tree is for the generation living before the final seven-years. By generation he means the church because the world does not recognize prophecy.

Now let us view these verses in the context of the chapter and see the confusion brought about by the pretrib teaching. Here is the interpretation according to pretrib teaching in Matthew's account of the Olivet Discourse-Rapture or Second Coming?

Matthew 24:32-42

24:32 Now learn a parable of the fig tree; When his branch is yet tender, and putteth forth leaves, ye know that summer is nigh:
Rapture: before the tribulation.
24:33 So likewise ye, when ye shall see all these things, know that it is near, **even at the doors**:
Rapture: before the tribulation.

24:34 Verily I say unto you, **This generation** shall not pass, till all these things be fulfilled:
Rapture or Second Coming: Depending on which pretrib teacher you listen to.

24:36 But of that **day and hour knoweth** no man, no, not the angels of heaven, but my Father only:
Rapture: before the tribulation.

24:37 But as the **days of Noe** were, so shall also the coming of the Son of man be:

Rapture or Second Coming: Depending on which pretrib teacher you listen to.

24:40-41 Then shall two be in the field; the **one shall be taken, and the other left.** Two women shall be grinding at the mill; **the one shall be taken, and the other left.**
Rapture or Second Coming: depends on which pretrib teacher you listen to.

24:42 Watch therefore: for **ye know not what hour your Lord doth come:**
Rapture: before the tribulation.

Matthew 24:50 The lord of that servant shall come in a day when he looketh not for him, and in an hour that he is not aware.
Rapture: before the tribulation.

Matthew 25: 13 Watch therefore, for ye know neither the day nor the hour wherein the Son of man cometh.
Rapture: before the tribulation.

As we see, pretrib teachers pick and choose how they want to interpret these verses to fit their theory. They cannot have it both ways: either the Olivet Discourse is strictly for Israel during the tribulation, which is after the rapture; therefore, NONE of these verses should be used as rapture verses. Or, Matthew 24 is for the church and Israel in the tribulation, which will lead up to the rapture at the second coming. The prewrath commentary on these verses is that this is the rapture and the second coming of Christ after the great tribulation is cut short.

#18) v.36   That Day

> 36. But of **that day** and hour knoweth no man, no, not the angels of heaven, but my Father only.

This verse cannot be speaking about the rapture if the previous verses in the chapter are talking about the second coming at the end of the 70th week. The phrase "that day" when taken within the context of the chapter must refer to the same topic being discussed. You cannot be talking of one thing throughout a subject and then refer to something different in the same context of the subject being discussed. Let's say you witnessed a crime and you were telling the events to someone about a man being shot to death, and during your story you say, "That was a terrible thing that happened." The · terrible thing you just described must refer to the crime you were talking about, not something else. Another example would be: While talking to your friends on Monday about your uncle John, who you haven't seen in two years, is scheduled to come visit on Friday for the weekend. And you tell them when your uncle shows up he is going to take you fishing on Saturday; and you say, "that will be great when he gets here." Contextually, you cannot be referring to his arrival the last time you saw him two years ago. Yet, pretrib teaching is that the reference to "that day" is indeed the rapture before the 70th week, seven years prior to the subject matter being discussed throughout Jesus's teaching in the chapter. Prewrath teaches "that day" is talking about the return of Christ at the rapture along with the previous verses in this chapter- plain and simple.

#19)   The Days of Noah and Lot

I have read and heard pretrib teaching using several Old Testament illustrations when trying to describe the rapture. Such are, Enoch when he was translated; Elijah when he was taken up in the fiery chariot; Isaac and Rebekah when they met for the first time. However, in our Lord's discourse of the subject he only describes two Old Testament events when comparing His return, which are Noah and Lot. I will bypass Matthew's account about Noah and will look at Luke's teaching here, which gives more details of the story.

> And as it was in the **days of Noe,** so shall it be also in the **days of the Son of man.** They did eat, they drank, they married wives, they were given in marriage, until **the day** that Noe entered into the ark, and the flood came, and destroyed them all. Likewise also as it was in the **days of Lot**; they did eat, they drank, they bought, they sold, they planted, they builded; But the **same day** that Lot went out of Sodom it rained fire and brimstone from heaven, and destroyed them all. Even thus shall it be in **the day when the Son of man is revealed**. (Luke 21:26-30)

This was pointed out by Marvin Rosenthal in his book "The Pre-Wrath Rapture of the Church" that Christ was teaching when He returns it will be on the very *same day* that God pours out His wrath; just as He did in the days of Noah and Lot. In those two events, both teach a deliverance and judgment on the same day.

In verse 27 it states that judgment did not take place until *the day* Noah entered the ark. Look at this account in Genesis chapter 7.

> In the six hundredth year of Noah's life, in the second month, the seventeenth day of the month, **the same day** were all the fountains of the great deep broken up, and the windows of heaven were opened. And the rain was upon the earth forty days and forty nights. In the **selfsame day entered** Noah, and Shem, and Ham, and Japheth, the sons of Noah, and Noah's wife, and the three wives of his sons with them, **into the ark;** (Gen. 7:11-13)

Noah was told to gather the animals and put them in the ark; so, for the final seven days before the flood he did accordingly. When completed, Noah and his family entered the ark on the final day and God Himself shut the door to the ark (Gen. 7:15).

Jesus also used the example of Lot's deliverance at the time of destruction on Sodom and Gomorrah, when, on the *same day* (v.29) Lot was taken outside the city, and then God rained the fire of judgment upon the cities.

The world in Noah's and Lot's time lived according to their way and *knew not until the judgment came.* The world conditions will be similar in the 70th week, they will be saying peace and safety and then sudden destruction comes upon them. It's the world who are saying peace and safety because they are following the Antichrist; however, the saints will be persecuted. This also makes the case that the world will not be experiencing any type of supernatural judgment in the great tribulation until God intervenes. There will be war and famines in different places around the world, but the concentrated persecution will be towards believers.

Only Noah and his family and Lot and his two daughters escaped God's wrath. This matches the continual warnings of Christ and the other writers of the Bible about being watchful, ready, sober, awake, and to look out for false prophets who will deceive many. The temptation to follow the world and the Antichrist will be great upon the *multitudes in the valley of decision* (Joel 3:14), many will *fall away* from the faith (2 Thessalonians 2:3; Matthew 24:12-13).

Notice in Revelation 9:20-21 that after the first six trumpet judgments of God are poured out on the world, the inhabitants who are not killed, fail to repent. Repentance after the rapture takes place will become impossible, it is simply too late.

When God shut the door to the ark, salvation was impossible to attain. Parallel this when God cuts short the great tribulation in the final week, He will shut the door on salvation, because it will be at this time when He raptures and resurrects His saints. We will see this in Paul's teaching in Thessalonians 2 in the following chapter of this book.

Go back in chapters nine and ten of my book and reread some of the pretrib quotes comparing the wrath of God to the flood of Noah. They did not even realize the discrepancy in their pretribulation theory they caused by teaching this. My question to the pretrib is: tell us when would the wrath of God take place in the tribulation when compared to Noah? If they say the wrath is at the beginning of the seven-years, then destruction occurs immediately, which contradicts the seal events in Revelation 6 and chapters 13-14. If the wrath occurs at the end of the seven-years, then their reasoning that all the seven-years is the wrath of God falls apart, and the rapture no longer becomes pretribulational. Their teaching certainly does not line up with Christ's comparison with the days of Noah and Lot.

As a side note, when Luke gives a description of the days of Noah and Lot, when listing the events of Lots society, marriage is not mentioned. Sodom was known for its perversion of God's plan for the family, which certainly and foremost includes marriage. I cannot but help think how here in America and world-wide, the definition of marriage is being redefined, because of the perversion of the homosexual movement. Satan has been having a hey-day in destroying what God first instituted in His creation- the marriage. This prophecy about the comparison of Lots day to the coming of Christ is coming true right before our eyes.

Matthew 25- The Parable of the Ten Virgins

1. Then shall the kingdom of heaven be likened unto ten virgins, which took their lamps, and went forth to meet the bridegroom.
2. And five of them were wise, and five *were* foolish.
3. They that *were* foolish took their lamps, and took no oil with them:
4. But the wise took oil in their vessels with their lamps.

5. While the bridegroom tarried, they all slumbered and slept.

6. And at midnight there was a cry made, Behold, the bridegroom cometh; go ye out to meet him.

7. Then all those virgins arose, and trimmed their lamps.

8. And the foolish said unto the wise, Give us of your oil; for our lamps are gone out.

9. But the wise answered, saying, *Not so*; lest there be not enough for us and you: but go ye rather to them that sell, and buy for yourselves.

10. And while they went to buy, the bridegroom came; and they that were ready went in with him to the marriage: **and the door was shut.**

11. Afterward came also the other virgins, saying, Lord, Lord, open to us.

12. But he answered and said, Verily I say unto you, I know you not.

13. Watch therefore, for ye know neither the day nor the hour wherein the Son of man cometh.

Matthew 25 is the continuation of the Olivet Discourse. What Christ is now teaching, like He always does, He makes practicable application to His listeners regarding the subject matter He just spoke about. The subject here is obviously His coming back in the future. The emphasis is Christ's warning about preparedness. We will see more in-depth later the seriousness of taking heed to the warning signs given by Christ. Simply, the ten virgins are about ten women who have a relationship with the coming groom who is set to receive his bride; but He has been away for a very long time. Unfortunately, five of these women "let" their lamps go out, which they obviously had knowledge of. This is the emphasis of the parable. Many will have abandoned their belief about Christ, as we seen in this study, and will be left behind when He comes. There's nothing magical about this teaching, it's plain and simple. You can abandon your faith in what you once believed and you will suffer the same fate as the lost world and be judged so. This passage also teaches individual accountability. If the story was simply about needing oil, the others could have simply shared; but it's not, its teaching self-responsibility.

Final Remark

With Jesus just completing a detailed account of His coming and the signs that are associated with His return; I would like to turn your attention to what is said by Christ to the apostles in the book of Acts 1:6-8 at His ascension. Let's look at the verses.

> 6. When they therefore were come together, they asked of him, saying, Lord, **wilt thou at this time restore again the kingdom to Israel?**
>
> 7. And he said unto them, **It is not for you to know the times or the seasons** which the Father hath put in his own power.
>
> 8. 8. But ye shall receive power, after that the Holy Ghost is come upon you: **and ye shall be witnesses** unto me both in Jerusalem, and in all Judaea, and in Samaria, and **unto the uttermost part of the earth**.

Did you notice the comparison to the same question that was asked of Christ in Matthew 24:3? But this time Jesus gives them a different response to their similar question. Jesus pointily told them *"It's not for you to know the times or seasons."* Yet, in contrast, at the Olivet Discourse, Jesus was basically explaining to them the times and the seasons of His coming as summed up with the analogy of the budding of the fig tree, *When his branch is yet tender, and putteth forth leaves, ye know that summer* is *nigh.* What Jesus was telling them in Matthew 24 was a sequence of events in the future because the signs and seasons will be for those living at the end of the age. Jesus is saying here in Acts 1 to the disciples that His coming will not happen in their lifetime; therefore, they need not worry about the establishment of the kingdom. Jesus is nullifying an imminent rapture in His statement to them. This is further evidenced by Jesus statement to go preach the gospel that will eventually over time reach the world. And to add even more evidence, after Jesus was taken up in a cloud they stood watching, two angels appeared and made this statement: *"why stand ye gazing up into heaven?* The angels were basically saying, quit wasting your time looking into heaven, didn't Jesus just tell you to go preach the gospel? They immediately left and went to Jerusalem, and a short time later were filled with the Holy Ghost. From that time, they began to preach the gospel.

CHAPTER FOURTEEN

1 & 2 THESSALONIANS

Now we come to another major problem text for pretribulationism, the rapture in 1 & 2 Thessalonians in relation to the day of the Lord. This is the classic rapture texts regardless of your position on the rapture.

1 Thessalonians 4:13-18

> But I would not have you to be ignorant, brethren, concerning them which are asleep, **that ye sorrow not,** even as others which have no hope. For if we believe that Jesus died and rose again, even so them also which sleep in Jesus will God bring with him. For this we say unto you by the word of the Lord, that we which are alive and remain unto the **coming of the Lord** shall not prevent them which are asleep. For the Lord himself shall descend from heaven with a shout, with the voice of the archangel, and with the trump of God: and the dead in Christ shall rise first: Then **we which are alive and remain shall be caught up together with them in the clouds, to meet the Lord in the air:** and so shall we ever be with the Lord. Wherefore **comfort one another** with these words.

Doubtless, these verses teach the rapture (the living will not see death) and the resurrection (dead will be raised). All sides agree here, no matter what your position is on the timing of the rapture. I would like to point out that in these verses; the promise of Christ's return is the "blessed hope" for the believer, not an escape of the tribulation. Remember, the foundation for the pretribulation rapture is the blessed hope is the "escape" from the tribulation, and we are supposedly to comfort one another with this. However, the "comfort" that we are to encourage each other with is the dead will rise again (v.14) when Christ comes again. Believers in Thessalonica were suffering persecution, and many believers were killed because of this (1 Thess. 2:14-15). Paul is giving them comfort that their love ones would be raised and they will be reunited at the return of Christ. We see this in Titus 2:13 where we as the redeemed will live with Christ for eternity. The "blessed hope" in Titus 2 is the same as here in 1 Thessalonians 4- we will live with Christ, not escape some tribulation. Also, just a thought: would the statement by Paul *"the coming of the Lord"* in verse 15 be the "second" coming of Christ? I ask my pretrib friends, if not, then why does Paul call Christ return here-coming?

Chapter 5

5:1-4

1. But of the times and the seasons, brethren, ye have no need that I write unto you.
2. For yourselves know perfectly that **the day of the Lord** so cometh as a thief in the night.
3. For when **they** shall say, **Peace and safety; then sudden destruction cometh upon them**, as travail upon a woman with child; and **they shall not escape**.
4. But **ye, brethren**, are not in darkness, **that that day** should overtake you as a thief.

Paul's continues his teaching about the rapture in chapter five. Paul now identifies that the day of the Lord is directly tied to the rapture (v. 2). He tells the believers that *"that day should not overtake you as a thief."* Believers will be well aware what is transpiring up to this time. Unfortunately for unbelievers, that day will catch them off guard. The question here for the pretribulation believers is: If the rapture is at the beginning of the 70th week how can there be "sudden destruction?" At the opening of the first seal the world is not seen suffering God's wrath. Many pretrib teachers say that for the first three and half years there is peace and security. Also, we looked at how the world is giving honor to the Antichrist at the "middle" of the 70th week, therefore no wrath yet.

5:5-11

5. Ye are all the **children of light**, and the **children of the day:** we are **not of the night, nor of darkness.**

6. Therefore let us **not sleep**, as do others; but **let us watch and be sober.**

7. For they that sleep sleep in the night; and **they that be drunken are drunken in the night.**

8. But let **us, who are of the day, be sober, putting on the breastplate of faith and love; and for an helmet, the hope of salvation.**

9. **For God hath not appointed us to wrath**, but to obtain salvation by our Lord Jesus Christ,

10. Who died for us, that, **whether we wake or sleep**, we should live together with him.

11. **Wherefore comfort yourselves together**, and edify one another, even as also ye do.

We recalled previously in our study that the Bible talks about watching in relation to our lifestyle regardless of the circumstances, because we know that Christ is coming back. Let's look at these verses again that reference this in the context of the Lord's return.

As believers, we are to be sober and alert in conducting our lifestyle, because a sober person thinks strait and a drunk person is impaired and has a hard time discerning the conditions that surrounds them. As Christians, we have a hope of eternal salvation, where in contrast, the world's hope is mainly in this temporal life only. Verse 9 is the pivotal verse teaching we are *not appointed unto wrath.* The wrath is associated with the day of the Lord in this context. The final two verses emphasize whether a Christian who is alive or dead, we are to comfort one another with the fact that we will eventually live together with Christ. Accordingly, this comfort in the context of the rapture passages has nothing to do with an escape from the tribulation, as pretribulationism would have you believe.

Now let's turn our attention to Paul's second letter to the Thessalonians.

2 Thessalonians 2

2:1-2

1. Now we beseech you, brethren, by the **coming of our Lord Jesus Christ**, and by **our gathering together unto him,**
2. That ye be not soon shaken in mind, or be troubled, neither by spirit, nor by word, nor by letter as from us, as that **the day of Christ is at hand.**

Here I will show you how pretribulation teachers jump through hoops and over hurdles to interpret this chapter from their biased pretribulation view. Instead of taking the plain language of the Scriptures and allowing them to teach us, the pretrib teachers are in overdrive as they try to make the Scriptures fit their theory.

First, we need to understand the topic being discussed here in this chapter. Paul makes it clear in verse 5 that he had previously instructed these believers about the subject matter, *Remember ye not, that, when I was yet with you, I told you these things?* What Paul brings out in chapter 2 had already been discussed with these believers.

In the plain language, we see in verse 1 the reference to the coming of the Lord. This coming and our gathering together unto Him is when the rapture/resurrection of the church takes place. This is the same teaching from Paul's letter in 1 Thessalonians, which would be the context of Paul previous instruction to these believers. In verse 2, Paul equates the rapture/resurrection to the day of Christ, which again, is the same event as in 1 Thessalonians chapters 4-5. No problem so far, we should all be in agreement. What has arisen in verse 2, Paul tells the Thessalonians not to be troubled or shaken that the day of Christ is about to begin. Apparently, there was teaching contrary to what Paul taught about the rapture and the day of the Lord. Perhaps Paul addressed Timothy on this matter in his second epistle, when he says in chapter 2 that Hymenaeus and Philetus taught a false belief; *Who concerning the truth have erred,* **saying that the resurrection is past already; and overthrow the faith of some.** These believers at Thessalonica thought they missed the rapture/resurrection according to Paul's teaching in his first epistle.

The Thessalonians were suffering hard times living for Christ, chapter 1:4 *So that we ourselves glory in you in the churches of God for your patience and faith in* **all your persecutions and tribulations that ye endure:** Because of the hardships they were experiencing, this helped reinforced the rumor that the day of Christ was at hand. Christ himself taught that there would be severe persecution before He returns (i.e. the tribulation, Mat. 24:9-10). However, we will see that Paul says in verses 3 and 4 that several events, specifically two, need to take place first "before" the day of the Lord can occur.

In all the pretribulation writings, they teach that the rapture is imminent (about to happen) based on the Scriptures use of the phrase, "at hand" or "I come quickly." Nowhere do they teach that any of these phrases are past or present tense, but future, except one. And here in 2 Thessalonians they change the meaning of "at hand" from future tense to have already begun in the present tense. Why? They want to make this passage sound as though the Thessalonians thought they had already entered the tribulation; hence, Paul was correcting their mistake by teaching a pretribulation rapture. This is not the case; he is teaching a prewrath rapture- not entering the day of the Lord.

Here is a classic example of manipulation of Scripture by pretribulationist Todd Strandberg of Rapture Ready; instead of allowing the text to say what it means, he interjects his pretribulation theory to make the Scripture "fit" their doctrine.

Confusion over Confusion: 2 Thess. 2:1-6

Because Paul in 2 Thessalonians, said the Antichrist would be revealed before the Day of the Christ, post and pre-wrath adherents frequently try to cite this passage as one that refutes the pre-trib rapture.

To quell the Thessalonian's **misunderstanding that they had somehow "entered" the tribulation**, Paul told them the **Antichrist must first be revealed**. By telling them they had no reason to panic, Paul is clearly disputing the idea that the Thessalonians could someday find themselves facing the **tribulation hour.**

I'm constantly being irked by Post-trib and pre-wrath folks' consistent, or better yet deliberate, failure to accept the simple fact that the pre-trib doctrine calls for a rapture and a second coming. Because they only glean the prophetic word for one event--the second coming--they're unable to recognize pre-trib rapture passages.[120] (bold letters mine)

Taking Strandberg's statement at face value, he is saying that the Antichrist must be revealed "before" the 70th week. He does not even address the "falling away" that occurs at the midpoint of the seven-years, which is when the revealing of the Antichrist takes place, not at the beginning of the 70th week.

As I have been stating, the day of the Lord is not the tribulation as we have previously seen, but an event "inside" the final seven-years. If these believers missed the rapture, then they would fall under the wrath and judgment of God; hence, the day of the Lord. Paul is saying that the day of the Lord is "future," so they had not missed the rapture- plain and simple. The believers here were not concerned about events in the tribulation, i.e. persecution by Antichrist, which Paul will verify this in the next few verses. Strandberg makes it sound as though Paul is talking about a "present" event. Here is a statement by John Walvoord on this passage.

> *The Rapture in 2 Thessalonians 2."* In the period between the writing of 1 and 2 Thessalonians certain teachers had arrived in Thessalonica who taught the people that they were **already in the Day of the Lord**.[121] (bold letters mine)

Walvoord is partially correct by saying the day of the Lord instead of the tribulation, even though he incorrectly equates in his teaching the tribulation is the same as the day of the Lord. He also follows the typical pretrib teaching of present tense vs. future tense.

In an article by pretribulationist Paul Feinberg, he responds to Robert Gundry's teaching on the posttribulational Rapture in 1 and 2 Thessalonians. Here is Feinberg's on 2 Thessalonians 2:2, which is the same as Walvoord's belief.

> An important reason for Paul's writing this second epistle so shortly after the first is found in these verses. The false teaching that was troubling the Thessalonians came to them either by a variety of means (a prophecy, a report, a letter) or by one of these means. **The content of this false teaching is clear "The Day of the Lord has come"** (2:2). The teaching was that these believers

were in the day of the Lord. This teaching was unsettling and alarming them. Paul writes to correct this false teaching, which was also incorrectly attributed to him.[122] (bold letters mine)

If this was true for the Thessalonian's it is also true for us today. No rapture until these two events occur, which is what Jesus taught in the Olivet Discourse in Matthew 24. And Paul is about to correct the Thessalonians on their misunderstanding of the coming day of the Lord.

I need to address another pretribulation Houdini effect on their rapture teaching. Many pretribulationist realize what Paul is correctly teaching about the day of the Lord; therefore, to help buffer their teaching errors they try to separate the terms- day of Christ and the day of the Lord as being two totally separate events. They teach that the day of Christ is the rapture, and the day of the Lord is judgment. Back in verses 1 & 2, verse 1 says coming of Christ, and verse 2 says the day of Christ. Therefore, both verses are supposedly restricted to the rapture (deliverance), not wrath. My first rebuttal is that Christ and the Lord are the same- that's a no-brainer. These names (Christ and Lord) are used interchangeably throughout the Scriptures. Second, back in 1 Thessalonians 4 it calls the rapture "the coming of the Lord," not the coming Christ. Thirdly, in chapter 5 of 1 Thessalonians, when it says the day of the Lord will catch the unbelieving world by surprise (thief), but for "you" (believers) it will not overtake you. Believers will be here when that day occurs. Even pretrib teachers agree with this. I have already proven by the Scripture that the rapture occurs on the very same day as the day of the Lord begins. Therefore, even by separating the two terms it really doesn't matter because they occur simultaneously. The rapture is identified with the coming of Christ/Lord for believers because that's who saved us from sin and who will save us from wrath.

The term "day of the Lord" used throughout the Old Testament is a natural rendering, because Christ (the Lord) has not been revealed yet. Just like trying to bait and switch the tribulation with the day of the Lord, pretribulationist do so with the day of Christ and day of the Lord. If you recall, pretribulationist insist that the seals are the wrath of God (I proved otherwise) because they say it is "Christ" who opens the seals. So, would this be the day of Christ or the day of the Lord according to pretrib definition? Doesn't the Scriptures teach there is a wrath of the lamb (Rev. 6:16)? Now here's another prime example of pretribulation Scripture manipulation.

The problem now arises for the pretribulation rapture folks, because their doctrine of imminence is about to be called into question. If prophesied events precede the rapture then the pretribulation rapture falls apart, as we saw in chapter seven and eight of this book.

The Falling Away

2:3-4

3. Let **no man deceive** you by any means: **for that day shall not come, except there come a falling away first, and that man of sin be revealed, the son of perdition;**

4. Who opposeth and exalteth himself above all that is called God, or that is worshipped; so that **he as God sitteth in the temple of God, showing himself that he is God.**

Let me preface my remarks by pointing out that Paul forewarns these believers "not to be deceived about Christ's coming" just as Jesus warned the apostles in Matthew 24. If we allow the plain text to be interpreted correctly, we realize that the day of the Lord will not come "until" two events take place. First, is the "falling away" or the apostatizing (Greek- apostasia); second, is the "revealing" of the man of sin- the Antichrist. This revealing of the Antichrist will take place at "abomination of desolations," which is what Christ spoke of in Matthew 24:15, *When ye therefore shall see the **abomination of desolation**, spoken of by Daniel the prophet, **stand in the holy place**, (whoso readeth, let him understand:).* The statement in verse 4 *showing himself* is the revealing being spoken of in 2 Thessalonians. Both verses in 2 Thessalonians 2 and Matthew 24 are the exact same event. This matches the seal judgments in Revelation where the Antichrist will at first be viewed as a hero, a man of peace (possibly first seal), then at the midpoint like Daniel 9:27 points out, he will be revealed when he breaks the covenant which kick-starts the great tribulation (Rev. 12:12-14; 13:5-18; 14:9). As I have stated previously, the peace covenant that is going to be signed will not be intended as a "seven-year" covenant. Most of the professing Christianity and certainly Israel will not know that this is the man of sin.

Here is a question for our pretribulation friends: If in Matthew 24, the Olivet Discourse- specifically the "abomination of desolation"- is for Israel in the tribulation, why is Paul using this for a sign to the church at Thessalonica? Also, we saw pretrib teach the coming of Christ in Matthew 24 is the second coming of Christ after the abomination of desolation's event and not the rapture; however, here in 2 Thessalonians the discussion is about the rapture, not a (pretrib) second coming. Since these two chapters parallel each other, then this verifies the subject of Christ's return in Matthew 24 is the rapture (that occurs at Christ's second coming).

Next, we have phase two of the pretribulation manipulation of these verses by changing the meaning of the verse pertaining to the "falling away."

> What precisely does Paul mean when he says that "the falling away" (2:3) must come **before the tribulation?** The definite article "the" denotes that this will be a definite event, an event distinct from the appearance of the Man of Sin. The Greek word for **"falling away", taken by itself, does not mean religious apostasy or defection.** Neither does the word mean "to fall," as the Greeks have another word for that. [*pipto*, I fall; TDI] **The best translation of the word is "to depart."** The apostle Paul refers here to a definite event which he calls "the departure," and which will occur just before the start of the tribulation. **This is the rapture of the church.**[123]
>
> (bold letters mine)
>
> Paul Lee Tan

First, Lee Tan proves my point about changing the meaning of the context. See how he makes the perception that Paul is talking about the tribulation, when in fact he is talking about the day of the Lord. Also, the definite article "the," that Lee Tan points out is not an event distinct "from" the appearance of the man of sin, but in relation "to" his revealing, which is seen in the context of Paul's teaching. In other words, the appearance of the man of sin is associated with the falling away as the Scripture reads.

Second, the problems are compounded for pretribulationism by Paul's teaching that the falling away is "before" the day of the Lord, now they go through great pains to re-define the meaning of "the falling away." This is exactly what Lee Tan does by saying the falling away is the rapture of the church.

Here is Thomas Ice in a debate with Richard Thomas at the Prophecy conference in 2001.

> **Dr. Thomas Ice**: "Ok, I just finished a article on Matthew 24:29-31 that will be out in our Pre-Trib Perspectives in January 2002. We do not publish a Pre-Trib Perspectives in December we take the month off. And that grew out of a debate I had with Irving Baxter, you heard of him. He is a big Post Tribber... Then you get to 2 Thessalonians 2:3 that the word **apostasia, very likely refers to the rapture**. It is a word that is only used twice as a noun in the whole New Testament, as it is used there. It is used as an ellipsis which means there is no object and so he says unless the departure occurs first and he doesn't have a subordinate clause or and adjustable phase explaining what the departure is. It was something that the Thessalonians knew about and something that Paul knew. (bold letters mine)

Instead of the falling away being a defection from the truth, the pretribulation changes it to the rapture itself. Therefore, Ice is really saying: that before the rapture can occur, the falling away (i.e. rapture) has to happen first. He destroys his own reasoning. If this were the rapture, I believe Paul would have used the same word (Greek- harpazo) in describing the falling away like he did in 1 Thessalonians. However, not all pretribulation teachers change the meaning. Charles Ryrie says in his *Study Bible* that the falling away is a time when people turn away the truth they once held.[124] He is exactly right on this, which matches the context of these Scriptures. Clarence Larkin acknowledges that the falling away is apostasy.

> 2. Apostasy
> In II Thess. 2:3, we are told that "THAT DAY (the Day of the Lord) shall not come, except there come a 'FALLING AWAY' first." This 'falling away' is evidence on every hand.[125]

As I noted in Matthew 24:36 about the reference to "that day," we saw that it had to refer to what was being taught in context to Christ's coming at the rapture. The same can be said here about "that day" in verse 2 and 3, denoting its referring to the rapture in verse 1. What I would like for you to also realize is that "that day" is independent to the falling away. In other words, "that day" cannot happen until another event, "falling away" occurs first; these cannot be the same.

Once again, there is confusion in the pretribulation camp over a simple verse that surrounds the teaching on the rapture. Plain and simple: verse 1 is the coming (2nd) of Christ and our gathering (rapture) with him. Verse 2 is instructions to these believers that God's wrath/judgment (Day of the Lord) is still future, which occurs after the rapture. Next, in verse 3 Paul says two events will have had to happen before the return of Christ and the rapture can occur, which these two events are connected to each other: the falling away (abandonment of the faith) and the revealing of the Antichrist. Paul goes on to state in the next verse, so there would be no mistake when the falling away and the revealing would happen, which is when the man of sin goes into the temple and declares himself God. This is the "abomination of desolations" which occurs at the middle of the 70th week.

Walvoord agrees that the falling away teaches rebellion, not the rapture.

> Don't let anyone deceive you in any way, for that day will not come until the "rebellion" occurs and the man of lawlessness is revealed, the man doomed to destruction.[126]

The Antichrist deceives millions of people on the earth at this time, and many will fall away from the truth of God and will embrace him as their God. From this event, he will cause all people to receive his mark, which the Bible calls the "mark of the beast" (Rev. 13:16-18; 20:4). I wonder how many people at this time will have believed in a pretribulational rapture, only to find they are in the great tribulation, and reject God? This is why the pretribulational rapture is so dangerous with its escapism mentality.

If we look back at 1 Thessalonians 4 about the rapture of believers, the Scriptures teach that people who are not only alive, but "remain" will be raptured (4:15, 17). The remaining in chapter 4 is compared with the falling away (not remaining) in 2 Thessalonians 2. If you go back and read the context of 1 Thessalonians 4 you will see in the context that Paul is addressing "Christian behavior" compared to those who do not know the Lord (e.g. v.5). This is why I believe Paul's continuation of the subject of the Lord's return in the next chapter briefly mentions Christ's coming, then he deals in-depth with contrasting the saved and the lost.

Remember, the word "offended" in Matthew 24 means to "stumble or fall away." Also, if you recall Jesus's description of those disciples in John chapter 6 who became offended (v.61) and walked away from Jesus (v.66).

This would match perfectly the sequence of events described by Paul to the Christians and Thessalonica.

Renald Showers in his book "Maranatha Our Lord, Come," teaches correctly that the falling away is apostasy.

> **The Revelation of the Man of Sin:** In order to prove to the Thessalonians that the Day of the Lord had not begun, Paul presented two things that had not yet happened but that must happen before the Day of the Lord can begin: "first the apostasy" (literal translation) and the revelation of the "man of sin."
>
> Since the revelation of the man of sin is the latter of the two things, it, rather than the apostasy, will take place closer to the beginning of the Day of the Lord. Therefore, when trying to determine when the Day of the Lord will begin, it is more crucial to discern when the man of sin will be revealed than when the apostasy will take place.[127]

In Shower's acknowledgment, he is correct, the revealing of the man of sin needs to be determined first, and then only afterwards can the day of the Lord occur. And the context states that this will happen when he goes into the temple at the midpoint of the 70th week. Consequently, the day of the Lord does not begin until this event.

In closing, I would like for you to understand the word concerning "apostasy." The only other time it's used in the New Testament is in the book of Acts 21:21, when Paul was accused of "departing" from the Law of Moses by the religious leaders in Israel. The context is a spiritual departure, not a physical (rapture) departure. To make the "falling away" the rapture is nothing more than tampering with the evidence as we saw in the case with the John Darby Bible.

One more quick point needs to be made here. Some pretrib folks will argue that the falling away is something that was even occurring in the early church, therefore the prewrath argument for abandonment of the faith by believers before the rapture does not disprove pretribulationism. They say there has always been some type of general abandonment from the faith in every generation. But what pretrib folks fail to acknowledge is how Revelation paints a very somber picture with the event when Antichrist forces everyone to give him allegiance, even to the point of death for refusal. This certainly would parallel 2 Thessalonians better than the pretrib answer, and matches what I have been saying. There will be "the" falling away, which is labeled by Paul and Jesus as a land-mark event, not something that is common every day.

The Restrainer 2:6-7

6. And now ye know what withholdeth that he might be revealed in his time.
7. For the mystery of iniquity doth already work: only he who now letteth will let, until he be taken out of the way.

There is much debate in prophecy as to whom or what is the restrainer in 2 Thessalonians. Based upon the pretribulation teaching, it is believed the restrainer mentioned here is none other than the Holy Spirit himself. Concluding then, since the restrainer is removed, the church is removed as well. Therefore, when the Holy Spirit is gone along with the church, then wickedness will be free to run its course.

However, if we look at these verses in their context, we see that the restrainer is removed only when the man of sin is revealed (v.8). As we have seen, his revealing does not take place until the middle of the 70th week. In reality, the pretribulation teachers are espousing a midtribulation rapture. The real clincher for the pretribulation teachers is if the Holy Spirit is removed before the 70th week how do folks get saved after the Holy Spirit is gone? Only by the leading and moving of the Holy Spirit does a person become born again (cf. John 3:5-8; 16:7-14). In fact, Jesus told the disciples in Matthew 13:11 *not to meditate when you are tried, because the Holy Ghost will lead you in what to say.* This will be the case during the tribulation period.

Another important point needs to be seen here in the context of verse 7 is that the restrainer is taken out of the "way," which does not imply that it taken to heaven. If the restrainer is not taken to heaven, obliviously the church is not taken to heaven as well (per pretrib teaching). Restraining simply means to hold back something from happening. The verse also identifies the restrainer as "he," which is singular not plural. If the saints were to be identified with the restrainer, then the plural form word (us and we) would be used. The church saints are to be salt and light to the blind world.

The restrainer (he), is none other than Michael the Archangel mentioned in concurrence with the 70th week, referenced in (Daniel 10:21; 12:1-8). Marvin Rosenthal does an excellent job describing how Michael is the restrainer in his book "The Pre-Wrath Rapture of the Church." Michael has a special role where he fights against Satan (Jude 9; Rev. 12:7-12). It is Michael who will fight against the devil and his angels in Revelation 12, which will take place at the mid-point of the 70th week. Satan is thrown out of heaven and cast to the earth, which fits exactly in the timing when Satan indwells the Antichrist in the middle of the 70th week. When Satan is kicked out of heaven, Michael quits fighting (restraining). The restrainer cannot be the Holy Spirit being removed with the church as the pretribulation theory prescribes.

This is further reinforced in the continuation of Paul's teaching in 2 Thessalonians 2:8-11.

> 8. And then shall that **Wicked be revealed**, whom the Lord shall consume with the spirit of his mouth, and shall destroy with the brightness of his coming:
> 9. Even him, whose coming is after the working of Satan with **all power and signs and lying wonders,**
> 10. And with all deceivableness of unrighteousness in them that perish; because **they received not the love of the truth,** that they might be saved.
> 11. And for this cause God shall send them strong delusion, that **they should believe a lie:**

These verses within their context are teaching the same thing; the Antichrist will be revealed in the middle of the 70th week of Daniel, which will in effect, start the great tribulation. The world rulers will also give the man of sin unprecedented power over the masses. When Satan is cast out of heaven at the middle of the 70th week, he will be given the power (political and supernatural) to do things to deceive the world. We also need to be reminded that the fallen angels that rebelled with Satan will be cast to the earth with him. There will be unprecedented demon possession taking place on earth. This can be seen within the context of these events in Revelation 13.

> And I beheld another beast coming up out of the earth; and he had two horns like a lamb, and he spake as a dragon. And he exerciseth all the power of the first beast before him, and **causeth the earth and them which dwell therein to worship the first beast,** whose deadly wound was healed. And he doeth **great wonders, so that he maketh fire come down from heaven on**

the earth in the sight of men, And deceiveth them that dwell on the earth by the means of those miracles which he had power to do in the sight of the beast; saying to them that dwell on the earth, that they should make an image to the beast, which had the wound by a sword, and did live. (Rev. 13:11-14)

In Revelation 13 we have further evidence of the account in 2 Thessalonians 2 pertaining to the events at the mid-point of the tribulation.

To reinforce the position of the prewrath rapture of the church, Jesus teaches the same thing in the Olivet Discourse in Matthew 24.

Then shall they deliver you up to be afflicted, and shall kill you: and ye shall be hated of all nations for my name's sake. And then shall many be offended, and shall betray one another, and shall hate one another. And many false prophets shall rise, and shall deceive many. And because iniquity shall abound, the love of many shall wax cold. (Matt. 24:9-12)

These verses are the same as 2 Thessalonians 2:9-10 and Revelation 13:12-15, which will result in the rebellion against God. The persecution against those who say they are Christians will be momentous; sadly, many will turn away from Christ. This will exponentially multiply in the great tribulation, yet, before the day of the Lord, which is what each of these passages teach. This is one of the reasons pretrib teachers will change the meaning of Matthew 24-25 to say this is for Israel and not the Church; however, Paul teaches what Christ taught in Matthew 24-25 to the church in Thessalonica, not Israel.

I recall attending in our church, Friday night Bible studies, and the subject of the rapture came up quite often. One predominate question pertaining to the rapture subject was: will there be a great revival during the tribulation? The answer was yes, because there is a multitude seen in heaven that came out of the great tribulation in Revelation 7:9. I was told these were the tribulation saints, because the church was already in heaven. Knowing what I know now about the rapture, the answer is completely opposite. There will be the greatest rebellion and abandonment of God since Noah's time. Sadly, we all are familiar with former church members that once walked with Christ but now embrace ungodly and worldly aspirations.

Rejecting the Truth

8. And then shall that Wicked be revealed, whom the Lord shall consume with the spirit of his mouth, and shall destroy with the brightness of his coming:

9. Even him, whose coming is after the working of Satan with all power and signs and lying wonders,

10. And with all deceivableness of unrighteousness in them that perish; **because they received not the love of the truth, that they might be saved.**

11. And for this cause God shall send them strong delusion, that they should believe a lie:

12. That **they all might be damned who believed not the truth,** but had pleasure in unrighteousness. (2 Thess. 2:8-12)

Another pretribulation straw man has been erected to justify their theory by their interpretation of these verses, which we have read once already. The setup is supposedly that if a person rejects the gospel before the rapture takes place, then these same folks will not be able to get saved during the tribulation itself. Instead of allowing the context to interpret what it means, pretrib teaching is forced to take this position, because these verses do state that those who rejected the truth will be damned. Also, for pretribulationism, this helps account for the multitudes saved in the 70th week.

Prewrath teaches, as we saw that as the days of Noah, those who rejected Noah's message did not enter the ark; consequently, when God shut the door it was too late to be saved. What happened immediately following the closing of the Ark's door was God's wrath was poured out upon the world. The same will be at the rapture at the day of the Lord.

We see this in the context of 2 Thessalonians that the Antichrist has been revealed for who he is (v.8), which will take place at the mid-point of the 70th week. Verse 9 shows the ability of Satan usurping his control over the people by using great deception. Verse 10 is the key to this passage, which states, because those who did not receive the love of the truth will not be saved. This rejection of the truth is not before the 70th week begins, **but after the revealing of the Antichrist** (middle of the 70th week), which is what the context teaches. God's strong delusion in verse 11 is tied to those rejecting Him and believing "the lie," which is to embrace the Antichrist and receive his mark. At this time, Antichrist will cause unparalleled signs and lying wonders, along with the demonic activity, which will deceive vast multitudes and cause many professing believers in Christ to fall away (reject their once-held belief in Jesus). The lost world is given the delusion base on their "not receiving the love of the truth." I believe they will reject the final gospel message to the world about what is transpiring. Jesus said the gospel would be preached up to the end of the world. I will add that I do not believe everyone in the world will be subjected to the Antichrist's mark.

Folks, there is nothing here even to minutely suggest the pretribulation view that the rejection of the truth is "before" the final week in these passages.

Allow me to make one final observation related to the pretrib teaching about folks being saved during the final week after the rapture takes place. As previously stated, the pretrib belief is all the final week is the day of the Lord, which is God's wrath. I want to point out this fallacy by looking at 2 Peter 3:9-10.

> 9: The Lord is not slack concerning his promise, as some men count slackness; but is longsuffering to us-ward, **not willing that any should perish, but that all should come to repentance.**
> 10: But the **day of the Lord** will come as a thief in the night; in the which the heavens shall pass away with a great noise, and the elements shall melt with fervent heat, the earth also and the works that are therein shall be burned up.

We see from verse 9 that this is saying God does not want anyone to end up in hell. God is patient to lost sinners, desiring that they would repent and come to a saving knowledge of Christ. God, being *longsuffering to us-ward,* is saying He is withholding His judgment on the earth. We know this because the very next verse references the "day of the Lord." The day of the Lord speaks of a world-wide judgment, as we have previously seen. What I would like to point out is the implied comparison of man needing to repent prior to the coming day of the Lord. Simply, Peter is teaching that when the day of Christ occurs, repentance will be impossible. This is why the "longsuffering" of God is explained; because when God's mercy and grace comes to a halt, then His judgment begins. Peter does not separate folks who heard the gospel and rejected it before the tribulation from those who need to repent.

He lumps everyone in all together that is not saved, they all need to repent before the day of the Lord begins.

Peter's teaching matches perfectly with the prewrath rapture teaching, the day of the Lord cannot occur at the beginning of the 70th week, because we do see individuals being saved during the tribulation. Read the previous verses in 2 Peter (vv. 3-6) that compares Noah and the flood to the future day of the Lord (vv.9-10). We pointed out in our study in Matthew 24 when God's judgment begins, salvation becomes impossible for everyone -same as Peter's teaching. (I will address Gentile nations going into the millennium in my closing remarks). Here is further proof that parallels Peter's teaching in Acts 17.

> 30. And the times of this ignorance God winked at; but now **commandeth all men every where to repent:**
> 31. Because **he hath appointed a day, in the which he will judge the world in righteousness by** *that* man whom he hath ordained; *whereof* he hath given assurance unto all *men*, in that he hath raised him from the dead.

Conclusion

It should be clear to the reader that when 1 & 2 Thessalonian are studied together in their context, we can deduce several truths.

1. Believers at Thessalonica were suffering severe persecution. 1 Thess. 1:6; 2 Thess. 1:6; 2 Thess. 1:4
2. The rapture of the church is taught in both books. 1 Thess. 4:15-17; 2 Thess. 2:1
3. The rapture is called the day of the Lord in both books. 1 Thess. 5:2; 2 Thess. 2:2
4. There is no mention of believers comforting one another by escaping the tribulation. The comfort is for those believers who have lost loved-ones (believers), when Jesus comes back He will resurrect them.
5. Believers thought they had missed the rapture; therefore, they were concerned with entering the day of the Lord, not the tribulation. To enter the day of the Lord would mean that a person is not a true

believer in Christ. This was the main concern for the Thessalonians, due to the false letter being read among the Thessalonians.

6. Paul taught two specific events need to take place before the rapture: First, the Antichrist must be revealed. Paul stated as Christ did in Matthew 24 that the Antichrist will be revealed at the "abomination of desolations." This event was foretold in Daniel in chapter 9:27, which will occur in the middle of the 70th week. Second, there will be a great falling away in association with the revealing of the Antichrist (2 Thess. 2:3). This is none other than professing believers who reject their "held" belief. Note: I have heard numerous teachers teach this verse and say we are experiencing the falling away at the present hour (Clarence Larkin taught this). This shows a simple fact on how biblical passages can be misapplied. This verse has nothing to do with the present day; only in the context surrounding the 70th week can this be applied correctly.

7. When the Antichrist is revealed he will have tremendous ability to perform signs and wonders, solely for one purpose- to deceive the world (2 Thess. 2:9-10; Rev. 13:7, 12-15).

8. The sudden destruction spoken of in 1Thess. 5:3 occurs when the world declares "peace and safety," and Paul taught this occurs before the rapture because the day of the Lord has not occurred yet. I believe the peace and safety announcement by the world will take place sometime after the Antichrist declares himself to be God at the mid-point of the 70th week. Conversely, the sudden destruction before the 70th week begins, which is taught by pretribulationist, is not a possibility, because the world doesn't experience destruction in the beginning.

9. The restrainer cannot be the Holy Spirit; one reason is multitudes are saved during the tribulation, which requires the Holy Spirit to work in the people's hearts to awaken them to their lost condition (c.f. John 16:11-16).

10. Rejection of the truth occurs by those who fall away (no longer remaining) during the tribulation when the Antichrist appears, not before the 70th week as pretrib teaches.

CHAPTER FIFTEEN

REVELATION 4-5

According to the pretribulation teaching, Revelation 4 is the pivotal chapter on the timing of the rapture in the book of Revelation. It is supposedly here the rapture takes place; after all, they teach that from this point John is explaining the things that are *hereafter* (c.f. Rev.1:19). The foundation in which the pretrib teaching stands upon is that the tribulation is the wrath of God, as we noted multiple times. Therefore, their conclusion is that the rapture "has" to take place here in chapter 4 for the church to be exempt from the tribulation.

David Hocking, in an article on the Pre-Trib Research Center website makes the following statement regarding the rapture taking place in Revelation 4.

THE PLACE OF JOHN IN HEAVEN
Revelation 4:1

"After this I looked, and, behold, a door was opened in heaven: and the first voice which I heard was as it were of a trumpet talking with me; which said, 'Come up hither, and I will shew thee things which must be hereafter.'"

Revelation 4:2 adds: *"And immediately I was in the spirit."* The definite article *"the"* is not in the Greek text. John simply says that he was *"in spirit."* The same thing is found in Revelation 1:10. By some means of spiritual transference, John was ushered into heaven where he could view the events that would transpire on the earth in the future. He also heard a voice like a *"trumpet"* talking with him; The words of I Thessalonians 4:16 include *"the trump of God."*

The very fact of this detail would point to a possible Rapture that would precede the coming tribulation. **John**, both as an apostle and as a believer, would certainly **picture such an event**.[128] (bold letters mine)

We see he states the typical pretribulation view on why the rapture must take place here in chapter 4, because John is now seen in heaven. I must say however, further in the book of Revelation John makes observations from the earth, not from heaven. Are there multiple raptures? NO! Finally, why does Hocking use the term "picture" in reference to John being the church? I will show you shortly why he says this.

Pretribulation teachers also emphasize that the word "church" is not mentioned after chapter 3 until it is mentioned again in chapter 19, when Christ comes back at the battle of Armageddon with His armies, which is the church triumphant.

And the **armies** which were in heaven followed him upon white horses, clothed in fine linen, white and clean. And out of his mouth goeth a sharp sword, that with it he should smite the nations: and he shall rule them with a rod of iron: and he treadeth the winepress of the fierceness and wrath of Almighty God. And he hath on his vesture and on his thigh a name written, KING OF KINGS, AND LORD OF LORDS. (Rev. 19:14-16)

An article by Dr. Robert Gromacki of the **Pre-Trib Research Center** echoes the prevailing thought by pretribulationist that the church is exempt on the earth during the tribulation because the word "church" is missing.

Where is "the Church" in Revelation 4-19?
OVERVIEW

Where is the church during the seven-year Tribulation, as outlined in Revelation 4-19? If posttribulationism were correct, you would expect to see the **church mentioned** as being on earth during this time. However, that is not the picture one sees in Revelation 4-19. This writer demonstrates through investigating many of the details of Revelation 4-19 that the church is pictured in heaven with Christ, having been raptured before the Tribulation began.

You can become informed of the overwhelming support for the pretribulational understanding of this issue through this essay.[129]

Gromacki's observation falls short in his argument on several accounts, but first, notice that the word "church" is not mentioned in chapter 19 either. In fact, the word church is not mentioned until chapter 22 when John brings a conclusion to his writing of the book of Revelation.

> I Jesus have sent mine angel to testify unto you these things in the **churches**. I am the root and the offspring of David, and the bright and morning star. (Rev. 22:16)

I believe I will give the reader ample arguments on why the word church is not mentioned from chapter 4-22. Also, take note that in chapter 22 that John is writing to the "churches" about the events in Revelation, not "Israel."

Arguments against the Rapture in Chapters 4 & 5:

First Argument

When John is told to *write the things which he has seen, the things which are, and the thing which shall be* (Rev. 1:19), he is following the natural progression of the book of Revelation. To make a statement as pretribulation teachers do that chapter 4 must be the rapture of the church, because what John writes is future, has no merit. John is simply stating what God is showing him- how future events will unfold.

Second Argument

I would like for the reader to rate the rapture event on the scale of one to hundred, compared to all the biblical events recorded in the Word of God. Where would you rate the rapture-resurrection in the course of human events? Just think of all of God's dealing with mankind: Noah and the flood; the tower of Babel; the destruction of Sodom and Gomorrah; God's judgments on Egypt forcing them to let Israel go free; the walls of Jericho falling down; David's victory over Goliath; the three Hebrews in the fiery furnace; Daniel in the lion's den; etc. What about the New Testament? We see the virgin birth of Jesus; the miracles of Jesus; the miracles of the Apostles in the book of Acts.

Outside of what Christ fulfilled in His life, death, burial and resurrection (which made it possible for mankind to come into a relationship with the Father), the rapture-resurrection would be off the scale compared to all other events. Just think about the implications of this event, the very thought of death itself being overcome and the reuniting with loved ones in heaven is phenomenal.

> So when this corruptible shall have put on incorruption, and this mortal shall have put on immortality, **then shall be brought to pass the saying** that is written, **Death is swallowed up in victory.** (1 Cor. 15:54)

This event is the total fulfillment of the redemption of what Christ did for every person on planet earth who places their faith in Him. The victory over death is what shall be brought to pass at the rapture/resurrection. When Christ rose from the grave three days after His crucifixion, He became the first-fruits of the resurrection, and the rapture/resurrection is the completion of the first resurrection.

> Blessed and holy is he that hath part in the **first resurrection**: on such the second death hath no power, but they shall be priests of God and of Christ, and shall reign with him a thousand years. (Rev. 20:6)

Since the fall of Adam in the garden, mankind has been under the penalty and the curse of death is the result. It has been estimated that there have been about 100 billion inhabitants on earth in recorded history (Wikipedia), and except for two people, Enoch and Elijah, every single human being has stepped into eternity through death.

Currently, there is an estimated seven billion living on earth, and outside of the rapture of the saints at the Lords coming, the clear majority of these people will die as well.

The final victory over death at the rapture-resurrection is huge compared to God's intervention in human affairs of mankind. For the believer who has put their faith and trust in our Lord and Savior Jesus Christ, this is our blessed hope, to be victorious over the curse of sin and death. For the unbeliever, they will be cast out from the presence of the Father and Jesus Christ to suffer God's judgment of wrath for all of eternity.

I would like to set the stage in your minds-eye of Revelation 4 from the pretribulation perspective. John, who represents the raptured church, has been called up into heaven to record the future events about to unfold. Now we have in heaven all of God's people standing in the presence of the Father, who have just been brought to Him by Jesus Christ (1 Thess. 3:13; Jude 24). What a joyous day that will be when we are reunited with our love ones and standing in the presence of the Father and the Son. Are you picturing this scene in your minds-eye? So, with this in view, what do we see in chapter five? John, who is detailing these events, is in heaven CRYING! And he is not only crying, but crying out WHO IS WORTHY?

> And I saw a strong angel proclaiming with a loud voice, Who is worthy to open the book, and to loose the seals thereof? And no man in heaven, nor in earth, neither under the earth, was able to open the book, neither to look thereon. And I **wept much**, because **no man was found worthy** to open and to read the book, neither to look thereon. (Rev. 5:2-4)

According to pretribulation theology, when we are raptured to heaven we will cry out in defeat, because we do not know who is worthy to open the book to bring to pass the final judgment on mankind and for Christ to usher in His kingdom? Here is the greatest victory for believers since the fall of man in the Garden of Eden, and we are supposedly dejected. Friends, this cannot possibly be the rapture here in chapter 4 & 5. We are not going to be wailing in disbelief after the greatest event ever. Jesus gave us this assurance in John's gospel when He told His disciples; *let not your heart be troubled,* when describing His return to gather His people (John 14:1-3).

Furthermore, how is it that John is just now being introduced to Christ in Revelation 5 when he supposedly "met" Christ in the air before this in Revelation 4? I Thessalonians 2:19 "*For what* is *our hope, or joy, or crown of rejoicing?* Are *not even ye in the **presence of our Lord Jesus Christ at his coming**?*"

The Bible is simply stating that John is in heaven recording the events that are about to unfold. John's record here has nothing to do with a pretribulation rapture.

Third Argument

After John is seen in heaven in chapter 4 he begins in chapter 6 recording the future events, which are related to the final seven-years (i.e. first three-and-half years, the great tribulation, the Antichrist, trumpet judgments, vial judgments and the battle of Armageddon).

Here is another example of the pretrib view that it is John who pictures the raptured church in chapter 4.

> 4: The church is absent in Revelation chapter 4 through chapter 18.

> The church is mentioned in the first three chapters of Revelation, but after **John (a member of the church)** is called up to heaven in chapter 4, he looks down on the events of Tribulation which begin in chapter 4 and the church is not mentioned or seen again until chapter 19 when she returns to earth with her bridegroom at His glorious appearing. Why? The answer is obvious: She isn't in the Tribulation. She is has been "caught up" to be with the Lord before it begins.[130] (bold letters mine)

Again, I equate much of the pretribulation teaching to the magician Houdini and his magic show like I said in my commentary of Matthew 24. The disappearing act became one of the most popular tricks performed by magicians. Pretribulationism teaching gets in on the magic act with their interpretations. With one wave of their wand (interpretation), they make the church mysteriously disappear, and then only to reappear again, this time as the person, John the apostle. If you recall, pretribulationist say that when Jesus gave His discourse to the disciples in Matthew 24, (John being one of them) he is referring to Israel. However, here in Revelation 4, for the sake of pretribulationism, John is not only a member of the church: he is "the" church- how convenient!

Go back and read the previous statement by David Hocking about Revelation 4:1 where he says that John pictures the raptured church.

Here is another example by Tim LaHaye from his book "Rapture Under Attack" in the section titled "Why is the Church Missing in Revelation 6-18."

> Then in chapter 4, John is called up into heaven with the words, "Come up here, and I will show you things which must take place

after this." **While we cannot use this as a primary Rapture teaching, it is interesting that John, a member of the church,** is called up into heaven immediately prior to the Tribulation, just as the church will be raptured prior to the tribulation. Calling John in vision up into heaven, where he can look down on Tribulation events, offers an allusion to the Rapture. If not, it has to be an amazing coincidence.[131] (bold letters mine)

Why wouldn't God use a member of the church to record the events in Revelation? Where in any other book in the Bible did God use someone, who was not part of God's people to record anything? John was called to heaven now to set the stage for the unfolding of the future events. His first recording was to reveal that Christ is worthy to open the book to bring to pass the events that would usher in the kingdom. Why wouldn't he be in heaven to record these events if this is the natural flow of events that are to unfold? Furthermore, when John gives the account of "who is worthy" to open the book, read the book and look inside. The seals must be "broken" first in order to look and read. I addressed this in dealing with the seals in Revelation chapter 6.

Tim LaHaye goes on to say in another section of the same book about the church being raptured in heaven in Revelation 4.

"The Events of the Tribulation Period According to Revelation"

1. Revelation 4:1-2 John, a **symbol** of the church, is taken up to heaven.[132]

The Twenty-Four Elders

We will now see the pretribulation rapture magic show continue to evolve with their bag of tricks. Not only did John become the church in chapter 4, now the church is seen in heaven as the twenty-four elders. Here is the typical teaching about the twenty-four elders from the pretribulation view.

Quoting David Hocking again on this subject, he argues that the twenty-four elders seen in heaven in chapters 4 and 5 are indeed representatives of the church age believers.

The description of these 24 elders in Revelation 4:4 connects them with the **promises to church-age believer**s in Revelation 2 and 3. The words about them sitting on thrones remind us of Revelation 3:21; the reference to them being clothed in white raiment connects us with the words of Revelation 3:5; the picture of them with crowns of gold on their heads reminds us of Revelation 2:10 and 3:11.[133] (bold letters mine)

David Jeremiah states this in his book "Escape the Coming Night."

"The Twenty-Four Elders, our Personal Representatives."

I believe these elders **represent** the church in the same way the twenty-four elders of the Old Testament represent the entire body of Priest.[134] (bold letters mine)

Here is H.A. Ironside:

Whatever view we may take of the **symbolic elders**, or **representing the entire heavenly priesthood,** which to me is clearly the true interpretation, there is this to bear in mind; they are seen crowned in Heaven before the judgments begin.[135] (bold letters mine)

We see they continually use such words as, symbol, member, picture, and represent to define the raptured church. This is the similar terms they use to define the tribulation and the day of the Lord. I quoted Tim LaHaye in chapter two who accused non-pretribulationism: "those who **refuse** to take prophecy as **literally** as they do other scriptures."

Here are my questions for my pretribulation brothers about the rapture of the church in Revelation 4. Follow my line of arguments against this and see if you agree?

1. According to pretribulationism, John in chapter 4 "represents" the church, and his being caught up to heaven is a "picture" of the church raptured before the tribulation.

2. According to pretribulationism, when John arrives in heaven he sees around the throne of God the twenty-four elders, who again, "represent" the church-age believers before the tribulation.
3. Finally, pretribulational belief that the multitude in Revelation chapter 19, is the church coming back after the tribulation at the battle of Armageddon with Christ at His second coming.

My questions are:

1. Is John a "representative" of the church, or is he the "literal" church body being caught up to heaven in chapter 4?
2. Are the twenty-four elders in heaven a "representative" of the church, or are they "literally" the church?
3. Is the multitude in chapter 19 "representative" of the church coming back with Christ, or are they "literally" the church?
    According to pretribulationist teaching, John and the twenty-four elders "represent, symbolize, picture, seem to be the church;" however, in chapter 19 the multitude is the "literal" church.
4. How does the "symbolic," John in chapter 4 and the twenty-four elders in chapters 4-5, turn into the "literal church" in chapter 19 by biblical interpretation?
5. How does one (John) transition into twenty-four (elders), then the twenty-four elders transition into a multitude?
6. Where does this literal multitude in chapter 19 come from?
    Furthermore, when reading Revelation 19 we see in heaven the multitude (v. 1), and the twenty-four elders (v. 4), and John (v. 16) altogether at the same time. Obviously, all three groups here are "distinct" from one another, and are literal themselves, not symbolic.
7. How were the twenty-four elders "already" seated in heaven "before" the rapture took place?
8. If the twenty-four elders, which picture the church are supposedly excluded from the tribulation: were they exempt from the church-age itself since they were already in heaven before John got there?

Here is one more example of pretribulational attempt to justify their view of the rapture in the book of Revelation.

> Whatever view one holds in regard to our Lord's return, one thing is clear in prophetic Scripture the marriage occurs *in heaven* (Revelation 19:7-9) *before* the triumphal return of Christ with His redeemed church at His side (Rev. 19:11-16)
>
> Non-pretribulationist are at a virtual loss to explain how the church got to heaven prior to returning with Christ at the battle of Armageddon.[136]

The fallacies of pretribulation teaching again reach its apex when discussing the book of Revelation in relation to the rapture. Pretribulation teachers switch the burden of proof to those who don't agree with them, in all the while, they have no proof whatsoever to support their belief how the church gets to heaven. They just simply reinterpret scripture to make it fit whatever they want to.

Here is the prewrath belief on this subject. One, John is none other than John recording the things which Christ is revealing to him; just as Ezekiel or Isaiah recorded the things they saw in heaven. They are literal as much as John is here. Two, the twenty-four elders are literal, but more than likely the "number" twenty-four represent the twenty-four courses of the priesthood that David set up to do the work of the temple in the Old Testament. In 1 Chronicles 24 we are given the account of this and in verse two it states: *And he gathered together all the **princes** of Israel, with the **priest** and **Levites**.* The princes can be equated to the elders with the priest.

The twenty-four elders in heaven are seated around the throne (Rev. 4:4), where in the Old Testament system there were no seats in the temple, simply because the work of the sacrificial system would not be complete until Christ finished the work on the cross. In Hebrews 10:12 it records that Christ "sat down" after He offered one sacrifice for sins. It would stand to reason that these twenty-four elders would be seated around the throne as a testament to Christ's finished work.

Third, the multitude in chapter 19 is at least part of the same multitude in chapter 7 seen before the throne declaring salvation. We believe this army is the literal church coming back with Christ at the end of the 70th week of Daniel. Chapter 19 also records that the "wife" had made herself ready. The wife is the multitude in verse 1-2 that is praising God for His salvation and judgment upon the great whore. Reversing the statement used by Hindson, "**Pre-tribulationist** (not prewrath) is at a virtual loss to explain how the church got to heaven prior to returning with Christ at the battle of Armageddon."

Fourth Argument

Another reason why pretribulation teaches the rapture occurs in chapter 4, because the word "church" is not mentioned in chapters 4-19; however, it is mentioned nineteen times in chapters 1-3. Their Conclusion then, is there is no reference to the church being persecuted on earth; therefore, it must be in heaven during this time.

Here is why I believe the "word" church is not found throughout the chapters in question. First, though the book of Revelation, according to scholars, was written around AD 95, it has direct reference to the seven "literal" churches of Asia at that time.

> John to the **seven churches** which are in Asia: Grace be unto
> you, and peace, from him which is, and which was, and which is
> to come; and from the seven Spirits which are before his throne;
> (Rev. 1:4)

There are direct references to the seven churches in Asia; however, when John is describing future events, these churches are not individually in view (i.e. church-ages), but will encompass "all" of Christianity. The church in general, before Christ's return, is experiencing all what Christ admonishes to these churches.

Second, within the context of every church that John describes in chapters 2 and 3, the Lord warns "individuals" within these churches that those who are not truly Christians need to repent. The Lord purposely uses the word "saints" when describing those after chapter 4 and not the word "church," so there is to be no mistaking who are true believers. Churches are filled with many professors of Christianity, but have not been truly born again. Throughout the New Testament when describing our Lord's return, the word church is never mentioned concerning who is to be raptured, only true believers. Remember how I pointed out in our study of 1 & 2 Thessalonians that the word "remain" is a direct reference to genuine believers who will not capitulate to the Antichrist by receiving his mark. And they are the only ones that will be "caught up" to meet the Lord in the air. The saints are said to be caught up with Christ, not the church (1 Thess. 4:14, 17).

2: Beloved, now are **we** the sons of God, and it doth not yet appear what **we** shall be: but we know that, when he shall appear, **we** shall be like him; for **we** shall see him as he is.

3: And **every man** that hath this hope in him purifieth **himself**, even as he is pure. (1 John 3:2-3)

In the book of Ephesians chapter 5 Paul makes the statement that Christ will present His church as a glorious church without spot or wrinkle. However, the rapture is not implied in the context, only the fact that we shall be presented as a glorious church.

In the book of Romans, the word "church" does not appear until the last chapter (16), and then it is not referencing the church at Rome to whom the letter is written. The letter is written to the saints (1:7; 8:27; 12:13), servants (6:18-19, 22), brethren (1:13; 7:1,4; 8:12, 29; 10:1; 11:25; 12:1; 15:14-15, 30; 16:14). These are the same names as those being described during the tribulation in the book of Revelation.

We acknowledge that these servants here in Romans are members in the body of Christ, the church, even though the word "church" is not found. Also, in chapter 2:17-29 Paul writing to believers, calls them Jews who are boasting in the law; is he writing to Israel or the church?

First Corinthians the word church is mentioned in 1:2, and not again until chapter 7, and this is referencing all the churches. Even in the classic rapture text in 1 Corinthians 15:51-52, it say's "we" not the church.

In 2 Corinthians, the word church appears in 2:1, and never mentioned again in the following twelve chapters.

In Galatians Paul calls believers, brethren, in the churches of Galatia, and only reference the word church again in verse 13 when he acknowledges how he persecuted the churches (individual in scope).

In 1 & 2 Thessalonians, the word church is only mentioned in the opening verse and not mentioned again. As I pointed out, at the rapture it does not mention Christ coming for His church, but believers only who make up His church.

In 1 Peter, Peter calls his audience "strangers" in verse 1 and "elect" in verse 2. Only in chapter five does he mention the word church, and this is a greeting from another church.

Even in the book of Hebrews the word church appears twice. In the book of Acts, the name church in chapter 7 is in reference to "Israel" in the Old Testament. In chapter 8 it mentions the Church at Jerusalem twice; however, when persecution came the Bible says in verse 4 "they" were scattered when it referenced the church being persecuted.

The Saints

I brought this to your attention to show you that though the word church is used sparingly it is still implied that all these individuals who are called brethren, brothers, believers, elect, and saints are indeed members of Christ's bride- the Church. Here are some verses describing the saints.

Matthew 27:52 "many bodies of the saints which slept arose"
Acts 9:13 "saints at Jerusalem"
Acts 26:10 "saints did I shut up in prison"
Romans 1:7 "called to be saints"
Romans 8:27 "intercession for the saints"
1Cor. 16:15 "ministry of the saints"
1 Cor. 14:33 "churches of the saints"
2 Cor. 1:1 "church with all the saints"
2 Cor. 8:4; 9:1 "ministering to the saints"
Ephesians 1:1 "to all the saints"
Ephesians 1:15 "love unto the saints"
Philippians 1:15 "saints at Philippi"
Colossians 1:2 "saints and faithful brethren"
1 Thessalonians 3:13 "coming of the Lord Jesus Christ with all His saints" (not the church at the rapture)
2 Thessalonians 1:10 "When he shall come to be glorified in all his saints" (not the church at the rapture)
Hebrews 6:10 "minister to the saints"
Jude 3 "faith delivered to the saints"

Saints themselves are not mentioned in the seven churches in Revelation, because the Lord is addressing certain aspects, which describe each church. Here again the Lord is careful not to give the impression that every church member is a Christian. Furthermore, when the Lord is addressing believers in the time of trials in the great tribulation, he does address them as saints.

5:8 "prayers of the saints"
8:3 "prayers of the saints"

13:7 "make war with the saints"

Rev. 11:18: The word servants, prophets, and saints are used in describing the rewards to be given and the word church is not used in relation to any of these groups.

14:12 "patience of the saints"

16:6 "blood of the saints"

18:24 "blood of the prophets and of the saints"

For pretribulation teachers to argue from silence pertaining to the church, it just does not add up. Question: Is John up in heaven describing different scenes that are taking place? Yes! When John is in heaven, does he mention the church while he is there? No! Consequently, pretribulation teaching is not justified in arguing from silence, because the same can be said about their argument. I maintain the belief that the word "church" is not used throughout the events in the tribulation because it will be the church as a whole that will capitulate to the man of sin, yet numerous individuals in various church assemblies will hold to their beliefs that only Jesus is Lord.

Now let's compare this to the seven churches in Revelation 2 and 3, and look at the warnings to "individuals" within these churches to take heed to what the Spirit of God is telling them.

The Church at Ephesus:

Revelation 2:2- I know thy works, and thy labour, and thy patience, and how thou canst not bear **them which are evil**: and thou **hast tried them which say they are apostles, and are not, and hast found them liars:**

The Church at Smyrna:

Revelation 2:9- I know thy works, and tribulation, and poverty, (but thou art rich) and I know the blasphemy of **them which say they are Jews, and are not,** but are the synagogue of Satan.

The Church at Pergamos:

Revelation 2:14-15 But I have a few things against thee, because thou hast there **them that hold the doctrine of Balaam,** who taught Balac to cast a stumblingblock before the children of Israel, to eat things sacrificed unto idols, and to commit fornication. 15: So hast thou also **them that hold the doctrine of the Nicolaitanes**, which thing I hate.

The name Nicolaitanes is taken from two words, Nico (which means to conquer, like the company Nike (which means to overcome or to conquer), and Laity (which means common people). Apparently, there were people trying to separate Christians into two classes of people, those who held special positions - as though they held a unique significance toward God - and the common believer.

Christ told His disciples in Matthew 23 that we are to call no one master, Rabbi, or father, but brethren. Christ taught that His children were equal, and every individual had the same right access to the Father as any other. Christ expounded on this in the Olivet Discourse when He said many would come in His name, as though they were speaking for Him, because they had some special right when others did not. Religion wants to bestow "titles" upon individuals, as though they are "super Christians." Jesus even said these individuals will set in the "uppermost" seats to be seen of men along with a public display of affection by being honored among God's people. Jesus said that if He is "lifted up," He would draw men unto himself.

The Church at Thyatira:

Revelation 2:20-21 Notwithstanding I have a few things against thee, because thou sufferest that woman **Jezebel, which calleth herself a prophetess,** to teach and to seduce my servants to commit fornication, and to eat things sacrificed unto idols. 21 And I gave **her space to repent** of her fornication; and **she repented not**.

The Church at Sardis:

Revelation 3:4 Thou hast a few names even in Sardis **which have not defiled their garments**; and **they** shall walk with me in white: for **they** are worthy.

Christ states that some (few) have not defiled themselves, which implies many have defiled themselves and will not be accepted, but rejected.

The Church at Philadelphia:

Revelation 3:9 Behold, I will make them of the synagogue of Satan, which **say they are Jews, and are not, but do lie;** behold, I will make them to come and worship before thy feet, and to know that I have loved thee.

The Church at Laodicea:

Revelation 3:17 Because thou **sayest,** I am rich, and increased with goods, and have need of nothing; and **knowest not that thou art wretched, and miserable, and poor, and blind, and naked:**

The Lord's warning is clear; everyone who claims to be a Christian needs to do self-examination of their faith (2 Cor. 13:5). Christianity will be faced with the ultimate test of its faith when it meets evil face-to-face in the person of the Antichrist. Many within the church will be exposed for who they are, only Christian by name, but not in reality. It makes sense for the Word of God to distinguish His coming for His saints, which are members of His true church instead of saying the church in general.

Another aspect of this is that the Lord is warning His church through these seven churches to remain true to Him. Why would Christ challenge His bride to remain true in the ultimate test, only to remove (rapture) them before the test is given? And I am not intending to use the word "test" loosely. Another way to say this, would be that this time during the great tribulation is the time for Christian saints to glorify God by remaining true to Christ. Even many pretribulationist say that the tribulation will be a "time of testing for Israel."

Revelation chapters 12-14 are in context during the tribulation period when the Antichrist is unleashed upon the world. Here are a few examples of God's exhortation to the believers during this time.

> And they **overcame him by the blood of the Lamb,** and by the **word of their testimony;** and they **loved not their lives** unto the death. (Rev. 12:11)

> And the dragon was wroth with the woman, and went to make war with the remnant of her seed, which **keep the commandments of God, and have the testimony of Jesus Christ.** (Rev. 12:17)

And it was given unto him to make war with the **saints**, and to overcome them: and power was given him over all kindreds, and tongues, and nations. (Rev. 13:7)

Here is the **patience of the saints**: here are **they that keep the commandments of God, and the faith of Jesus.**

And I heard a voice from heaven saying unto me, Write,

Blessed are the dead which die in the Lord from henceforth: Yea, saith the Spirit, that they may rest from their labours; and **their works do follow them**.

(Rev. 14:12-13)

And I saw thrones, and they sat upon them, and judgment was given unto them: and *I saw* the souls of them that were **beheaded for the witness of Jesus, and for the word of God,** and which had not worshipped the beast, neither his image, neither had received *his* mark upon their foreheads, or in their hands; and they lived and reigned with Christ a thousand years. (Rev. 20:4)

This concludes our study in Revelation 4 on the supposed pretrib rapture of the church. Again, like everything I state, you weigh the evidence. We will now follow up in the next chapter that exposes, yet, another fallacy that is central to the pretrib theory.

CHAPTER SIXTEEN

KEPT FROM THE HOUR

7. And to the angel of the church in Philadelphia write; These things saith he that is holy, he that is true, he that hath the key of David, he that openeth, and no man shutteth; and shutteth, and no man openeth;

8. I know thy works: behold, I have set before thee an open door, and no man can shut it: for thou hast a little strength, and hast kept my word, and hast not denied my name.

9. Behold, I will make them of the synagogue of Satan, which say they are Jews, and are not, but do lie; behold, I will make them to come and worship before thy feet, and to know that I have loved thee.

10. Because thou hast **kept the word of my patience**, I also will keep thee **from the hour of temptation**, which shall come upon all the world, to try them that dwell upon the earth. (Revelation 3:7-10)

Revelation 3:10 is another key verse for the pretribulation rapture theory. This one is pulled from their bag of magic tricks more than any other verse when trying to exempt the church from the tribulation. Here is Tim LaHaye stating the typical pretribulation explanation of this verse.

The Promise of Revelation 3:10

One of the best promises guaranteeing the church's rapture before the tribulation appears in Revelation 3:10. As you read it, keep in mind it is one of our Lord's promises.

> Because you have kept My command to persevere, I also will keep you from the hour of **trial,** which shall come upon all the whole world, to test those who dwell on the earth. (Revelation 3:10)

> This verse teaches that the **faithful church** of the open door, which will **not deny my His name,** but will **practice good works, evangelism, and missions,** will be kept out of the hour of the trial (the Great Tribulation) that shall try the whole earth. The guarantee of rapture before the Tribulation could hardly be more powerful. No wonder one writer labeled it "a cardinal Scripture."[137] (Bold letters mine)

First, is LaHaye claiming that "only" the faithful church is raptured? Is he distinguishing between those believers who "practice" good works will be raptured, while those who don't are left behind? In his Left Behind series he never states that a backslidden believer is left behind, only the lost are left. As a reminder, the great tribulation does not begin until midway through the 70th week (Dan. 9:27); therefore, he is advocating a midtribulation rapture. If this verse promises "escape" from the great tribulation, how does pretrib teaching handle Revelation 2:10?

> And unto the angel of the church in Smyrna write; These things saith the first and the last, which was dead, and is alive; I know thy works, and **tribulation,** and poverty, (but thou art rich) and I know the blasphemy of them which say they are Jews, and are not, but are the synagogue of Satan. Fear none of those things which thou shalt suffer: behold, the devil shall cast some of you into prison, that ye may be tried; and **ye shall have tribulation ten days: be thou faithful unto death,** and I will give thee a crown of life. (Rev. 2:8-10)

Here the Lord is telling these believers to be faithful *unto death* and He would give them a crown of life. The Lord did not say if they were faithful he would deliver **from** death, but **through** death they would receive the crown of life. The crown of life (eternal salvation) is the goal the Lord wants individuals to attain, which is priceless when compared to the struggles and hardships of this life (Rom. 8:18).

Another false claim by some pretribulationist; they will say that the reference in verse 8 and 10 about those who have "kept my (God's) word and not denied my (Jesus) name is referring to the saints throughout church history. Therefore, because of the faithfulness of the church-age saints, the promise is given to the future church at the end of the age that they will be kept from the world-wide tribulation (v.10). I'm not sure why we today, supposedly, the Laodicean 'unfaithful' church will rest on the martyrs of the past? Also, I ask the pretribulationist; how does the "dark-ages" fit in with their Bible hermeneutics?

Now back to our verse in question, which we will see is beyond just the topic about the tribulation. The Scripture text does not say **trial**, it says, "I will keep thee from the **temptation**." I need to make it clear that I believe the King James Bible is correct in its wording of Revelation 3:10. It uses the word "temptation" while some other versions use the word "trial." Like all other Scripture passages we need to allow the Scripture to say what they mean, not what we want them to say. We know they are kept from the temptation, not the trial, because in the same context to the church at Philadelphia in verse 8 it says;

> I know thy works: behold, I have set before thee an open door, and no man can shut it: for thou hast a little strength, and **hast kept my word, and hast not denied my name.**

These believers are not kept from the trial, but from the temptation "in" the trial. By not denying the Lord, "He set the open door that no man could shut." In verse 10, it states these faithful saints have "kept the word my patience," which is teaching that patience comes from the midst of perplexity, persecution, or tribulation.

We saw in Paul's letter to the Thessalonians that those who "remain" have not "fallen away;" therefore, will be raptured at His return. Christ warned about the evil servant in Matthew 24:48 that thought his master delayed his coming and began to smite his fellow servants and eat and drink with the drunken. Christ gave the same warning in the parables of the seed and the sower in Matthew 13:20-21. He stated that one type of person is one who received the word with "joy" (20); however, when "tribulation or persecution" came they "rejected" the word because they were "offended." Many have a false impression of salvation and will reject its truths when the great tribulation arises?

In the context of the letters to the seven churches we can discern the main point of emphasis to each of the seven churches being described. It is warning and encouragement not to forsake the Lord, and remain faithful to Him. This is the consistent theme throughout the teachings of Christ as they pertain to His return.

1.) Ephesus: 2:4-5 "has left thy first love"; "fallen"
2.) Smyrna: 2:10 "be faithful"
3.) Pergamos: 2:13 "holdest fast my name"; "hast not denied my faith"
4.) Thyatira: 2:25-26 "hold fast till I come"; "keepeth my works unto the end". The admonition to these believers at Thyatira is to stay faithful "unto the end." This is what Christ told the disciples in Matthew 24:13 "but he that shall endure unto the end the same shall be saved."
5.) Sardis: 3:1-3 "thou livest, and art dead"; "strengthen the things which remain, that are ready to die"; "hold fast, and repent"
6.) Philadelphia: 3:8 "hast kept my word, and not denied my name"
7.) Laodicea: 3:15 "I would thou wert cold or hot"; "I counsel thee to buy me gold tried in the fire" (not out of the fire).

In each case, the Lord was telling some members of these churches that they are in danger, because they had already or were about to forsake the Lord in some way. He encouraged them to maintain the things that are true, and challenged them to continue in those things.

Let's look in the following example of someone we are familiar with who did not heed the warning about temptation; and apply its truth relating to the end-times.

Lot's Wife

> And delivered just Lot, **vexed** with the filthy conversation of the wicked: (For that **righteous man dwelling among them,** in seeing and hearing, **vexed his righteous soul** from day to day with their unlawful deeds;) The Lord knoweth how to **deliver the godly out of temptations,** and to reserve the **unjust unto the day of judgment to be punished:** (2 Peter 2:7-9)

We already talked briefly in chapter thirteen about Lot and his wife in relation to God's deliverance from His wrath that was poured out on

Sodom and Gomorrah. I would like to look just a little deeper into this regarding the current topic we are dealing with, namely temptation. Notice how Peter described the conditions of the society in Sodom when Lot was living in there. Lot was "vexed," as he saw and heard (not participated) the unrighteous lifestyle of the inhabitants of Sodom.

We all know the story how the Lord brought Lot, his wife and two daughters out of the city before the destruction. However, having disobeyed God's command not to look back, Lot's wife was turned into a pillar of salt (Gen. 19:26). The question I propose is: why did she turn back to look? First, we need to see the reason why the cities were destroyed in the first place; the answer is given in Genesis 18:20. *And the LORD said, because the cry of Sodom and Gomorrah is great, and because their sin is very grievous;*

The sins of Sodom and Gomorrah had become so vile that the Lord came out of His place in heaven to put a halt to the iniquity of those cities. With this context, we see the stern warning given to Lot in Genesis's chapter 19.

> And when the morning arose, then the angels hastened Lot, saying, Arise, take thy wife, and thy two daughters, which are here; **lest thou be consumed in the iniquity of the city.** (Gen. 19:15)

Lot's wife looked back towards Sodom because that was where her heart was leading all along. Physically, she left the city; however, her natural inclination was to look back at the thing she really desired in her heart. Her heart was consumed with all the sinful allurements and attractions that Sodom had to offer.

Now let's fast-forward to the teaching of Christ according to Dr. Luke. We briefly looked in chapter 13 about Lot's deliverance in relation to the day of the Lord; now let's look at it with Lot's wife in mind.

In Luke's gospel chapter 17, Christ was teaching about His coming kingdom, because the Pharisee's demanded that he tell them when the kingdom of God was to come (Luke 17:20). Christ gave His answer by stating that the kingdom of God is "not with observation" (vs. 20), but is "within you" (vs.21). He was teaching a deeper truth here to the Pharisees so that they would not miss His intentions in His answer to them.

He illustrates His point with two events from the Old Testament. One was Noah, verses 26-27; the other was Lot, verses 28-29. He speaks of His revealing in the end-time in verse 30; then in verse 31 he issues a warning, "in that day," which is the context of the great tribulation, not to turn back for things in your house (temporal security). Then he continues His warning to those working in the field not to turn back, which speaks of (temporal substance).

Christ gives a three-word warning in verse 32 in relation to what he is teaching: "REMEMBER LOT'S WIFE." Lot's wife, whom we have seen in Genesis 19, was consumed in the iniquity of the city. And in Luke 17, which is the context of the great tribulation, Christ warns those who "profess" Christianity not to turn back. How does one turn back? Verse 33 answers the question: *Whosoever shall seek to **save his life shall lose it**; and whosoever shall lose his life shall preserve it.*

In the context to save one's life is to capitulate to the Antichrist and receive his mark (Revelation 13:15-17). However, for the ones who will lose their lives physically; they will save it eternally. By accepting the Antichrist, many will think they are saving their life; this will eventually come to a screeching halt at the day of the Lord, followed by the eternal rejection of Christ in hell (Rev. 14:9-11).

Let's look at an example of this in the New Testament about remaining true to Christ in light of His return.

1 John 2:15-29

15: Love not the world, neither the things that are in the world. **If any man love the world, the love of the Father is not in him.**

16: For all that is in the world, the lust of the flesh, and the lust of the eyes, and the pride of life, is not of the Father, but is of the world.

17: And the **world passeth away**, and the lust thereof: but he that **doeth the will of God** abideth for ever.

18: Little children, it is the last time: **and as ye have heard that antichrist shall come,** even now are there many antichrists; whereby we know that it is the last time.

19: **They went out from us, but they were not of us; for if they had been of us,** they would no doubt have continued with us: but they went out, that they might be made manifest that they were not all of us.

20: But ye have an unction from the Holy One, and ye know all things

21: I have not written unto you because ye know not the truth, but because ye know it, and that no lie is of the truth.

22: **Who is a liar but he that denieth that Jesus is the Christ? He is antichrist, that denieth the Father and the Son.**

23: Whosoever **denieth the Son**, the same hath not the Father: (but) he that **acknowledgeth the Son** hath the Father also.

24: **Let that therefore abide in you,** which ye have heard from the beginning. If that which ye have heard from the beginning **shall remain in you**, ye also **shall continue** in the Son, and in the Father.

25: And this is the promise that he hath **promised us, even eternal life.**

26: These things have I written unto you **concerning them that seduce you.**

27: But the anointing which ye have received of him **abideth in you,** and ye need not that any man teach you: but as the same anointing teacheth you of all things, and is truth, and is no lie, and even as it hath taught you, **ye shall abide in him.**

28: And now, little children, abide in him; that, **when he shall appear, we may have confidence,** and **not be ashamed** before him at his coming.

29: If ye know that he is righteous, ye know that **every one that doeth righteousness is born of him.**

These verses teach:

15-17: Comparing our love for Christ to the world and God's warning is that anyone who loves this world God's love is not in them.

18-22: The Antichrist will come, and because of the types of antichrists that are present in their day many denied Christ and left the faith.

23-24: This is contrasting between those who denied Christ (fall away) and those who are still abiding (remaining).

25: The end-result for the believer is eternal life.

26-27: Warning to believers, there are those who will seduce you from believing the truth.

28-29: We are to have confidence (Hope) that He is coming, and if this hope is real in our life we will continue in righteousness (believing in the Lordship of Christ).

Christ taught the same thing in His Olivet Discourse in Matthew 24. The only difference between the two passages is the context of 1 John is mainly for Christians throughout the church-age, whereas, Matthew 24 is a specific time at the "end of the age." However, the warning is the same- do not forsake Christ.

> 3: Blessed be the God and Father of our Lord Jesus Christ, which according to his abundant mercy hath begotten us again **unto a lively hope** by the resurrection of Jesus Christ from the dead,
> 4: To an **inheritance** incorruptible, and undefiled, and that fadeth not away, **reserved in heaven for you,**
> 5: Who are kept by the power of God through faith unto salvation ready to be revealed in the last time.
> 6: Wherein ye greatly rejoice, though now for a season, if need be, **ye are in heaviness through manifold temptations:**
> 7: That the **trial of your faith**, being much **more precious** than of gold that perisheth, though it be **tried with fire**, might be found unto praise and honour and glory at the appearing of Jesus Christ: (1 Pet. 1:3-7)

There are several observations I would like to make pertaining to these verses. Pretrib teachers make a big deal about the blessed hope in Titus as though it pertains to escaping the tribulation. We saw that the blessed hope in Titus has nothing to do with an escape from the tribulation, but a completion of our salvation when we stand righteous before our Lord and Savior in heaven. The same application is made here in these verses. What is our *lively hope* pertaining to? This is answered in verse 4 when we are in heaven, which is not an escape of some physical persecution.

Peter goes on to make this applicable to his readers by stating that these believers were facing *manifold temptations*, that is to say, multiple and various temptations. These temptations come during the trial in which Peter calls the trial itself, "more precious." The temptations are not precious, because they come from the flesh and the devil; these are not of God. However, in contrast, the trials are what develop and mature the believer to become the Christian whom God can use for His glory and the kingdom.

> My brethren, count it all joy when ye fall into **divers temptations;**
> Knowing this, that the **trying of your faith worketh patience**.

> But let **patience have her perfect work**, that ye may be perfect
> and entire, wanting nothing. (James 1:2-4)

As James opens his letter to the twelve tribes scattered abroad, he is addressing those who have fled because of the persecution they were experiencing. Specifically, these folks are mainly Jewish (v. 1 the twelve tribes) who have fled Jerusalem because of their faith in the Messiah, Jesus the Christ. James acknowledges that these folks were facing temptations that were "trying" their faith. He tells them to accept the fact that temptations are real and a part of life. He will express this fact in verse 13 that temptations themselves are not from God. *Let no man say when he is tempted, I am tempted of God: for God cannot be tempted with evil,* **neither tempteth he any man:**

Temptations are the mechanism that Satan uses to get people to reject God's truth. However, the temptations in most cases show up during a time of trial. The trial is the test to help someone grow in their faith, but the temptation is evil influence that weighs in on the person's faith to trust God. Temptation will tell you to quit, but the trial is to teach you to trust God.

James goes on to say in verses 14-16 of chapter one.

> But every man is **tempted**, when he is **drawn away of his own
> lust, and enticed.** Then when lust hath conceived, it bringeth
> forth sin: and sin, when it is finished, bringeth forth death. Do
> not err, my beloved brethren.

God does not bring a trial upon someone to bring death; temptation in the trial will draw the individual's heart to abandon their position where they once stood. This is produced by their lust or desires when they start to think and act independently from God's truth.

Paul acknowledged this important truth of trials in 2 Corinthians 12:7-9 when he petitioned God three times to take away the thorn in his flesh. He knew that Satan was "buffeting" him, and God's response to his request was that *God's grace is sufficient.* God telling him that His grace is sufficient for him to endure in his personal trial. It would have been Satan's desire to derail Paul in his Christian walk with God.

Jesus taught this truth in His "Sermon on the Mount," beginning in Matthew 5.

> Blessed are they which are persecuted for righteousness' sake: for
> theirs is the kingdom of heaven. Blessed are ye, when men shall

revile you, and persecute you, and shall say all **manner of evil against you falsely,** for my sake. **Rejoice, and be exceeding glad**: for great is your **reward in heaven:** for so persecuted they the prophets which were before you. (Matt. 5:10-12)

Jesus acknowledges trials will come upon His children through persecution, and for them to rejoice and accept by faith what they were experiencing would be rewarded in the eternal- heaven.

When Jesus taught the disciples how to pray in Matthew 6, he included that when we pray to ask God not for us to be led into "temptation."

And **forgive us** our debts, as **we forgive** our debtors. And lead us not **into temptation**, but deliver us from **evil:** For thine is the kingdom, and the power, and the glory, for ever. Amen. For if **ye forgive men** their trespasses, your heavenly Father will **also forgive you:** But if **ye forgive not** men their trespasses, **neither will your Father forgive your** trespasses. (vv. 12-15)

Temptation mentioned here is tied in with; *deliver us from evil,* not the trial. The evil is anything that goes against nature and character of God. God hates evil! Jesus said in John 3:20, *He that doeth evil, hates the light.* The light here is God himself, which speaks of His holiness and moral attributes. Temptations ultimate conclusion is to draw us away from God and the good for which He exhibits. This would fit perfectly in Revelation 3:10 where the deliverance from temptation is "in" the trial, not "from" the trial. As a side note, Christ speaks of forgiveness in this context of Matthew 6, and the temptation not to forgive is the one serious action that can destroy a person's walk with God. Forgiveness demonstrated by a person's life is the main building block that a person has with the Lord, and without it brings serious consequences.

Jesus told His disciples in John 16:33, *These things I have spoken unto you, that in me ye might have peace.* ***In the world ye shall have tribulation:*** *but be of good cheer; I have overcome the world.*

Paul acknowledge this point in Acts 14:22

Confirming the souls of the disciples, and exhorting them to continue in the faith, and that **we must through much tribulation** enter into the kingdom of God.

According to some pretribulationist, Paul had the "persecute me" syndrome; apparently, Paul "wanted" to go through the tribulation. No! Paul was a true servant of Christ and stood the test for whatever situation he faced.

Temptation in the Wilderness

> **Harden not your hearts**, as in the provocation, in the **day of temptation** in the wilderness: When **your fathers tempted me**, proved me, and saw my works forty years. Wherefore I was grieved with that generation, and said, They do alway err in their heart; and they have not known my ways. So I sware in my wrath, They shall not enter into my rest.) **Take heed**, brethren, lest there be in any of you an **evil heart of unbelief, in departing from the living God.** But exhort one another daily, while it is called To day; lest any of you be **hardened through the deceitfulness of sin.** For we are made partakers of Christ, **if we hold the beginning of our confidence stedfast unto the end;** (Heb. 3:8-14)

Here we have a perfect example of what temptation is talking about in relation to evil. The children of Israel had just been delivered from Pharaoh by the mighty hand of God, but, many harden their heart because of unbelief. Through their unbelief, they began to complain and question God through Moses, which led to many hardening their heart and turning from believing and trusting God.

Jesus taught in Matthew 13 in the parable of the sower of the seed, because of tribulation, professing Christians will turn from walking with the Lord.

Revelation 3:10 has created a lot of attention when it comes to the subject of the tribulation. The phrase *word of my patience* does indicate some type of hardship. The word patience in the New Testament is associated with trials, not from trials.

> Knowing this, that the **trying of your faith worketh patience**. But **let patience have her perfect work,** that ye may be perfect and entire, wanting nothing. (James 1:3-4)

> Take, my brethren, the prophets, who have spoken in the name of the Lord, **for an example of suffering affliction, and of**

patience. Behold, we count them **happy which endure.** Ye have heard of the **patience of Job,** and have seen the end of the Lord; that the Lord is very pitiful, and of tender mercy. (James 5:10-11)

And not only so, but we glory in **tribulations also: knowing that tribulation worketh patience;** (Romans 5:3)

4: But in all things approving ourselves as the ministers of God, in **much patience, in afflictions**, in necessities, in distresses,
5: In stripes, in imprisonments, in tumults, in labours, in watchings, in fastings; (2 Cor. 6:4-5)

Strengthened with all might, according to his glorious power, unto all **patience and longsuffering** with joyfulness;

(Colossians 1:11)
So that we ourselves glory in you in the churches of God for your **patience and faith in all your persecutions and tribulations that ye endure:** (2 Thess. 1:4)

But thou hast fully known my doctrine, manner of life, purpose, faith, longsuffering, charity, **patience, Persecutions, afflictions**, which came unto me at Antioch, at Iconium, at Lystra; what persecutions I endured: but out of them all the Lord delivered me. (2 Tim. 3:10-11)

I John, who also am your brother, and companion in **tribulation**, and in the kingdom and **patience** of Jesus Christ, was in the isle that is called Patmos, for the word of God, and for the testimony of Jesus Christ. (Rev. 1:9)

He that leadeth into captivity shall go into captivity: he that killeth with the sword must be killed with the sword. **Here is the patience and the faith of the saints.** (Rev. 13:10)

And the smoke of their torment ascendeth up for ever and ever: and they have no rest day nor night, who worship the beast and his image, and whosoever receiveth the mark of his name.

Here is the **patience of the saints**: here are they that keep the commandments of God, and the faith of Jesus. And I heard a voice from heaven saying unto me, Write, Blessed are the dead which **die in the Lord** from henceforth: Yea, saith the Spirit, that they may rest from their labours; and their works do follow them. (Rev. 14:11-13)

There is a common thread woven throughout the Scriptures which speaks of patience during trials and hardships. The word patience itself is interlocked with temptations, because the trials themselves bring forth the opportunity to the person to quit enduring. That is why Revelation 3:10 the word *patience* and *temptation* are tied together in the same phrase in this verse. A person who exercises patience in the trial will not be tempted to quit or reject the Lord Jesus. Those who lose their patience will be tempted to "fall away" from the truth that they proclaimed they believed in.

Jesus spoke of this in Luke's account of the Olivet Discourse in chapter 21, which is in the context of the tribulation.

And ye shall be hated of all men for my name's sake.

But there shall not a hair of your head perish. In your **patience possess ye your souls.** (Luke 21:17-19)

I like to add one final thought about this particular subject. Jesus said in John 17:15 in his prayer to the Father *I pray **not** that thou shouldest take them out of the world, but that thou shouldest keep them from the evil.* Pretribulation teachers are silent in their writings about this statement by Christ. I am confident if Christ had said when he prayed, that His followers "would be taken" out of the world, pretribulation teachers would be all over this verse trying to prove their theory. However, this verse teaches the opposite, nothing here is said about Christians escaping the tribulation, but being kept from the evil.

CHAPTER SEVENTEEN

THE FINAL CONCLUSION

We have completed a detailed study of the fallacies of the pretribulation rapture, now here are my closing remarks.

1.   Chapter (Two): In this chapter, we looked at the psychological mind-set of some who believe in the pretrib rapture. Even to question the validity of the pretribulation doctrine is taboo. Many who have deep concerns about pretribulation discrepancies are usually silenced through intimidation. This doctrine is echoed so loudly in the pulpits and airways, unfortunately, many simply do not like to make waves with their questions, so they just keep quiet.

The "blessed hope" is the backbone of the pretribulation rapture. They cry out: "How could you dare to take away my hope from escaping the coming tribulation!" We all agree that we are on the Titanic, and the ship is sinking. However, that's ok, because many believe that since they hold to the pre-tribulation rapture theory that gives them a first-class ticket to the row boats, while the doubters are left behind with the "third class" passengers to sink with the ship.

We saw that the "blessed hope" was not an escape from the tribulation, but the surety that as Christians we will be with Christ for eternity. Nowhere in the rapture passages did we see any verses pertaining to a hope of escape from the great tribulation. The blessed hope is just as good for those who have already died in the Lord (1 Thess. 4:14-15) as those who are alive at His coming. During the tribulation period, the blessed hope will be the only assurance given to believers who will be experiencing the most dreadful conditions.

Jesus is not punishing His bride as pretribulationist would have you believe. However, the conclusion can be easily made when God's wrath takes place, and it's certainly not against believers. One more note about the bride of Christ. We read in Revelation 21:2 "And I John saw the holy city, new Jerusalem, coming down from God out of heaven, **prepared as a bride adorned for her husband**. This is clearly referring to Israel, which is called the bride. In the same chapter, we can read in verse 9 *"And there came unto me one of the seven angels which had the seven vials full of the seven last plagues, and talked with me, saying, Come hither, I will shew thee the bride, the Lamb's wife."* If you continue to read the remaining verses you will see this is referring to Jerusalem and the twelve tribes of Israel. We see this again in Revelation 22:17 "And the Spirit and **the bride** say, Come. And let him that heareth say, *Come. And let him that is athirst come. And whosoever will, let him take the water of life freely."* Pretribulationist insist the book of Revelation is for Israel, yet, they will bypass these verses that unquestionably point to the church.

2.   Chapter (Five): Dispensationalism is the Trojan horse that has entered the church: This pretribulation led doctrine was brought into the church by John Darby. His biased belief in the pretribulation rapture led him to dismantle the Bible that disrupts the harmony and continuity of the Scriptures. The vain attempt to separate Israel and the church falls short in its dissertation.

3.   Chapters (Six and Seven)-Imminence: Imminence is the illegitimate child of dispensationalism. We saw in this chapter that signs do indeed precede our Lord's coming, which dispels imminence. Pretribulation teachers, while espousing imminence, spend large amounts of energy in their teaching about the "signs of the times" of the last days that disproves their own doctrine. How do we really know, as many pretribulation teachers believe, that we are closer to our Lord's return today if the signs are not a factor? As pretribulationist Clarence Larkin closes out his book "The Second Coming of Christ," he lists eleven events that precede the rapture. He prefaces this list by saying: "While we cannot name the exact date of the Lords Return its nearness may be known by the **character** of the times."[138] Inevitably, this typifies the abundance of discrepancies between the pretribulation camps in this chapter. You would have better luck mixing oil and water than reconciling the discrepancies between the different pretribulation teachers over signs of Christ's return.

While pretribulation teaching suggests that Christ can come back at any moment; Jesus indicated that a long period of time would elapse before His return. Phrases used such as; *wheat and tares grew together; the bride groom tarries;* and *went to a far country* are just a few examples indicating long periods of time.

We now know this time is when Christ would be building His church for the kingdom, which has been two thousand years and counting (e.g. Matt. 13:24-30; 21:33-41; 22:1-10; 25:1-13).

When Peter spoke about the last days, as he stated in 2 Peter 3:3-4; *Knowing this first, that there shall come in the last days scoffers, walking after their own lusts, And saying,* **Where is the promise of his coming?** *4: for since the fathers fell asleep,* **all things continue** *as they were from the* **beginning of the creation.**

Peter foretells what the world's attitude in the last days toward Christ and His promised return would be by comparing God's previous judgment on the world in the following two verses: (5) *For this they* **willingly** *are ignorant of, that by the word of God the heavens were of old, and the earth standing out of the water and in the water:* (6) *Whereby the world that then was, being overflowed with water,* **perished.** Peter was speaking about the lethargic and careless attitude of mankind as it related to God's coming judgment in Noah's day.

Now Peter will fast forward to another judgment that is future as it relates to Christ's second coming.

> But the heavens and the earth, **which are now,** by the same word are kept in store, reserved unto fire against the day of judgment and perdition of ungodly men. But, beloved, be not ignorant of this one thing, that one day is with the Lord as a thousand years, and a thousand years as one day. The Lord is not slack concerning his promise, as some men count slackness; but is longsuffering to us-ward, not willing that any should perish, but that all should come to repentance. But the **day of the Lord** will come as a thief in the night; in the which the heavens shall pass away with a great noise, and the elements shall melt with fervent heat, the earth also and the works that are therein shall be burned up. Seeing then that all these things shall be dissolved, what manner of persons ought ye to be in all holy conversation and godliness, **Looking for and hasting unto the coming of the day of God,** wherein the heavens being on fire shall be dissolved, and the elements shall melt with fervent heat? Nevertheless we, according to his promise, **look for new heavens and a new earth, wherein dwelleth righteousness.** (vv. 7-13)

Peter tied both Christ's first coming with His second. The point he is making is that God's final judgment at Christ's second coming will be the same as it was in Noah's day. They were willingly (choice) ignorant, and the same will be true at the end as well. Peter emphasized steadfastness for the believer by maintaining a clear-cut testimony for Christ just as Paul taught.

4. Chapter (Nine) – The Glorious Appearing: Pretribulation teaching is at a cross roads when trying to define Scripture verses pertaining to the glorious appearing of Christ. Even though several Scriptures (e.g. Titus 2:13) are talking about the rapture, pretrib teachers are at a loss as to the "appearance" of Christ, because at the rapture His coming is supposed to be secret. Pretribulation teaching is forced to make a distinction between the rapture and the second coming, which the Bible teaches that this is the same event. Consequently, pretribulation teaching forces upon the Word of God an invisible rapture, which the Bible never gives any hint of the world being frightened as to the disappearance of millions worldwide. By saying there are two comings of Christ, pretribulationism is forced to reinterpret many passages that brings disharmony to the Scriptures. The Scriptures overwhelmingly speak of a visible appearance at His coming.

5. Chapter (Ten) – Watch and be Ready: A large portion of this book dealt with the true emphasis for professing Christians to be alert and watchful as to Christ's return. Pretrib rapture teaching maintains that as Christians we could be raptured any-moment; therefore, we need to be watching for Christ's return any day now. I pointed out that all the Scriptures that talked about Christ coming again emphasized the professing believer needs to be examining themselves as to what they profess. Many Scripture passages warned folks by example how some grew tired waiting upon the arrival of their lord, and began to live and act contrary to what they professed. This exposes the true nature of their heart. When the church enters the tribulation period, many will be exposed for whom they truly are and reject the truth about the coming kingdom. They that sleep in the night will live as lost people; and they that are not of the night, will be alert to the events occurring and will remain faithful to Christ.

6. Chapters (Eleven and Twelve) - The Day of the Lord: This is the primary emphasis on the prewrath teaching. While the pretribulation teaching scantly covers this topic, it drives to the heart the rapture debate. We saw in these chapters that the event of the day of the Lord is where the Lord will come out of His place (heaven) in a supernatural way to punish the sinners in this

world. Furthermore, on the very same day, God will have raptured (rescued) His saints, then will begin to pour out His wrath and judgment on the unbelieving world (this will be the true left behind). In Revelation chapter 6, beginning at the sixth seal, God's wrath will be realized for the very first time during the final seven-years. The world is giving praise to the Antichrist at the mid-point of the seven years, which proves again that God's wrath has not yet begun. In Luke 21 we saw that men's hearts fail them for fear because of the impending destruction from the Lord. Certainly, men's hearts are merry at the mid-point of the 70th week - not failing them.

I ask my pretrib friends to explain from their rapture position; when does the "sudden destruction" upon the world take place in relation to the 70th week and the rapture?

We saw numerous discrepancies between pretribulation teachers in defining what is going to take place in the tribulation. Walvoord correctly stated that the tribulation was Satan's wrath on believers, where Thomas Ice said the tribulation was God's wrath on Israel. Many pretrib teachers believe that peace will dominate the first three-and-half years of the seven-years, while other pretrib teachers say there will be devastation. Some pretribulationist will try to equate the term "tribulation" with the birth pangs spoken by Christ in Matthew 24 as being part of the final week. Yet, I noted the "birth pangs" described by Christ start well before the final week, and pretrib adherents never distinguish between what occurs "before" the final week and what takes place in the beginning of the final week. They do not define a clear separation between the birth pangs before the final week and those that occur in the final week. In other words, they are not justified in calling the beginning of the final week-the tribulation, nor the birth pangs as God's wrath?

We also saw the distinction between the seal judgments which are the Antichrist's wrath, and the trumpet judgments which are God's wrath. In every instance, when the pretribulation teachers tried to identify God's wrath in Revelation they always acknowledged (correctly) the sixth seal as God's wrath. Furthermore, we saw when the sixth seal is opened the world cries out the "great day" has come, which is the same reference in Zephaniah 1:14 to the "great day." Pretrib teachers continuously referenced this verse when making their argument for a pretribulation rapture; yet, Zephaniah's quote matches the sixth seal, which is opened after the great tribulation begins sometime in the latter part of the 70th week, nullifying a pretribulation rapture.

7. Chapter (Thirteen) - Pretribulation teaching is posed with a dilemma by claiming Matthew 24 teaches an imminent pretribulation rapture, quoting verses that say we "do not know the day or hour of our Lord's return" (vv. 36, 42, 44, 46, 50). However, they also teach that Matthew 24 is written for the nation of Israel **after** the rapture and not for the church. Also, thrown into the mix, they claim Matthew 24 is about the second coming at the end of the tribulation, yet, claim these verses in the same context speak of the rapture. We saw "that day" in verse 36 has to be applied to the rapture, while keeping the context and harmony of the chapter.

The teaching by Christ in Matthew 24 is reiterated by Paul's teaching to the Thessalonians about the timing of the rapture in relation to the appearance of the Antichrist in the middle of the final week. If Matthew 24 is meant to be for Israel; why does Paul teach the same thing to the church at Thessalonica?

In the Olivet Discourse in Matthew 24 when Christ describes the events He NEVER makes reference to the world's unbelievers receiving divine judgment. However, there is reference to believers enduring a time of suffering and persecution along with a warning to not be deceived by false prophets and sin that turns the heart away from God.

We saw that the cosmic events in Matthew 24 matched the same events in Revelation 6 at the opening of the sixth seal. These events identified the "sign" that the disciples asked about at the beginning of the Olivet Discourse. The signs in the heavens are also identified with the day of the Lord passages throughout the Old Testament.

8. Chapter (Fourteen): 1 & 2 Thessalonians proved that before the rapture the Antichrist must be revealed and the apostasy (falling away) must take place first. These two events complement each other when they occur simultaneously. This will happen at the mid-point of the 70th week, disannulling the pretribulation rapture theory. Both Christ and Paul teach that the rapture occurs after the "abomination of desolations."

We saw where the pretribulation teachers attempted to explain the simple meaning of "falling away" (apostasy), and reinterpreted this to mean the rapture itself. What pretribulation is really saying, that before the rapture occurs there must be the falling away, and this falling away is the rapture itself. In other words, they are saying the rapture must occur before the rapture can happen. Moreover, they tried to make the passage sound as though the Thessalonians believed they were entering the tribulation, hence, missing the rapture; whereas, Paul was teaching that they would not enter the day of the Lord; therefore, will not miss the rapture, but are exempt from God's coming wrath.

In all the pretrib teaching on imminence, they say the phrase "at hand" means Christ's impending **future** return. However, we saw in their interpretation of 2 Thessalonians that they say the phrase "at hand" is **present** tense. This is to get you to believe that the passage is teaching a pretribulation passage; in reality, it is teaching a prewrath passage – rapture before God's wrath.

9.   Chapter (Fifteen) – Revelation 4 and 5: I laid out a fourfold argument showing the pretribulation biasness for a rapture in Revelation 4. John, is summoned to heaven to record future events, but is replaced by the church being raptured according to pretrib interpretation. It has been admitted by pretribulation teachers that it would **seem** that the rapture occurs here, with no scriptural proof to back this up. They teach that John, symbolizes, is a type, a member, pictures, among others, as the church, yet no multitude is seen in heaven in Revelation 4. While accusing their opponents of misapplying biblical hermeneutics, they are truly the guilty ones.

If pretribulation teachers believe they interpret the Bible literally, then they need to explain their understanding of the trumpet mentioned in Revelation 4. They identify the rapture with the blowing of the trumpet in 1 Corinthians 15:52; then teach that Revelation 4:1 is the same trumpet used to call John up to heaven. However, in Revelation 4:1 the verse says "I heard a voice 'as' a trumpet." The contextual meaning of this is it is not a "literal" trumpet. This is just another example where pretribulation teachers "do not" interpret Scriptures as they claim. These two Scripture passages are not one in the same.

Another point I would like to make regarding the pretrib belief that John represents the church: Jehovah's Witnesses claims they are the 144,000, and we as Christians know this is not true. This group is even identified by tribes (Judah, Benjamin, etc.) However, before the pretrib teachers blast the Jehovah's Witness for their false interpretation, they need to take heed in calling John, the church. How can one man represent millions of people; especially when this future event is supposed to literally occur? Where is the literal church when the literal tribulation period begins?

We saw why the word "church" is not used by the Lord in chapters 4-21 because the Lord is distinguishing between the lost church members from the saved. This would lead to a false impression that everyone who might be a member of a church will be raptured. As a reminder, the word "church" is not used to describe anyone in heaven during this time as well. Many pretribulational teachers will argue their point from silence by claiming the word church is absent in chapter 4 until chapter 19. However, their analogy carries no weight, specifically, when the word "church" is absent in chapter 19 as well. They defeat their argument about silence, by saying this is the church is in chapter 19.

Allow me to interject one more observation pertaining to the multitude in 7:9. In the context of this scene we see: the throne (v.9); the lamb (v.9); the multitude from the great tribulation (v.9); the angels (v.11); the twenty-four elders (v.11); and the four beasts (v.11). My simple question is: where are the previously raptured saints? Why aren't they listed here is a distinct group declaring God's salvation and glory apart from the others?

Invariably, and very important, we see in chapter 7 of Revelation the saints before the throne shouting "salvation." These are the saints who came out the great tribulation. This fits perfectly with the picture of Noah and Lot being delivered on the very "same day" when God's wrath begins. This is what the apostle Paul spoke of in 1 Thessalonians 5:9 that *we are not appointed unto wrath, but to obtain **salvation.***

At the beginning of Revelation chapter 7, Israel (the 144,000) will be sealed at this time for special protection from God's impending wrath. This does not take place before the first six seals, proving again, God's wrath is absent until now. We also saw the four angels in Revelation 7 standing at the four corners of the earth holding the four winds, which would match perfectly Matthew 24:31 where the four angels gather God's elect from the four corners of the earth. We see the gathering of this multitude on Revelation 7:9-10 coming out of "great tribulation," which is the raptured church. This will allow for God to maintain a presence in the earth, which transitions back to Israel that will enter into the millennium. Moreover, Christ taught, and Paul affirmed, that there would be a great "falling away" before He returns. To the contrary, pretribulationism is forced to say there will be a great "revival" in the great tribulation, because many saints come from this event. Prewrath believe that the saints will be the ones who enter the tribulation and remain faithful to Christ, and the ones who fall away are the ones who once falsely acknowledged Christ but abandoned the faith.

In Revelation 8 we see the "prayers" of the saints that go up before the throne of God after thirty minutes of silence where the Lord is now going to send His wrath on the world. These prayers are a result of the fifth seal when the saints cry out for vengeance upon those who persecuted them during the tribulation. This scene in Revelation 8 is happening in rapid succession from the sixth seal event of Christ's return. Again, this matches our Lord's teaching of Noah and Lot that on the "same day" of deliverance of God's people there was judgment upon the inhabitants of the earth. After a time of God's supernatural judgment (trumpet and vials) on the earth, the Antichrist will muster one last attempt to stop Christ's coming kingdom at the battle of Armageddon. The Antichrist and those who took the mark of the beast will be defeated at this battle. After this, the Jews will enter the millennium where God fulfills His covenant with the nation of Israel. All the saints throughout history will be part of the millennial reign of Christ, as well.

10. We saw that the "fullness of the Gentiles" is completed at the rapture, which takes place at the beginning of the day of the Lord. We saw in Acts Chapter 2, the signs associated with this fulfillment (sun, moon, and stars), where "all" of Israel will be saved. Pretribulation rapture teachers differ when teaching on the "fullness of the Gentiles." Some say this fulfillment is at the rapture before the tribulation-even though you still have Gentiles being saved during the tribulation. And some have the "fullness of the Gentiles" completed at the end of the 70th week, yet both theories conflict with their own dispensational teaching.

Christ spoke to His disciples in Matthew 24 about the world conditions before His return. Two days later, at the upper room, Christ told the disciples that he would come again and received them unto himself (John 14:3). This is universally taught that Christ is referring to the rapture of the church. The same disciples are the ones given the Great Commission in Matthew 28 to go and preach the gospel to *all the world;* and Christ promised us that He would be with us "to the end of the world." This end would bring the fulfillment of the "fullness of the Gentiles" spoken of in Romans chapter 11. The fullness of the Gentiles cannot be completed before the 70th week of Daniel, because there are Gentiles saved that come out of the great tribulation.

In Acts 1:6-8 the disciples asked the angel when Christ would restore the kingdom, the angel replied: *it is not for them to know the times our seasons, but go and be witnesses to the entire world.* This matches perfectly our Lord's teaching in Matthew 24 that the gospel would be preached to the entire world before the end would come. Furthermore, we saw the pretribulation fallacy where they believe the rapture could happen years well before the final 70th week. This creates a big problem, because what happens to those Gentiles saved after the rapture, yet before the final week starts? This also creates more problems with the dispensational teaching of the pretrib doctrine. Dispensationalism has no definitive category between the rapture and 70th week; biblically this does not exist.

11. Chapter (Sixteen) - Kept from the Hour: I pointed out in this chapter the distinction between "temptation" and "trials." While pretribulation teachers try to explain that Revelation 3:10 is saying that the church will be exempt from the tribulation. Christ is actually teaching those who are faithful will not fall away in "temptation" to capitulate during world-wide trial. If we traverse through Revelation, we see that the temptation happens when the world is required to receive the Antichrist's mark (allegiance).

The warnings are given to each of the seven churches for their members to be faithful to the Lord. In Revelation 2:10 the Lord charges these believers to be faithful "unto death," not from death. These warnings corresponded with our Lord's teaching to be watching (faithfulness), because he is, in fact, coming back to establish His kingdom. There will be many Judases on that day who will sell out Christ for a temporal deliverance from the persecution of the Antichrist. However, those who are faithful in the Lord will be like the five wise virgins who had their lamps (light in their lives) trimmed (prepared). As emphasized already, this matches perfectly with the "falling away" when the abomination of desolations takes place (2 Thess. 2:3-4).

Pretribulation False Assumptions

Here is a list of false assumptions made by pretribulationist about the rapture.

1. The tribulation is the 70th week (seven-years).
2. The great tribulation last seven years.
3. The tribulation is God's wrath.
4. The tribulation is the day of the Lord.
5. The day of Christ is different than the day of the Lord.
6. The rapture is not part of the second coming.
7. The blessed hope is the escape from the tribulation.
8. The seals in Revelation are God's wrath.
9. The seals are called the judgments of God
10. The tribulation is for Israel.
11. The rapture occurs in Revelation chapter four.
12. The apostle John is symbolic of the raptured church.

13. The twenty-four elders are symbolic of the church.
14. The church is absent on earth between Revelation chapters 4-19.
15. The 144,000 are evangelist during the tribulation.
16. The rapture is invisible- saints just disappear.
17. The rapture is signless- no notable events prior to the rapture.
18. Christ's return is invisible.
19. Christ's return is only seen by the saints, no one else.
20. The Olivet Discourse is only for Israel.
21. Christ's coming, taught in Matthew 24, is not the rapture but the second coming.
22. If a person who hears and rejects the gospel before the tribulation they cannot get saved after the tribulation begins.
23. The restrainer is the Holy Spirit.
24. The Christians at Thessalonians thought they were in the tribulation, not the day of the Lord.
25. The falling away (apostasy) is the rapture, not the rejection of a once-held belief.
26. The elect is only Israel, not the saints.
27. The early church believed in a pretribulation rapture.
28. To watch and look up means you expect Christ to come today.
29. The rapture is imminent.
30. The rapture is pretribulational.

Prewrath Problem Text

As I have spent a considerable amount of time exposing the fallacies of the pretribulation rapture, it is incumbent upon me to address a scripture text that poses a problem for us who hold to a prewrath rapture.

Daniel 7:25-26

> And he shall speak *great* words against the most High, and shall wear out the saints of the most High, and think to change times and laws: and they shall be **given into his hand until a time and times and the dividing of time.**

> But the judgment shall sit, and they shall take away his dominion, to consume and to destroy *it* unto the end.

As I believe that I have built a solid case for the great tribulation being cut-short by the day of the Lord and the rapture of the saints; however, this verse in Daniel 7:25 says that the saints are given (subject) to the Antichrist for the full 3-1/2 years. Conversely, if we are raptured before the completion of this the full 3-1/2 years how is this reconciled?

First, this falls under the category of the posttribulationism argument. They teach that believers will be here for the completion of the full seven-years. The saints will be protected during the trumpet and vial judgments towards the end, then as the battle of Armageddon draws closer the saints are raptured.

My first rebuttal I sufficiently proven the great tribulation is cut short-persecution of believers by Antichrist. When we are raptured at the beginning of the day of the Lord the Antichrist's reign is still ongoing until the battle of Armageddon. As an example, in comparison, during the Gulf War, Saddam Hussein was rendered defeated in the first one-hundred hours, yet, his captivity did not come until nine months later.

Second, there are two subjects addressed in verse 25- wearing out the saints and the changing of the times and laws. The question is, does the reference to the "they" in the same verse refer to the saints? I do not believe so. I believe the consensus of Scripture is that this is referring to those who are subject to the "changing of the times and laws." Revelation 13:1-4 states the Antichrist is given great power and authority by the world. The world is given into his hand for the remaining time and it's the world that agrees with Antichrist. They are the ones who follow the laws made by Antichrist. The world follows Antichrist for the 3-1/2 years up to the battle of Armageddon, and they are defeated with him by Christ.

Third, verse 26 uses the pronoun "they" as a reference to the defeat of Antichrist. It is not the church that defeats Antichrist at the end, but Christ. And the "they" is certainly referring to someone different than the "they" in verse 25.

I believe it is not well proven by neither posttribulationist nor pretribulationist that this is speaking of church saints up until the end of the 70th week.

Pretrib Strongholds

With our study of the rapture completed, in closing I would like to finalize my argument against the pretribulation rapture by citing the typical pretribulation strongholds used to support their position. I purposely waited to address this, because I believe the solid case I have already built shows that the rapture is prewrath/posttribulational.

1.   Populating the Millennium:

Pretrib teachers say that one main reason for the church raptured pretribulational is because there must be believers that come out of the 70th week (specifically God's wrath) to populate the millennium. These people are called "tribulation saints" by pretrib definition. If the church is raptured prewrath or posttribulation, then this supposedly defeats the purpose for the millennium which will include "earthly Gentile believers." I would counter this pretrib argument by pointing out that according to the book of Zechariah, there will be many Gentiles that are not killed in the day of the Lord. 14:16 *"And it shall come to pass,* that *every one that is **left of all the nations which came against Jerusalem** shall even go up from year to year to worship the King, the LORD of hosts, and to keep the feast of tabernacles."* This verse alone proves that not everyone will be destroyed in the day of the Lord's wrath. These folks were not saved; therefore, they were not saved at the time of the rapture, and were participants in God's wrath. For whatever reason, these folks survived the day of the Lord and now will be part of the millennial reign. Here's another verse stating the same thing, there will be other nations in the kingdom.

> 13. I saw in the night visions, and, behold, *one* like the **Son of man** came with the clouds of heaven, and came to the Ancient of days, and they brought him near before him.
> 14. And there was given him dominion, and glory, and a kingdom, that **all people, nations, and languages, should serve him:** his dominion *is* an everlasting dominion, which shall not pass away, and his kingdom *that* which shall not be destroyed. (Dan. 7:13-14)

I spent a considerable amount of time comparing God's wrath to Noah and Lot, teaching that there was deliverance then wrath. At the time of Noah, every single inhabitant on earth was killed, so no one survived except Noah's family. What a pretribulationist might say is that my paralleling the events in Noah's day and those that enter the millennium is flawed. Because I am saying that after wrath in the day of the Lord there are survivors. First, my main emphasis about Noah and Lot, was that on the "same day" there was deliverance and wrath. There was no time separating the two events like the pretribulation rapture teaches. Second, God clearly has laid out, starting in the Old Testament, His coming kingdom on earth. So really there is no discrepancy between the two events as they pertain to the rapture topic. Even pretribulationist teach there will be Gentiles that enter the millennium as well. Finally, I don't believe that every single person on earth will have taken the mark of the beast. For whatever reason, maybe because of seclusion or hiding in remote parts of the world, many will not be subjected to receiving the mark. Also, just because someone had not received the mark of the beast does not mean they are saved, therefore they will not be raptured with the saved saints. What I can say for certain is that anyone who took the mark of the beast will not enter the millennium.

2. Rapture or Second Coming.

Here is a list of pretribulationist points attempting to separate the rapture from the second coming.

1. Pretrib: Christ comes "for" saints at the rapture/Christ comes "with" His saints at the second coming.
    Prewrath: We believe at the second coming Christ comes "for" His saints and returns with His saints at the battle of Armageddon.

2. Pretrib: Christ only comes in the air/second coming Christ comes to the earth.
    Prewrath: Rapture, Christ comes only to the air to deliver His saints from His impending wrath. Christ comes to the earth at the end of His wrath on the lost so He can establish His earthly kingdom.

3. Pretrib: At the rapture the earth is not judged/At the second coming the earth is judged.
    Prewrath: I have demonstrated that we are raptured which allows Christ to judge the earth, which begins on the same day. Does pretrib believe that only at the second coming, which occurs at the battle of Armageddon, that this is the first-time judgment comes upon the earth?

4. Pretrib: The rapture is signless/the second coming there are signs that precede Christ coming.

   Prewrath: I demonstrated that signs do precede the rapture. Pretrib vainly teach that "shadows" of signs precede the second coming, deceptively denying that they are signs indeed. However, analyzing this pretrib belief, isn't is strange that we can "see" the foreshadowing signs of the second coming but not the rapture, yet by their definition the second coming happens years after the rapture.

5. Pretrib: Rapture affects believer's only/second coming affects the whole earth.

   Prewrath: The rapture event does indeed affect the whole earth because the world cries out that "God's wrath has come," and they try to hide from the presence of Christ.

6. Pretrib: Rapture is "before" God's wrath/ second coming is "after" God's wrath.

   Prewrath: Rapture "before" God's wrath/same day God's wrath begins which is well before Christ's coming at the end of the 70th week.

7. Pretrib: At the rapture, only the saved see Christ coming/second coming all the earth sees Christ.

   Prewrath: This is never proven by pretrib that Christ comes invisible at the rapture. Revelation 6, specifically, the 6th seal, the world sees Christ which is well before the end of the 70th week. The verse says that those left on the earth cry out "hide us from the presence (appearance) of the lamb…"

In response to the pretrib attempt to separate the rapture form the second coming, here is an excellent explanation that I retrieved from a Facebook post by John McKay who was explaining the meaning of the Greek word parousia as it relates to Christ's coming.

"Parousia" is first and foremost a THING, not an ACTION. "Parousia" is a NOUN, and not a VERB. The biggest, consistent error I see is that 'parousia' is interpreted as a verb. When used as Jesus next trip from heaven to earth, that is using it as a verb, not a noun. The repeated criticism of prewrath of having multiple comings and goings to heaven entirely misses the point. Once you properly interpret parousia as a noun those issues disappear.

Jesus's first Parousia entails everything that happened from conception to ascension. So too, the second parousia will entail everything that happens from the moment of His appearance in the sky (the rapture, per prewrath) until he delivers up the kingdom to the father after the millennium (although, to be fair, there are different opinions about the end of the second parousia). Regardless, the point is that a parousia is (a) term that has nothing to do with a specific moment in time but encompasses a range of time and a sequence of events.

In scripture, parousia is used multiple times and the details given often seem to contradict each other. Both pre-trib and post-trib have resolved the issue in different ways: pre-trib typically manufactures multiple parousia's, post-trib typically interprets parousia as a verb and/or crams all the associated details into a single moment event. Both resolutions are false. The former because scripture is clear that there is only one, future parousia. The latter because parousia is a noun, not a verb and there is no need to make all the details align at a specific moment.

Once you realize that parousia is a general term that represents the entire sum of Jesus next active participation with those on the earth, the problems vanish, and the sequence and details fall into place in large fashion. Some passages use parousia but give details about early things that happen (rapture, triple sign, etc.). Other passages use parousia but give details on later things that happen in sequence. They occur at different times in the chronology, but they are all part of the Second Parousia.[139]

McKay sums up the intent of Christ's coming, which disqualifies the pretrib declaration for separating the rapture and second coming. Simply, one second coming with many activities. If you traverse through the Scripture passages pertaining to Christ's coming, they are never in the plural form, but singular. Even the verses that pretribulationist insist that are second coming verses, they are singular- coming. The rapture passages are the same as well.

I recall a radio debate on the rapture between pretribulationist Dave Hunt and Marvin Rosenthal. Hunt, continually tried to hammer-home his belief that the Scriptures teach two separate events as his way to reconcile the different passages about the rapture and the second coming. In other words, there was no way the Bible could be talking about one (same) event. I would counter his argument in another way than which I have already proven. In the doctrine of salvation, there are passages that seem to teach predestination (God alone chooses), and passages that teach free-will (man's responsibility to choose or reject the gospel). Using Hunt's line of reasoning, obviously, there are two ways of salvation that the Bible teaches to get to heaven. So, when we get to heaven there will be two groups of people, those who God chooses and those who chose God. No, there is only one way of salvation, and this only can be reconciled by applying the totality of Scripture, as with the rapture.

3. Prewrath and Posttribulationist teach a works salvation:

The pretrib argument is that only a pretribulational rapture allows for Jesus Christ to be the sole author of one's salvation by faith. If, as prewrath teaches, those who enter the tribulation, they must "not" accept the mark of the beast by enduring, then in essence, they are the one's responsible for their salvation into heaven by maintaining their faithfulness.

My first response is, don't pretrib teach that the ones who get saved in the tribulation must "not" accept the mark as well or they will be lost? Is this a "works" salvation?

Next, doesn't the Bible teach that by "faith" a person is saved? Does not evangelical Christianity teach there is a "saving" faith one embraces to become a Christian? We equate this faith with not only believing on Jesus, but trusting Him as well. Would we consider this "saving faith" to be a work? No! Yet, there are some within Christianity that "profess" faith, but truly are not saved. What is it that separates their "false" faith from those who have a "true" faith? I conclude then, that when the saints are in the great tribulation, many will give up their faith in the only one who can deliver them, exchanged for a temporal deliverance. They will choose to reject the one they once accepted. The pretrib argument is no different than prewrath here.

I'm reminded of the biblical account of the Jews in Babylonian captivity when Nebuchadnezzar built the tower and commanded everyone to bow and worship this very large embellished statue. The Bible records that out of the vast multitude only three people did not bow their knee. Only three men out of this large assembly refused to follow the king's decree and trust God. These men even resided to the fact they most likely would have faced death by burning, yet remained faithful to God.

The Verdict Please!

If a person who has no knowledge of the rapture topic and became stranded on a deserted island with only a Bible to read, what do you suppose they would believe about the return of Christ? Do you believe they would believe in the invisible pretrib rapture with its elaborate scheme developed by the pretrib teaching, or simply allow the Scriptures to speak for themselves and believe in a visible prewrath rapture? Finally, using the equivalence of a courtroom trial, if we weighed the evidence, beyond a shadow of a doubt, we would see there is no, invisible, signless, pretrib rapture taught in scripture. The rapture is clearly taught to be "after" the tribulation. We also saw how; not only does pretribulationism cover up the evidence against their doctrine, but they plant false evidence to mislead the facts.

A prominent figure in the Niagara Prophecy Conferences, and a former pretribulationist and Darby follower, Nathaniel West, wrote:

> [The Pre-Trib Rapture] is built on a postulate, vicious in logic, violent in exegesis, contrary to experience, repudiated by the early Church, contradicted by the testimony of eighteen hundred years...and condemned by all the standard scholars of every age (The Apostle Paul and the "Any Moment" Theory, p. 30). Nathaniel West (1826-1909)

Final Warning

I trust and pray that this book on the rapture will be a catalyst for your desire to know and understand the teaching on the rapture. I trust that you will be honest with the Scriptures as you study this topic. As I teach the men in my Bible study in the prisons, I challenge them to get into God's word and seek His truth. You and I will not only be accountable for what we believe, but what we teach others as well.

This is not an attempt as some would accuse me of to steal your hope in Christ. The rapture topic is not a theological subject where you can believe in wishful thinking- truth will win in the end. You can wish a cancer to go away and deny it exists; however, if you don't treat it, the consequences will be disastrous. You can believe in the pretribulation theory if it makes you feel better, but someday a generation of Christians will awaken to the reality that they will enter the 70th week and face the horrific conditions of the great tribulation. We continue to see the advancement of the technology where we are steadily being engulfed into a world system that is invading our privacy and controlling our everyday actions, socially, politically, and particularly in finances and healthcare. There is a cashless system coming to where people will be forced to some degree or another to conform to the political decisions of governments. The term "new world order" has been a theme by the world's political leaders since WWII. The driving force to implement this age-old agenda is the world's cry for peace and safety. There is an enigma that continues to grow at an exceedingly rapid rate throughout the world.

Jesus's Admonition

When Jesus taught the Sermon on the Mount in Matthew 7 he gave a fourfold warning to the multitude about being a true believer (saving faith). First, Christ warned that many are on the road to destruction, thinking they are on the right path.

Next, Christ spoke of two trees, one bearing fruit the other being unfruitful, identifying who is truly born again.

Third, multitudes will be standing before Christ in heaven saying, Lord, Lord, only to be rejected by Christ who will tell them, "depart I never knew you."

Finally, there is the parable of two houses being built; in appearance, they looked identical. However, when the true test came, this being the storm, one fell and the other stood. The one that stood proved that it was built upon Christ and His word. *Therefore whosoever heareth these **sayings of mine, and doeth them**, I will liken him unto a wise man, which built his house upon a rock:* (Matt. 7:24).

As the book of Revelation ends, we see in chapter 20 the "great white throne judgment." This is where the lost will have their final sentencing for all of eternity, which will result in them being cast into the lake of fire (20:15).

I find it interesting that in the next chapter 21, John heard a voice saying: *"**and God shall wipe away all tears from their eyes** and there shall be no more death, neither sorrow, nor crying, neither shall there be any more pain:"* (v.4). There are two possibilities pertaining to this statement; first, this could be a general statement that God is giving assurance to believers that everything will be all right in the end. On the other hand, this could be in the context of the chronological order of events as they have unfolded in Revelation. If the latter is true, as I believe, part of this statement could be that believers have just witnessed this great white throne judgment in chapter 20. And if this is the case, then we will witness the rejection of our friends, family, and love ones who will be condemned for all of eternity. Many Christians will realize the wasted opportunities they had to be a true witness for Christ.

Solomon certainly hit the nail on the head when he stated in Ecclesiastes 7:2. *It is better to go to the house of mourning, than to go to the house of feasting: for that is the end of all men; and the living will lay it to his heart.* There is really no comparing this life with its fleeting pleasures to the eternal promise's God has for us. This is the realization that Solomon came to. We know the story of Lot, when God told him of the impending judgment upon the cities, and Lot tried to warn his family- they thought him to be a fool. What about Noah? The world rejected his message and paid the ultimate consequence- an eternity in hell for their rejection of the truth.

Paul warns Christians in 2 Timothy 3 that in the last day's society as we know it will be turned on its head.

> This know also, that in the last days perilous times shall come. For **men shall be lovers of their own selves**, covetous, boasters, proud, blasphemers, disobedient to parents, unthankful, unholy, Without natural affection, trucebreakers, false accusers, incontinent, fierce, despisers of those that are good, Traitors, heady, highminded, **lovers of pleasures more than lovers of God; Having a form of godliness,** but denying the power thereof: from such turn away. (2 Tim. 3:1-5)

We are truly seeing these things come to pass before our very eyes. We tend to view the Scriptures through the lens of America; however, we can see that these things are taking place world-wide. America certainly has a "form of Godliness," and our cities are filled with churches everywhere you go. The prosperity doctrine and the positive thinking movement has become the focal-point in many churches. More and more churches are embracing a worldly philosophy than Gods truth, with a self-pleasing, self-driven, materialistic lifestyle, apart from what God wants for them, which is personal, spiritual walk with Him regardless of their social status. Christ taught in John's gospel that He came to give true peace to you and I (John

14:27). This peace will allow the Christian to endure the hardships this world cast upon us.

As I close out this book, I ask, are you truly prepared for eternity? As I have proven that the rapture is not imminent; however, your death is imminent. There are no prophesied events that must precede your and mines death. Thousands of people around the world are entering eternity every day without notice. Sadly, and frighteningly, many will never enjoy being with God. If you have never repented of your sinful condition and confessed Jesus Christ as Lord and savior, you can commit your life to him today. You can by faith, trust the Lord Jesus Christ, the one who lived a sinless perfect life, died on the cross for your sins, and rose again the third day. Jesus did not come to make bad people good, he came to make dead people alive. He came to give us life so we can live for Him. Christ came to give us the righteousness needed to stand in the presence of the Father (2 Cor.5:21). God desires a personal relationship with you through the working of the Holy Spirit. He lives today to make intercession for you: will you trust and live for him?

> I tell you that he will avenge them speedily. Nevertheless when the Son of man cometh, **shall he find faith on the earth**?
>
> Luke 18:8

ABOUT THE AUTHOR

Billy Broadwater is a born-again believer in Christ Jesus. He grew up and graduated from high school in Bay City, Texas. He attended Wharton County Junior College for two years. He was saved in 1984 after attending a Baptist church for over two years when he embraced Christ's righteousness by faith in Jesus alone. He has been faithful in serving Christ through soul-winning, the Master Club ministry, and currently the Prison Bible study for over 26 years. He has a private library of books, tapes, CD's, and videos, which he has used to advance his understanding of the Bible. He is a construction superintendent, and has built many buildings around the Austin, Texas area. He is married to his wife Beatrice and they have seven children: Melissa (Travis), Kyle, Rebekah (Jonathan) with granddaughters Kenzie, Andrew (Julie), Laura, Katherine, and Matthew.

Contact info:

Email is prewrath.billy@yahoo.com

APPENDIX

From Chapter Three: Sodom and Gomorrah and the Birth of Isaac:

I would like to consider the **timing** of the destruction of Sodom and Gomorrah as it relates to the birth of Isaac. It is interesting that the birth of Isaac came **after** the destruction of Sodom and Gomorrah (Genesis 19), even though God promised Abraham and Sarah a son **twenty-five years** earlier. Both, the destruction of these two cities and Isaac's birth were supernatural events brought forth by God. The destruction of Sodom and Gomorrah came when the Bible says their sins finally reached an apex (Gen. 18:20). And Isaac's birth came twenty-five years after God first announced to Abraham that he would have a son; concluding that Sarah was long passed the child-bearing years (Gen. 17:1; 18:10-11). Tying these two supernatural events together, I believe they foreshadow certain events in God's future prophetic clock, which involves God's coming judgment of the world and the restoration of the nation of Israel back to God.

Because of Abraham's faith, we saw that God establish His promises to the nation of Israel as a whole. Even though Israel became known as God's chosen people, they were obligated to maintain a separation from the pagan nations that surrounded them and to honor and worship Jehovah. After all, it is God who would be their deliverer and salvation.

When Israel obeyed the statutes of God they received God's blessings. However, when Israel disobeyed they received the chastening hand of God. Unfortunately, there were longer periods in Israel's history that they were receiving God's hand of judgment than His blessings. Eventually, because of Israel's continual rebellion and ultimately the rejection of God's son Jesus, Israel received the harsh judgment from God. This judgment would be the temporary setting aside Israel as God's authority in performing His work on the earth. Therefore, spiritually, since Christ's rejection by Israel, particularly Israel's religious leadership, they have been dead.

Paul alludes to this in Romans in his teaching about Israel being "temporarily" cutoff.

> I say then, Hath God cast away his people? **God forbid**. For I also am an Israelite, of the seed of Abraham, of the tribe of Benjamin. **God hath not cast away his people** which he foreknew. Wot ye not what the scripture saith of Elias? how he maketh intercession to God against Israel, saying,…I say then, Have they stumbled that they should fall? God forbid: but rather through their fall salvation is come unto the Gentiles, for **to provoke them to jealousy**…For if the casting away of them be the reconciling of the world, what shall the **receiving** of them be, **but life from the dead?** (Rom. 11: 1-2, 11, 15)

Jesus says in Matthew.

> O Jerusalem, Jerusalem, thou that killest the prophets, and stonest them which are sent unto thee, **how often would I have gathered thy children together**, even as a hen gathereth her chickens under her wings, and **ye would not! Behold, your house is left unto you desolate**. For I say unto you, Ye shall not see me henceforth, till ye shall say, **Blessed is he that cometh in the name of the Lord**. (Matt. 23: 37-39)

Jesus is pronouncing the death sentence upon Israel. Notice the timing of the prophecy: when they see Christ coming again, then they will say *blessed is he that comes in the name of the Lord* (vs.39). This prophecy cannot be fulfilled at the beginning of the 70th week of Daniel's prophecy, but sometime during the 70th week.

God states in Ezekiel 37 that Israel would eventually be received back again to Himself; however, this restoration will only take place after Israel is brought back from **death** to life.

> The hand of the LORD was upon me, and carried me out in the spirit of the LORD, and set me down in the midst of the **valley which was full of bones,** And caused me to pass by them round about: and, behold, there were very many in the open valley; and, lo, they were very dry. And he said unto me, **Son of man, can**

these bones live? And I answered, O Lord GOD, thou knowest.
(Ezek. 37: 1-3)

The Lord questions Ezekiel if he believed these bones could receive life again, even though they are very dry —symbolizing Israel has been dead for a long period of time. God ultimately declared to Ezekiel that He will be faithful to the promises he made to Israel.

> Again he said unto me, Prophesy upon these bones, and say unto them, O ye dry bones, hear the word of the LORD. Thus saith the Lord GOD unto these bones; Behold, **I will cause breath to enter into you, and ye shall live:** And I will lay sinews upon you, and will bring up flesh upon you, and cover you with skin, **and put breath in you, and ye shall live; and ye shall know that I am the LORD**...Then he said unto me, Son of man, **these bones are the whole house of Israel:** behold, they say, Our bones are dried, and **our hope is lost: we are cut off for our parts.** Therefore prophesy and say unto them, Thus saith the Lord GOD; Behold, O my people, **I will open your graves, and cause you to come up out of your graves, and bring you into the land of Israel.** And ye shall know that I am the LORD, when I have opened your graves, O my people, and brought you up out of your graves, **And shall put my spirit in you, and ye shall live, and I shall place you in your own land**: then shall ye know that I the LORD have spoken it, and performed it, saith the LORD. (Ezek. 37: 4-6, 11-14)

These Scriptures, widely understood by futurists, are a reference to Israel in the millennium, to which many pretrib teachers agree. Ezekiel's prophecy is directly correlated to Romans 11 where Israel would receive life only after death.

According to the prophet Ezekiel, these dry bones come to life only after they are placed in the (promise) land, followed by the indwelling Spirit of God. Israel which was restored as a nation again in 1948; yet, they still are living in unbelief that Jesus is the Messiah, therefore, a portion of this prophecy is still future.

Comparing the future event of Israel's restoration back to God to the destruction of Sodom and Gomorrah, I asked: could there be any significance in the timing in the destruction of Sodom and Gomorrah occurring between the promised birth of Isaac and the actual birth of Isaac? Is it coincidence that the sequencing of these events took place the way they did? I think not! I believe the correlation is that this destruction depicts God's wrath being poured out upon the world in the final days, because the world's rebellion of God will come to fullness during the final 70th week. This will culminate at the abomination of desolations when the world accepts Antichrist and rejects Christ. This will be followed by God's supernatural judgment of wrath. Then Israel will experience the covenantal blessings promised by God in the millennium when Israel receives life (spiritual), and is a blessed nation again.

Jesus verifies this truth to the Pharisees when they ask him in Luke 17:20, "when will the kingdom of God come?" Jesus's answers:

Likewise also as it was in the days of Lot; they did eat, they drank, they bought, they sold, they planted, they builded; But the same day that Lot went out of **Sodom it rained fire and brimstone from heaven, and destroyed them all**. 30: Even thus shall it be in the day when the Son of man is revealed. (Luke 17: 28-30)

God will give Israel life only after the revealing and the return of Christ. This is truly a beautiful picture we have of God's prophetic time clock for the nation of Israel! Just as the deadness of Sarah's womb in her old age (Romans 4:19) when all hope seemed lost, she was miraculously able to give birth to Isaac, which came after the destruction of Sodom and Gomorrah. The same will be for Israel after the judgment on the world during the latter part of the final seven-years, then all of Israel will be saved (Romans 11:25-27). The question you might ask – how does this relate to the rapture debate? According to Romans chapter 11 in the context of our discussion, we read in verse 25 -26.

> For I would not, brethren, that ye should be ignorant of this mystery, lest ye should be wise in your own conceits; that **blindness in part is happened to Israel, until the fullness of the Gentiles be come in**. And so all Israel shall be saved: as it is written, There shall come out of Sion the Deliverer, and shall turn away ungodliness from Jacob:

According to these two verses the spiritual blindness of Israel will be lifted only after the fullness of the Gentiles is complete, and the Deliverer comes. We saw from our study that this will occur at the rapture. If you recall

Matthew 23:39, Israel will say, "blessed is he who comes in the name of the Lord," at the time of their repentance. Therefore, the blindness of Israel cannot be lifted at the beginning of the 70th week; concluding, the rapture is not pretribulational?

It still is a supernatural event pertaining to the birth of Isaac at Abraham's and Sarah's age, regardless when it took place in the Bible. This in itself is a beautiful picture of life being restored from death. I believe, however, the timing of Isaac's birth after this well-known destruction of Sodom and Gomorrah parallels the end-time sequence of the final week.

From Chapter Six: Israel's Feasts and the 70th Week:

I would like to make a personal observation on the timing of three particular feast of Israel: the Passover, Yom Kippur (Day of Atonement), and Hanukkah (Dedication of the Temple) as they relate to the 70th week of Daniel. There is a very interesting scenario that could be played out in the timing of the "abomination of desolations" event, which occurs directly in the middle of the 70th week.

In the book of Daniel it gives a very detailed account of the prophetic days as they relate to the final week.

> And I heard the man clothed in linen, which was upon the waters of the river, when he held up his right hand and his left hand unto heaven, and sware by him that liveth for ever that it shall be for a **time, times, and an half**; and when he shall have accomplished to scatter the power of the holy people, all these things shall be finished. And I heard, but I understood not: then said I, O my Lord, what shall be the end of these things? And he said, Go thy way, Daniel: for the words are closed up and **sealed till the time of the end.** Many shall be purified, and made white, and tried; but the wicked shall do wickedly: and none of the wicked shall understand; but the wise shall understand. And from the time that the **daily sacrifice** shall be taken away, and the **abomination that maketh desolate** set up, there shall be a **thousand two hundred and ninety days**. Blessed is he that waiteth, and cometh to the **thousand three hundred and five and thirty days**. But go thou thy way till the end be: for thou shalt rest, and stand in thy lot at the end of the days. (Dan. 12:7-13)

In verse 7 it states that a time (1 year), times (2 years), and half (1/2 year) equals 1260 days, based on 360 day calendar year. Verse 11 speaks of the daily sacrifice that is taken away, which is part of the "abomination of desolations" event. From this event, verse 11 adds an extra 30 days, which brings the total to 1290 days. Going to the next verse we see another 45 days added, bringing the total to 1335 from the abomination of desolations.

Yom Kippur (Day of Atonement) is a time for Israel as a nation that mourns over their sin, which occurs once a year on the 10th of Tishri. Seventy-five days later on the Jewish calendar the dedication of the Temple (Hanukkah) occurs, which takes place on 26th of Kislev.

Now here is the interesting aspect of this scenario. If you subtract 1260 days from Yom Kippur, in many cases, **but not always**, you come to 3-4 days after the feast of Passover has taken place. In Revelation 13:3 it is giving a description of the Antichrist being killed and coming back to life. The world wonders in amazement and worships the Antichrist in verse 4. In verse 5 it says that the Antichrist is given 42 months to "continue." This 42 months equals the time, times, and half a time or three-and-half years, or 1260 days. We see back in chapter 12 of Revelation when Satan is kicked out of heaven he is cast to the earth; he immediately persecutes the woman- Israel (12:4). In verse 6 it gives the number of days that Israel will flee from Satan, which is *a thousand two hundred and threescore days,* or 1260 days.

Could it be that the Antichrist, at the time of the Jewish feast of Passover, goes into the temple and there is killed, and three days later comes back to life? This would be the ultimate counterfeit of Christ by the devil himself. It will be at this time the world gives honor and praise, which is followed by the world being required to take mark of the beast. This event triggers the great tribulation, which we have discussed already. Three days following Passover when the Antichrist is killed, he comes back to life; if you add 1260 days you come to Yom Kippur. I believe it is at this time Jesus Comes back at the end of the 70th week (not rapture); Israel mourns for their rejection of Christ (as pictured in the Day of Atonement). For the next 30 days the bowl judgments of God's wrath is poured out on earth, followed by the battle of Armageddon, which will complete the day of the Lord's judgment. Then for the next 45 days, is the time of cleansing for the dedication of the temple for the millennium, which fulfills the feast of Hanukkah.

Let's look at an example of what I am saying. I took a random date of 1970. In 1970 the Jewish Passover was on April 21, where on the Jewish calendar it was Nisan 15th. If Antichrist was killed at Passover (21st), then three days later he would have rose on the (24th); then starting on the (25th) you and add 1260 days, you come to the date October 6, 1973, which is exactly the day of Yom Kippur. Seventy-five days later you come to December 20th, which is Hanukkah. Is this coincidence? Maybe, maybe not!

Give it a try! Pick a date from the past or future and work the numbers and see what your results are. As I stated, the dates do not always match perfectly, but will be within a few days. Let me state plainly, this is not an attempt of any kind of date-setting. What I am proposing has absolutely NO bearing on the rapture debate. When I discovered this, it was just a fun exercise that I found intriguing, nothing else.

PRE-WRATH RAPTURE OF THE CHURCH

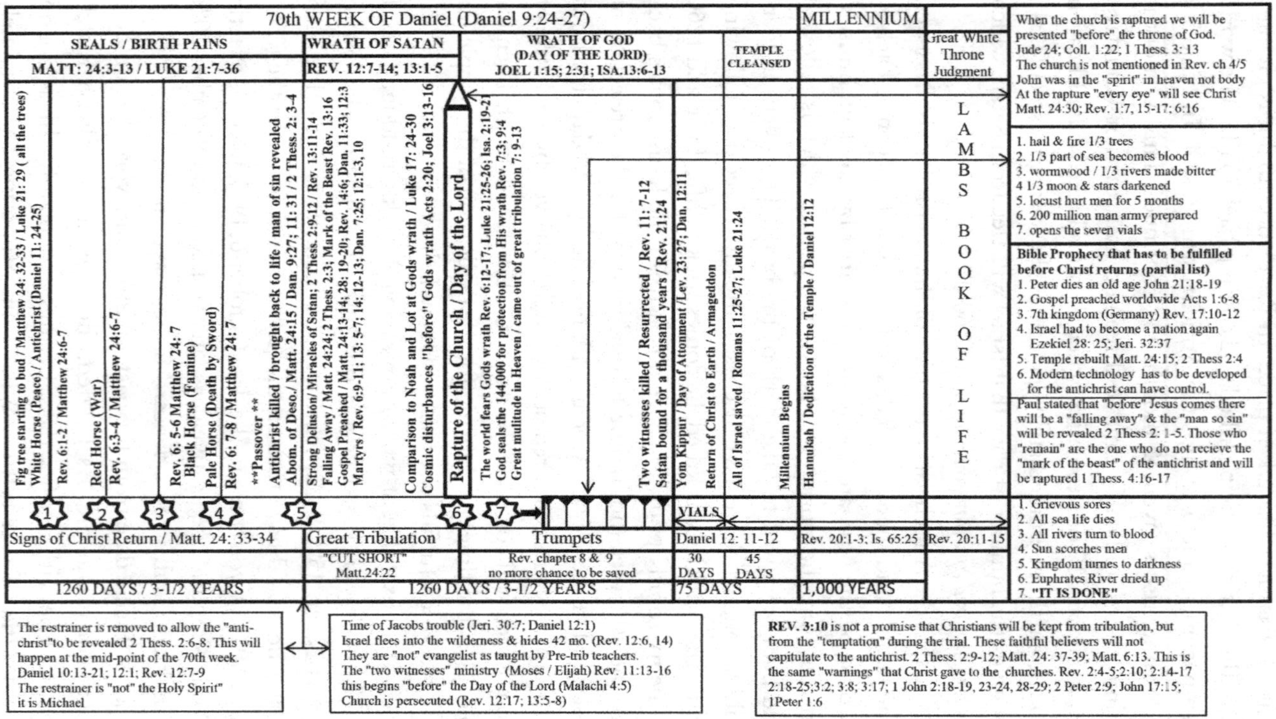

70th WEEK Of Daniel (Daniel 9:24-27) | MILLENNIUM

Column headers (left to right)

SEALS / BIRTH PAINS — MATT. 24:3-13 / LUKE 21:7-36

WRATH OF SATAN — REV. 12:7-14; 13:1-5

WRATH OF GOD (DAY OF THE LORD) — JOEL 1:15; 2:31; ISA.13:6-13

TEMPLE CLEANSED

Great White Throne Judgment — Rev. 20:11-15

Timeline rows (bottom to top / earliest to latest)

- Fig tree starting to bud / Matthew 24: 32-33 / Luke 21: 29 (all the trees)
- White Horse (Peace) / Antichrist (Daniel 11:24-25) — Rev. 6:1-2 / Matthew 24:6-7
- Red Horse (War) — Rev. 6:3-4 / Matthew 24:6-7
- Black Horse (Famine) — Rev. 6:5-6 Matthew 24:7
- Pale Horse (Death by Sword) — Rev. 6: 7-8 / Matthew 24: 7
- **Passover**
- Antichrist killed / brought back to life / man of sin revealed
- Abom. of Deso./ Matt. 24:15 / Dan. 9:27; 11: 31 / 2 Thess. 2: 3-4
- Strong Delusion/ Miracles of Satan: 2 Thess. 2:9-12 / Rev. 13:11-14
- Falling Away / Matt. 24:24; 2 Thess. 2:3; Mark of the Beast Rev. 13:16
- Gospel Preached / Matt. 24:13-14; 28: 19-20; Rev. 14:6; Mark 13:16
- Martyrs / Rev. 6:9-11; 13: 5-7; 14: 12-13; Dan. 7:25; 12:1-3, 10
- Comparison to Noah and Lot at Gods wrath / Luke 17:24-30
- Cosmic disturbances "before" Gods wrath Acts 2:20; Joel 3:15-16
- **Rapture of the Church / Day of the Lord**
- The world fears Gods wrath Rev. 6:12-17; Luke 21:25-26; Isa. 2:19-21
- God seals the 144,000 for protection from His wrath Rev. 7:3; 9:4
- Great multitude in Heaven / came out of great tribulation Rev. 7:9-13
- Two witnesses killed / Resurrected / Rev. 11: 7-12
- Satan bound for a thousand years / Rev. 21:24
- Yom Kippur / Day of Attonement /Lev. 23: 27; Dan. 12:11
- Return of Christ to Earth / Armageddon
- All of Israel saved / Romans 11:25-27; Luke 21:24
- Millennium Begins
- Hannukah / Dedication of the Temple / Daniel 12:12

Lower timeline bands

Signs of Christ Return / Matt. 24: 33-34 — 1260 DAYS / 3-1/2 YEARS

Great Tribulation "CUT SHORT" Matt. 24:22 — 1260 DAYS / 3-1/2 YEARS

Trumpets — Rev. chapter 8 & 9 — no more chance to be saved

VIALS

Daniel 12: 11-12 — 30 DAYS — 45 DAYS — 75 DAYS

Rev. 20:1-3; Is. 65:25 — 1,000 YEARS

Right-side notes

When the church is raptured we will be presented "before" the throne of God. Jude 24; Coll. 1:22; 1 Thess. 3: 13
The church is not mentioned in Rev. ch 4/5
John was in the "spirit" in heaven not body
At the rapture "every eye" will see Christ
Matt. 24:30; Rev. 1:7, 1:5-17; 6:16

1. hail & fire 1/3 trees
2. 1/3 part of sea becomes blood
3. wormwood / 1/3 rivers made bitter
4. 1/3 moon & stars darkened
5. locust hurt men for 5 months
6. 200 million man army prepared
7. opens the seven vials

Bible Prophecy that has to be fulfilled before Christ returns (partial list)
1. Peter dies an old age John 21:18-19
2. Gospel preached worldwide Acts 1:6-8
3. 7th kingdom (Germany) Rev. 17:10-12
4. Israel had to become a nation again Ezekiel 28: 25; Jeri. 32:37
5. Temple rebuilt Matt. 24:15; 2 Thess 2:4
6. Modern technology has to be developed for the antichrist can have control.
Paul stated that "before" Jesus comes there will be a "falling away" & the "man so sin" will be revealed 2 Thess 2: 1-5. Those who "remain" are the one who do not recieve the "mark of the beast" of the antichrist and will be raptured 1 Thess. 4:16-17

1. Grievous sores
2. All sea life dies
3. All rivers turn to blood
4. Sun scorches men
5. Kingdom turns to darkness
6. Euphrates River dried up
7. "IT IS DONE"

LAMB BOOK OF LIFE (vertical)

Bottom-left box

The restrainer is removed to allow the "antichrist" to be revealed 2 Thess. 2:6-8. This will happen at the mid-point of the 70th week. Daniel 10:13-21; 12:1; Rev. 12:7-9
The restrainer is "not" the Holy Spirit' it is Michael

Lower-middle box

Time of Jacobs trouble (Jeri. 30:7; Daniel 12:1)
Israel flees into the wilderness & hides 42 mo. (Rev. 12:6, 14)
They are "not" evangelist as taught by Pre-trib teachers.
The "two witnesses" ministry (Moses / Elijah) Rev. 11:3-16
this begins "before" the Day of the Lord (Malachi 4:5)
Church is persecuted (Rev. 12:17; 13:5-8)

Lower-right box

REV. 3:10 is not a promise that Christians will be kept from tribulation, but from the "temptation" during the trial. These faithful believers will not capitulate to the antichrist. 2 Thess. 2:9-12; Matt. 24: 37-39; Matt. 6:13. This is the same "warnings" that Christ gave to the churches. Rev. 2:4-5;2:10; 2:14-17 2:18-25;3:2; 3:8; 3:17; 1 John 2:18-19, 23-24, 28-29; 2 Peter 2:9; John 17:15; 1Peter 1:6

Bottom paragraphs

Pre- Trib teaching says that John represents the raptured Church in Rev. chapter 4. However, if the greatest victory ever had just taken place through the rapture, then why does the Bible say in Rev. 5:1-5 that John "wept much- because no one was found worthy." This cannot be true if the rapture happens here. Also, if John "represents" the church being raptured in chapter 4, how can the armies coming back with Christ in Rev. 19 be the "literal" Church? Where is the transition from one (John) to the armies (Church)?

The Pre-Wrath teaching says that the rapture takes place in Revelation 6 at the opening of 6th seal which is when the church sees Christ and cries out that the "wrath of God has now come."

Following next in chapter 7 is the great multitude (church) before the throne of God. Chapter 8, the prayers of the saints from the 5th seal are answered, which God will "now" judge the world.

Also in Rev. 7 before God pours out His wrath in chapter 8: God seals the 144,000 for protection from the judgment of the "Day of the Lord."

* **Passover:** From the passover at the start of the 70th week the antichrist is killed. Three days later the antichrist is raised to life (Rev. 13:3) which begins the "great tribulation states he must continue for 42 months. This 1260 days (42 mo) will end on the feast of Yom Kippur (when Israel repents). 75 days later the millenium begins.

ENDNOTES

Chapter 1: Psychology 101

[1] Robert Van Kampen, *The Rapture Question Answered* (Grand Rapids, Mich.: Fleming H. Revell, 1997)pp. 9-10

[2] Ibid.,11

[3] Tim LaHaye, *Rapture Under Attack* (Sisters, Or.: Multnomah Publishers, 1998), 12

[4] Ibid., 19-20 (emphasis mine)

[5] Hal Lindsey, *The Late Great Planet Earth* (Grand Rapids, Mich.: Zondervan, 1970), 54

[6] Garance Burke, Associated Press, Tuesday May 24, 2011

[7] Chuck Smith, *"Future Survival,"* www.concernedchristians.com pp. 16-17

[8] Tim LaHaye, *The Beginning of the End* (Tyndale House Publishers,1972), 165

[9] Tim LaHaye, *The Beginning of the End* (Tyndale House Publishers,1991), 193

[10] Todd Standberg, *"Defending the Pre-Tribulation Rapture,"* www.gospeloutreach.net

Chapter 4: Early Roots of Bible Prophecy

[11] John Hagee, *From Daniel to Doomsday"*(Nashville, Tenn.: Thomas Nelson Publishers, 1999), 90

[12] Jack Kinsella, *Does Jesus Beat His Wife*, www.omegaletter.com

[13] Tim LaHaye, *Rapture Under Attack* (Sisters, Or. :Multnomah Publishers, 1998), 150

[14] Ibid., 102

[15] Ibid., 26

[16] Tim LaHaye, *No Fear of the Storm*, (Sisters, Or.: Multnomah Publishers, 1994), 172-182

[17] Ibid., pp.13-14 (parenthesis mine)

[18] Thomas D. Ice, *"Biblical perspectives, the Origin of the Pre-trib Rapture, Part 1"* (January/ February 1989), pg.6

[19] Joseph Smith, *"Doctrine And Covenants 130:14-15"*; 1835

[20] Joseph Smith, *History of the Church*, vol. 5, pp. 336-337

[21] Joseph Smith, *History of the Church*, vol. 2, p.182

[22] Ellen G. White, (Early Writings, pg. 64, 1882 Edition)

23   Ellen G. White, (White 1888, pg. 333-334)
24   Ellen G. White, (Spiritual Gifts, Vol.1, p. 189)1858
25   Ellen G. White, (White, testimonies Vol. 1, p. 131)1855
26   Ellen G. White, (Testimonies for the Church, Vol. 1, p. 259)1855
27   Charles Taze Russell, *"Zion's Watch Tower"*, July, 1879, p. 4
28   Charles Taze Russell, *"Zion's Watch Tower"*, September, 1879, p. 26
29   Charles Taze Russell, *"Zion's Watch Tower"*, October, 1879, p. 4
30   Charles Taze Russell, (The Time is at Hand, 1908 ed.; p. 99)
31   Bernard Ramm, *After Fundamentalism* (San Francisco: Harper and Rowe, 1963), 186
32   Robert Cameron, *Scriptural Truth about the Lord's Return* (New York: Flemming H. Revell, 1922), 146-47

Chapter 5: Dispensationalism- The Trojan Horse

33   Didache, XVI
34   Tommy Ice, Israel's Fall Feast and Date- Setting of the Rapture, www.Pretrib. org/articles
35   Philip E. Hughes, *Interpreting Prophecy* (Grand Rapids: Eerdmans, 1976), 104
36   Sermon outline by Joe Temple, *"Dispensation of Conscience,"* www.livingbiblestudies.org
37   www.gcoh.org/2011-sunday-school-schedule/230html
38   C.I. Scofield, *Scofield Reference Bible*, 1909, 1917 [notes on John 1:17, sec.2 pg. 1115]
39   John Macarthur, Jr., *The Gospel According to Jesus* (Grand Rapids: Zondervan, 1988), 25
40   J. N. Darby, "The Collected Writings of J. N. Darby," *A Reply To Defence Of The Doctrine Of Baptismal Regeneration"* [Ecclesiastical No. 4, Volume 20] www. plymouthbrethren.org/ article/ 10884

Chapter 6: The Seventy Weeks of Daniel

41   Sir Robert Anderson, *The Coming Prince* (Grand Rapids: Kregel Publishers, 1894)
42   Thomas Ice and Timothy Demy, *The Truth About the Tribulation* (Eugene Oregon: Harvest House Publishers, 1996), 39
43   Thomas Ice and Timothy Demy, *The Return* (Grand Rapids: Kregel Publications, 1999), 29
44   H.A. Ironside, *Not Wrath but Rapture: Will the Church Participate in the Great Tribulation?* (Neptune, New Jersey: Loizeaux Brothers, Inc. 1941), 1
45   H. A. Ironside, *Not Wrath but Rapture: Will the Church Participate in the Great Tribulation* (Neptune, New Jersey: Loizeaux Brothers, Inc. 1941), 66 % digital
46   John F. Walvoord, *Major Bible Prophecies* (Grand Rapids, Mich.: Zondervan, 1999), 283
47   Thomas Ice, *Is it Time for the Temple: www.pre-trib.org/articles*

[48] Tim LaHaye and Ed Hindson, *Global Warning: Are We on the Brink of WWIII* (Farmington Hills, Michigan: The Gale Group Publishers, 2008), 123

Chapter 7: Imminence Part One

[49] John A. Sproule, *In Defense of Pretribulationism* (Winona Lake, Indiana: BMH Publishers, 1980), 12
[50] Thomas Ice, *Imminence and The Rapture (Part 1): www.pre-trib.org/articles*
[51] John Hagee, Letter, February 22, 2011: www.tribulation-now.com/2011/02/pray-up-pack-up-hagee-warns-of-rapture.html
[52] Gerald B. Stanton, *Kept From The Hour: Biblical Evidence for the Pretributational Return of Christ* (Haysville, N.C.: Schoettle Publishing, 1991), 108
[53] Ed Hindson, "The King is Coming Broadcast", 2010
[54] Grant Jeffrey, *The New Temple and the Second Coming* (Colorado Springs, Co.: WaterBrook Press, 2007), 4
[55] Grant Jeffrey, *The New Temple and the Second Coming* (Colorado Springs, Co.: WaterBrook Press, 2007), 4
[56] Thomas Ice, *Imminency and the Any-Moment Rapture*: www.pre-trib.org/articles
[57] Tim LaHaye, *Rapture Under Attack* (Sisters, Or.: Multnomah Publishers,1998), 26
[58] John Walvoord, *Major Bible Prophecies of the Bible* (Grand Rapids, Mich.: Zondervan, 1999), 341
[59] Chuck Smith (Commentary on Titus 2:13 The Blue Letter Bible)
[60] H. A. Ironside, *Not Wrath but Rapture: Will the Church Participate in the Great Tribulation?* (Neptune, New Jersey: Loizeaux Brothers, Inc. 1941), 61% digital
[61] David Jeremiah, *What in the World is Going On* (Nashville: Thomas Nelson Publishers, 2010), *99-101*
[62] Marvin Rosenthal, *The Pre-Wrath Rapture of the Church* (Nashville: Thomas Nelson Publishers, 1990), 96-97
[63] Stanley Ellisen, *The Apostasy as it Relates to the Lord's Return: www.pre-trib.org/articles*
[64] Ibid.,

Chapter 8: Imminence Part Two

[65] Tim LaHaye, *Rapture Under Attack* (Sisters, Or.: Multnomah Publishers, Inc., 1998), 164;
[66] Clarence Larkin, *The Second Coming of Christ* (Glendale, Pa.: Rev. Clarence Larkin Estate, 1922), 42
[67] Todd Strandberg, *Defending the Pre-Trib Rapture*: www.raptureready.com/rr-pre-trib-rapture.html

[68] John Hagee, *From Daniel to Doomsday* (Nashville, Tenn.: Thomas Nelson Publishers, 1999), 47

[69] Clarence Larkin, *The Second Coming of Christ* (Glendale, Pa.: Rev. Clarence Larkin Estate, 1922), 53

[70] Elmer Towns, *Tim LaHaye Study Bible* (AMG Publishers),1450

[71] Clarence Larkin, *The Second Coming of Christ* (Glendale, Pa.: Rev. Clarence Larkin Estate, 1922), 55

[72] John Walvoord, *Major Bible Prophecies* (Grand Rapids: Zondervan Publishing House, 1991), 312-313

[73] Thomas Ice and Timothy Demy, *The Return* (Grand Rapids: Kregal Publications, 1999), 188-189-section written by Tim LaHaye

Chapter 10: The Glorious Appearing

[74] Thomas Ice, www.biblicist.org/bible/america.shtml

[75] Tim LaHaye, *The Rapture Under Attack* (Sisters, Or.: Multnomah Publishers, Inc. 1998), 69

[76] Quoted by Thomas Ice; *Perhaps Today: The Imminent Coming of Christ:* www.prophecy. org

[77] Jack Van Impe; The Jack Van Impe Show, 1-27-1999

[78] Mal Couch, *Major Terms and Passages:* www.pre-trib.org/articles

[79] Ed Hindson, *The Rapture and the Glorious Appearing of Christ:* www.pre-trib.org/ articles

[80] Wayne Bridle, *Biblical Evidence for the Imminence Rapture:* www.pre-trib.org/articles

[81] Tim LaHaye, *Rapture Under Attack* (Sisters, Or.: Multnomah Publishers, 1998), 35

[82] Ibid., 38

[83] Thomas Ice, *Rapture Myths:* www.pre-trib.org/articles

[84] Todd Stanberg, *Defending the Pre-Tribulation Rapture:* www.gospeloutreach.net

[85] S. P. Tregelles, *The Hope of Christ's Second Coming, How it is Taught in Scriptures and Why?* (Great Britain, 1864), 35

[86] Dwight Pentecost, *Things to Come* parenthesis mine

[87] Adrian Rogers, *In the Twinkling of an Eye- Jesus Christ Return* (Love Worth Finding-Devotional) March 29, 2007

[88] David Jeremiah, *What in the World is Going On* (Nashville: Thomas Nelson Publishers, 2010), *99-101*

Chapter 11: The Day of the Lord

[89] Tim LaHaye, *The Prophecy Study Bible* (AMG Publishers, 2001), 1035

[90] J. Randall Price, *The Return* (Grand Rapids: Kregal Publications, 1999), 32-33

[91] John Walvoord, *The Day of the Lord*, Journal of Ministry and Theology Vol. JMAT 04:2 (Fall 2000)

[92] John Hagee, *From Daniel to Doomsday* (Nashville, Tenn.: Thomas Nelson Publishers, 1999), 97

[93] Tim LaHaye, *Rapture Under Attack* (Sisters, Or.: Multnomah Publishers, 1998), 211

[94] Tim LaHaye, *Tim LaHaye Prophecy Study Bible* (AMG Publishers), 1035

[95] Ibid. Joel 2:11

[96] Tim LaHaye, *Tim LaHaye Prophecy Study Bible* (AMG Publishers), 751

[97] Dwight Pentecost, *Things to Come* (Grand Rapids, Mich.: Zondervan, 1965), 195

[98] Thomas Ice, Timothy Demy; *Facts on Bible Prophecy From A to Z* (Eugene Oregon: Harvest House Publishers, 1997), 64

[99] Charles Ryrie, *The Ryrie Study Bible* (Chicago; Moody Press, 1978), 1353

[100] Tommy Ice and Timothy Demy, *The Tribulation* (Eugene Oregon: Harvest House Publishers, 1996), 11

[101] John Walvoord, *Every Prophecy of the Bible* (Colorado Springs, Colorado: Chariot Victor Publishing, 1999), 287

[102] John Walvoord, *Major Bible Prophecies* (Grand Rapids, Mich.: Zondervan, 1999), 287

[103] Thomas Ice and Timothy Demy, *The Return* (Grand Rapids: Kregel Publications, 1999), 47

[104] John Walvoord, *Every Prophecy of the Bible* (Colorado Springs, Colo.: Chariot Victor Publishing, 1999), 555

[105] Tim LaHaye; *Rapture Under Attack* (Sisters, Oregon: Multnomah Publishers, 1998), 60

[106] Tommy Ice and Timothy Demy, *The Tribulation* (Eugene Oregon: Harvest House Publishers, 1996), 25-26

[107] Renalde Showers, *What on Earth Is God Doing* (Neptune, New Jersey: Loizeaux Brothers, 1973), 109-110

Chapter 12: The Timing of the Day of the Lord

[108] Tommy Ice and Timothy Demy, *The Tribulation* (Eugene Oregon: Harvest House Publishers, 1996), 27

[109] David Reagan, *The Wrath of God is it Myth or Reality?* (www.lamblion.com/articles/articles_tribulation4.php)

[110] Thomas Ice and Timothy Demy, *The Return* (Grand Rapids: Kregel Publications, 1999), 104

[111] Tim LaHaye, *Rapture Under Attack* (Sisters, Oregon: Multnomah publishers, 1998), 58

[112] John Hagee, *Can America Survive* (New York, NY. Howard Books, 2010), 221

[113] John Walvoord, *Major Bible Prophecies* (Grand Rapids: Zondervan Publishers, 1991), 286

[114] Dr. Gerald B. Stanton, *A Critique of the Pre-Wrath Rapture Theory, Biblical Perspectives*, vol. IV, no. 1,2 (January/February 1991)

[115] Marvin Rosenthal, *The Pre-Wrath Rapture of the Church* (Nashville: Thomas Nelson Publishers, 1990), 144

[116] Thomas Ice and Timothy Demy, *The Truth About The Tribulation* (Eugene Oregon: Harvest House Publishers, 1996), 16

[117] Thomas Ice and Timothy Demy, *The Truth About The Tribulation* (Eugene Oregon: Harvest House Publishers, 1996), 8

Chapter 13: Matthew 24

[118] Thomas Ice and Timothy Demy, *The Return* (Grand Rapids: Kregel Publications, 1999), 135

[119] Mark Hitchcock, *The Complete Book of Bible Prophecy* (Wheaton, Illinois: Tyndale House, 1999), 127

Chapter 14: 1 & 2 Thessalonians

[120] Todd Strandberg, *Defending the Pre-Trib Rapture: www.raptureready.com/rr-pre-trib-rapture.html*

[121] John Walvoord, *Major Bible Prophecies* (Grand Rapids: Zondervan Publishers, 1991), 274

[122] Paul D. Feinberg, *2 Thessalonians 2 and the Rapture:* www.pre-trib.org/data/pdf/Feinberg-ArguingAbouttheRaptur.pdf

[123] Paul Lee Tan, *The Interpretation of Prophecy* (Winona Lake, Indiana: Assurance Publishers, 1974), 341

[124] Charles Ryrie, *Dispensationalism Today* (Chicago: Moody Press, 1965), 151

[125] Clarence Larkin, *The Second Coming of Christ* (Glendale, Pa.: Rev. Clarence Larkin Estate, 1922), 66

[126] John Walvoord, *Major Bible Prophecies* (Grand Rapids: Zondervan Publishers, 1991), 274

[127] Renald Showers, *Maranatha our Lord, Come* (Bellmawr, New Jersey: The Friends of Israel Gospel Ministry, 1995), 65

Chapter 15: The Rapture and the Day of the Lord

[128] David Hocking, *The Rapture in Revelation:* www.pre-trib.org/articles

[129] Dr. Robert Gromacki, *Where is the Church in Revelation 4-19:* www.pre-trib.org/articles

[130] Article in the website www.areweliinginthelastdays.com/article/rapture/rapture.htm

[131] Tim LaHaye, *Rapture Under Attack* (Sisters, Oregon: Multnomah Publishers, 1998), 53

[132] Ibid., pg. 58

[133] David Hocking, *The Rapture in Revelation:* www.pre-trib.org/articles)

[134] David Jeremiah, *Escape the Coming Night* (Nashville: Thomas Nelson Publishers, 2001), 103

[135] H.A. Ironside, *Not Wrath but Rapture: Will the Church Participate in the Great Tribulation?* (Neptune, New Jersey: Loizeaux Brothers, Inc. 1941), 66% digital

[136] Edward Hindson, *The Rapture and the Return: Two Aspects of Christ's Coming* (Grand Rapids, Mi.: Kregel Publications, 1999), 100

Chapter 16: Kept From the Hour

[137] Tim LaHaye, *Rapture Under Attack* (Sisters, Oregon: Multnomah Publishers, 1998), 49-50

Chapter 17: The Final Conclusion

[138] Clarence Larkin, *The Second Coming of Christ* (Glendale, Pa.: Rev. Clarence Larkin Estate, 1922), 65

[139] John McKay, Facebook post.

BIBLIOGRAPHY

Robert Anderson, *"The Coming Prince"*
Wayne Bridle; *"Biblical Evidence for the Imminence Rapture"*
Garance Burke, Associated Press
Robert Cameron, *"Scriptural Truth about the Lord's Return"*,
Mal Couch, *"Major Terms and Passages"*(
J. N. Darby, "The Collected Writings of J. N. Darby,
Timothy Demy, *"The Return"*
H. A. Ironside, *"Not Wrath, but Rapture: Will the Church Participate in the Great Tribulation"*
Stanley Ellisen, *"The Apostasy as it Relates to the Lord's Return"*
Paul D. Feinberg, *"2 Thessalonians 2 and the Rapture"*
Robert Gromacki, *"Where is the Church in Revelation 4-19"*
John Hagee, *"From Daniel to Doomsday"*
Ed Hindson, "The King is Coming Broadcast
Philip E. Hughes, *"Interpreting Prophecy"*
Thomas D. Ice, *"Biblical perspectives, the Origin of the Pre-trib Rapture, Part 1*
Mark Hitchcock; *"The Complete Book of Bible Prophecy"*
David Hocking, *"The Rapture in Revelation"*
Grant Jeffrey, *"The New Temple and the Second Coming"*
David Jeremiah, *"What in the World is Going On"*
Tim LaHaye, *"No Fear of the Storm"*
Tim LaHaye, *"Rapture Under Attack"*
Hal Lindsey, *"The Late Great Planet Earth*
John Macarthur, Jr., *"The Gospel According to Jesus"*
Dwight Pentecost, *"Things to Come"*
J. Randall Price, *"The Return"*
Bernard Ramm, *"After Fundamentalism"*
David Reagan, *"The Wrath of God is it Myth or Reality?*
Adrian Rogers, *"In the Twinkling of an Eye- Jesus Christ Return"*

Marvin Rosenthal, *"The Pre-Wrath Rapture of the Church,"*

Charles Taze Russell, *"Zion's Watch Tower"*

Charles Ryrie; *"The Ryrie Study Bible"*

Renalde Showers, *"What on Earth Is God Doing"*

C.I. Scofield, *"Scofield Reference Bible"*

Clarence Larkin, *"The Second Coming of Ch*rist"

Todd Standberg, *"Defending the Pre-Tribulation Rapture*

Chuck Smith (Commentary on Titus 2:13 The Blue Letter Bible)

Joseph Smith, *"Doctrine And Covenants"*

Joseph Smith, *"History of the Church"*

John A. Sproule, *"In Defense of Pretribulationism"*

Gerald B. Stanton, *"Kept From The Hour: Biblical Evidence for the Pretributational
    Return of Christ",*

Paul Lee Tan, *"The Interpretation of Prophecy"*

Joe Temple, *"Dispensation of Conscience,"*

Elmer Towns, *"Tim LaHaye Study Bible"*

S. P. Tregelles, *"The Hope of Christ's Coming,"*

Jack Van Impe, (the Jack Van Impe Show)

John F. Walvoord, *"Major Bible Prophecies"*

Ellen G. White, (Early Writings)

Ellen G. White, (Spiritual Gifts)

Ellen G. White, (Testimonies for the Church, Vol. 1)

Ellen G. White, (White, testimonies Vol. 1)

Ellen G. White, (White 1888, pg. 333-334)

Printed in the United States
By Bookmasters